Seldovia, Alaska

An Historical Portrait of Life in Zaliv Seldevoe ~ Herring Bay

Susan Woodward Springer

Blue Willow, Inc.
Littleton, Colorado

Copyright © 1997 by Susan Woodward Springer

All rights reserved. This work is protected by international copyright laws. Unauthorized reproduction of this work in any form is a violation of the rights of the copyright owner and may expose you to civil and criminal penalties. All rights are reserved.

Page layouts and typography by Thomas J. Glover
Cover photograph "Seldovia, Alaska - June, 1950" courtesy of
  William Wakeland © 1950, reprinted with permission
Cover design by Robert Schamm and Thomas J. Glover
Back cover photo by Gail Richards of Alaska Close-up Images

For information about this book, please contact:

  Blue Willow, Inc.
  P.O. Box 621227
  Littleton, Colorado 80162
  (303) 932-1600

Printed in the U.S.A.

Library of Congress Number 97-074728

ISBN 1-889796-03-4

AUTHOR'S NOTE

I loathed history in school. Through some fast-talking and cajoling, I convinced the Dean at Lawrence Academy to let me skip European History and study famous law trials instead. I received an A-plus in the latter class, but left school with no idea of nor interest in what had happened in the world before the Beatles and bellbottoms. What an unlikely person I am then, to compile and record Seldovia's history. What a fascinating process it has been!

Although post-earthquake Seldovia is quaint and lovely, it today speaks little of the thriving seaport and trading post it once was. The voices of the past are hidden everywhere here: in vacant lots, old houses, ruined docks, and in the memories of the elders. In five years of research and interviews, I've become close friends with the past. Often I feel as though I stand with a foot in each world. The more I unearthed, the harder it became to bring this project to closure. But I have been reminded that it is a researcher's obligation to share that which has been discovered.

Undoubtedly, many great tales of Seldovia are still to be told. I have learned that the history of a place is never completely written, for one good story seems to spark and set fire to the tinder of another. We plan to update this book as subsequent editions are printed and I would be most grateful to anyone who is willing to share their photographs and reminiscences.

It is my hope that this book will preserve history, memories, stories, and pictures all in one place, as would a museum. Seldovia needs a museum, for it would help us understand our past and give us insight into the present. Museums open our eyes to the layers of humanity that existed before us. Our here-and-now importance diminishes as we recognize that in the greater scheme of things we are as transient as the fleeting Alaskan summer.

I wrote this book for the people of Seldovia, to share my research with the people who love this place the most. It is also written for the visitor. Many folks come here and are taken with our community. Perhaps this book will help them understand why.

To Jack English,
  for inspiring me to begin this project.

To Janet Klein,
  for hounding me to finish this project.

And to my husband, Ray,
   for granting me a sabbatical from the real
   world so that I could undertake this
   project in the first place.

Seldovia, Alaska - 1997. Photo courtesy of Tom Glover.

CONTENTS

Introduction · · · · · · · · · · · · · · · · 6	Fur and Fin (cont.)
Acknowledgments · · · · · · · · · · · · · · · 7	The Salmon Fishery in the 1920's and 30's · · · · · 135
Present Day Seldovia · · · · · · · · · · · · · 9	Great Depression Weakens the Salmon Fishery · · · 139
The Prehistory · · · · · · · · · · · · · · 19	Working in the Cannery: Elsa Pedersen's
The Past is Discovered · · · · · · · · · · 19	Reminiscences · · · · · · · · · · · · · · · · 141
Seldovia's Ancient Artifacts · · · · · · · · 25	The Wartime Fishery · · · · · · · · · · · · · 141
Seldovia Midden Found in 1993 · · · · · · 28	Postwar to Present · · · · · · · · · · · · · · 142
Early Exploration · · · · · · · · · · · · 37	Crab · 146
Glacial Influence · · · · · · · · · · · · · 37	Clams · 148
Early Explorers · · · · · · · · · · · · · · · 40	Halibut · · · · · · · · · · · · · · · · · · · 149
Seldovia Bay is Named · · · · · · · · · · · 46	Shrimp · · · · · · · · · · · · · · · · · · · 150
American Exploration · · · · · · · · · · · 48	Diversified Catch Today · · · · · · · · · · · 151
Seldovia's Modern Beginnings · · · · · · · 51	Mining Around Seldovia · · · · · · · · · · · 151
Russian Retirement Community? · · · · · · · 51	Chrome Mining · · · · · · · · · · · · · · · 154
Or Native Village? · · · · · · · · · · · · · 51	Harvesting Trees · · · · · · · · · · · · · · 157
Seldovia or Akedaknak? · · · · · · · · · · 54	Tourism · · · · · · · · · · · · · · · · · · · 159
Seldovia's Native Culture · · · · · · · · · 56	**Life in Old Seldovia** · · · · · · · · · · · 165
Preserving Tanaina Culture · · · · · · · · 57	Seldovia School Days · · · · · · · · · · · · 165
Ways of the Seldovia Tanaina · · · · · · · 59	Special Delivery: Seldovia's Post Office · · · · 173
Russian Culture and Influence · · · · · · · 71	Law and (dis)Order in Early Seldovia · · · · · 176
Orthodox Church Provides Seldovia Census · · · · · · 72	Raise Yer Jug: Bootlegging in Seldovia · · · · · 182
Travel Journals of the Russian Orthodox Priests · · · 74	On the Boardwalk · · · · · · · · · · · · · · 185
St. Nicholas Orthodox Church · · · · · · · 89	Business on the Boardwalk · · · · · · · · · · 191
Russian Orthodox Celebrations and Observances · · 92	Read All About It In the Seldovia Herald · · · 196
Fur and Fin · · · · · · · · · · · · · · · 99	The Seldovia Women's Club · · · · · · · · · 200
Seldovia's "Furst" Industry · · · · · · · · · 99	Behind the Scenes: Public Utilities and Services · · 203
Fur: Trapping and Hunting Give Way to Farming. 102	Fourth of July: A Seldovia Celebration · · · · · 210
There's Gold up the Inlet! · · · · · · · · · 109	Childhood Scrapbook: Growing up in Seldovia · · · 211
Herring · · · · · · · · · · · · · · · · · · 121	**The Earthquake and Urban Renewal** · · · 217
Salmon · · · · · · · · · · · · · · · · · · · 128	Water Torture · · · · · · · · · · · · · · · · 221
Moving the Fish · · · · · · · · · · · · · · 129	Urban Renewal: To Be or Not To Be · · · · · · 224
Salted Salmon · · · · · · · · · · · · · · · 131	The Reshaping of Seldovia · · · · · · · · · · 227
Canning Overview · · · · · · · · · · · · · 132	Final Thoughts · · · · · · · · · · · · · · · · 233
	Glossary · · · · · · · · · · · · · · · · · · 217
	Index · 238

INTRODUCTION

Seldovia's rich past is buried, not only figuratively, but literally due to Urban Renewal after the 1964 Good Friday Earthquake. There is a sense of urgency to capture and preserve the flavor of old Seldovia. Most of those who resided here at the beginning of the century are dead. The whereabouts of those who moved away after Urban Renewal are largely unknown. While still picturesque and quaint, Seldovia today is but a ghost of its former self. The present day visitor has few clues to the importance of this community to all of South-central Alaska in the late 19th and early 20th centuries.

This book is a historical portrait of Seldovia as opposed to a definitive history, replete with neat chronological stepping stones. A portrait differs substantially from a photograph in that it omits some of the sun and shadow, many of the lines, and some of the imperfections. So in its way does this portrait of a small town. The reader looking for a year-by-year account of history may be disappointed. Look instead for a sense of place in history: how it felt to be here and how those here at the time painted the picture for us to admire now. While some of the sources are archival, much of the information is from the reminiscences of individuals, and many of the photographs are from private collections, lovingly preserved in dusty boxes and old albums. Two people seldom remember an event in exactly the same way, and although that may handicap a historical textbook, to a historical portrait it serves to remind us of the wonderful diversity of humanity that has always characterized Seldovia, and in fact all of Alaska.

I was introduced to "old Seldovia" by our unwitting purchase in 1985 of the oldest house in town, and by my subsequent introduction to Jack English, one of the town's earliest residents. Jack had suffered a stroke, and couldn't always make his mouth say what his mind was thinking, so we spent a number of quiet afternoons simply sitting together at his former office, looking at old pictures. For Jack they were poignant remembrances of a full and fascinating life in a bustling Alaskan town. For me they were the doorway to a place that no longer exists. Luckily, it had been his habit to carefully type captions, often with dates, across the top or bottom edge of his photographs, and in this way he assured that old Seldovia was perhaps one step closer to immortality.

After Jack died in 1989, his heirs graciously gave me full use of his collection. The more I learned about old Seldovia, the hungrier I became. After a time, word got out that I was working on a book about Seldovia. Whenever a former resident came back for a visit and inquired about a museum or began going on about "the good old days," they were referred to me. Some of these accidental meetings provided rich material. I hope that my book does justice to everyone who shared their time, papers, and photographs with me, and most of all I hope it does justice to my home—Seldovia.

ACKNOWLEDGMENTS

Jack English, and his grandchildren **John and Suzie-Q Gruber** for their generosity in loaning me countless photographs and historical papers.

Ted Anderson, son of Juanita and Ralph Anderson who built our log house in 1915, for donating a number of his parents' photographs to this book, as well as contributing many fine stories and writing some great essays.

Jim Busey, son of Lester and Mary Louise Busey who published Seldovia's first newspaper, *The Seldovia Herald*, in the early 1930's, and Jim's wife **Marian**, for their informative interview and letters.

Steve Zawistowski, long-time resident of this area, for his stories and for his photograph of our house in the 1930's.

Lou Collier, construction superintendent during Urban Renewal, for his patient recounting of all that took place during that turbulent time.

Candy Hendrix, Elsa Pedersen, Lavake Renshaw, Dana Stabenow, and **Gene "Whitey" Wadsworth**, whose written and oral memories, reports, and photographs breathed life into this book.

Janet Klein, Homer historian and archaeologist, who convinced me to write this book, and shared with me her wealth of material. Janet was my support system. We spoke every few weeks, and when we did she reignited my sense of purpose.

Seldovia was the boyhood home of former resident Ted Anderson (left), here shown greeting Seldovia elder Nick Elxnit. Both men were invaluable sources of material for this book. Photo courtesy of Janet Klein.

Fred Elvsaas, lifelong resident of Seldovia and president of the *Seldovia Native Association*, who provided many colorful stories, and to the **Seldovia Native Association** staff who made their historical files available to me.

Nick Elxnit, a retired fisherman who came from Kodiak to Seldovia as a child with his family after the 1912 Katmai eruption, and whose anecdotes about Seldovia rival Fred's.

Barbara Sweetland Smith, historian, who guided me to the treasure trove of Russian language archives she has so carefully researched and indexed.

Mina Jacobs and **Sergei Chulaki**, who translated the Seldovia material from those archives for me, and Mina, who dug through the Anchorage Museum photo collections.

Dr. Frederica de Laguna, whose hallmark archaeological work on Yukon Island put into perspective for me that the 19th and 20th century south shore Kachemak

Bay settlements are but a small link in the long chain of human occupancy of this area, and who kindly consented to put on paper for this book her impressions of Seldovia in the early 1930's.

The staff at Homer Public Library, especially **Dave Swarthout and Cathy George**, who assisted me with many interlibrary loans.

Dr. Richard A. Pierce, of the History Department at the University of Alaska Fairbanks (UAF) and the Limestone Press, for his help and encouragement during my visit to UAF, and more so for his determination to translate and publish Russian works of history—having access to this material was key to my project.

Katherine Arndt, also of UAF, for her keen eyesight while reading faint Russian script microfilm, and for her command of the language.

Dr. Gregory Wiles, the Kachemak Bay glacier specialist, of Columbia University's Lamont-Doherty Earth Observatory.

Ellen Fitzgerald and Gladi Kulp, of the Alaska State Library, Historical Collections, Juneau, for being two of the most helpful and kind people a researcher could hope to meet.

Jan Cevene, John B. Child, Denita Higman, and **Gail Richards** for their generous contribution of photographs.

William Wakeland of Anchorage for his skill in photo-documenting Seldovia in the 1950's, and for his kindness in sharing his wonderful photographs.

Savannah S. Lewis, whose patient and meticulous proof-reading and editing really polished the manuscript, and **Tom Glover** of Blue Willow, Inc. whose dedication and expertise have helped to make this book a reality

Thank you all for your sharing and your help!

Point Naskowhak at the mouth of Seldovia Bay. View looking west from Gray Cliffs. Photo courtesy of Tom Glover.

Present Day Seldovia

An Overview of the Community in the 1990's

Seldovia, on the south shore of Kachemak Bay, is located 240 miles southwest of Anchorage. Because of the numerous fjords and glaciers on the south shore of Kachemak Bay, there is no road to Seldovia. Accessible only by air or water, Seldovia is served year-round by two bush airlines and in the summer by three tour boat companies. The state ferry, M/V *Tustumena*, page 14 , comes one to two times per week for about ten months of the year. The community relies on the state ferry to bring vehicles, building materials, and other large supplies. While the tour boats dock inside the protection of the small boat harbor, the state ferry ties up at the City Pier at the northern end of town. The Seldovia Airport is a 1,845 foot gravel strip, rated for VFR (good weather/daylight) only. Floatplanes land on Seldovia Bay, taxi into the boat harbor, and tie up at a designated float.

Seldovia nestles into the eastern shore of the mouth of a north-south running fjord. The rolling hills of the community rise to a ridge whose peaks reach up to over three thousand feet in elevation. A similar ridge follows the western shore of the fjord. The community of Seldovia is nearly surrounded by water: Seldovia Bay to the west and south, Kachemak Bay to the north, and the Seldovia Slough and Lagoon (both salt water tidal bodies) to the east. Several miles away at the head of Seldovia Bay, the Seldovia River twists through a valley floor. In town, Fish Creek empties into the Seldovia Slough. Both watercourses are fed by mountain snow-melt. All this water surrounding Seldovia helps to moderate the local climate. Normal winter temperatures in Kachemak Bay range from 16 to 36 degrees Fahrenheit, but there is usually a week of near zero. Normal summer temperatures range from 40 to 60

Present day Seldovia photographed from a boat in Seldovia Bay. View looking to the East. Photo courtesy of Tom Glover.

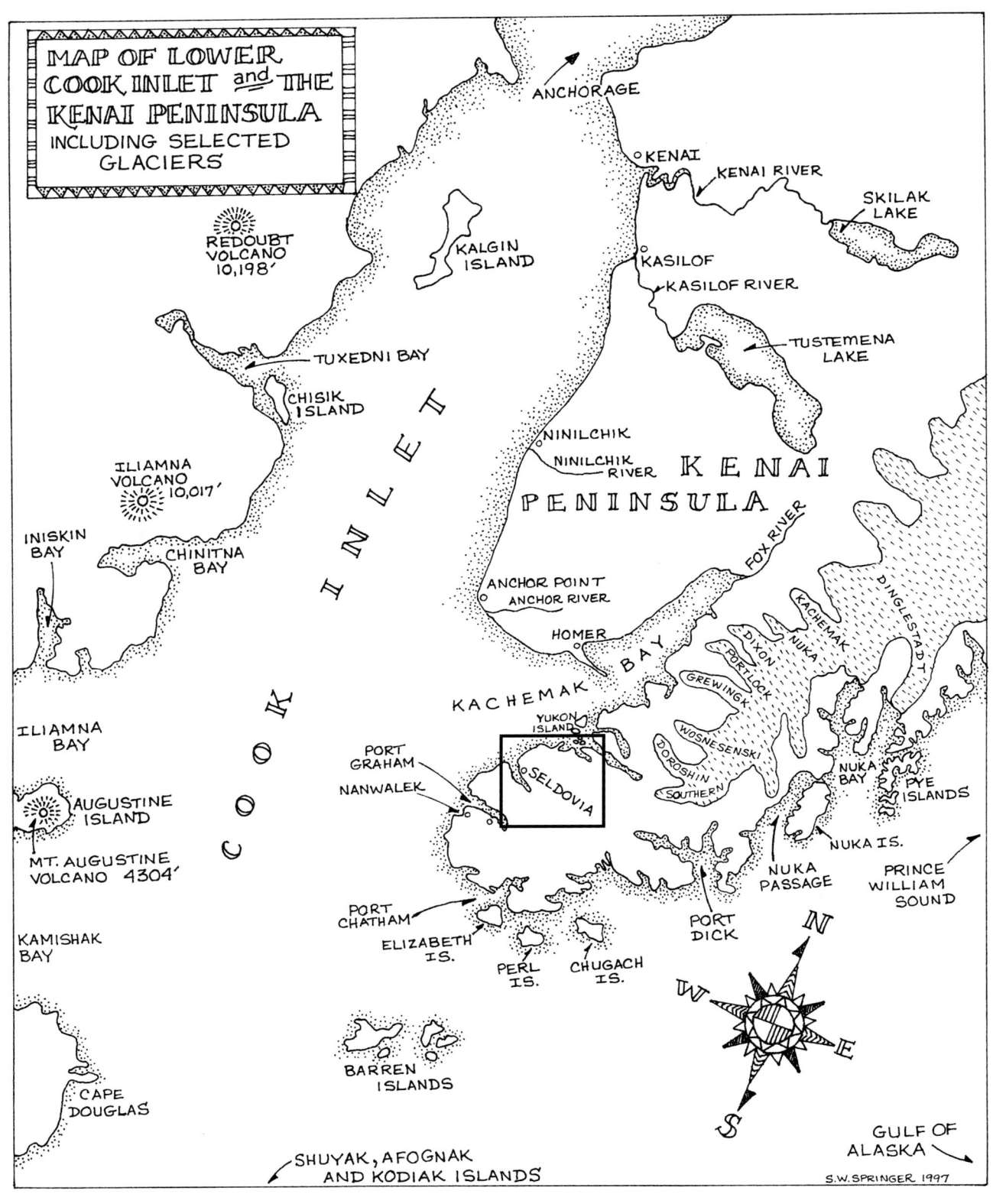

LOWER COOK INLET AND THE KENAI PENINSULA. Square outlined area around Seldovia is shown in more detail in the map on the facing page. Map by Susan W. Springer © 1997.

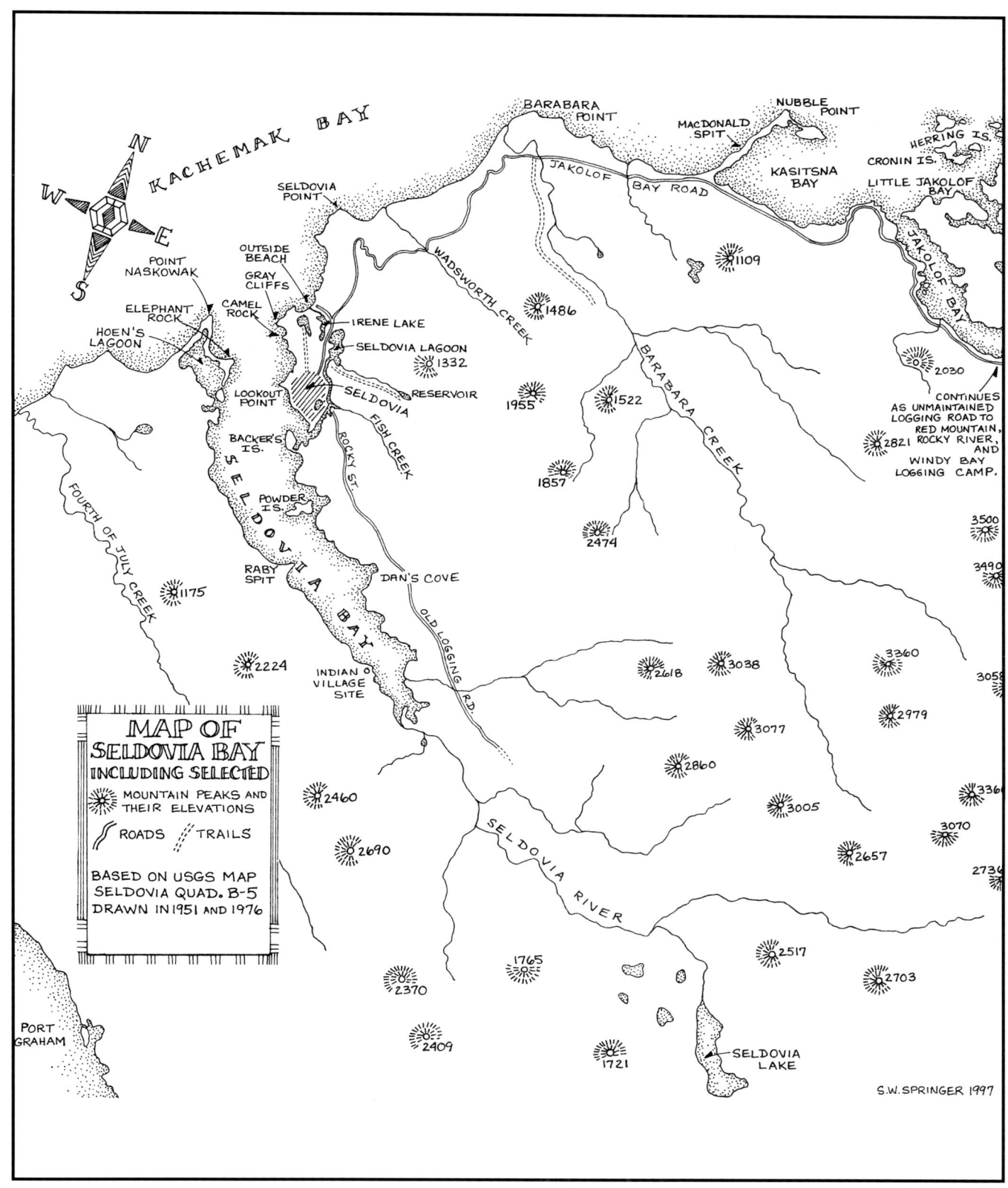

SELDOVIA BAY, KACHEMAK BAY, AND COOK INLET. Shielded by mountains on three sides, Seldovia is somewhat protected from the weather systems that move across the Gulf of Alaska and lower Cook Inlet. This map is a blowup of the square outlined area of the facing page map. Map by Susan W. Springer © 1997.

Sport fishing for halibut is great fun and one of the primary summertime pursuits in Seldovia. Photo courtesy of Tom Glover.

degrees Fahrenheit. In some years, many days in the high 50's and 60's are enjoyed. The annual precipitation is 34.5 inches, in the form of rain and snow. In Seldovia Bay, the tidal range is impressive. At its extremes, the tide varies from around minus 5 feet to plus 22 feet.

Seldovia is a first class city, incorporated in 1945. It is one of the southernmost communities in the Kenai Peninsula Borough. Governed by an elected six member council and mayor, Seldovia employs a City Manager, Harbormaster, Police officer, and roughly ten additional full and part-time workers. The city is served by a volunteer fire department, and volunteer emergency medical technicians assist a resident physician. In the city-owned clinic, the physician keeps regular office hours and each week flies his own plane to Homer to attend patients at South Peninsula Hospital in Homer.

The 1990 census listed the population within city limits as 316. From the city limits north to Jakolof Bay, there are over 100 additional people. In the summer, seasonal residents living along the local road system and on the western shore of Seldovia Bay add perhaps another 100. Roughly 30% of the population is Native, with Eskimo, Aleut, and Tanaina Indian tribes represented. Descendants of 19th century Russian settlers, and early 20th century Scandinavian immigrants also make their homes in the community.

The Susan B. English School with a staff of 12 serves roughly 80 to 90 students in grades K through 12. The school facilities include a gymnasium, swimming pool, library and computer room. On the grounds are tennis courts and a ball field. In addition to the school library, the Seldovia Public Library lends books, periodicals, and videos, and is staffed entirely by volunteers. The school is one of the major employers in the community, along with the grocery store and the Seldovia Native Association.

The majority of homes and buildings in Seldovia were constructed after the 1964 Good Friday earthquake, although a number of pre-earthquake structures are still in use. Heating oil, delivered by barge to a local distributor, is the fuel of choice, although a number of homes employ wood or electricity. Electric power comes via an underwater cable from Homer to Jakolof Bay where poles carry it

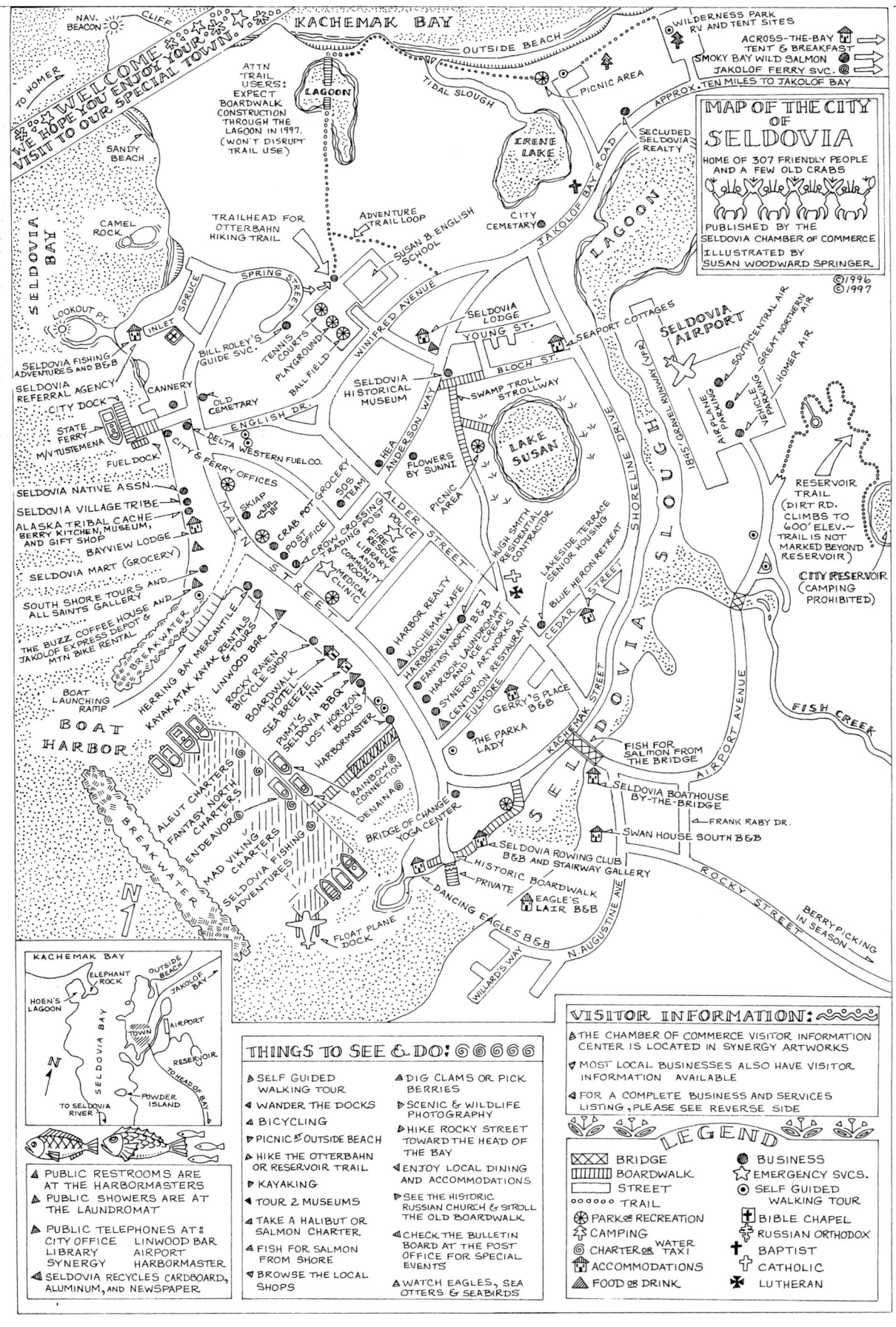

The state ferry, M/V Tustumena, comes to Seldovia one to two times per week for about ten months of the year. Photo courtesy of Tom Glover.

Seldovia Harbor. View looking to the west from the main pier. Photo courtesy of Tom Glover.

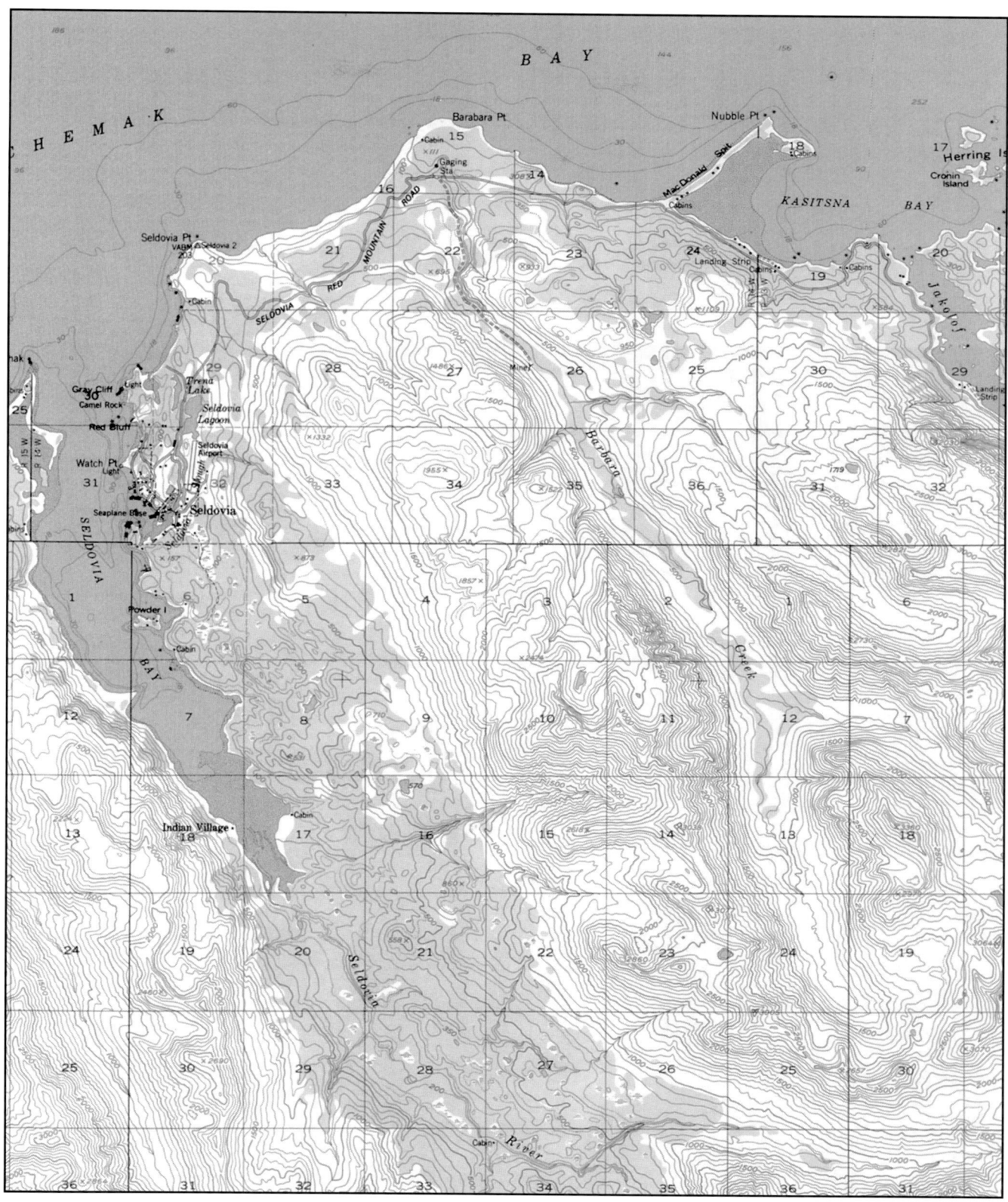

Seldovia (B-5) Quadrangle, USGS 15 Minute Topographic Series. Scale approximately 1:84,480 (1"=7040')

the eleven miles into Seldovia. A local oil-fired, turbine-driven power plant provides electricity during extended outages. Water within city limits comes from a reservoir at 600 feet elevation, fed by mountain run-off. Piping carries the water down to a storage tank about 100 feet above sea level. A back-up reservoir is located near the mouth of Fish Creek. Sewage is collected at a community holding tank and then the harmless effluent is piped to an ocean outfall at the northern end of town. Homes outside city limits rely on wells and individual septic systems. A landfill located about one and a half miles south of town serves the area's solid waste disposal needs.

U.S. Mail arrives in Seldovia five days a week by bush plane, depending on weather. Almost all residents have telephone service, and Seldovia is part of the Homer local exchange. Anchorage television stations are received in the community via a microwave relay and satellite dishes provide additional viewing access. The Seldovia area has less than twenty miles of regularly maintained road. Within city limits, most streets are paved. Outside city limits, dirt roads are maintained by a resident State Department of Transportation employee. Old logging roads heading toward the head of Seldovia Bay, Jakolof Bay, and Red Mountain are not maintained and are navigable with 4-wheel-drive vehicles or ATV's.

Commercial fishing and tourism are Seldovia's primary industries. Although the last processing facility closed in 1989, the community is still home port to a number of small and large fishing boats which participate in the salmon, herring, halibut, cod, and crab fisheries. Catches are delivered to Homer or Kenai. A city-operated boat haul-out and

A drizzly fall day doesn't stop Mr. Tim Ray Volstad from an afternoon outing on Seldovia Bay. Photo courtesy of Tom Glover.

Winter temperatures normally range from 16 to 36 degrees Fahrenheit and there is usually a week of near zero readings. Photo courtesy of Tom Glover.

storage facility provides winter quarters for both recreational and commercial vessels. Seldovia's tourist season runs from May through September, with July 4th customarily the peak. Contributing to this is the old-fashioned Independence Day celebration, for which the community has become well known. The rich history of the area has spawned two small museums, a self-guided walking tour, and several guided tour operations. A number of retail businesses, eateries, and hotels and B&B's flourish seasonally, and the city operates a camping area and RV park.

Both residents and visitors enjoy sport-fishing for salmon and halibut, recreational boating, hiking, kayaking, mountain biking, berry picking, and cross country skiing. A number of artists make their homes here, and classes are frequently offered to the community. The Hospital Guild sponsors Bingo, and community groups organize swim classes, basketball and volleyball, and aerobics and weight-training. A community Christian Church is active, and the local Catholic Church holds periodic services when clergy visit from Homer. The Russian Orthodox Church conducts services several times a year, officiated by clergy from the Anchorage diocese.

Although winter brings the snow and cold and darkness, there always seems to be time for fun. Photo courtesy of Tom Glover.

Peace at its best. View of Mt. Iliamna looking northwest across Kachemak Bay from MacDonald Spit. Photo courtesy of Tom Glover.

THE PREHISTORY

Through Archaeology, a Look at the Seldovia Area Prior to the 18th Century

The coastline on and around Seldovia Bay has been populated for many hundreds of years. With its temperate climate and abundant natural resources it is hardly surprising that the area has been used for millenia for everything from hunting camps to seasonal and year round settlements.

The fjord that is Seldovia Bay is situated on the south shore of Kachemak Bay, off the great northern reaching arm of the Pacific known as Cook Inlet. At a latitude of 59° 27' 45" N, it is well below the Arctic Circle, and thus not subject to the extreme temperatures that characterize the Interior of Alaska. The placement of Seldovia Bay near the tip of the Kenai Peninsula exposes it to the moderating influences of the sea in nearly every direction: Kachemak Bay to the north and east, Cook Inlet to the northwest, the Gulf of Alaska to the south, and Prince William Sound to the southeast. A mountain range separates and somewhat protects Seldovia Bay from the strong winds blowing in across the Gulf and up the Shelikof Strait, and there is safe anchorage in nearly all weather.

The verdant hills and mountains on either side of Seldovia Bay offer tall, straight spruce for fuel and lodging, and abundant game: moose, goat, black bear, and various smaller mammals. Snowmelt from the mountain range gathers into countless freshwater streams, and their outflows provide the breeding grounds for salmon. The ocean itself is probably the richest area resource and is the habitat for halibut, rockfish, cod, crab, shrimp, mussels, and clams, among other edibles.

The Past is Discovered

As obvious as it would seem, then, that the Seldovia area would have been long used by humans, this fact remained speculation until the 20th century. The door to Seldovia's ancient past was opened in 1930 by a young graduate student from Bryn Mawr, Pennsylvania, Frederica de Laguna. In an East Coast museum, Dr. de Laguna had studied a stone lamp listed as being found by a farmer in Cook Inlet, Alaska. Although Cook Inlet was a region known to have been inhabited by Dena'ina Athabaskan Indians, the stone lamp was of Eskimo design. That Eskimo may have lived in Cook Inlet was only a theory, but it was one that Dr. de Laguna felt merited further study.

On a hunch, she came to Alaska in the summer of 1930, and teamed up with Seldovian Jack Fields. In his gas boat, the *Dime*, Fields and de Laguna scoured Cook Inlet for the origins of the mysterious lamp. Although they inquired about ancient sites at any village or cannery they passed, none of the leads they were given panned out. Finally, in Kachemak Bay, Fields led de Laguna to Yukon Island and showed her the beach where he'd found a bone point protruding from the bank, and upon digging further had unearthed a female skeleton wearing a shell bead necklace. [1]

Jack Fields "Loaded for bears or stone lamps", Seldovia, September 13-14, 1930, negative #30-10-9, 1930-295. Photo courtesy of Dr. Frederica de Laguna

Pausing from her archaeological work on Yukon Island in the summer of 1932, Dr. Frederica de Laguna is joined by her expedition crew: her mother, Grace, and friends Bill Newman and Dana Street. Captain Jack Fields is at far right. Photo courtesy of Dr. Frederica de Laguna. Dr. de Laguna shot this photo with a self timer on her camera. Ref. Neg. #32-9, 1932-13

Dr. de Laguna remembered her trip down Cook Inlet for this book:

> My first impression of Seldovia, in September 1930, was a confused one. I had come down the Inlet from Anchorage in a gas boat belonging to Jack Fields, looking for archaeological sites. Since Jack was "the Crew and Captain, too", it is understandable that I had to be enlisted for quite a few unexpected shipboard duties, not the least of which was taking the wheel during a really bad storm while Jack pumped out the bilge. Although we had been unable to discover suitable archaeological sites on the way down, my luck changed dramatically when we reached Kachemak Bay, where Jack was able to guide me to some really old village sites on Yukon Island and Cottonwood Creek. The stresses and strains of the trip, with its disappointments and dangers, and the sudden change to safe waters and exciting prospects of good digging, had naturally left my head in something of a whirl, when we ran in to Seldovia to renew supplies. It was not until the following years, 1931 and 1932, that the peculiar charms of this town had a chance to register. [2]

In test digs, first at Cottonwood Creek and then on Yukon Island, de Laguna found what she had journeyed to Alaska to seek: the probable source of the stone lamp. She turned up a fragment of a stone lamp similar to the museum piece and this gave her the impetus to return the following year to conduct a full excavation. [3]

The Seldovia Herald *of September 27, 1930 reported on de Laguna's visit:*

RESEARCH WORK TOUCHING OLD ALASKA LIFE AND CUSTOMS – THAT'S MISS de LAGUNA'S JOB

Seldovia had the interesting and interested visitor last week in the person of Miss Frederica de Laguna, representing the University Museum of the University of Pennsylvania, and who also compiles information for the Columbia University, New York. She is traveling about Alaska making a first hand study of old native villages, taking voluminous notes of customs, manner of life long-gone by. Her tour is a prelude to the invasion of a scientific expedition to be undertaken next year that she will head, that is expected to make an exhaustive research into Alaska Indian antiquities. Miss de Laguna made a leisurely trip down the inlet from Anchorage on the Seldovia owned gas boat Dime, captained by Jack Fields, the voyage required two weeks, all points of possible interest being visited and reviewed by the young archaeologist. Not only is the young lady an avid student of her favorite subject, but is an eager and willing assistant in navigating a boat. Takes her trick at the wheel, lays out her own course, ties up the ship in true sailor fashion. From here Miss de Laguna made a trip up Kachemak Bay. She expects to make early connection with a passenger ship for the Outside.

By the following year, de Laguna was prepared to begin her excavations. Being the closest town to Yukon Island, Seldovia was the obvious supply and service base for the project. (At the time, Homer was inferior in size and services to Seldovia.)

A 1931 Seldovia Herald *article reports:*

SELDOVIA MECCA FOR ARCHEOLOGICAL RESEARCH PARTY FROM EAST–YUKON ISLAND WILL BE DELVED BY MUSEUM

Advices from Philadelphia indicate that Miss Frederica de Laguna, of the museum of the University of Pennsylvania, will make Seldovia her headquarters this coming summer when she comes north to again take up archaeological research work. Besides an associate archaeologist Miss de Laguna will be accompanied by her mother and brother. According to the present understanding the party will get here about June 18. Native settlements of a near ancient period flourished on Yukon Island and at Cottonwood Creek, and it is at these two points most of the digging will be done. Miss de Laguna, who visited this and other sections last year, had intended making survey of varied regions, Prince William Sound particularly interesting her, but later reflection decided on the Seldovia program. The gas boat Dime, operated by Jack Fields and Harry Lewis last year under charter to the young archaeologist, will be used by the research party.

De Laguna remembers:

> *My mission in Kachemak Bay was to excavate archaeological sites at Cottonwood Creek on the north shore, and on Yukon Island near the south shore, and we did not stay longer in town [Seldovia] than was necessary. I was accompanied in 1931 and 1932 by two male undergraduates from Haverford, my brother's college. On the first trip, my companions were my brother and a classmate, Ed Newman, who later became a psychologist. In 1932, Ed was replaced by his easy going brother, Bill, and my brother by Dana Street, then taking pre-med courses. My mother joined us half-way through the first summer, and came with us the second, ostensibly as guest of the expedition both times, although she soon assumed charge of getting breakfast, since we could not be trusted to wake up on time.* [4]

With mother Grace acting as alarm clock, then, the de Laguna dig got down to business in June of 1931. By the time she had finished a second summer at Yukon Island, de Laguna had concluded, based on artifacts found, that four distinct layers of early Eskimo culture existed. Dr. de Laguna named this the "Kachemak Culture" (today known as the Kachemak Tradition) and theorized that the four layers corresponded to four periods in time. From other excavations around Kachemak Bay we know that the Kachemak Tradition spanned over a thousand years. At sites farther up Kachemak Bay, the First Period dates to approximately 500 B.C., the Second Period dates to about 0 A.D., and the layer closest to the surface, the Third Period, dates to about 500 A.D. It is only in recent years that any dates have been determined for the Kachemak Cultures. It must be remembered that the technique of radiocarbon 14 dating was developed in 1949, well <u>after</u> de Laguna conducted her excavations on Yukon Island! [5]

For the people of Seldovia, de Laguna described her work and her findings in three articles published in the *Seldovia Herald* in 1931 and 1932:

The Seldovia waterfront as Dr. de Laguna would have seen it in the early 1930's. Photo courtesy of the Alaska State Library, Early Prints Collection, #01-2563.

NOTED ARCHAEOLOGIST REVEALS INTERESTING RESULTS OF YUKON ISLAND EXPLORATIONS

Miss Frederica de Laguna, noted young archaeologist from the University of Pennsylvania, contributes important information regarding her Alaskan research work in the following letter to THE HERALD, the receipt of which is acknowledged with thanks. To the editor of the SELDOVIA HERALD: Sir: The many Seldovians who have helped me in my work may be interested in the results of my investigations and why I have returned to Yukon Island this summer. All the evidence shows that the first inhabitants of the Kachemak Bay region were Eskimo like those of Port Graham, Kodiak Island and Prince William Sound (popularly called "Aleuts," but who should be distinguished from the true Aleuts of the Aleutian islands). The Indians who live here are recent immigrants having come according to their own traditions from the region about Skilak and Tustumena Lakes.

Eskimos First On Inlet

Though our own researches along the upper inlet were not very successful, there is strong evidence that the Eskimo were the first inhabitants in that part of the country. The Indians of Cook Inlet form a branch of the great Athabascan race who inhabit the interior of Alaska and western Canada, and who have pushed down to the sea only on Cook Inlet and perhaps at the mouth of the Copper river. Not only in southwestern Alaska, but further north, they have been readily pressing toward the coast, driving out the earlier Eskimo inhabitants from whom they learned how to adapt themselves to their new environment. However, until their culture was destroyed by the white man, it still bore the deep imprint of their life in the Interior, below, as it were, the new layer of sea culture, borrowed from the Eskimo. It was this Eskimo-like Indian culture which Dr. Osgood was studying last summer. The Indian sites in Kachemak Bay probably do not date back more than a few generations.

Four Stages

The older sites are all Eskimo and show a development of culture through four stages. Our work last year was chiefly in the layers of the last two stages. It is impossible to date them in years, but I should be surprised if the beginning of the third period were not least 1,000 or 1,500 years ago. Our Kachemak Bay Eskimos at this time had evidently lost much of their northern culture and had come under the influence of the Indians of Southeastern Alaska and British Columbia. Because of this mixture their culture was very rich. The stone lamps with human figure in the bowl from the upper inlet and the lamp with whale figures found by Mr.Tansy in Tutka Bay illustrate this mixture.

Carving not Eskimo

Stone carving, and in particular the style of the decorations are Indian, not Eskimo, and these decorations can be closely duplicated by carvings from the ancient shell heap at the mouth of the Fraser River and on Vancouver Island. The stone lamp with plain knobs in the bowl is an old Eskimo type, found from Greenland to southwestern Alaska, and it is from these plain knobs that the elaborate figures have been evolved under Indian influence. It is probable that the earlier periods of the Kachemak Bay culture will show a purer Eskimo type, free from Indian influences. It is to test out this hypothesis that I have returned to Yukon Island. The ideal of the archaeologist is to dig so carefully and to keep his notes so well that at the end of the season he could, if necessary, put everything back in the ground just as he found it. If the specimens from the various layers were not kept apart, it would be impossible to trace the development of culture, indeed. It would not even be suspected. Any excavation, no matter how careful, destroys evidence, and the conscientious archaeologist will never clear out a whole site, but leave something for the problems and better methods which are sure to be found in the future. It is because of this need for scientific exactness that the law was made prohibiting the excavation or destruction of archaeological sites and monuments, except by permission of the government to a representative of an accredited institution. The remains of ancient civilizations in Alaska should not be excavated by the amateur pillager, or collected for private gain by the curio collector, but should be preserved for science and for the enjoyment of everybody.

ARCHAEOLOGIST DELVES INTO SIGNS OF ANCIENT CULTURE ON KACHEMAK BAY

I am often asked how old are the ruins which I have been investigating. This is a question for which I would give much to know the answer. As I have already explained, we know that a few hundred years ago the Eskimo left the Kachemak bay region which was taken over by Indians coming down from the Interior. But when the Eskimo first came here and whether they or some other people were the original inhabitants, I do not pretend to say. It is certain that no one could have lived here before the retreat of the great glaciers at the end of the Ice Age, which occurred about 10,000 years ago, as many geologists claim, but when in the course of those many centuries the first Eskimo settled on Yukon Island it is impossible to estimate. Since that time the land has sunk at least 16 feet, for the top of the 16-foot shell-heap which we excavated is now covered over by beach gravel, and the bottom is only 11 feet above mean lower low water, so that the tide drained in and out of our hole. At Cottonwood Creek, on the north side of Kachemak bay, is a shell heap ten feet thick, covered by two feet of earth, an accumulation that must represent a great lapse of time. This site is younger than most of the shell-heaps on Yukon Island, yet it must have been inhabited before the silting up of the north shore of the bay destroyed the shellfish. Perhaps it was this which caused the abandonment of the village. When the geologists have determined how long it has taken for the sinking of the land and for the formation of those mud flats, only then can we hope to date the older village sites. Including the rubbish from the modern Indian village, said to have been inhabited only fifty years ago, there is evidence of five different settlements on Yukon Island, built one on top of the other, and showing the development of Kachemak bay Eskimo culture through four stages. Most of our material comes from the Third Period, which apparently had the richest culture, but we made small collections from the First and Second periods, while the material which we gathered last year illustrates the Fourth Period.

WITH KACHEMAK'S ANCIENTS

It is the development of this culture which has most interested me. In the last two periods we find a wealth of types including bone heads for harpoons, darts, knives and scrapers, adze blades, saws for cutting stone, drills, wedges, mawls, grinding stones, lamps, awls, fishooks, needles with eyes so small that they cannot carry thread coarser than number 50, beads, ivory pendants, dolls, and slate mirrors. The most common objects are stones, from one to six inches long, pointed at both ends, and used, I believe, as weights for bolas, similar to those of ivory employed by the northern Eskimos for catching birds. The main differences between the upper and lower layers is shown in the stone technique. In the earlier periods there was very little polished slate and almost all of the stone blades were chipped, but in the Third and Fourth Periods polished slate blades were abundant and chipped stones rare. There was no evidence of sawed stones in the First Period. The first harpoon heads are all of a very primitive type, now no longer in use anywhere, but formerly known from Alaska to Greenland; in the Third Period more elaborate forms appear. It is, however, the notched stones which mark the divisions most clearly. In the upper layers only small specimens, none over two inches long, are found. A little lower, in the Third Period, a few of the larger type occur. In the layers of the Second Period the small stones are very rare, while the large ones are found in great numbers. In the First Period, suprisingly enough, there are none at all. The grooved stone in warfare and hunting, also show changes in type. The single find which pleased us most and which brought our work to a fitting conclusion was a lamp with human figures carved in the bowl. I had already argued that lamps of this type were of Eskimo workmanship made under the influence of Indian art style, and that they belonged to the Third Period of the Kachemak bay culture. The finding of such a lamp, when only five others are known to exist was, of course, just luck, but it is a matter of great satisfaction to me that its position in a layer of the Third Period should thus verify my theory, and that now the problem of the origin of these lamps, which first brought me to Cook Inlet three seasons ago, should be solved. It is with great regret that I say goodby to Seldovia, for I have been very happy here, both in my work and in the many friends I have found. My warmest thanks go to Jack Fields, without whose intimate knowledge of the region and untiring enthusiasm I should have accomplished very little.

Although de Laguna's Yukon Island finds were a landmark in the archaeology of the southern Kachemak shore, they did not provide a prehistory for Seldovia Bay, nor for the village that became the present townsite. While there may never be proof of the latter, de Laguna did gather anecdotal evidence of artifacts found in Seldovia Bay and along the Kachemak south shore towards Yukon Island. Because of her attention to and documentation of these finds, we have at least been able to capture a glimpse of prehistoric habitation in Seldovia Bay.

Seldovia's Ancient Artifacts

De Laguna turned to Fitka Balishoff, a Seldovia native and a reliable man knowledgeable in the lore of the area. (Fitka was at the time assisting Cornelius Osgood of Yale University in gathering ethnographic information about the Seldovia natives. More on Fitka and his work can be found in the chapter "Seldovia's Modern Beginnings.") Fitka told de Laguna that he had found "a stone knife on the middle part of the spit at the western side of the bay." [6] Upon investigation, de Laguna found a site on the spit and another on a small island that stood at the entrance to a lagoon behind the spit. The lagoon is known today as Hoen's Lagoon. The island site consisted of two middens, with small shell heaps. The clam shells in the northernmost midden showed evidence of having been roasted in a fire. Below the island, on the beach, de Laguna found a stone maul head.[7] The Seldovia Native Association also has a 10" long slate tool (an ulu or scraper?) with a hole drilled in it, found at Hoen's Lagoon in 1976.

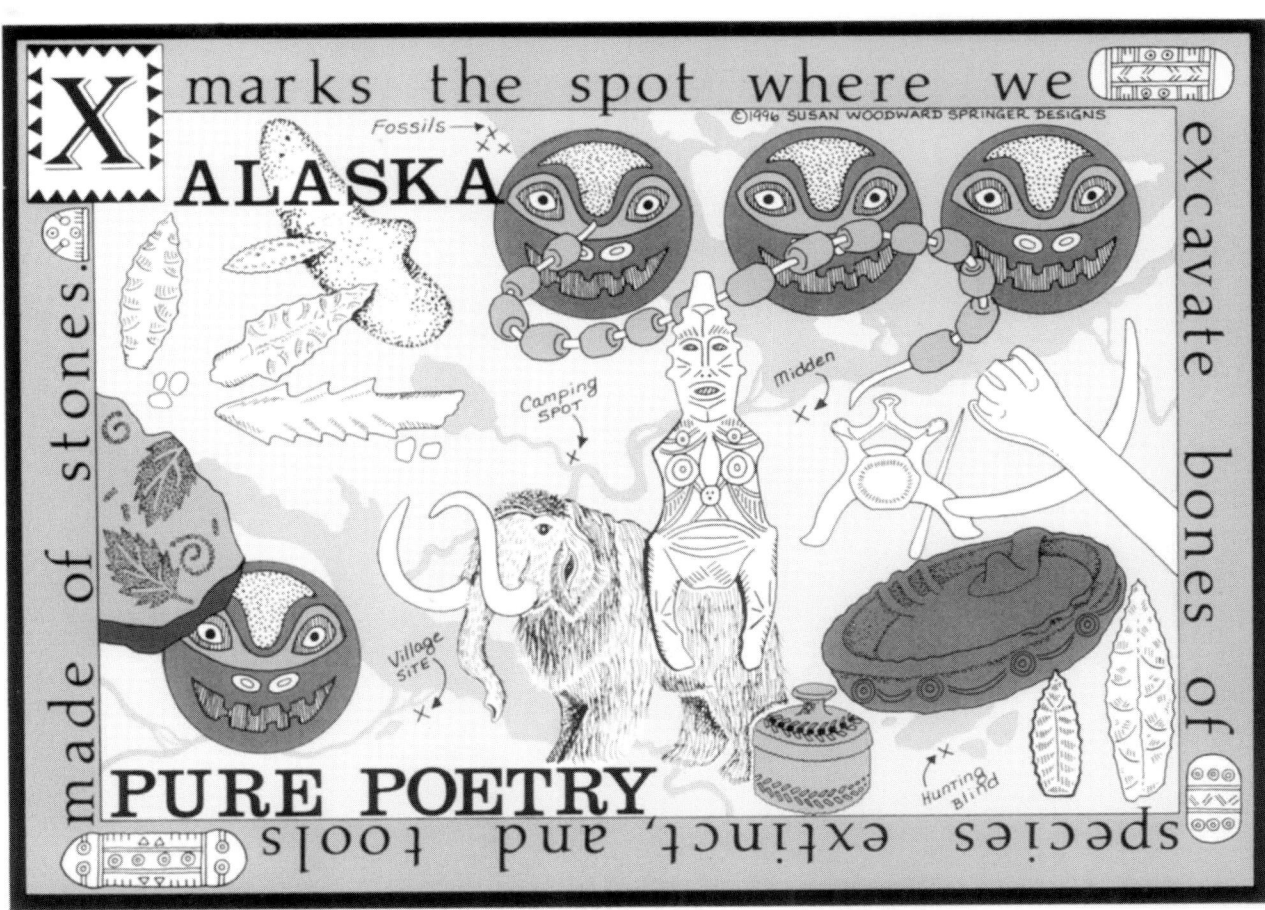

A card honoring archaeology in Alaska, drawn by the author.

In the village of Seldovia, de Laguna was told of a grave that had been found underneath a house by an Indian boy. The grave appeared to be older than the structure. A carved ivory figure[8] had been found on the beach below the Blue Fox Cafe and was in the possession of a local woman. A chipped knife blade[9] had been found on the bank behind the Seldovia House, and was given to de Laguna by Mr. W. Lloyd. De Laguna noted that holes dug along the beach for pilings had not turned up any evidence of a midden below the surface of the beach. She theorized that the old village site must have been on the hill where the Russian Orthodox Church stands.[10] A slate tool, grooved stone, and whale vertebrae bowl have all been found along the Seldovia Slough in the years since de Laguna first visited here. The slate tool is 6" long and is similar to the 10" one found at Hoen's Lagoon, both in its shape and in the placement of the drilled hole. The grooved stone measures about 4" long, and has perpendicular grooves. De Laguna found such stones rather common, and confined to the Third Kachemak Tradition.[11] The whale bone bowl is 8" in diameter by 6" high. Its walls are approximately 1" thick and the bowl is 4" deep.

It is believed likely that the bulldozers employed in the post-earthquake (1964) Urban Renewal destroyed or scattered any remains of a prehistoric village site. However, if de Laguna is correct in placing the site on the hill by the church, it is also very possible that prehistoric evidence could lie slumbering (undisturbed by Urban Renewal) beneath the church and modern homes.

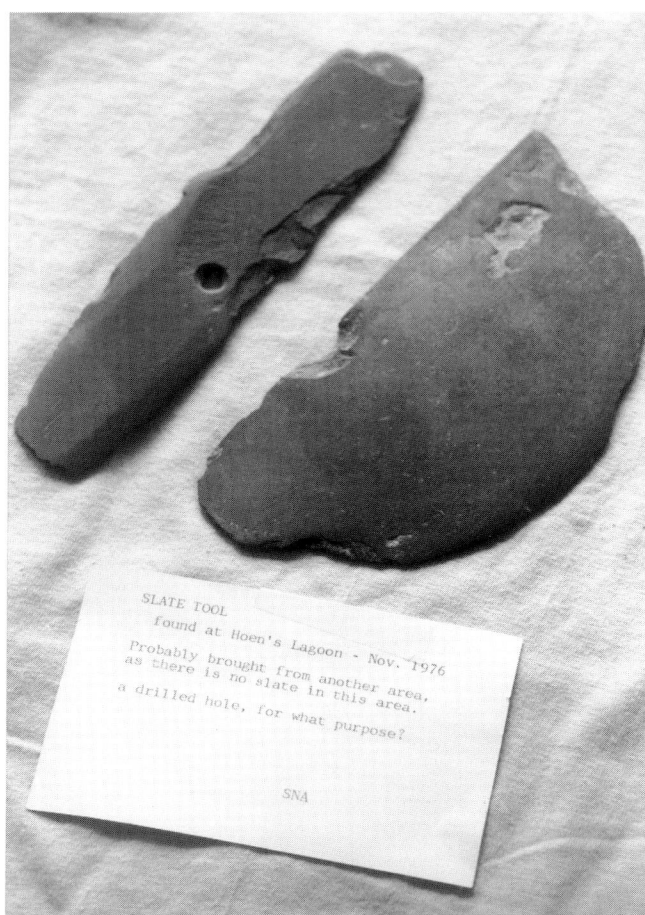

These slate tools were found at Hoen's Lagoon on Seldovia Bay in 1976 and are on display at the Seldovia Village Tribe Museum. Photo courtesy of Gail Richards.

This whale vertebrae bowl found in 1976 in the Seldovia Slough is on display at the Seldovia Village Tribe Museum. Photo courtesy of Gail Richards.

De Laguna received a report of an old Indian camping spot on Barabara Point, but did not investigate. She was given as a gift from Jack Fields a stone lamp that had been found on the east side of MacDonald Spit on the beach which faces Kasitsna Bay. This prompted her to examine the area, and upon closer inspection, she did find a one-foot thick midden. Near the midden were two house pits, one smaller than the other. Neither the midden nor the housepits appeared to be very old, and de Laguna couldn't find any artifacts to convince her to the contrary. She did conclude however that the stone lamp was undoubtedly of Eskimo origin.[12]

In recent years, several human bones were found on MacDonald Spit, and were given to the Seldovia Native Association. The bones, a left upper arm and a lower jaw bone, were sent to the state coroner's

These artifacts were found along the eastern shore of Seldovia Bay during the 1980's. Clockwise, beginning at the top, they are a stone ax, a slate scraping tool, and a slate knife blade. Photo courtesy of Dede Higman.

office for analysis. The lab report confirmed them to be Eskimoid, male, age 35, and stated that the time of death was probably prehistoric. It thus would appear that there may indeed be prehistoric sites on MacDonald Spit as yet undiscovered. The Seldovia Native Association has reinterred on Yukon Island ancient bones returned by museums, and did likewise with these bones found on MacDonald Spit.

Just inside the entrance to Jakolof Bay, and apparently near the location of the present state dock and a private cabin, de Laguna found yet another site:

"Jakolof's place ... is just to the east of a projecting rock which forms an island at high tide. At the west end of the little flat on which Jakolof's cabins are built, and under the shelter of the cliff, is a small midden. A shed is built on top of it. According to Tollak Olstead, Seldovia, when Jakolof was digging the cellar for the shed he came upon human bones, together with one or more splitting adzes, a slate knife, and the ivory statuette now in the collection of Mrs. Meehan." [13]

The ivory figure was found about 12 feet down, said Allen Peterson, Seldovia resident who observed the cellar construction, and greatly scared the natives who were helping Jakolof (then spelled Yakoloff). They were convinced the statuette, with its malevolent eyes, was evil, and would not touch it. [14]

De Laguna conducted a small excavation beside the shed and found three layers of midden, the lowermost two evidently pre-Russian, as no sign of European goods such as china, beads, or metals were found. The topmost layer did contain china and a

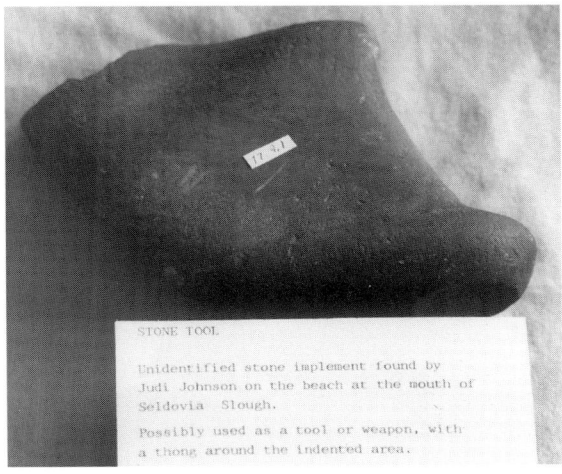

These stone tools, found in the Seldovia Slough and elsewhere around the community, suggest the distribution of artifacts is not limited to just one area of Seldovia Bay. These stone tools are on display at the Seldovia Village Tribe Museum. Photos courtesy of Gail Richards.

bone that had been cut by an iron knife, so it was cited as post-Russian contact. She did note, however, that the condition of the bones and shells in the first and third layers did not differ much from one another, and also that the land must have sunk, exposing the site to tidal action.

De Laguna went on to investigate reports of middens and places where artifacts had been found on the bays around Yukon Island. She apparently did not travel up Seldovia Bay, where a local resident found a stone maul, a scraping tool, and a knife blade. Around 1983 the resident and her son were playing on an east side beach, just up the bay from the town. The boy was throwing rocks into the water, enjoying the splash they made. One rock in particular caught his eye and the child paused moments before he launched it seaward and took it to his mother instead. This rock was positively identified by de Laguna in 1993 as an ulu or scraping tool.

Very little, if any, archaeological work has been done on Seldovia Bay since de Laguna visited here in the 1930's. There exists yet another midden in the area, unreported by de Laguna. This site lies on the north side of a tiny cove which is just south of the entrance to the lagoon. It is on Seldovia Native Association property. I measured the shell midden there in April of 1993 and found the exposed portion of it to measure 84" across and to run from 16 to 24" below the surface. Readily apparent are clamshells, mussel, cockles, triton, chiton, charcoal, and fire-cracked rocks. Unfortunately, as is the case with many coastal sites, exposure to tidal action and to the weather is eroding this midden.

In contrast, the rest of Kachemak Bay has played host to a number of archaeologists testing and expanding upon de Laguna's hallmark work. With the advent of radiocarbon dating and with many more artifacts and sites to study, de Laguna's theories about the Kachemak cultures, or traditions, have now taken their place in a broader spectrum of known cultures.

In 1989, Janet Klein discovered a site in Aurora Lagoon, farther up Kachemak Bay. Radiocarbon-14 testing on materials from the dig gave a date of 4500 years BP (Before Present), or roughly 2500 BC. The dates and artifacts found suggest the site is of the Ocean Bay tradition. The next known culture is the Arctic Small Tool tradition, or Basal Component, identified from a dig on Chugachik Island, which is near the head of Kachemak Bay and off its south shore. This culture dates to 4000 years BP, or about 2000 BC. De Laguna's Kachemak Tradition is now combined into two periods, an older and a younger. The entire tradition is felt to span the period from 1000 BC to 500 AD, although these dates are open to continuing debate and testing.[15] The Late Prehistoric Period covers the years from 500 AD to 1750 AD, with the Historic Period, or post-European contact, continuing from 1780 to 1900 AD.[16]

Some pieces of Seldovia's historic and perhaps prehistoric past were sold off as curios. Steamship passengers disembarking at Seldovia around the turn of the century often roamed the village in search of souvenirs. Ella R. Higginson, writing in 1909, described stopping at Seldovia on a steamer. She climbed down a rope ladder and into a dory for the trip ashore with her friends. She quickly concluded that this was not the place to buy baskets, for she watched one member of her party purchase a poorly made and poorly colored basket for the hefty price of $5.00. After a walk about the village, Higginson's party came upon a barabara where they found "real treasures—old bows and arrows, kamelinkas, bidarkas, virgin charms, and ivory spears."[17] These they bought straight away and carried back to the steamer. This was undoubtedly a scenario oft repeated here, with the result that very few artifacts have been passed down to the present day.

Seldovia Midden Found in 1993

Until 1993, the most recent pre-European or Late Prehistoric Period site known to exist on Kachemak Bay was in Halibut Cove. This site dates from around 1200 AD. In April of 1993, the picture began to change when I stumbled across a layer of broken shells protruding from a cut bank near Seldovia's Outside Beach. My journal entries from April 2nd and 4th describe this find which I, at the time, merely thought was "neat," but which would later turn out to be of significance in the prehistoric timeline of human habitation in Kachemak Bay.

From an original linoleum block print by the author.

April 2, 1993

Today as I was walking the Outside Beach with the dogs, I decided to continue on up to the new city camping park. Public access ends in the park, so I made it the terminus of our walk and turned to come back down the path to the beach. A mussel shell protruding from the bank caught my eye, and I scraped at it with my boot. Out tumbled more bits of mussel, from earth that looked markedly different than the surrounding bank. Intrigued, I found a sharp flat rock and began to scrape away the dirt. It was laden with the shells of chiton, limpet, snail, mussel, and clam. There were many tiny greenish bits that looked like fresh spruce needles, but upon closer inspection turned out to be sea urchin fragments. As I dug, I found charcoal from a fire, and a smooth stone such as one would use to ring a fire pit. It was at this point I sat back and thought that I might have found something old. I looked out to sea and imagined a band of hunters, stopping here for the night, keeping watch over their bidarkas hauled high on the beach and feasting on food gathered from the rocks. As I looked at the barely exposed fire pit, it became dark and I heard the hunters laughing and talking. I watched the sparks from their fire spit toward the sky. I felt the moist chewing sounds as they pulled the hot morsels from the shells with their teeth. The word "delicious" sat in my mind and would not leave.

I brought home samples of the firepit contents and called my archaeologist friend Janet Klein. I learned that:

a. I screwed up by exposing part of the site, but at least I had not committed the fatal error of tossing the diggings back into the hole.
b. the site might not date back older than 200 years because there were sea urchin shell fragments present. These are some of the first things to decompose, unlike the sea urchin spines. However, if no man made materials such as glass, china, beads, or ammunition were found, then the site could be much older, and simply well preserved, which would allow for the presence of the sea urchin shell fragments.
c. radiocarbon dating was possible, but the samples had to be extracted carefully and, as Janet put it, "scientifically"—that means we wear white lab coats and carry notebooks on clipboards, and take lots of measurements, and have intelligent discussions and spirited arguments. Things like cigarette smoke, plastic wrap, and salty sea spray can mess up the accuracy of a radiocarbon date.

Janet promised that she and her partner Peter Zollars would be over by month's end to excavate these sites properly for us. I can hardly wait. I will go back out to the beach site tomorrow to cover it with spruce boughs so it can remain undisturbed for a few more weeks.

April 4, 1993

A secret is not worth having unless it is shared with at least a few other people. I shared the secret of the discovered midden with Lynn, and with Bob and Mary Lindemann. Lynn and I searched in vain for a midden by her house. She will have to talk to the man who claims to have found it, and who told her, "Oh, I'm surprised you haven't seen it before. It's in an eroding hillside RIGHT BY your house." Lynn and I discovered this afternoon just how many eroding hillsides there are "right by" her house!

We convinced Lynn's son to go see the Outside Beach midden site with us, after assuring him that we would not be excavating any ancient graves, the disturbed inhabitants of which he feared might haunt his sleep. The dogs were glorious with mud, and we all piled in the Willy's to pick up Bob and Mary. They squeezed into the back seat, pressed against friendly and filthy dogs, and we were off.

Bob had brought frozen Snickers bars, which he distributed once we arrived at the beach. They kept us happily occupied until we reached the site. The party was duly impressed with my find, and everyone examined the surrounding bank. We found that the firepit seemed to extend 48" across the bank, with stray shells another three feet on either side. We imagined the hunters sitting in a circle around the fire, and tossing empty shells over their shoulders. We had a lengthy discussion on why the hunters chose this spot, concluding that it afforded them the best view of the bay and the coastline to the west on the left, and to the east on the right. Rival hunting parties could be seen approaching in their bidarkas from far away, and the Russian ships that ran between Kodiak, Fort Alexander, and Kenai, would have been in plain sight. Mary found a bone sticking out of the bank, but we restrained ourselves from digging.

We walked the beach, all of us now ripe with desire to find more evidence of ancient habitation. I walked ahead, looking up at the cliffs with their Rastafarian cap of eroding soil laced with dredlocks of tree roots. A clam shell poking its head from the dirt high above merited closer inspection, and I climbed up the rotten rock face for a look. There, hidden under the exposed roots of a tree, was the clamshell, and beside it two bones. I did not remove them, but I could see that both appeared to be vertebrae of some kind. After announcing my find, the challenge was on, the gauntlet thrown. Every square centimeter of that cliff was analyzed by four other pairs of eyes, but no more potential sites were found.

The timing of my find was most fortuitous, for in less than two weeks, Dr. de Laguna herself was scheduled to be in the Kachemak Bay area for perhaps a last look at the places of her youthful pursuits. She was in Alaska to be honored at an anthropological conference, and was making a number of side trips, Kachemak Bay among them. From Homer she was to come to Seldovia and spend the night with us. Who better to shed some light on my discovery!

After an impressive round of public receptions and gatherings in Homer honoring Dr. de Laguna, a party of 25 archaeological groupies boarded a small cruise boat for Seldovia. But first we would point the bow towards the head of Kachemak Bay, bound for Chugachik Island, the beginning of Dr. de Laguna's 1930's haunts on the south shore. Some four and a half hours and many ancient sites later, we arrived in Seldovia. De Laguna had not returned here since 1932. For her, Seldovia must have borne little resemblance to the bustling boardwalk town of the 1930's. Because of my telephone introduction to and resultant correspondance with her for the past several months, I had fallen into the honor of hosting her quite by accident, there being almost no one left in town who knew her when she was here before. I was thrilled at the opportunity to get to know this great woman one-on-one.

The adoring crowd having dispersed, Dr. de Laguna became "Freddy," and Freddy announced that she would like a walk. No one had permitted her to walk, she said, for almost the last month she had been travelling. I had shared with her the secret of my discovered midden, and she was eager to see it for herself. After a brief stop at the house, we set off to walk the two miles to the Outside Beach and the site, accompanied by a reporter and trailed by a photographer and my dogs in our Willys jeep. The dogs were thoroughly confused at our strange and slow procession, but I would not permit them to run wild down the dirt road; I needed to concentrate on getting this very determined 86 year old woman with replaced hips and a cane over the gravel and potholes without incident.

We made it almost all the way to the site before vast pools of standing water from the melted snow forced us to detour to the gravel beach. I had been dreading such a detour, for the soft beach gravel was piled high and was littered on top with strands of bull kelp and driftwood: a veritable mine-field for an older person. Freddy approached a small streamlet, her feet slipped, and down she went, although gracefully. I stood by with arms flailing impotently (convinced I would live forever in disgrace and infamy as the jerk who wiped out Frederica de Laguna) as she deftly scrambled to her feet. With a laugh, she motioned ahead and we continued on to the site.

I showed Freddy the midden, and how I'd measured the distribution of the shell fragments. She poked and dug lightly at the bank with her cane and with her hands. The photographer danced about, shooting almost non-stop. I had been adamant that no photographs were to be taken which might reveal the location of the site, since I was determined to keep it undisturbed until a proper excavation could be done. The photographer readily agreed.

I pointed out to Freddy the bone and shell fragments high on the cliff overhang above the beach. In less than two weeks, heavy rains had eroded the precipitous dirt and clumps of it laden with clamshell had tumbled down to the beach. I climbed up. "Gee Freddy," I called, "It looks like these bones might fall out of the bank if I don't retrieve them. What do you think?" "Absolutely!" she called back, without hesitation. Bones thus retrieved, I climbed down and presented them to her. One appeared to be the lower leg bone of a small animal, she said, but what kind of animal she could not ascertain. The other seemed to be the ankle or heel bone of a larger animal. I also displayed two rocks that had caught my eye: one smooth on a side and sharply broken on another. Freddy identified this as fire-cracked rock. The other had what I thought were a series of four tiny holes bored or worn into it. I rinsed it so they could be more clearly seen. "Ahh," said Freddy with great ceremony as we watched, anxious for her pronouncement, "This is a rock!"

The author clings to exposed spruce roots for a closer look at bits of shell and bone protruding from the midden, while Dr. Frederica de Laguna waits below for a report. Photo by Bill Roth, courtesy of the Anchorage Daily News.

The excavation is visited by Seldovia Native Association President Fred Elvsaas and his wife, Gladys, in May 1993. The author is at left, and archaeologist Pete Zollars is at right. Photo courtesy of Janet Klein.

I circled around, intending to approach the bank from on top, lying on my stomach out over the cliff. Once up there, though, I found the bank sloped down too much for my comfort, so I sat in the grass and waited for Pete to complete his inspection. Admiring the spring shoots and wild plant starts, I looked down and at my left hand was a small pile of fresh dirt atop the grass. The dirt was heavily mixed with sea urchin spines and shell fragments! Excitedly I called down to Pete and up he came. He took one look at the little pile and said, "Okay—we dig here."

We would later find that the little pile of earth which signalled Pete like a beacon was due to the presence of a small creature, probably a hoary marmot, whose burrow we

Before she left Seldovia, Freddy cautioned me that my find was probably a small midden, which might not turn up anything of interest in the way of artifacts. She felt it to be a temporary campsite, as opposed to evidence of a more permanent habitation. Although I took her caution under advisement, it could not dampen my enthusiasm for excavating the site.

Homer archaeologists Janet Klein and Peter Zollars had agreed to do the excavation, donating their time. I had them flown to Seldovia in May and housed them for our weekend test dig. It turned out to be the best investment I could make, as early on in our dig we "struck gold." Where exactly to begin digging was somewhat of a question and the three of us first did an extensive visual survey of the area. I showed Pete the exposed shell fragments in the dirt atop the cliff, but there wasn't room for two of us to cling to the cliff face.

These artifacts were found during the SEL-248 dig in 1993. From left are an incised and shaped piece of bone (possibly a labret), a bone awl, a bone spear point, a stone knife blade tip, and three pieces of cut or carved bone. These artifacts are on display at the Seldovia Village Tribe Museum. Photo courtesy of Janet Klein.

excavated in the midst of our test site. Pete and I worked from the cliff face toward the forest and Janet worked toward us from the forest seaward. The test pit dimensions would end up being 1.5 meters (about 60") from east to west, by 82 cm. from north to south. In the course of two days, we took this rectangular pit down to a depth of 28-30 cm. (11 to 12").

Janet turned up the first artifact, right under the tangled mat of grasses and roots. Neither archaeologist had seen anything like it, and we could only guess that it might be some kind of decorative facial ornament, such as a labret. For the remainder of that day and all of the following, we scraped carefully away at the sides and the bottom of the hole. Seven artifacts in all were found, together with a large array of bones and shells. Near the bottom of

The author digs a smaller pit through the floor of the primary test pit, and reaches volcanic ash. Beneath this is sterile earth, undisturbed by humans, which signals the bottom of the midden. Photo courtesy of Janet Klein.

the pit we even found piles of berry seeds, and I found my first (and only) artifact: a bone awl lying just above a large roll of birchbark. Janet and Pete were thrilled with the birchbark, for now we could get a good radiocarbon 14 date. Although we had found an adequate amount of charcoal for this purpose, birchbark produces a far more accurate reading. In addition, its proximity to the bottom of the pit ensured it would be free from contaminants such as salt water.

The weather had been cold and wet and windy, not atypical for Seldovia in early May but tiresome for working outside. I was not unhappy when we began to reach volcanic ash on the floor of the pit. This does not necessarily signal the bottom layer of a midden, as evidenced in the Kachemak Tradition sites farther up Kachemak Bay,

This piece of birch bark, found by the author during the SEL-248 dig in close proximity to a bone awl, was used to carbon date the site. Although charcoal was found at the site, birch bark produces a more accurate radio carbon-14 date. Photo courtesy of Janet Klein.

but it did in our case: a smaller pit dug through the floor of our primary test pit showed that beneath our volcanic ash layer was sterile earth.

Once photographs and measurements were taken, it was time to fill in our hole.

Plastic sheeting was laid in the pit before we refilled it with dirt. This is so that subsequent archaeologists who might dig here could readily see the extent of our test pit. Once filled in, the sod was replaced and the cliff face stabilized with tree branches. Atop the sod we dragged branches and scattered grasses and duff from the forest floor. Within a month the wildflowers had begun to sprout as if they had never been disturbed at all.

Now began another difficult period: waiting while the birchbark was being analyzed and dated. The site had been assigned a state identification number of SEL 248, and would be known as the Hawkey site (chosen by me to honor my father). By late June, the report from Washington State University was back. The birchbark sample, now known as SEL 248.8/WSU 4471, showed the midden dated to the late 15th or early 16th century, with a calendar date of 1478, plus or minus 90 years. This would put the site in the late prehistoric period[18] or the period of human habitation prior to European contact.

> From my journal:
> To see a 500 year old artifact in a museum is to acknowledge the foggy existence of early man. To find that same artifact in provenience, to pick it out of the dirt and to touch it (perhaps being the first to do so since its original owner), is in some small way to know early man, and to feel a tangible link with him.

By speciating the shells and over 400 bones we retrieved from the test pit, it is possible to know what these people ate.

Some bones bore puncture marks, which could indicate the presence of domestic dogs. It is interesting to note that de Laguna's Yukon Island excavations revealed the presence of Eskimo dog bones. They appeared with regularity in the first and second Kachemak periods, somewhat less in the sub-third period, and rarely in the third period. In her excavations of sites from the third or last period of Eskimo occupation, she notes the emergence of bones from a Plains Indian type of dog. She felt that the Eskimo brought sled-pulling type dogs with them from the north, but found them to be ill-suited for travel around the Bay area. As the dogs were bred less, their numbers declined. The appearance of the Plains Indian type dog bones would indicate the Eskimos had had contact with Indians coming to the area.[19] Janet Klein notes that it was not uncommon for dogs to be

BONES AND SHELLS FROM THE TEST PIT

Shellfish
Arctic Rock Borer —*Hiatella arctica*
Barnacle — *Balanus sp.*
Barnacle, Thatched — *Semibalanus cariosis*
Blue Mussel — *Mytilus edulis*
Chiton, Black Katy — *Katharina tunicata*
Cockle — *Clinocardium nuttallii*
Dogwinkle — *Nucella lima*
Limpet — *Notoacmea scutum*
Moon Snail, Aleutian —*Natica aleutica*
Pacific Littleneck Clam — *Protothaca staminea*
Periwinkle — *Littorina sitkana*
Ridged Whelk — *Neptunea lirata*
Sea Urchin, Green — *Strongylocentrotus droebachiensis*
Surf Clam — *Spisula polynyma*
Washington Clam — *Saxidomus giganteus*
Whelk, Big Mouthed — *Volutharpa ampullacea*

Fauna-Birds
Waterfowl
Cormorant, possible

Fauna-Land Mammal
Black Bear — *Ursus sp.*
Hoary Marmot — *Marmota caligata*
Deer family (antler) — *Cervidae*

Fauna-Marine Mammal
Seal — presumed to be harbor seal, but could be another species; found bones from both immature and mature animals, however most were immature;

Fauna-Fish
Halibut
Salmonoid — unspeciated
Otoliths (ear bones) of Pollock or Cod—definitely not of halibut, salmon, or rockfish

Flora
Seeds, unidentified species
Birch bark, unworked

SEL 248 ARTIFACT LIST
(from the unpublished site report by Klein and Zollars, 1993)

SEL 248-1 .... *Unidentified implement (an ornamental piece? a labret?)
 *Long, rectangular piece with knob on one end, slightly curved, concave surface, decorated with incised lines
 *Material: bone
 *Overall measurements: 8.5 cm Long x 0.9 cm Wide x 0.2 cm Thick
 *Provenience: 20 m below surface (BS), not directly associated with urchin midden

SEL 248-2 .... *Slate point tip
 *ground edges, break suggests clean snap
 *Measurements: 3.2 cm Long x 1.3 cm Wide x .30 cm Thick
 *Provenience: 20 cm BS, within lower shell midden complex

SEL 248-3 .... *Worked Antler
 *Worked on all surfaces, two incised lines visible
 *Measurements: 3.10 cm Long x 2.00 cm Wide x 1.10 cm Thick

SEL 248-4 .... *Cut Antler
 *Possible remnant of worked piece similar to SEL 248-3
 *Measurements: 1.50 cm Long x 1.00 cm Wide x 1.20 cm Thick

SEL 248-5 .... *Cut Bone-Land or Marine Mammal
 *Bone splinter with straight decorative lines; appears to be part of a larger worked piece
 *Measurements: 7.6 cm Long x 0.08 cm Wide x 0.06 cm Thick

SEL 248-6 .... *Dart Point
 *Bilaterally barbed, 4 barbs, broken
 *Material: Land Mammal Bone
 *Measurements: 3.80 cm Long x 1.82 cm Wide x 0.4 cm Thick
 * de Laguna calls this a barbed dart head (ref Plate 40-4)

SEL 248-7 .... *Awl, splinter
 *Material: Bird Bone
 *Measurements: 7.5 cm Long x 0.8 cm Wide x 0.3 cm Thick
 *Found above and in direct association with piece of birch bark which was submitted for C-14 dating

eaten once their useful working life (as, for example, pack animals) was over.[20]

A small number of the bones were calcined or charred. An unusual amount of green sea urchin fragments, including spicules (spines) and the mouth plates (Aristotle's lantern) were found. The deposit of these fragments was uncommonly thick.[21]

The SEL 248 site is interpreted by Klein and Zollars to be definitely pre-historic, but there are insufficient tools and diagnostic artifacts to assign to it a particular culture. The tentative analysis is that the site was a seasonal camp for people subsisting on marine mammals and invertebrates, land mammals, and fish. Stone, bone, and antler were worked to fashion tools and possibly ornaments. The fact that deep sea fish and seal bones were found would suggest these people were both mobile and maritime-adapted. The presence of bones from young seals suggests that the encampment was occupied in late spring or early summer.[22]

With a C-14 date of around 1478 AD, SEL 248 replaces the Halibut Cove (approx. 1200 AD) site as the most recent prehistoric find on Kachemak Bay.

The Halibut Cove site is presumed to be prehistoric Dena'ina by archaeologists, but SEL 248 does not fit their cultural pattern, primarily because the Dena'ina were known for leaving clean campsites. The SEL 248 site cannot be associated with any known culture at this time, but it does make the gap between prehistoric and historic people that much narrower.

In the weeks following our SEL 248 dig, I found a similar cliff midden near Seldovia's Inside Beach and one at Lookout Point. The same clues of shells protruding from an overhung bank can be seen. Knowing now the significance of the SEL 248 site, it is my hope that funding can be secured to conduct a full scale excavation there, as well as test digs at other sites that are discovered. In 1994, Janet Klein and I climbed into harnesses and lashed ourselves to a tree in order to better inspect the Inside Beach cliff midden. With the permission of the landowner, we excavated a small test pit on top of the cliff. Although we found remnants of shells similar to SEL 248 we also found 20th century bullet casings. Given this contradictory evidence, we chose not to proceed further. Whether this is a relatively new site or an old site that has suffered recent disturbance is not known. Only through more site samplings, radio carbon-14 datings, and artifacts to analyze will the picture of prehistoric life in Seldovia and Kachemak Bay come into focus.

Wearing climbing harnesses, the author and Janet Klein inspect a cliff top midden near the Inside Beach. Photo courtesy of Janet Klein.

Endnotes

[1] Frederica de Laguna, *The Archaeology of Cook Inlet*, 2nd ed. (Anchorage: Alaska Historical Society, 1975) 29; Tom Kizzia, "Honoring a Lifetime of Discovery,"*Anchorage Daily News* 26 April, 1993: B1-2 .

[2] De Laguna, "Impressions of Seldovia in the Early Nineteen-Thirties," unpublished essay written for this book, 1993.

[3] *Anchorage Daily News,* 26 April, 1993.

[4] De Laguna, "Impressions."

[5] Janet Klein, personal communication, Sept. 94.

[6] De Laguna, *Archaeology* 17.

[7] De Laguna, *Archaeology* Plate 21-6.

[8] De Laguna, *Archaeology* Plate 52-9.

[9] De Laguna, *Archaeology* Plate 30-1.

[10] De Laguna, *Archaeology* 17.

[11] De Laguna, *Archaeology* 55.

[12] De Laguna, *Archaeology* 17.

[13] De Laguna, *Archaeology* 18.

[14] Alice Cushing Lipke, *Under the Aurora* (Los Angeles: Suttonhouse, 1938) 255, 270. Author's note: I stumbled across this book while on a research trip to Juneau. The book is long out of print, but a signed copy of it was waiting, seemingly just for me, in a rare book store there. I made numerous phone calls to try to locate the publishing house to seek reprint permission. I was unable to find Suttonhouse, nor anyone who knew which publisher might have bought their rights. A search for Lipke heirs was equally unproductive.

[15] William B. Workman, "Archaeology of the Southern Kenai Peninsula,"paper, North Pacific Maritime Cultures Seminar, Honolulu, June 1993: 8-10.

[16] Workman, "Archaeology" 11-12.

[17] Ella R. Higginson, *Alaska: The Great Country* (New York: MacMillan, 1909) 302-303.

[18] Workman, "Archaeology" 11.

[19] De Laguna, *Archaeology,* 31-32.

[20] Klein, personal communication, 1993.

[21] Janet R. Klein and Peter Zollars, "SEL-248," unpublished site report, 1993.

[22] Klein and Zollars.

EARLY EXPLORATION

The Cook Inlet Travels of Some 18th and 19th Century Explorers, As They Relate to Seldovia

There is no unbroken line of recorded or evidential (archaeological) history for Seldovia or Kachemak Bay. Until the discovery and carbon-dating of the Hawkey SEL 248 site, a gap between known cultures stretched from a presumed Dena'ina site in Halibut Cove dating from about 1200 AD to the broadly accepted "first mention" of modern Seldovia: Ivan Petroff's 1880 census. The Hawkey site, with its 1478 AD date, narrows the gap between known cultures. Even so, a period of a little over 400 years of unknown habitation remains.

To an historian, this is a curious situation. To begin with, the Golden Age of Alaskan exploration began in the latter half of the 18th century. Starting in the 1780's, European Captains Cook, Portlock, Dixon, Meares, and Russian Captains such as Bocharov, Izmailov, Golikov, and Shelikov all sailed up Cook's Inlet on various trading and exploratory missions. Bocharov himself reported to his superiors (in 1789) that "many European ships were seen...at Kenai Bay...".[1] [Kenai Bay would also be known as Cook or Cooks Inlet.] With all that activity just beyond the mouth of Seldovia Bay, that there is no mention made of a deepwater fjord here, nor of any civilization, no matter how transient, is a point that bears further consideration.

How could an area so attractive to humans just three hundred years before now apparently be ignored by explorers from Russia, England, America, Spain, and France? Although we'll likely never know for sure, a study of the logs of these explorers, and of the climatic and socioeconomic forces in place at the time may allow a reasonable explanation to be formed.

Glacial Influence

The south shore mountains of Kachemak Bay are peppered with glaciers, with at least six fingers of ice that reach down toward (but no longer come close to) the fjords. Although no glacier has commanded the head of Seldovia Bay for at least 10,000 years, there are several massive icefields above Kachemak Bay, and it is here the modern glaciers reside. The Grewingk-Yalik Ice Complex, with its Southern and Doroshin glaciers, is closest to Seldovia Bay, beginning just south of Tutka Bay and stretching 40 km to the east. Almost adjoining it is the Harding Ice Field, which pushes east another 80 km. The proximity of these glaciers dictated much of the climate of Kachemak Bay in prehistoric times, and it is thus appropriate to note their activity within the last millenium.

In 1850, Dr. Constantin Caspar Andreas Grewingk published a geological study of Alaska. Although he did not visit Alaska personally, he was able to compile a comprehensive survey based on reports from visiting Russian scientists who had studied Alaska over the previous ten years. While his book made note of the Kachemak Bay glaciers, it was not until a century later that modern scientists began tracking their movement and influence.

In the early 1990's, Dr. Gregory Wiles of the University of New York at Buffalo studied the glaciers on the south shore of Kachemak Bay. He was able to identify in the late prehistoric era a period of significant ice advancement known as the Little Ice Age. "As early as 1488 AD, the study glaciers were once again advancing into the forest. The initial date of this event is determined by radiocarbon ages on wood incorporated in two lateral moraines at Grewingk Glacier and in an end moraine at Tustumena Glacier. The age of trees (about 150 years) and lichen diameters (about 60 cm) suggest retreat from terminal positions occurred during the early to middle 19th century."[2]

The Little Ice Age in Kachemak Bay lasted until the mid 1800's, when a trend of global warming began that continues today. The Little Ice Age glacial retreat began before or by 1858 AD from the Grewingk terminal moraine, and from the

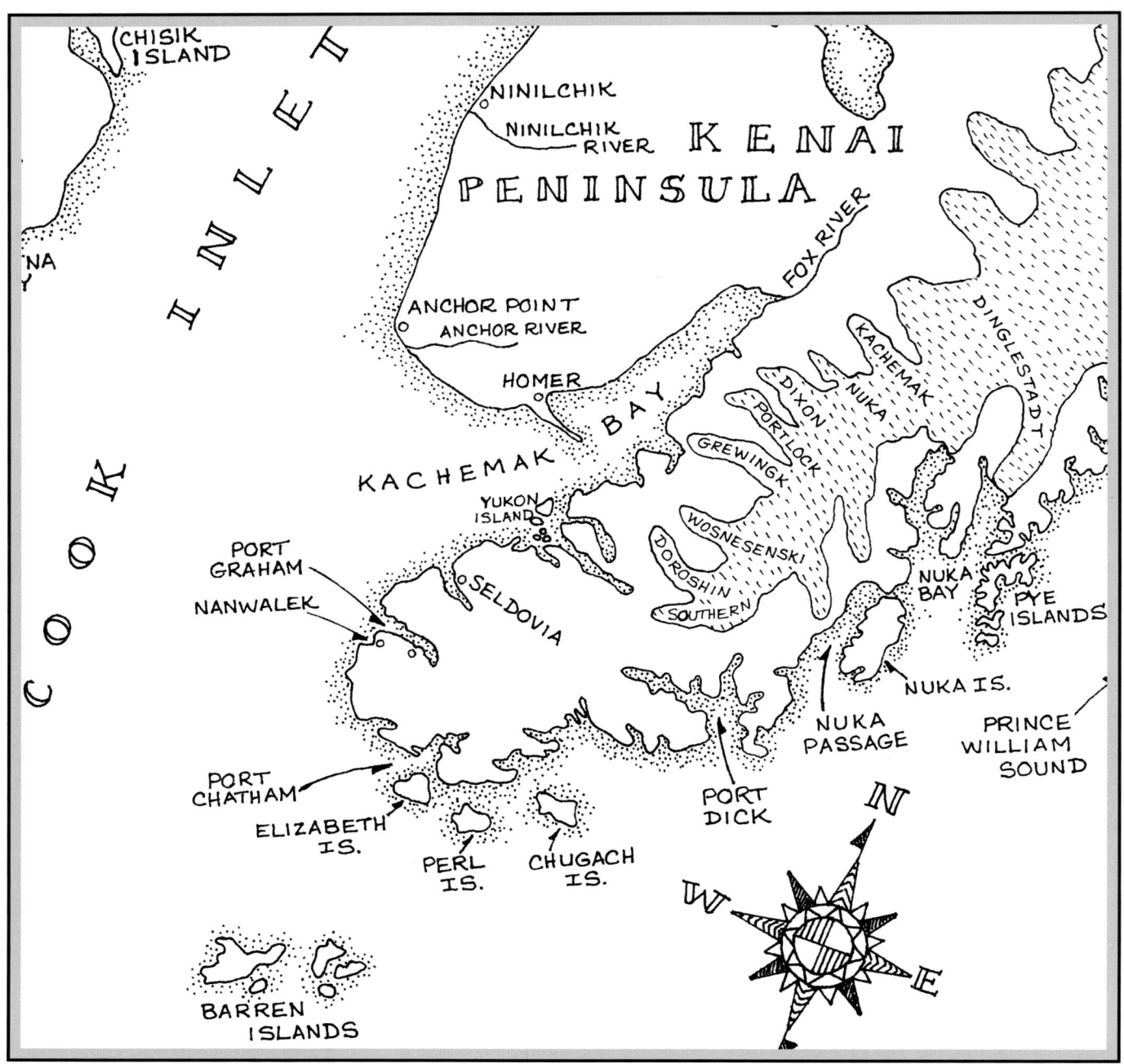

Although there is no longer a glacier at the head of Seldovia Bay, a number of the fjords farther up Kachemak Bay are crested by these ice age remnants. Map by Susan W. Springer © 1997.

Wosnesenski Glacier by 1828 AD.[3] These are the two glaciers within closest proximity to Seldovia Bay, and have had, one might presume, the greatest climatic influence. The height of the glacial advance is thought to have occurred from the 1600's to the 1800's, and the local climate is felt to have been affected by a 1-2 degree centigrade drop in temperature.

It is curious that the apex of the Little Ice Age in Kachemak Bay occurred during the time of initial European exploration, namely the 1700 and 1800's. The July 1786 logs of Captains George Dixon and Nathaniel Portlock, aboard the English vessels *King George* and *Queen Charlotte*, lend credence to the effects of the advancing glaciers on the local climate. This excerpt was written in Coal Harbor, (present day Port Graham): " Cook's River 25th July 1786: ...The more distant mountains, whose lofty summits reach the clouds, are totally covered with snow, and have the appearance of everlasting winter. ....let it suffice for thee at present to know, that though this is the latter end of July, the weather is in general cold, damp, and disagreeable, with frequent showers of snow or sleet, and the surrounding prospect barren, dreary, and uncomfortable."[4] Dr. Wiles notes, "It is

Giant ice cakes are left stranded along the banks of the Seldovia Slough, deposited there during the high tides. This photograph dates from the winter of 1946/47. Photo courtesy of the Gene Wadsworth Collection.

tempting to say that this time interval [the Little Ice Age] was a period of harsh cold that kept people away from this region." While we cannot know this for certain, it is apparent at least that the Dixon/Portlock expedition did not consider it the Promised Land.

Dr.Wiles notes that at no time in the last 10,000 years did the glaciers reach the tidewaters of Kachemak Bay. "Only in the Kenai Fjords did ice reach tidewater. Many maps drawn in the 1800-1900's show glaciers near the water. From the ocean, many glaciers appear to terminate near the water, however they did not." [5] He also feels that Kachemak Bay, even with the increased fresh water glacial runoff, did not freeze over for long periods.

While this may be true, it is worth noting that older residents of Seldovia today remember Kachemak Bay freezing sufficiently in 1946/47 to permit travel from the south shore to the Homer Spit.[6] This memorable winter boasted a cold snap that lasted from January 16 through February 4, with only one recorded temperature above zero during that time. Ice destroyed the Homer dock, and in Seldovia Bay it carried two boats onto the rocks and wrenched three others from their moorings. On Kachemak Bay, vessel traffic was at a standstill. In the Seldovia Slough, the ice pack was finally blasted free with dynamite after it nearly wiped out the bridge, the Lippincott home, and several other waterfront buildings.[7]

Homer pioneer Della Banks reported that at the turn of the century a boat discharging its passengers (herself among them) at the Homer Spit could not

Drifting ice cakes and extreme high tides conspired during the winter of 1946/47 to create significant damage to boats tied along the banks of the Seldovia Slough. In this photograph, the F/V Sea Scout was frozen to the ground and thus swamped during the tide. Photo courtesy of the Gene Wadsworth Collection.

get on the beach due to icebergs. The month was April, and she remembered having to scramble over the ice to get to shore.[8] Such icing conditions may not have been the norm, but it is worth noting that they occurred *after* the 1880's onset of the present global warming trend. The question becomes, then: if such severe icing took place in Kachemak Bay *after* the Little Ice Age, what were the conditions *during* its reign?

The theory of severe sea-icing caused by the Little Ice Age would neatly explain the absence of year-round settlement in Seldovia Bay prior to the late 1800's. The 1478 AD C-14 date from the SEL-248 site, if it turned out to be the most recent prehistoric site found on Kachemak Bay, would coincide almost exactly with the onset of the Little Ice Age in 1488. One could assume that the Little Ice Age did in fact create climatic conditions so harsh that Kachemak Bay was not used or visited at all. Unfortunately, there are too many unknowns to lend such a theory much credence. To begin with, until all the prehistoric sites on Kachemak Bay are discovered and dated, such a conclusion cannot be drawn. In addition, we simply do not know much about the typical weather patterns during the Little Ice Age.

Dr. Wiles asserts that silting of Kachemak Bay, rather than freezing, may have discouraged human habitation during the Little Ice Age. "Increased glacial activity during this time could have silted the waters too much for some marine life, which the people depended on for food." [9] In her article for the *Seldovia Herald*, de Laguna made reference to the silting up of the north shore of Kachemak Bay destroying the shellfish.[10] Such a decline in food resources could have been a compelling reason for humans to move away from the Bay.

Early Explorers

By studying the maps and accounts of some of the first Europeans to explore Cook Inlet, we are offered a tantalizing glimpse at Kachemak Bay during the last two centuries of the Little Ice Age. This glimpse reveals that despite the presumably harsh climate there very probably were human settlements on the Bay, although their location and permanence has never been established.

Many of the early maps either don't show Kachemak Bay, or simply indicate it as a featureless indentation off Cook Inlet. Some early Russian maps do suggest that Kachemak Bay was entered, but it is not until the mid 19th century that Seldovia Bay is shown as a named feature. Because of the competition, at first between rival Russian fur companies and later between explorers from different countries, maps were not always shared with fellow explorers. After all, the primary reason for most forays into new territory was to seek out new sources of marketable goods: sharing your sources of fur with your competitors made poor business sense.

One of the first known maps of the coastline to include Kachemak Bay was made in 1784 by the Russian navigator Dmitrii Bocharov. He was part of the trading company headed by Ivan Golikov and Grigorii Shelikov. The map was a detailed piece, used later to create a more general map, and is shown on page 42. Dr. Richard Pierce of the University of Alaska at Fairbanks translated this map and its annotations. An ethnographic note accompanying the map reads as follows, (with 18th century place names transcribed to modern day names): " Peoples living on the mainland as far as the Kamykshatsk [Kamishak] Bay, and on the islands indicated in this plan, are in general called Koniags, which have the same way of life and language. *The people living in Kamykshats*[Kamishak], *Kenai and Shugachik [Kachemak] bays and beyond are called Kinaitsy."* [11] This single sentence mentioning the Kinaitsy in Shugachik Bay in a casual sweep of the area is a careless ethnographic summary, and yet it could be evidence of 18th century settlements on Kachemak Bay - perhaps even Seldovia Bay - probably received second hand by the navigators.

In July and August of 1786, Englishmen George Dixon and Nathaniel Portlock captained two ships that sailed up Cook's Inlet. Captain Portlock found himself in Kachemak Bay, but was unable to anchor:

> July 26-27, 1786 (enroute from Port Graham) "During the night we had light airs, and the tide carried us very fast to the northeast into a deep opening, which is formed by Anchor Point, and the land to the northeast of Point Bede. *[This describes Kachemak Bay.]* Our depth of water was too much for anchoring, being upwards of sixty fathoms; so that we were put under the neccessity of waiting for a breeze to push us out again. At 5 o'clock in the morning a light breeze came on from the eastward, with which we stood north-northwest for Anchor Point, having got out of the opening with the ebb tide. The lead was kept constantly going, and we had soundings from 48 to 30 fathoms water, over a bottom of fine grey sand." [12]

At two PM on August 12th, observations showed Captain Dixon's party to be at 59° 28' North latitude, which would be just north of but in clear view of Seldovia Bay. The log reveals, however, the ship to be more concerned with catching a favorable tide for the trip down the Inlet than with venturing off into Kachemak Bay. Nevertheless, the observations made of the native people of the area

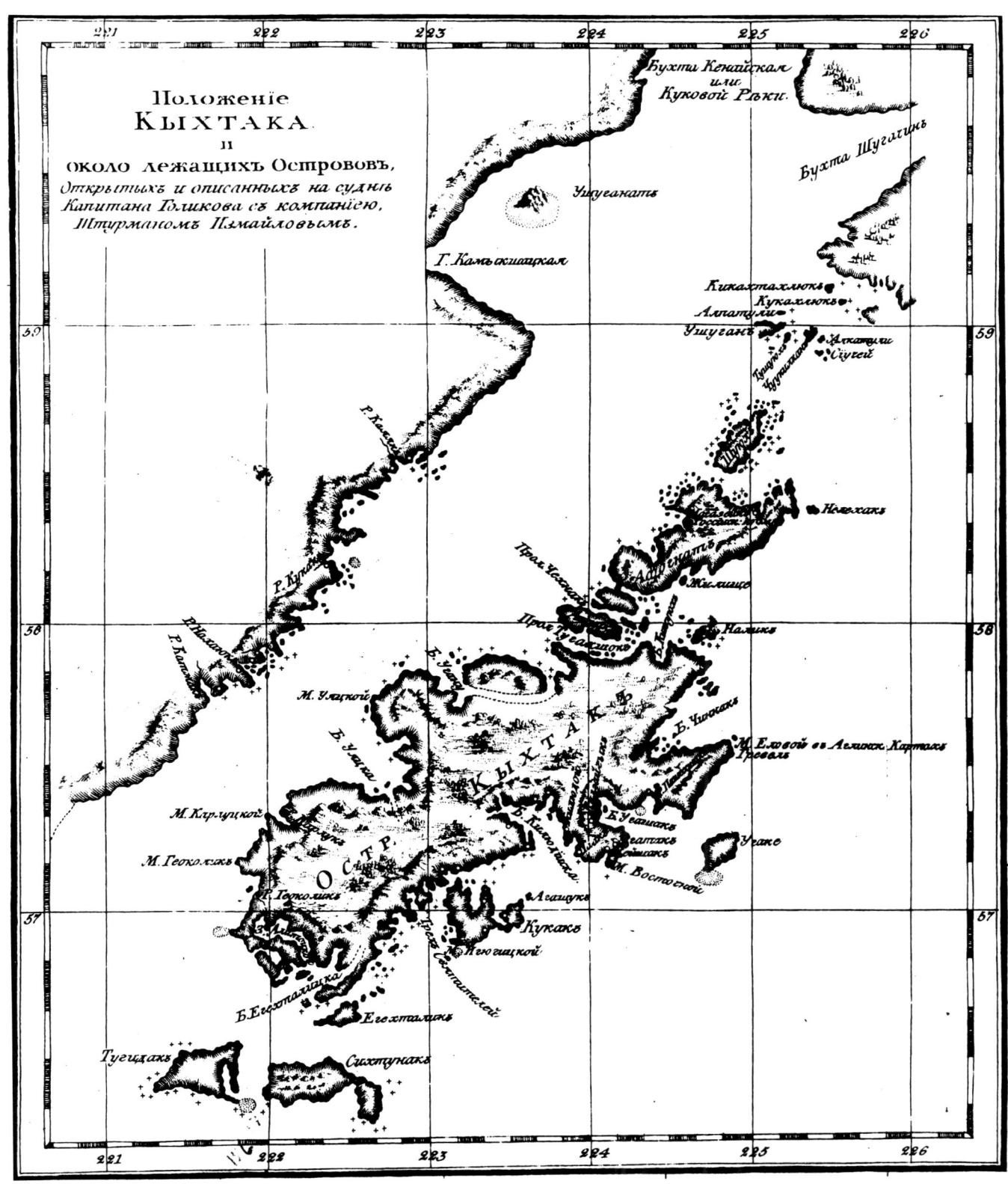

This is an inset from a Russian chart showing their North Pacific voyages made during the years 1728 through 1779. At the upper right corner of this inset map, the mouth of Kachemak Bay is drawn, although incompletely. While there is an opening in the coastline which would indicate the settlement of Alexandrovsk (today Nanwalek), there is none to indicate Seldovia Bay. Map courtesy of Rare Map Collection, Acc. #G9236/S12/1787/V5, Alaska and Polar Regions Dept., University of Alaska Fairbanks.

This 1784 chart made by the Russians Bocharov and Izmailov shows the mouth of Kachemak Bay. The number 1 has been printed on the map to show the location of the settlement of Alexandrovsk (now Nanwalek). The number 2 would approximate the location of Seldovia Bay, were it drawn on this chart. The number 3 designates Kachemak Bay. Map courtesy of Dr. Richard Pierce, History Department, University of Alaska Fairbanks.

are worth noting: "The inhabitants seem not to have fixed on any particular spot for their residence, but are scattered about here and there, as best suits their convenience or inclination. 'Tis most probable they are divided into clans or tribes, as in every large canoe we saw, there was at least one person of superior authority to the rest, who not only directed their traffic, but kept them in a proper degree of subordination. In their manners they seem harmless and inoffensive; But this might probably be occasioned by the different treatment they met with from us, to what the Russians had used them to...." [13]

Dixon goes on to describe in detail the appearance, dress, and implements of the native people, but it is his reference to their apparent migratory status that lends credence to the argument that Seldovia was perhaps a seasonal food gathering camp. Dixon must have observed the height of the salmon run in the Inlet, for he writes enthusiastically of the bounty of food encountered in a wilderness he found "barren and inhospitable." [14]

Two years later, in June of 1788, John Meares, another Englishman, followed much the same route. His log entry from Wednesday the 25th of June makes reference to native inhabitants: "About three o' clock in the afternoon of the 25th, two canoes came down the river, and brought a sea otter cut through the middle, and otherwise mangled. It appeared as if these natives thought that the flesh was wanted, and not the skin; but no satisfactory explanation could be obtained, as they did not understand any words that were addressed to them; and indeed gave no cause for supposing that they had ever traded with any European people. They had not a single bead of any kind in their possession; and the few which were now given them, seemed to attract that kind of admiration which is awakened by objects that have been never, or at least seldom seen before. It was conjectured that they were inland natives, who live up the country in the winter, and had descended some river which empties itself into *Smoky Bay*, as that was the quarter from whence they appeared to come...." [15]

It is of significant interest that Kachemak Bay has long been known as "Smoky Bay" due to its smoldering seams of coal on the north shore. However, even though Meares' ship was at this point in the vicinity of Anchor Point, it is difficult to say with any authority that the "Smoky Bay" he referred to in his log was in fact Kachemak Bay. On the 27th of June Meares anchored just south of Anchor Point in 17 fathoms of water, and most probably in clear view of Seldovia Bay, but his party did not linger in Cook's Inlet, for unlike Dixon they were in general disappointed with the meager supply of salmon and furs to be found there. [16]

Russian fur trading companies traveled Kachemak Bay in the early 1790's. Fur trading company head Alexander Baranov as early as 1792 sent men to the Kenai Peninsula in search of coal. Coal was needed to provide the high temperatures required to recast iron for the ship *Phoenix* being built in Resurrection Bay. It is probable that they would have entered Kachemak Bay, since its north shore, along with Port Graham, was a known source of accessible coal.

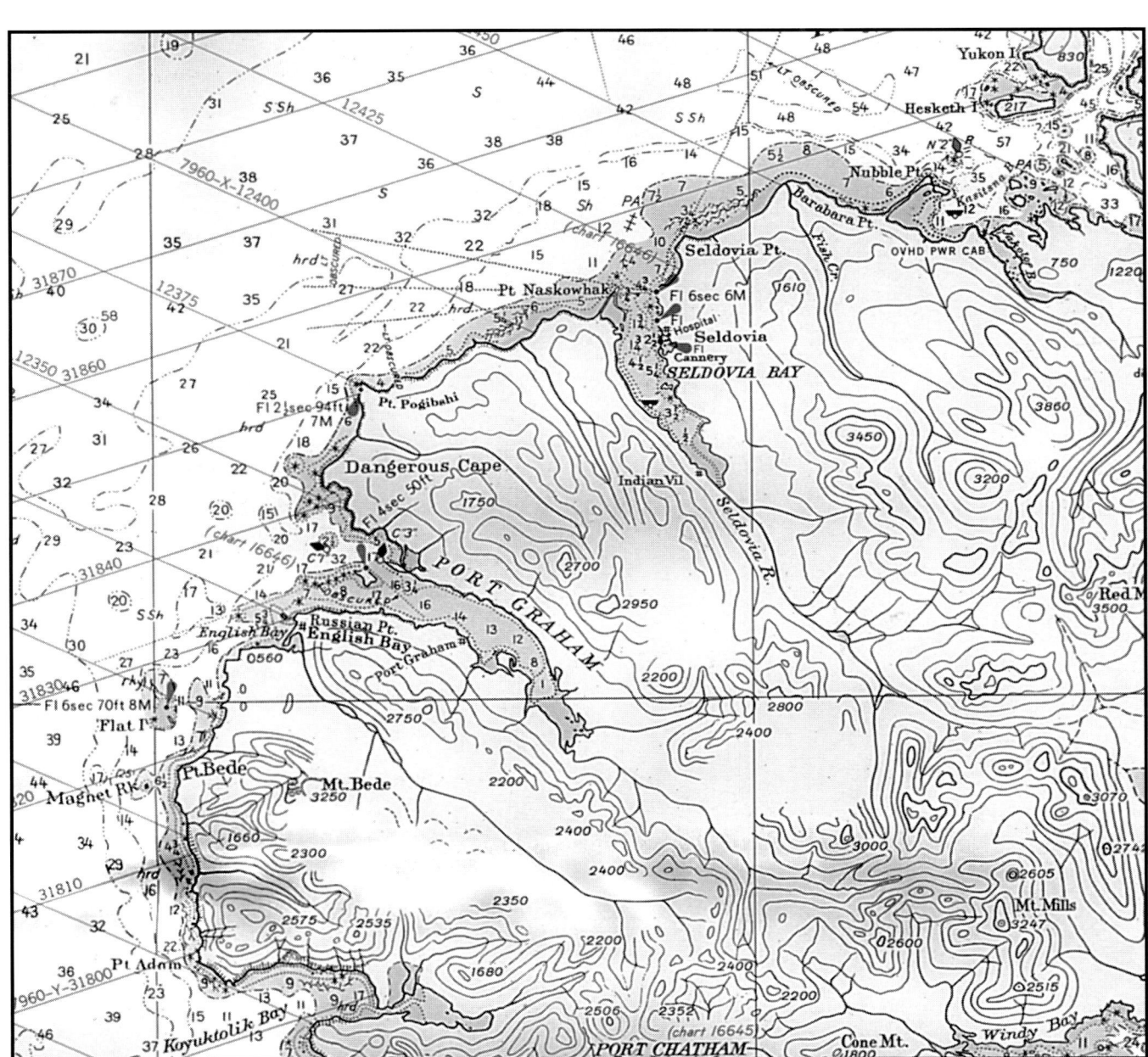

Nautical Chart of Cook Inlet/Kachemak Bay/Seldovia Bay. Scale is approximately 1:200,000 and soundings are in fathoms. NOAA Map 16640, 15th Edition, November 27, 1976..

Fur hunting was also taking place in Kachemak Bay at this time. On June 24th, 1793, Baranov wrote a lengthy report to his superior, Grigorii Shelikov, and complained of troubles between his men and those of a rival trading company headed by Pavel Lebedev-Lastochkin.

"Now I will explain to you our troubles with Lebedev's company. After Grigorii Konovalov was sent away, they with their two ships, the *Ioann* and *Georgii* tried to do as much harm to our company as possible. Trying to force us out, their first aim was to make us abandon Kinai Bay [Kenai]. They took possession of Kachikmat Bay, [Kachemak Bay] and settled a big crew there. They didn't let us trap foxes, even though our winter cabin (zimov'e) still stood there as proof that we were there first. I enclose a copy of an agreement in which Petr Kolomin states that along with other ground, this bay is our territory. In their locality, they made real slaves of the natives and forbade them to have any communication with us...." [17]

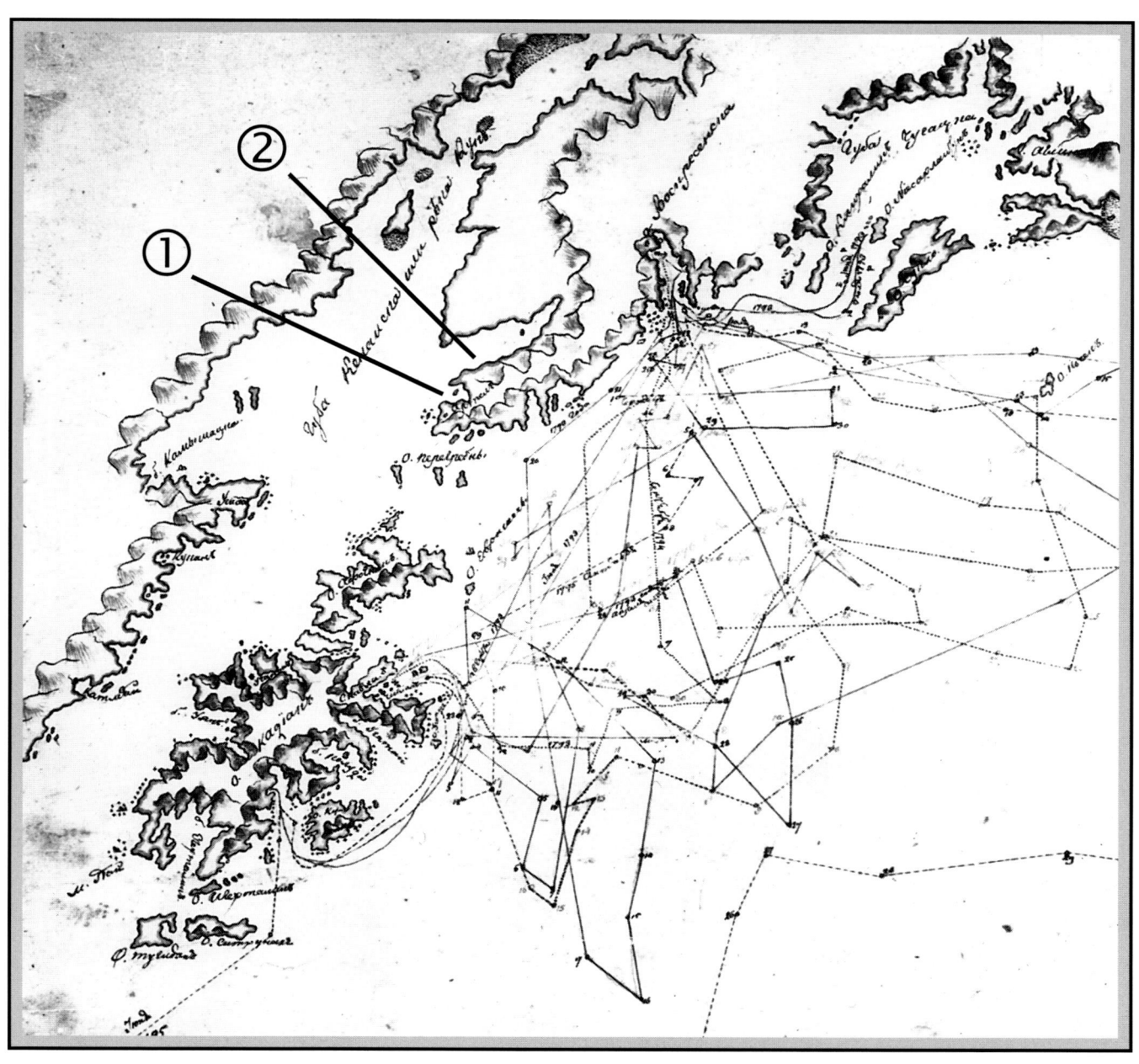

This map of Cook Inlet, Prince William Sound, and the Gulf of Alaska shows the 1793-1797 voyages of the Russian Lieutenant Shil'ts. The number 1 has been printed on the map to show the location of the settlement of Alexandrovsk (now Nanwalek), and the number 2 shows the approximate location of Seldovia Bay, were it included on this chart. From this map it is clear that the Russians knew the extent of Kachemak Bay, but for some reason had not explored or perhaps simply not charted its southern shore. Map courtesy of Dr. Richard Pierce, History Department, University of Alaska Fairbanks.

From 1793 to 1797, the Russian Lieutenant Shil'ts explored the coastline from Kad'iak (Kodiak) to Atkha (Atka), and in 1797 published a map which shows the full length of Kachemak Bay. Even though this confirms Russian knowledge of Kachemak Bay, there are still no south shore fjords shown. Apparently Shil'ts' expedition either did not explore them or else did not consider them important. The latter is perhaps the more plausible explanation, as the focus of Shil'ts' voyage was to look for more islands, particularly in Prince William Sound, known then as Chugach Bay.

In trying to put together an early history for Seldovia, I studied 19th century maps of the region at the University of Alaska at Fairbanks archives. A chronology of my findings appears below:

- 1802 Russian map shows only a small indentation in the coastline for Kachemak Bay; it is not named

- 1808 English map- similar to above

- 1816 Thomson's *New General Atlas* shows an indentation for Kachemak Bay and for Seldovia Bay, although neither is named; Alexandrovsk and Port Chatham are named

- 1821 Russian map clearly shows indentation for Kachemak Bay, but no indication of any south shore fjords; Kachemak Bay is not named, nor is Alexandrovsk

- 1825 French map shows no indentation for Kachemak Bay

- 1826 Russian map shows Kachemak Bay named Chugachik, and shows slight break in the southern shoreline to indicate Seldovia Bay

- 1827 French map shows Kachemak Bay between Anchor Point and Port Chatham; Seldovia Bay shows as a break in the southern shoreline

- 1828 English map shows the indentation of Kachemak Bay but with no name

- 1844 Russian map shows and names Kachemak Bay

- 1847 Ditto above, with slight indentation to indicate Seldovia Bay

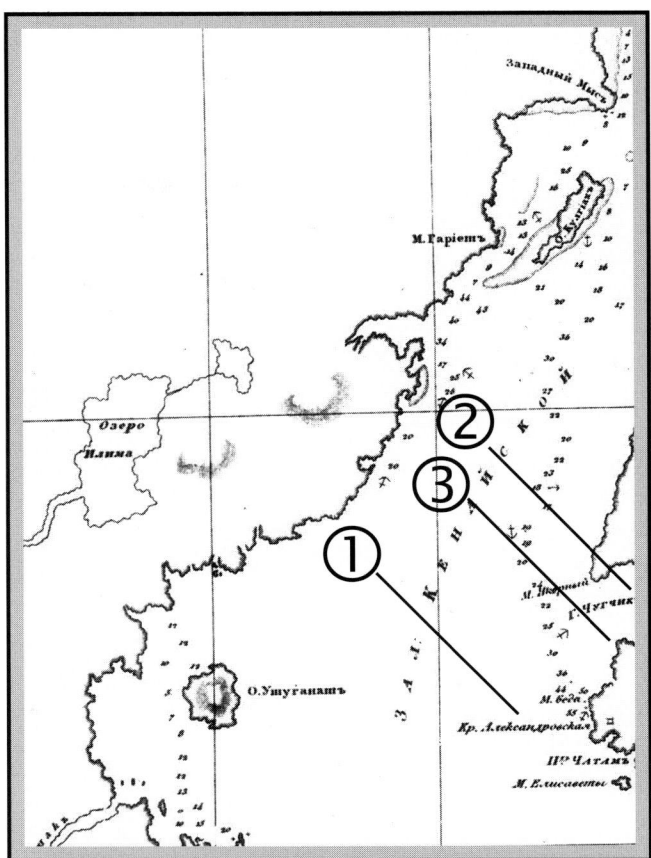

In this 1826 Russian Chart, the mouth of Kachemak Bay is shown. The settlement of Alexandrovsk is noted (1), and there is a break and indentation in the south shore (Kachemak Bay)(2) coastline where Seldovia Bay (3) is located. Map courtesy of Rare Map Collection, Acc. #VF915/K83/1824/R2, Alaska and Polar Regions Dept., University of Alaska Fairbanks.

It becomes clear that at least in the first half of the 19th century, the Russians had perhaps the best handle on the lay of the land. This knowledge of the coastline was not necessarily shared with explorers from other countries. The French map on page 46 suggests that some maps were published based on incomplete or inaccurate coastline data. Based on its absence from any of the early maps, it is unlikely that Seldovia was a year-round settlement or even a seasonal settlement of any consequence.

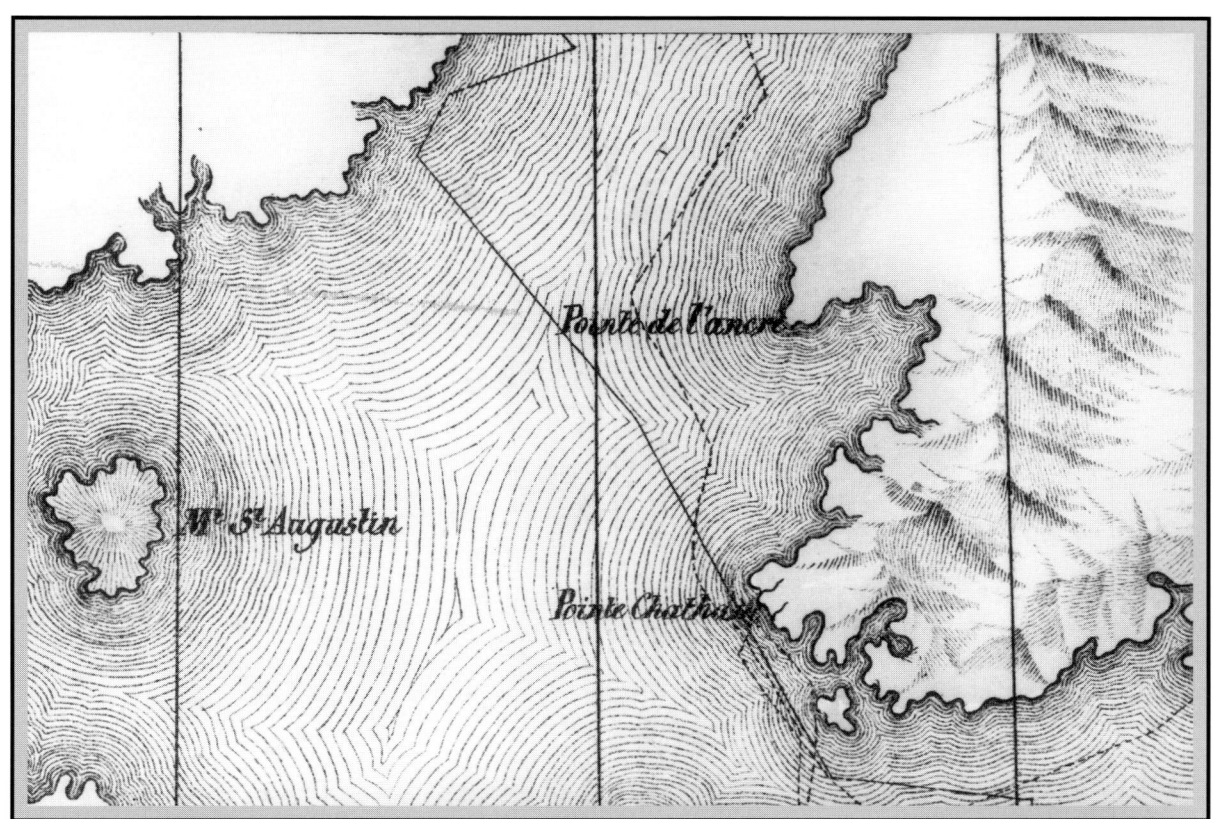

This 1827 French map is notable for its lack of detail and place or feature names. The dotted line suggests a route traveled by a ship, probably on a trade mission to Kenai, apparently with few stops made to explore or chart the country enroute. Photo courtesy of Rare Map Collection, Acc.# G3200/1827/M3, Alaska and Polar Regions Dept., University of Alaska Fairbanks.

Seldovia Bay is Named

The first published mention of Seldovia Bay occurred in 1852, in an atlas compiled by Mikhail Dmitrievich Teben'kov. Born in 1802, Teben'kov was a Russian naval cadet, and career seaman. In 1825 he joined the Russian American Company, and by 1844 had been appointed chief of the Russian colonies in North America. Teben'kov's tenure as chief manager was during a period of expansion in the company. Charts and maps that had heretofore been much respected were now found to be incomplete and inadequate as new trade routes and outposts were established.[18]

In the 1840's, Teben'kov secured government backing and arranged for a number of expeditions to survey the coastline of Alaska. Around 1846, he sent a party led by Captain Archimandritov to explore Kenai Bay (Cook's Inlet).[19] In addition to the data provided by his survey parties, Teben'kov "used the many ship's logs kept in the colonies [from 1782], personal observations on many places, and information given me recently by ship's commanders—-each of whom I asked to investigate something. I also examined published accounts of voyages and observations, the sketches of coasts made by natives, and information obtained by expeditions which I sent out expressly to determine little known locations."[20]

Although Teben'kov himself has long been credited with naming Seldovia Bay, it is unlikely that he visited the area. His notes accompanying the 1852 atlas state that descriptions are provided "only in those cases where they were lacking, or not in Russian, or where they were in supplements to publications, or in personal observations and information buried in journals."[21] It would seem that if the skipper Archimandritov did not name the bay, it came then from someplace in Teben'kov's collection of obscure published and unpublished observations. A loose translation of Zaliv Seldevoi would be "Bay of Herring," which would have been an accurate observation made by anyone in the bay during the spring herring run.

Teben'kov's supplemental narrative to his atlas provides little more information about Kachemak Bay. He reports that the north shore of the bay was described in 1834 by the Russian navigator Dingel'shtet, but it was not until 1848 that Archimandritov described the south shore. According to Teben'kov, the native population on Cook Inlet during this time was about 1000, and the Inlet froze in the winter as far south as Kachemak Bay. [22]

Teben'kov's Chart V shows Seldovia Bay, named, with three charted depths, which indicate that the bay was entered and sounded. Only when Archimandritov's personal notes are located and translated will we have an opportunity to learn if the survey party found evidence of human habitation in Seldovia Bay.

The frontispiece from Teben'kov's 1852 atlas.

> There is a local legend regarding Teben'kov and Seldovia Bay. It is said that when Teben'kov sailed into the bay in his ship, he brought with him a critically ill man, his ship's surgeon. A small boat was dispatched to the native village, and the shaman, or medicine man, was forced aboard. On the ship, Teben'kov ordered the shaman to cure the patient, or be faced with dire consequences. It is unclear whether the shaman refused, or did as he was instructed, but in any event, the patient succumbed. Teben'kov was furious, and ordered the shaman killed. Again the small boat was dispatched, with the unlucky shaman and an executioner and crew. On the east side of Seldovia Bay, near its mouth, is a rocky promontory known as Lookout Point. It is here that the shaman was taken, and made to dig his own grave. Upon completion of his work, he was shot and pushed in the hole, where the crew buried him. The terrible moans of the shaman could be heard even from below the dirt. This so unnerved the crew that they were compelled to dig him up. They buried him face down the second time, so that his unearthly wails would not reach human ears. [23]

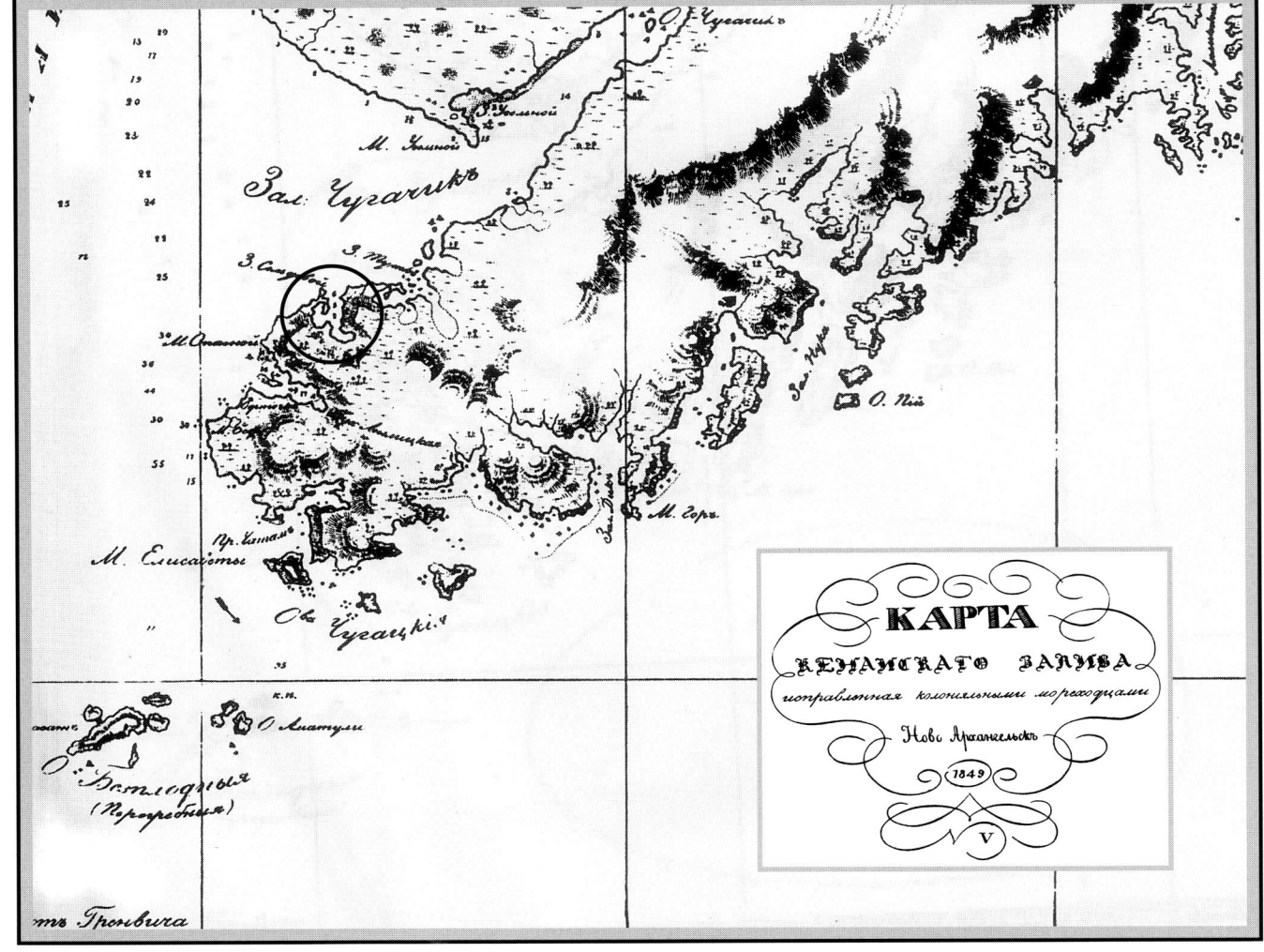

In 1849 the Russian Archimandritov charted the south shore of Kachemak Bay, including Seldovia, or "Bay of Herring" (see circled area). His map was published in Mikhail Teben'kov's 1852 atlas as Chart V. The complete Chart V shows Cook Inlet from the Barren Islands northward, and includes insets of Port Chatham and Nikolai. Only a portion is reproduced here. Map courtesy of the Kenai Community Library.

American Exploration

By 1867, the United States had purchased Alaska from Russia. In an 1867 address to the 49th Congress, President Andrew Jackson outlined the tasks to be undertaken regarding the new territory. One of the steps was to scour the coastline for possible sites for new military outposts. Of the locations cited for study, one was the mouth of Chugachik (Kachemak) Bay.

The address advises: "The unexpected delay in the arrival of the commissioners and the advance of the season, render it impossible to establish the other posts ordered for your district. Other troops, however, will be sent to you, as early as practicable in the spring. In the meantime you will inquire into and report upon the more prominent points in the district—their relative importance in regard to trade, to the probable settlement of the country, influence upon the Indians, &c. Among the places which have been suggested for military outposts are ...Chugachnick gulf, in Cook's Inlet...; As not more than four additional companies can be sent to your command next year, it is not proposed that you occupy all these points, but you will report on their relative advantages, and the means necessary for occupying those which you may select." [24]

The job was assigned to the United States Coast Survey, and was carried out by the Revenue Cutter Service. The Revenue Cutter Service, created in 1790, was the predecessor of the U.S. Coast Guard. It began as a maritime agency charged with collecting customs duties, and evolved to include functions similar to our present-day Coast Guard (law enforcement, maintenance of navigational aids, and search and rescue).[25]

The cutters *Wayanda, Wolcott, Reliance,* and *Lincoln* all came to Alaska in the 1860's and 70's, but only the *Wayanda* appears to have entered Kachemak Bay. The logs for the *Wayanda* are written in longhand, and there are few latitude/longitude readings to suggest where their course took them. We do know, however, that on Thursday, June 4, 1868, at about 11:30 a.m., the *Wayanda* left Coal Bay at Port Graham and proceeded up Cook's Inlet with three Indians as pilots. At 2:10 p.m. on the 4th, they "came to anchor at Kaney, in 10 fathoms of water".[26] This is an unlikely name for Kachemak Bay, and in all my research I've found no other reference to "Kaney" denoting a village, point of land or body of water in or around Kachemak Bay. To be sure, "Kaney" sounds close to "Kenai," but the cutter could not have made the trip from Port Graham to Kenai in roughly 2-1/2 hours. Furthermore, the following excerpts from the log sketch a picture that could only make sense if the cutter were in Kachemak Bay.

The Indian pilots were paid in bread and molasses and were discharged when the cutter anchored. Two boats in the charge of officers were sent to sound out the harbor, and "Capt. White with two officers visited the shore to examine for coal, and brought several specimens on board."[27] While it is unclear exactly where this harbor was, it would make sense to theorize that it was on the north or east side of Homer Spit, and referred to what is today known as Mud Bay. This would shelter the cutter from the prevailing southeast winds, and would have provided ready access to the coal seams.

On Friday the 5th at 8:30 a.m., a launch was sent ashore to gather coal, while the Captain went off to "examine a harbor on the east side of the inlet."[28] Halibut Cove or China Poot Bay are the likely targets of his examination, as he was back at the ship by noon. At 2:30 p.m., the Captain was off again to "examine the head of the bay" and was back in time for dinner.

On Saturday the 6th, a launch was sent ahead "to look for a sunken rock at the entrance of the passage."[29] This undoubtedly referred to the submerged rocks off Yukon Island, which had been charted by Teben'kov. By 9:45 a.m., the cutter got underway, and left the harbor and proceeded down the bay. At 11:30 they picked up the launch, but the weather had turned bad enough—"blowing fresh and weather thick"—that they were obliged to steam to the south shore for shelter. At noon, they came to anchor at "Kah-sits-nah Bay, or Jack's Harbor,"[30] referring to the present day Kasitsna Bay at the mouth of Jakolof Bay. A launch was sent to take some soundings, but all in all they sat tight until the 7th, when the weather let up enough for them to leave. The log shows that they made directly for Anchor Point to the north, and by late morning were off Ninilchik village on their way up Cook's Inlet.

This study of the *Wayanda*'s logs is of value in determining the history of the area for what it doesn't tell us. For example, there is no mention of civilization in all of Kachemak Bay. It is evident that Seldovia Bay was bypassed entirely, both on their way in and out of Kachemak Bay, in favor of the coal on the north shore. They took on a ton of the stuff, presumably to keep the boilers for the steam engines fired on the trip up Cook's Inlet. Had there been a settlement of any consequence in 1868 on Seldovia Bay, it is likely that it would have been reported by the Indian guides or the Russian pilot who was also on board, and it seems likely that the *Wayanda* would have visited it.

When George Davidson, at the direction of President Andrew Jackson, made his report of the coast in November 1867, he defined Tchugatchnek Bay (Kachemak Bay) as being that body of water to the north and east of the Homer Spit. His description of Seldovia Bay is tagged onto the end of his narrative on Graham's Harbor (Port Graham):

"Six and a half miles northeast by east of Dangerous cape is the opening of a small bay with shallow water, but anchorage close under the western point in four or five fathoms. According to Tebenkoff's chart, there is six fathoms in the entrance of the bay, which is about three miles long, north and south, and two-thirds of a mile wide. Rocks are laid down on the manuscript map close to each point, which are represented as bold and rocky. The points lie northeast and southwest of each other."[31]

It is doubtful a large sailing ship of the time would have considered Seldovia Bay a good anchorage because of its relatively shallow water, and breadth too narrow for maneuvering in and out against wind and tide. It is virtually the only bay in the region with both of these conditions. It is no wonder then, that it was so unexplored by early vessels. Today, thanks to modern surveying techniques and navigational aids, there is a marked channel into Seldovia Bay, traveled safely and often by vessels up to several hundred feet in length.

Endnotes

[1] P.A. Tikhmenev, *A History of the Russian American Company*, trans. and ed. Richard A. Pierce and Alton S. Donnelly, 2 vols., (Kingston, ON: Limestone, 1979) 2:22.

[2] Gregory C. Wiles and Parker Calkin, "Neoglaciation in the Southern Kenai Mountains, Alaska," *Annals of Glaciology,* 14: 10.

[3] Wiles and Calkin 11.

[4] George Dixon, *A Voyage Round the World: But More Particularly to the North-West Coast of America, Bibliotheca Australiana #37,* (New York: Da Capo, n.d.) 61.

[5] Gregory C. Wiles, letter to the author, Nov. 1993.

[6] Fred Elvsaas, personal interview, 1992.

[7] *Frontiersman,* [Seldovia] 5 Feb. 1947:1, 4; 8 Feb. 1947:1-3.

[8] Janet R. Klein, personal communication, 1993.

[9] Wiles, letter.

[10] Frederica de Laguna, "Archaeologist Delves Into Signs of Ancient Culture on Kachemak Bay", *Seldovia Herald* 17 Sept. 1932: 1.

[11] A.V. Efimov, ed., *Atlas Geograficheskikh Otkrytii V Sibiri I V Severo-Zapadnoi Ameriki., M..,* (n.p.: n.p., 1964) Map 178.

[12] Nathaniel Portlock, *A Voyage Round the World, But More Particularly to The Northwest Coast of America: Performed in 1785, 1786, 1787, and 1788 in the* King George *and* Queen Charlotte, *Capts. Portlock and Dixon* (London: Stockdale and Goulding, 1789) 109-110.

[13] Dixon 67.

[14] Dixon 63.

[15] John Meares, *Voyages Made in the Years 1788 and 1789 from China to the Northwest Coast of America* (London: Logographic, 1790) 312.

[16] Meares 312-313.

[17] Tikhmenev 32-33.

[18] M.D. Teben'kov, *Atlas of the Northwest Coasts of America,* trans. Richard A. Pierce (Kingston, ON: Limestone 1981) xi-xiii.

[19] Teben'kov xiii.

[20] Teben'kov Foreword 3-4.

[21] Teben'kov Foreword 4.

[22] Teben'kov 19.

[23] Mike Miller, personal interview, 16 June 1992.

[24] Andrew Jackson, "Message from the President of the United States," *Russian America,* U.S. 40th Cong., 2nd sess., House Ex. Doc. No. 177 (Washington: GPO, 1868) 305.

[25] *Alaska File of the Revenue Cutter Service 1867-1914,* a pamphlet accompanying Microcopy No.641 (Washington: National Archives, 1966) 1.

[26] *Wayanda 1864-1872,* Logs of the Revenue Cutters and Coast Guard Vessels, 1819-1941, Record Group 26, Box 2659, June 1868, Records of the U.S. Coast Guard, Revenue Cutter Service (National Archives) 4.

[27] *Wayanda* 4.

[28] *Wayanda* 4.

[29] *Wayanda* 5.

[30] *Wayanda* 5.

[31] *Wayanda* 5-6.

[32] George Davidson, "Report of Assistant George Davidson Relative to the Coast, Features, and Resources of Alaska Territory," *Russian America,* U.S. 40th Cong., 2nd sess., House Ex. Doc. No. 177 (Washington: GPO, 1868) 305.

SELDOVIA'S MODERN BEGINNINGS

The Growth of a Small, Nineteenth Century Native Village

There is no written record to mark the beginning of modern habitation in Seldovia. The commonly accepted earliest written record of Seldovia comes from Ivan Petroff's 1880 census. As a researcher, I've spent four years examining the question of Seldovia's origin from many different angles, endeavoring to establish a pre-1880 date. Following a new lead is a bit like searching for treasure, and there is always the promise of "the big find" just around the corner. As tantalizing as the search for Seldovia's modern origins might be however, there comes a point where the probability of finding an answer drops off sharply. Thus, the story of Seldovia's beginning as a modern village is not complete. There are pieces missing in the jigsaw puzzle. Nonetheless, the value of the search is that it has turned up some information heretofore unknown. From these widely divergent pieces of data, we can create a plausible story of Seldovia's beginnings. It should be stressed however, that this remains but a hypothesis.

Russian Retirement Community?

As it matured, the Russian American Company in the 1840's found that many of its employees were too old to be productive workers any more. These were men who had been brought from Russia before the turn of the century and now were ready for retirement. As employees, they were costing more to feed and house than they were worth. Faced with declining supplies of fur, and hence declining revenue, the Company was not in a position to send these men back to Russia, nor to support them indefinitely. Besides, many of them had long since married native women, and had established families and lives here that they did not wish to give up.

In 1971, Russian historian Svetlana Fedorova published *The Russian Population in Alaska and California, Late 18th Century-1867*. Regarding the retirement of Company workers, she writes:

"A 'Supreme Command' of 2 April 1835 permitted former employees of the Russian American Company with families to remain in the colonies permanently and to establish special settlements. It was recommended that 'similar settlements also be formed for the Creoles'.... At the mouth of the Ninilchik River an agricultural settlement of 'colonial citizens' was established, named Ninilchik. In 1844, the agricultural settlements of Kachemak, Kasilov, Kenai, Knyk, and Matanuska were founded on the east shore of Kenai Bay and Rossiiskoe selenie (Russian settlement) on the northwestern shore (the modern towns of Seldovia, Kasilov, Kenai, Knik, Matanuska, and Taionek)."[1]

As the source for the assertion that Seldovia was a retirement colony for Russian American Co. employees, Fedorova uses a paper entitled, *A Russian Matanuska Colony in Alaska in 1844*, written by James Wickersham. Unfortunately, Wickersham's paper is not footnoted, so we don't know the source of his information. Dr. Richard Pierce, scholar of Russian Alaskan history, feels that the Wickersham version of Seldovia's beginnings is not accurate. Other than Wickersham's paper, there is no other reference to Seldovia as a retirement colony in any of the Russian documents studied by Dr. Pierce and his associates.[2] In the 1870's, many of the Russian American Company archives were destroyed. Perhaps among them were records of the creation of these supposed retirement communities.

Or Native Village?

From 1865 to 1868, William Healy Dall worked for, and subsequently directed, the Western Union Telegraph Expedition in Alaska. In 1870, he published *Alaska and its Resources*, which includes descriptions of the indigenous people. From his account of the Kenai Indians we find yet another pre-Petroff reference to native peoples inhabiting Kachemak Bay.

"These Indians inhabit the country near Cook's Inlet, and both shores of the inlet *as far south as Chugachik Bay*. [author's italics] They are the 'true Thnaina' of Holmberg, and are called by the Yukon tribes Tehanin-Kutchin. Their customs are similar to those of the other Indian tribes of the vicinity, as far as we know. Capt. Iurii F. Lisiansky says that they use birch canoes, and bury their dead in wooden boxes, piling stones above the dead. They express their lamentation by spreading their faces with black paint, singeing their hair, and lacerating their bodies with knives. They are more intelligent than the neighboring Inuit tribes, and live by hunting and fishing. They kill large numbers of the mountain goat, and clothe themselves partly with the skins. Those near the coast use bidarkas, which they purchase from the Inuit. Their language is extremely guttural when compared with that of the Inuit."[3]

Russian American Company historian P.A. Tikhmenev notes that between 1842 and 1861 there were only 958 natives living on Kenai Bay (Cook's Inlet), that number being spread among 20 villages in an area reaching from Alexandrovsk (English Bay or Nanwalek) on the east side to the West Foreland cape on the west side.[4] Their number may have been far greater a generation or two before. A virulent smallpox epidemic in the Russian colonies raged from 1837 to 1839, and claimed many lives. It was carried to nearly all the native villages by traders and hunting parties, and struck down many people. Some of the natives had not had access to the Russian-supplied vaccinations, and many more simply refused the lifesaving shots as they rejected all things European. They preferred to rely on the village shaman, or medicine man. It was only after the epidemic, when they realized that very few of the vaccinated had perished, that the natives began to acknowledge any validity or superiority of the Russian practices. Not surprisingly, there was a post-epidemic interest among the natives in learning Christianity.[5]

According to Tikhmenev, the smallpox epidemic wiped out entire native settlements. Had there been a settlement at Seldovia in the early part of the century, it is not unreasonable to think that it could have been effectively obliterated by this epidemic. Any survivors may have moved away to live with relatives farther up the Kenai Peninsula. Thirty years after the epidemic, however, it became evident that either natives were returning to Seldovia, or else what had been a small post-epidemic remnant population was growing.

In my search for the origins of Seldovia, I turned to the Russian Orthodox Church parish records. Although they are written in Cyrillic longhand and recorded on microfilm, they are moderately legible to a scholar with a good command of the language. Mine being both elementary and rusty, I turned to Katherine Arndt of the University of Alaska at Fairbanks. Because she had studied these records

Seldovia village chief photographed in 1892. Photo courtesy of the National Archives, # 22-FFA-486.

while researching the history of the Ninilchik area, Katherine was very familiar with them.

Katherine found that the first reference to Seldovia in the church records occurs in 1875,[6] as a notation in the margin of some confessional records from the village of Chkitukskoe, which was near Kenai.[7] The notation is opposite the names of a family who used to reside in Seldovia, or who presently resided there but were currently in Chkitukskoe. Priest Nikolai Sorokovikov heard confession from Mikhael Nal'tun (age 39), his wife Anna (32), and daughters Daria (11) and Agafia (9). This "first family" of Seldovia was probably just visiting up north, as at least part of the family was back in Seldovia (according to parish records) the following year. Sadly, Mikhael was listed as a widower by 1876, so Anna must have died some time after the priest visited Chkitukskoe in 1875. For the first time, we know the names and a little something about actual Seldovians. More about these early residents can be found in the chapter "Russian Culture and Influence" (page 71).

By 1880, Petroff was conducting the census that includes what was previously the first known reference to Seldovia. Ivan Petroff was born in Russia, but came to America in 1861. By 1866 he was working in Alaska, and helped translate Russian source material for H.H. Bancroft's *History of Alaska*. He was appointed special agent to conduct the Alaskan portion of the 10th U.S. Census. Information was gathered in 1880 and 1881, and the report was published in 1884.[8]

Petroff puts Seldovia in the Kadiak (Kodiak) District, and lists the combined population of Seldovia and Ostrovski as 74.[9] Since "ostrov" is Russian for "island", and Yukon Island (in Kachemak Bay, to the east of the mouth of Seldovia Bay) is the only island in the immediate area known to have sustained inhabitants in modern times, it is assumed that Petroff's "Ostrovski" is Yukon Island.[10] It is unlikely that Petroff would have known the European name for the island, as it was just that same year (1880) that it was so designated by Dall.[11]

Petroff lists this combined population as being comprised of 38 Creoles (a person of mixed Russian and native heritage) and 36 Eskimo. No white or Athabaskan (Indian) residents are noted.[12] This is curious, because in 1875, the Russian Orthodox Church records show movement of some Kenai area villagers to and from Seldovia. The Kenai area villages were home to what we now call the Dena'ina, a branch of the Athabaskan Indians, (aka: Kenaitze — Russian term, Tinnats-khotana — Petroff's term, Tehanin-Kutchin — Dall's term[13]). Had there been only Eskimo, or Inuit (Petroff uses these terms interchangeably) in Seldovia, their kin would have been in the villages at Alexandrovsk (English Bay, or Nanwalek) and Chugach Bay (Prince

Native Seldovians pose with the elder chief at far left. The year was 1892. It is interesting to note that the western style of dress is represented by the three younger men on the right. The chief appears to be wearing a more traditionally styled garment. Photo courtesy of the National Archives, # 22-FFA-453

William Sound). Perhaps the "Creoles" to whom Petroff refers in his census entry for Seldovia are people of mixed Russian and Dena'ina heritage. This would at least explain their travels to and from Dena'ina villages. Another explanation is that, either from carelessness or ignorance, some explorers lumped native peoples into broad categories such as "Indian" or "Eskimo" and didn't necessarily note the precise ethnographic mix of a particular village.

Petroff defines the boundaries of the Indians and the Inuits in the narrative accompanying his census:

"The Kenaitze population proper is all located north of a line drawn from Anchor Point to the Ilyamna portage of the west coast of the inlet, south of the deep indentation of the Kenai peninsula called Chugachik or Kuchekmak gulf. This country is settled by Inuits, who have peopled the east coast of the peninsula, and from there eastward along the mainland nearly to the Copper River. Two of the trading-stations in the Kenai district are located among these Inuits at English Bay and Seldovia." [14] Petroff noted that "in ancient times, the Kaniagmute [i.e. Inuit] settlements extended much farther both north and south than they do now...and in the north were found by Captain Cook halfway up Cook's inlet as late as 1778." [15]

One would assume from this description that Seldovia was soundly placed in Inuit territory. However, later in his report, Petroff seems to cast some doubt when he writes "The settlements of Tinnats-khotana [Tanaina or Dena'ina] extend from Kuchekmak gulf on the Kenai peninsula around the inlet northward and westward, etc....." [16]

Frederica de Laguna, in her *Archaeology of Cook Inlet* was informed by a Kenai Indian woman that "in former times there were only Eskimo at Seldovia." From her other informants, from the scanty information that the 1930's Seldovia natives had regarding the Eskimo, and based on her excavations, de Laguna concluded that the (Tanaina) Indians migrated to Kachemak Bay from the interior and Kenai, supplanting the Eskimo, and that this migration and cultural transition occurred prior to the period of Russian occupation. [17]

That Seldovia was at a confluence of overlapping cultures seems the most plausible interpretation. The southern edge of Dena'ina territory extended to Seldovia, as did the northwestern edge of the Chugach Eskimo (Chugachmiut) lands. Influence was also felt from the Kodiak Eskimo (Koniagmiut, aka Aleut) culture. Petroff's 1880 census defines the Inuit population of Seldovia as Chugachmiut, similar in culture, he found, to the Koniagmiut. Yet ten years later, Porter's census referred to the occupants as Koniagmiut. [18]

Nearly twenty years ago, local elders informed anthropological researcher Carrie Reed that in former times, there was a village at the head of Seldovia Bay which was occupied by natives from Port Graham and English Bay (Nanwalek). Those villages would have probably been in Chugachmiut Eskimo territory. [19]

Elders also confirmed for Reed what other ethnographers have been told in the past; that there was a large Indian settlement on Yukon Island. According to legend, there was extensive contact between the two groups, ranging from trade to fighting. The Yukon Island Indians (who would have probably been Dena'ina) are said to have used the present townsite of Seldovia as a camping spot long before there was any kind of settlement here. [20]

Even today some of the members of the Seldovia Native Association refer to themselves as Aleut, or Koniagmiut, while others claim Dena'ina (once also known as Tanaina) as their heritage.

Seldovia or Akedaknak?

From 1881 through 1883, a museum collector named Johan Jacobsen traveled throughout Alaska. He visited native villages, both occupied and abandoned, in search of artifacts for the Berlin Museum. He published an account of his travels in Alaska, and made some interesting mentions of Seldovia.

Jacobsen visited many trading posts operated by the Alaska Commercial Company, which had supplanted the Russian American Company as the primary fur trading agents after the purchase of the Alaska Territory by the United States in 1867. He noted five trading posts or stations in Cook Inlet, each, as was the custom, under the direction of a white trader to whom the native hunters delivered skins. Company sailing vessels and steamers visited the stations each year, bringing trade goods (food, dry goods, general merchandise, etc.) to the stations and leaving with their loads of furs, bound for San Francisco. [21]

A rival company, the Western Fur Company, also operated in Alaska during this period. Their headquarters were in San Francisco too, and they shared trade routes with the Alaska Commercial Company. While the two companies were in business, natives enjoyed high prices for their furs, but in the spring of 1883, the Western Fur Company, after losing a quarter of a million dollars, ceased operations.[22]

While at Kenai, Jacobsen decided to go overland from the Kenai Peninsula to Prince William Sound. However, local traders convinced him instead to cross Kachemak Bay and make for Fort Alexander (today known as Nanwalek or English Bay) from whence he could go by sea to Prince William Sound. Bad weather necessitated a detour, and brought Jacobsen to Seldovia Bay:

> *"We spent the night at Anchor Point, or rather Leida, where a large number of sea otter hunters with their boats also spent the few hours until morning. About three o'clock in the morning the hunters left and I woke my crew so that they could make tea and prepare for departure. While I took a little more rest the crew did likewise, and when we woke again we found we had missed the tide for departure and had to wait until the afternoon. The stormy weather forced us to go far into Kachemak Bay before we could cross to the other shore, which we followed to the southwest, reaching Akedaknak in Seldovia Bay for our next night's camp. Here we found the dwellings that the sea otter hunters we met the night before had used. This village had been the location of a trading post of the Western Fur Trading Company that had been abandoned in May. Because of this the price of a good sea otter pelt fell from $112 to $35."* [23]

The word "Akedaknak" is similar to the name the Seldovia Dena'ina Indians called themselves: "Agidaknodana."[24] If one assumes that in the 1880's the village at the head of Seldovia Bay was still inhabited by Eskimo, and that the present townsite was a camping place for Indians from Yukon Island, then Akedaknak would most probably refer to a settlement at or near the present townsite. On the other hand, Alaskan writer Elsa Pedersen, in a 1958 *Alaska Sportsman* article about Seldovia, wrote that the village at the head of the bay was Indian.[25] Perhaps, in more recent times, the natives from Port Graham and English Bay (Nanwalek) retreated and the village was taken over by the Dena'ina from the Akedaknak or Yukon Island settlements.

Seldovia resident Dede Higman reports being told by a local elder that the Western Trading Post was at present day Schooner Beach. This beach was the location of Seldovia's first cannery, around 1912, and the informant noted that before that, a fur trading post was on the site. Reasons stated for the post having been at Schooner Beach were its deep water and good anchorage.[26]

Jacobsen is the first and only person to make reference to a village called Akedaknak on Seldovia Bay. A correspondence with a former curator of the Berlin Museum reveals that although Jacobsen kept a map of his travels, the document has been "relocated" as the result of a museum reorganization, and its whereabouts are currently unknown.[27] Such a map might show for certain the location of this mysterious village of Akedaknak.

Jacobsen ended up leaving Akedaknak for Fort Alexander (Nanwalek), only to find that the only sizable vessel was engaged for two weeks salmon fishing, and even the native bidarkas and their owners were occupied with sea otter hunting. Not wishing to cross the ocean in a bidarka, Jacobsen decided to wait until the schooner became available. To occupy him in the interim, the schooner captain suggested he return to Kachemak Bay to explore the abandoned Indian Village of Soonroodna. Jacobsen returned to Seldovia Bay, and at Akedaknak "engaged as a guide an old Indian whose father had lived in this abandoned village."[28] Jacobsen spent three days digging for artifacts at Soonroodna, whose location is unknown save to say that it is towards the head of Kachemak Bay from Seldovia. On the fourth day he began the journey back, and after running into stormy weather, "went farther into Seldovia Bay, where we spent the night with Captain Sand and Mr. Frank."[29] Jacobsen left the next day, and so ends our glimpse of the village of Akedaknak...almost.

After the Western Fur Company went bankrupt, the Alaska Commercial Company, its chief rival, purchased the assets and took over the operation of many of its trading posts, among them the post at Akedaknak. Hoping to find more about Akedaknak in the company archives, I searched repositories in California as best as I could by telephone and correspondence, since the headquarters of the Western Fur Co. had been in San Francisco. This proved to be a dead end and I turned instead to the Rasmuson Library at the University of Alaska at Fairbanks.

The only records of the Western Fur Company at Akedaknak were inventories of "Stock at Seldovia Station" dated "November 10th, 1881," "April 1882," and simply "1883." [30] The three pages consisted of the following items, reported by the author here in consolidated fashion:

- over 400 yards fabric, including calico, cotton ticking, and alpaca
- skirts, hats, caps, scarves, and drawers, and shawls ranging in price from $3.00 to $24.00
- Tule, hair nets, sou'westers, jumpers, shirts, and child's shoes
- beads, thread, metal boxes, combs, brass crosses, and zinc mirrors
- glass dishes, china tea pots, tea kettles, coffee kettles, and lamps
- thimbles, beer mugs, lamp glasses, and bowls
- cups, soup plates, dinner plates, and scissors
- snuff boxes, stove pipe, and panes of glass
- compasses, solder, cigar lighters, silver crosses, and vermillion
- vespers candles, grey blankets, ladies' cloaks, and infant shirts
- cardigan jackets, cotton pants, towels, overcoats, and vests

Although it may not seem that revealing, the inventory list does indicate something about the population of Akedaknak/Seldovia in 1881 through 1883. To begin with, the presence of dishes, kitchenware, and European fabric and clothing suggests that the population had been influenced by Western ways of dressing, cooking and dining. Finally, from the 2 dozen brass crosses, half a dozen silver crosses, and 10 boxes of vespers candles, it can be inferred that the population had been introduced to and had to some extent accepted the Russian Orthodox religion.

Seldovia's Native Culture

Little is known about the village at the head of Seldovia Bay during its time of occupation by Port Graham and English Bay (Nanwalek) Eskimos. By the time its existence was recorded, local informants called it the "old Indian village"; hence the supposition that it must have been taken over by the Akedaknak/Yukon Island Dena'ina.

However, in the *Cook Inlet Region Inventory of Native Historic Sites and Cemeteries*, the village is listed as being populated most probably by Port Graham Indians. The village was almost at the head of Seldovia Bay, at a prominent point above a gravel beach. The village site was in a field which slopes gradually from the beach about 500 yards uphill to alders and spruce. The inventory description is:

"Recent village site. The village in 1900 consisted of 10-15 barabaras and stretched along the beach for about 1/2 mile. It was primarily a fall and summer residence. People recall many fish drying in racks along the beach. Each house may have held one or several families. Date of origin of village is unknown, but it was no longer occupied by the 1920's. Probable inhabitants were Port Graham Indians. Presently housepits not visible due to vegetation overgrowth. The waterline has changed by 3 1/2 feet in Seldovia Bay, and a rock slide from the steep narrow crevasse above the site has changed part of the terrain to an undeterminable extent. Informants recall that various artifacts such as a stone knife and a lamp have been found on the beach." [31]

When the inventory was conducted in 1975, the housepits may well have been overgrown and invisible. Upon visiting the site in the last few years, however, I found at least three clearly visible square depressions in the field just back from the bank above the beach.

Local elder Nick Elxnit remembers the village from his childhood, roughly between the years 1913 and 1920. In 1913, he recalled, the village was used as a summer fish camp. The houses, called "barabaras," were made of big logs and driftwood. Smoke from cooking fires was released through a big hole in the roof. Sleeping pallets were fashioned from alder, with grass on top, and covered with bear or moose hides. Nick remembered that the black bear hide was the best for sleeping under. He recalled a trip up Seldovia Bay with his grandfather to the mouth of the Seldovia River. They stayed across the river from the village, in a barabara. The natives were seining pink salmon in the river, and hanging them on racks to dry for the winter. He described a banya as being attached to the side of the barabara, essentially an addition to the house, that was used for steam bathing purposes. Round red volcanic rock from the base of the cliffs at Pt. Naskowhak was gathered for use in the banyas, preferred because it did not crack or fall apart. The rock was heated "red-hot" on a bonfire and then moved using wooden paddles to a corner of the banya. Water was poured on the rock to make it steam, the door was shut, and the occupant enjoyed a steam bath. [32]

In addition to the barabaras at the head of Seldovia Bay, there were also small native encampments at the Outside Beach, toward the hills from the present airstrip, on the hill where the Russian Orthodox church stands, and on the spit of land where the first dock stood (near Schooner Beach). [33] For a people who lived off the land, these locations were strategic to food gathering, as they were near the summer fish runs.

The Seldovia natives of the late 19th and early 20th centuries were mainly Tanaina, also referred to as Kenaitze or Dena'ina. The census of 1900 lists 149 people in Seldovia. For the first time, names were given and limited personal data such as marital status, heritage, education, occupation, and date of birth were included. The natives are shown as Kenaitze (spelled there "Kenaites") without exception. There is no mention of the Inuit listed by Petroff twenty years earlier. Nearly all the men were shown as hunters/fishermen, with several occupied as laborers. (Two notable exceptions were Adam Bloch and John Wall Smith, two U.S. soldiers who were now trading company agents in Seldovia. They are listed as "merchants.") Only two of the natives are shown as being able to read and write. The oldest resident is a man, aged 89.

Surnames included Andreanoff, Berrystoff, Maxim, Barascovia, Lucco, Nicholi, Micuyal, Yakaloff, Stafeof, Delchuck, Simeon, Antoniva, Matway, Bayou, Putt, Ivanish, Sockoloff, Kloah, Kanetikut, Neana, Kevaloff, Walholamay, Gregory, Kankaluk, Balishoff, Bashiloff, Inglu, Balascovia, and Kaviak. A small number of residents are listed by first name alone. The Balishoff name is the only one to have been carried down intact to present day Seldovia. Descendants of Adam Bloch live here as well, but do not carry the name.

Preserving Tanaina Culture

As interesting as this census was, it did little to describe the rich culture shared by these early Seldovia natives and their ancestors. It was not until 1931 that this culture was recorded by Yale University ethnographer Cornelius Osgood. He spent a month in Seldovia, and then moved on to Iliamna, Eklutna, Tyonek, Susitna, and Kenai, in his effort to make a series of descriptive studies which would then be the foundation for a general analysis of the Athabaskan culture.

The *Seldovia Herald* in 1931 reported:

> C.B. Osgood, professor of anthropology at Yale University, and Mrs. Osgood, registered at Shortley's, are arranging for a season of research work among native Alaskans. A young man, and a graduate of the University of Chicago, he is personally and well acquainted with the present head of his Alma Mater, and has a fund of interesting stories to tell about the world's youngest university president. Professor Osgood's investigations into the origin of races have heretofore taken him into northern Canada, but this is his first trip to Alaska. He has not fully decided upon the main district to be covered, but believes that interesting facts might develop along the Inlet, and he may decide to confine his activities to this region.

At the time Osgood conducted his research, he estimated the Tanaina population of Cook Inlet to be about 650. This is considerably less than the population "high" of roughly 3000 in 1805.[34] Osgood attributed the decline of the Tanaina in part to the 1838 smallpox epidemic. Noting that relations between the Tanaina and the Russians had never been warm, Osgood pointed to a probable breakdown in Tanaina morale after the epidemic, and a corresponding downward trend in population.[35]

Osgood lamented his difficulty in gathering information, finding that only informants of age 50 or greater had any real memory of traditions. Osgood's lack of fluency in the Tanaina tongue, and his informants' lack of English, further hampered matters. Finally, he recognized that the culture he was recording was a post-European one, there being no one left living who could recall pre-European contact Tanaina culture. Indeed, he noted sadly that the aboriginal culture was almost completely gone.[36] The informant Osgood regarded most was from Seldovia:

Cornelius Osgood (far left) poses in 1937 at Mendenhall Glacier in Juneau with his wife and (2nd from left) Jim Fitzgerald, and (at far right) J. B. Mertie. Photo courtesy of U.S. Geological Survey.

"The informant to whom I am indebted most deeply is Fitka Balishoff of Seldovia who was born in that place about sixty-five years before my arrival. [author's note: This would have been about 1866, and is the only reference I have found that in any way places modern man in Seldovia prior to the Russian Church record reference of 1875.] Both his father and mother were Tanaina, the latter born in a village farther up Kachemak Bay and the former at Kenai. The only grandparent he could remember was his mother's father who came from the country to the south of Tustumena Lake. At the time of his childhood there were no Europeans in Seldovia, and one of his earliest memories was that of a ship anchoring outside the harbor. The natives fled to the woods, overlooking Fitka, who, being too young to run, hid in a corner of a house. When the white men came ashore, they found him very frightened and let him sit with them to share their meal. When they departed they left some food which his parents took away from him immediately on their return. All this left a vivid impression. Fitka's English had indisputable weaknesses but he had an inherent interest in the ways of his own people which with a retentive memory made him a valuable informant. His native intelligence would put to shame many of his white critics, and he had a philosophy of life which enabled him to live comfortably from day to day in a chicken coop which he for a period shared with a pet porcupine. (Osgood later notes that Fitka's pet porky followed him around and slept by his head.) Fitka was a chronic drinker, but his happy disposition never failed him at his worst. Some days with apologetic politeness he said, 'I guess I pretty drunk—I come back after.' And so he did through the weeks of our association. I left esteeming his friendship and protesting inwardly against the statement that he was 'old enough for died'." [37]

By 1933, Fitka had indeed passed away, but not before he and Osgood together captured and recorded the last remaining vestiges of the Tanaina culture in Seldovia.

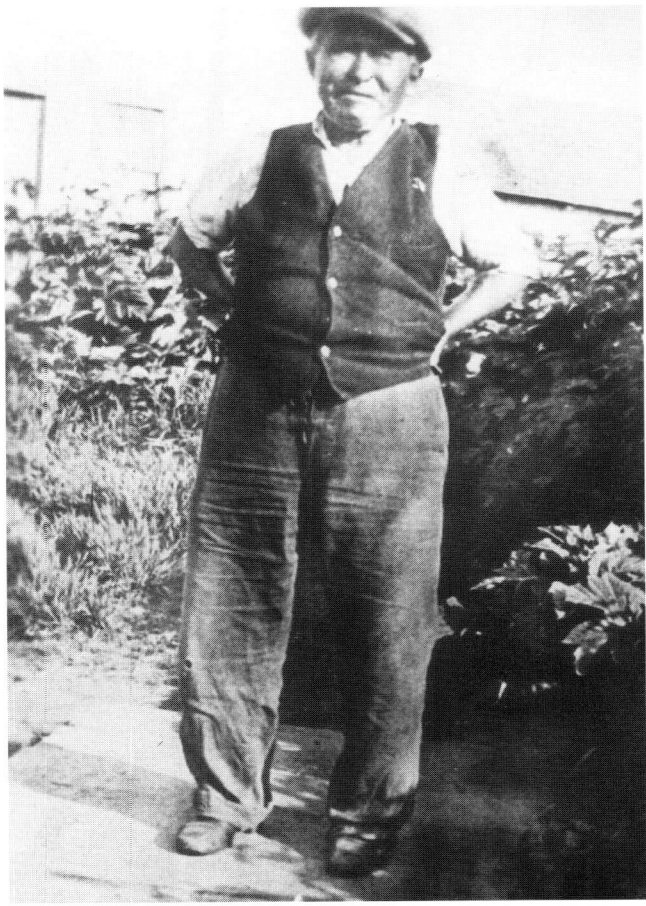

Fitka Balishoff about 1925. Photo courtesy of Jack and Susan B. English Collection.

As a researcher, I tried very hard to find the log of some vessel which would have anchored off the mouth of the bay sometime in the late 1860's to early 1870's, figuring that Fitka would have to have been four or five years old to retain a memory of the event, while being "too young to run." Logs of the revenue cutters seemed the most likely place to search, but a check of the logs of ships in Alaskan waters during those years yielded little. The event that so impressed little Fitka must also have touched the men coming ashore, perhaps so much so that there sits in some silent journal, in a museum somewhere, a grown-up's account of the encounter that took place that day.

Ways of the Seldovia Tanaina

The Kachemak Bay Tanaina enjoyed one of the richest food-producing areas in the Tanaina region. Ten species of saltwater fish, octopus, crab, mussels, clams, and sea mammals such as hair seal, fur seal, sea otter, sea lion, porpoise, and beluga whale were harvested from the sea.[38] Salmon were caught by damming a stream with a weir fashioned from logs and debris. As the fish swam through a small funnel opening, they were netted and killed with a club.[39] Halibut were caught using a configuration of sticks, spruce root line, a hook baited with salmon, and a rock heavy enough such that two men were required to lift it. The device was constructed on the beach at low tide and left in place. At high water, the halibut catcher was submerged, and the size of the bait discouraged small flatfish while attracting larger ones. Even though the sticks used might be broken by the struggles of the fish, the great stone held it in place for the natives to retrieve when the tide had receded again.[40] Fish were dried for winter, with the exception of the late fall run of silver salmon, which were buried in the ground in layers alternating with grass.

Land mammals were hunted using bow and arrow, and dispatched if needed with a spear. Osgood reports that the Kachemak Bay Tanaina removed their footwear for running down game, enduring severe bruising from the thorny devil's club plant in their belief that barefoot was the only way to outrun an animal. Black bear, moose, porcupine, and rabbits were common fare. The Kachemak Bay Tanaina reported hunting black bear by finding a den in autumn and memorizing the location. Come winter, they would return to the den and tease the sleeping bear awake, killing it while it was still groggy. Small fur-bearing animals such as ermine, fox, marten, mink, squirrel, and land otter were trapped, and their pelts used in clothing.[41]

Seals were hunted at low tide, as they hauled out to sun themselves on the beach. The hunter swam to the beach, dashed out of the water, and clubbed the animals to death. Seals were also hunted with bows and arrows and harpoons from bidarkas. Sea otters were hunted from bidarkas as well, with the men usually going out in groups of eight or ten. Sea lions, apt to turn on the hunter and destroy his bidarka, were hunted by a solitary man.[42]

Ducks, geese, loon, ptarmigan, and grouse were hunted using snares, or bow and arrow, or slingshots. Eagles and owls were also eaten, but sea gulls were only used for bait. The Kachemak Bay Tanaina lured young eider ducks by honking like the mother duck. The young birds became somewhat domesticated, and were consumed when they were fully grown.[43]

Women gathered blueberries, raspberries, currants, and low and high bush cranberries. The Kachemak Bay Tanaina also harvested two kinds of edible seaweed.[44] The primary meal of the day was taken in the evening, and since eating was done with the fingers, hands and faces were washed first, and then dried before the warmth of the fire, or with grass.[45]

Native hunters land on the beach at Seldovia c.1916. Photo courtesy of Anchorage Museum of History and Art, #143.

Thatched-roof barabara at Seldovia. Photo courtesy of Alaska State Library, J. E. Thwaites Collection, # PCA 18-17.

Native dwelling and food cache (at left) at Seldovia. Note the person standing beneath the cache, and the bidarka at the far left. Photo courtesy of the University of Alaska Fairbanks, George Talmadge Collection, acc.# 74-18-59.

A native family poses outside their thatched-roof log dwelling in Seldovia. Photo courtesy of Ted Anderson from the Ralph and Juanita Anderson Collection.

In this 1901 photograph, a group of Seldovia natives stands at the entrance to their dwelling. The photograph includes the notation that it was taken "above Seldovia", which may simply mean in the foothills above the beach. Photo courtesy of Anchorage Museum of History and Art, #142.

The Kachemak Bay Tanaina wore a loose unisex garment made from tanned caribou or sheep hides. Over this, they wore a shirt of the same material, the men "being somewhat shorter than the women." Decoration was limited to red paint and long beads laid vertically. Boots to the knee made of several types of skin were smeared with porcupine grease as a waterproofing agent. In the winter, the one-piece garment was traded for one similar but longer, and with the hair left on the hide and turned in toward the body. The overshirt was exchanged for a parka made of squirrel or lynx, which provided warmth but was not overwhelming for active work. Warmer furs were used for dressier parkas. Supplemental garments such as wind breakers, hunting parkas, coats, mittens, and caps were created as the need arose.

Because they spent a considerable amount of time on the water, the Kachemak Bay Tanaina made special waterproof parkas from the intestines of bear or beluga whales. The garments were constructed so that the bottom could be lashed around the opening of the bidarka, similar to the spray skirt employed by kayakers today. Bear hide boots were waterproofed by using the grease rendered from a pot of boiling porcupine. The marine outfit was completed by broad-brimmed woven spruce root hats, which protected the eyes from the glare off the water. [46]

The Kachemak Bay Tanaina adorned themselves with hyqua-shell beads, obtained indirectly through trade with Indians from Southeast Alaska. They also favored sea otter fur, and red paint made from ochre. Women wore their hair in long braids, while men wore theirs shoulder length and loose. Using a sinew blackened with charcoal, tattoos were made by using a needle to pull the sinew underneath the skin. In Kachemak Bay, vertical lines on the chins of both men and women were the only tattoo reported. Ear lobes, noses, and lower lips were pierced by wealthy people of both sexes, and bead, bone, and shell ornaments worn. [47]

Housing was provided by barabaras in the winter, and more lightly constructed smokehouses at the summer fish camps. The word barabara is a Russian term which means "native house."[48] The Kachemak Bay Tanaina name for their house was "níčił."[49] Although most barabaras were around 20 x 25 feet,

> ### NATIVE GOES HUNTING AND FAILS TO RETURN
>
> The Mysterious disappearance of Simeone Balishoff, a part Russian, part native resident of Seldovia, is agitating the native population of the Cook Inlet village. Balishoff, who was the most expert bidarka man on the inlet, departed from Seldovia on June 24 for Kachemak Bay on a bear hunt. He was unaccompanied and went in a single-hatch bidarka. Two days later natives found the bidarka near the big rock on Yukon Island. The top was crushed in. No sign could be found of the missing man, although several search parties have sought for him. It is the accepted theory that a whale struck the bidarka and killed the occupant. Like instances are not uncommon on the inlet, where whales of various varieties are numerous.

Travel by bidarka was not without its hazards, as this Seward Weekly Gateway *article from July 10, 1909 illustrates.*

some were as large as 25 x 40 feet. The lowermost part of the house was subterranean, with a pit dug down two to three feet, and log walls laid above that. The logs were not notched, but instead were placed between pairs of vertical poles driven into the ground. Moss was laid between the logs for insulation, and after each wall log was laid, the vertical poles were tied tightly with spruce root cord. Splitting adzes and straight-grained spruce provided planks, which were lashed vertically to create the gabled ends of the house. Internal posts held up a ridgepole, and rafters made of smaller poles were lashed from the ridgepole to the top course of wall logs. Large sheets of spruce bark were stripped from trees and flattened and lashed to the rafters to make a roof. The walls and sometimes the roof were water and wind proofed with beach grass thatching, and finally the excavated dirt was piled around the exterior. [50]

Rooms added on to the main structure included an entryway, a sweathouse or banya, a menstrual room, and sometimes an additional sleeping room for a large family. The interior of the house featured a central firepit, with a smoke hole in the roof above. Raised platforms built of planks ran along both sides of the central room. During the day, they were used as work areas. By night they became beds for boys and unmarried men. Married couples and girls slept under the platforms.

Sometime prior to European contact, the Kachemak Bay Tanaina presumably adopted from the neighboring Eskimo the kaiak (kayak) and the umiak. The kaiak was referred to by the Russians as

The Kachemak Bay Tanaina name for this three-hatch kayak was "wáidálgi." Photo courtesy of Alaska State Library, J. E. Thwaites Collection, PCA 18-436.

"bidarka." The Kachemak Bay Tanaina name for this craft was "wígídin," "qáiyíhgʷaq," or "wáidálgi," depending on whether it had one, two, or three hatches, or top openings.[51] The kaiak was fashioned from about ten seal skins, with paddles carved of spruce. The umiak was an open-topped boat, requiring from twenty to fifty seal skins to construct. The Tanaina were all reportedly able to swim.[52]

For land travel, the Kachemak Bay Tanaina blazed trees to mark a trail, and carried a backpack for longer trips. It was their custom to build camping shelters at the more popular hunting and fishing destinations.[53]

Although the Tanaina culture was not particularly nomadic, the Kachemak Bay people maintained friendly relations with Eskimos on the south coast of the Kenai Peninsula and in Prince William Sound. The Kachemak Bay region had a reputation for its rich and abundant food supplies, so there probably was little reason, other than trade, for the Tanaina of this area to travel. Tanaina from Tyonek sometimes had difficulty gathering food in the winter when Cook Inlet had frozen. They would travel overland to the north shore of Kachemak Bay and light a signal fire, which would alert the Kachemak Bay people to come for them. They would then stay until food gathering in their locale improved, sometimes until spring.[54]

For household goods, skins were tanned or smoked, mats were woven from grass, and coiled and woven baskets were made from spruce root. Ropes were made from sinew, skin, spruce root, and sometimes bull kelp. Fish spears were fashioned of spruce, with a bone point, and sometimes a whale rib. Bows were backed with sinew, and bore much resemblance to certain Eskimo bows. Wooden clubs and sling-shots made of skin were also used as hunting implements. Knives in the Kachemak Bay area were made of stone, as were oil burning lamps. Other implements were fashioned from bone, wood, and shell. Bear intestine was used to create waterproof pouches and bags.[55]

The Tanaina villages were not noted for fighting amongst themselves, but instead with the Eskimo in the region of Kodiak Island. The Eskimo were generally the aggressors, seeking to acquire possessions, such as skins, which were not in abundance in their locale. The Tanaina were generally successful in the battles fought. The bow and arrow and spears were used, and the Kachemak Bay Tanaina were known for making clubs from a hard type of knotted spruce. "Armor" made of skins and coated with layers of spruce gum and sand helped to protect the Tanaina warriors.[56]

Among other Tanaina ways were the use of indigenous plants as medicines, the sending of smoke signals, and the use of red and black "homemade" paints in artwork. Dancing was popular among the Tanaina, but they were not noted for the intricate steps of the Eskimo. Drums and sometimes rattles accompanied dance and song. Songs were sung to celebrate love, feasts, death, and to bring luck. The Kachemak Bay Tanaina sang a song to encourage luck in hunting and long life. An intricate ritual of fasting and immersion in the ocean or a stream was performed in conjunction with the song.[57]

Storytelling was considered an art, and games of all sorts were enjoyed. Among them were horizontal jumping, foot racing, bidarka races, high jumping, tug-of-war, wrestling, and a bow and arrow game played with teams and gambled on. Versions of blind-man's-bluff, hide-and-seek, and a game requiring acrobatic skill were popular. In Kachemak Bay, several games involving sticks and teams of men were played as well.[58]

The Tanaina were organized into a complex series of clans, and within each village existed several social classes, a village council, and a leader, or chief. The Russians referred to this (male) position as the "toyon," while the Kachemak Bay Tanaina name for it was " toyok."[59] Wealth was the basis for the class system, and was measured by the number of hyqua-shell beads an individual owned.

Visitors were in general regarded with enthusiasm, and the occasion of a visit called for much feasting and dancing. Women and men appeared to enjoy more or less equal power in the family unit, although women could be loaned as sexual commodities to the husband's best friend/blood brother, or "slocin" from another clan.[60]

The Tanaina had complex familial relationships, and engaged in much feasting at "potlatches" to mark a variety of special occasions. A young man's debut as a hunter, a marriage, a death, and, in Kachemak Bay, the completion of the building of an umiak were all reasons for a potlatch to be held. The "rules" governing potlatches were quite involved, depending on the occasion and the social position of the honoree. They all had in common much communal eating and the exchange of gifts, as well as singing and dancing.[61]

Although no potlatch was held for the birth of a child, it was considered desirable to bear children, and women birthed an average of seven children. For the Kachemak Bay Tanaina, the menstrual addition to the dwelling served as the birthing chamber, and the men of the house left to stay with other villagers for about five days. The infant was bathed and powdered with charcoal daily, and kept in a moss-lined sealskin bag. Young girls marked their entrance to adulthood with certain traditions observed at the first menstruation, and boys at around age 15 were sent into the woods for five days and allowed neither food nor water. A ceremony also marked their first successful hunt. [62]

Chastity in girls was highly valued, and although there was no marriage ceremony, a lengthy courtship was observed. The suitor spent a certain period of time living with his bride's family, helping to contribute to their support. This working apprenticeship could be waived in lieu of quantities of gifts. A wealthy man could have several wives. [63]

When a person died, his or her body was dressed in fine new clothes and burned. The residual bones were gathered into a bag and buried. A pole marked the gravesite, and strings were tied to the pole to record the number of potlatches given by the deceased. [64]

The Tanaina believed in reincarnation, and also believed that all natural objects had powers either greater or lesser than those of humans. They believed that inanimate objects could speak, and they also believed in spirits. They acknowledged the presence of monsters and evil spirits. Among these was the "Nakani," or bad Indian, who was noted for stealing people. "At Seldovia a Nakani once captured a woman who had the cleverness to drop at intervals the tails from her squirrel parka. Hunters following, discovered and saved her, but the Nakani escaped." [65]

There was also widespread acceptance of superstitions, and the use of amulets. Shamans, or medicine men, provided the link between the material world and the world of the spirits. Rattles, drums, and masks were used in affecting cures, and "devil sticks" and "devil dolls" were employed to drive out the evil spirits which made people sick.

The story is told of Mother Rick, an elderly native woman of Seldovia who lived with Fitka Balishoff. She was said to be the last remaining shaman. Newcomers to town were warned never to leave their washing on the line to dry overnight, for Mother Rick would come and take a piece of it, as she might want to use it in the future for working a charm on its owner. Mother Rick allegedly had a nine inch tall doll, whittled from wood, which she used in working her magic. Sitting on the floor, Mother Rick would dress the doll in the scrap of clothing from her intended victim, and would chant and sway. The doll is said to have danced also. Depending on the nature of the spell, the doll might be buried in the carcass of a dead crow or dog, and as the animal decomposed, so apparently did the life of the spell's victim. [66]

"Nakani Steals a Seldovia Woman", an original linoleum block print by the author.

Mother Rick was thrown in the Seldovia jail for three months once for interfering with the U.S. Marshal's arrest of a bootlegger. Upon her release, Mother Rick vowed that Jimmy Hill, the Marshal, would only live for three months, the exact length of her jail sentence. Her prophecy came true, when approximately three months from the time she uttered those words, U.S. Marshal Hill was shot and killed while investigating reports of a local still. [67]

There were a number of Tanaina myths related to Osgood, many of them by Fitka Balishoff. Three are selected for inclusion in this book, and they illustrate the Tanaina's belief that a killing, be it purposeful or accidental, upset the vital balance of society so much that some kind of compensation was deemed absolutely necessary. While this generally meant the taking of a life for a life, it on rare occasions could be settled through payment. Based on their marine setting, it is not implausible that these stories referred to the Kachemak Bay Tanaina. [These stories are reprinted from *Ethnography of the Tanaina* by Cornelius Osgood with permission of Yale University Publications in Anthropology, Human Relations Area Files Press.]

The First Sea Otter

A man married a chief's daughter. Then he wanted other women, so during low tide he put his wife out on a rock and left her. The tide came in and hit her feet and she sang a song, low and plaintive. Then the tide came up to her knees and the chief's daughter sang another song. When the water hit her waist she sang a third song, and another when the water reached her chest. When the water got to her mouth she sang the last and saddest song and sank into the water to become the first sea otter.

Several months later, in June, the sea otter recognized her husband's brother in his kaiak and went to him and asked, "Where is my husband?" The brother told her that he was hunting close to shore, so she went to her husband's boat and said to him, "You tried to kill me, but I am going to kill you this time." The sea otter went under water and bit a hole in the skin of the kaiak, so that her husband started to sink. His brother came to try to rescue him, but the wife said, "Don't pick up my husband or I'll tear your kaiak too." When the husband tried to swim, the wife sea otter would bite him, and then she killed him. And that makes even. The sea otter went to some other country and was never seen again. [68]

The Woman and the Ducks

Once there was a rich man who had one daughter. Many men wanted to marry her but her father would not let them. One day a rich man came and married the girl, and took her back to his country, which was across the bay. Every night he left her and did not return until the next morning. During the night he went to the country of his wife's people, and on each visit he killed one person when he left. In a year they were all dead. From each one that he killed he took out the viscera and hung the bodies up to dry. While he was on these nightly ventures, he employed two women from his own country to watch his wife so that she didn't go out.

But one time one of these women told his wife that her husband danced each night. She persuaded her to lend her clothes and then she covered her hair with grease. She also dirtied her face so that no one would recognize her. Thus disguised she went to her people's country for she wanted to see her family. She climbed on top of the barabara and there she saw her husband dancing inside. Hanging up around the walls were the dried skins of her father, her mother, and her brother. Her husband had fastened strings to the arms and legs to make them dance. After seeing this she went home and washed her face and laid down on the bed and started to cry.

When her husband came home in the morning he tried to talk to her but she would not answer. At last he asked if she wanted to see her mother. She answered, "Yes." And he said, "I will take you home then." When she was ready he put her in his one-hole kaiak and took her across the bay to her people's country. When they reached the shore he told her to get out. When she had done so he told her, "I will go behind you." As she walked toward the village, she looked for smoke but saw none and then she knew that everyone was dead. She turned back after going half way but her husband was already gone. She sat down and cried. Then she got up again and went to her father's home. She saw it was a long time since there had been a fire. She looked over all the town but everyone was gone. She came back to her father's house and built a fire and cooked some meat. There was plenty of food but no people. Every day she walked back and forth through the village and when she was hungry she came home and cooked some food.

Summertime came—the June month. She went out to take a walk along the little creek in the flat and when she saw a mallard duck go with young she followed them. After a little way, they came to a waterfall and the ducklings could not swim up so she caught them all and took them home. She kept them there and put soft food in a wooden plate and the ducks came and ate.

One evening when she was lonesome she started to dance. As she danced the little mallards lifted their wings and started to jump, to dance around and around the fire. After that, she did not let the ducklings go out because she was afraid that she might lose them. Every evening when she was lonesome she started to sing. Then the mallards began to dance. They had become full grown. One evening when they lifted their wings to dance, small hands grew out from under their wings. The next day the woman made small bows and arrows and she taught the ducks how to use them. They started to play and shoot at sticks at the opposite end of the barabara. At first they missed the sticks but afterwards they learned to hit them.

One day when the woman was out walking, she saw a one-hole kaiak. She called to the man in it to come ashore and told him to come to her barabara. Then she gave him plenty of food to eat and said, "I'll show you I have some dancing mallards." She started to sing and the mallards began to dance and play with their bows and arrows. The man had never seen such a thing. She told him to bring all the people from her husband's country and she would show them her wonderful babies.

The next day at noontime she saw many big skin boats and many kaiaks coming. Everybody from her husband's country was on the way to see her babies. She ran back to the village and in every barabara she built a fire and in each fire she put rocks to get hot. Then when they were heated she put them in every sweat house. Finally she filled a seal belly full of old oil. When the people from her husband's country arrived, she served food in every barabara. She fed them very well. Then when they wanted to see the ducks she said she would show her babies to them after everyone had taken a sweat bath. So everyone went into the bath houses and she closed the doors behind them. Then the mallards took the old seal oil and dropped some from the roof of the bath house on to the hot rocks. This made a black smoke. The mallards poured the oil on the hot rocks of all ten bath houses and the people were all killed before they saw the mallards dance.

Then the mallards went back to the creek and the woman followed them. There they met the old mother mallard coming down the creek and she said, "A man killed all your family—mallards killed all his family—that makes even." Then the woman went off and lived with the ducks. [69]

The Two Brothers

There were two brothers, married to sisters, daughters of a chief. The boys went out hunting, but the older brother never learned to shoot. The younger brother was a very good hunter and his kaiak was always full of food. The older brother was very angry that he couldn't shoot better than his brother. One day when they were out in the kaiaks he said to the younger brother, "Let's go ashore for dinner." They went and the older brother killed the younger and took all his catch and put it in his own kaiak. Then he went home.

When he returned home his wife asked him where his brother was. He answered that he had left him on the other side of the bay. But there happened to be a man in the woods hunting when the older brother killed the younger, and he came and told the young widow what had happened to her husband. The girl had never cried before, but she wept very hard. Then she told her father and her nine brothers. Three brothers stood on each side of the murderer's barabara so that he couldn't get away. Then the father of the girl called him out and said, "You killed your brother." He hit him on the head and then killed him with a bone knife. [70]

SELECTED KACHEMAK BAY TANAINA WORDS

Reprinted from <u>Ethnography of the Tanaina</u> by Cornelius Osgood with permission of Yale University Publications in Anthropology, Human Relations Area Files Press.[71]

ENGLISH	TANAINA
Humpback salmon	kóγonà
Dog salmon	a̦líma
Silver salmon	nóλáγe
Red salmon	toḱóya
King salmon	łoxága
Herring	kócínágóx̦a
Halibut	šáiyoq'
Jellyfish	tócáłin
Octopus	ámókok
Clam (a)	tálčímá
Clam (b)	čógoš
Clam (c)	stóga
Clam (d)	kézin
Mussel	q'áola
Crab	cnáλin
Black Bear	γaldaší
Porcupine	q'é'γé
Fox	káwiak
Land otter	táq'din
Mink	tagé·ča
Marten	ḱačaγóša
Ermine	káγólčína
Wolf	waḱikníyi
Sea otter	tóhges
Killer whale	áx̦lot
Geese	nodáke
Eagle	ńdáłíga
Duck (Mallard)	čahdoλ'íči
Grouse	ex̦łyín
Ptarmigan	télgémá
Blueberry (high bush)	kánca
Red Salmonberry (high bush)	ńgólga
Kelp (edible - a)	q'áλót
Kelp (edible - b)	žágáłq'a
Kamleika	wágízγe
Fur Parka	wíq'ó'tqóni
Mittens	góž
Woven spruce root hat	x̦ágíčax̦
Barabara	níčił
Dance house	káži
Smoke house	čagóŋγa
Sweat house	nλí

ENGLISH (cont.)	TANAINA (cont.)
Kaiak (1 hatch)	wíģídin
Kaiak (2 hatch)	qáiyíhgʷaq
Kaiak (3 hatch)	wáidálgi
Umiak	wádi
Paddle	tá·γe·
Spruce root line	kóŋgíláši
Fish spear	ƛ'óq'íške?
Detachable bone spear point	ésƛ'íní
Club	číknáγáltne
Snare	q'óq'eƛ
Bow	cíɬdén
Arrow	ízin
Stone Adze	ḱicáƛi
Stone Lamp	nánógáƛníga
Spruce root basket	x̥áge
Bear intestine bag	óq'is
Dance	ní·yo·c
Song	q'tálí
Village	káiyax̥
Family	dosnága
Potlatch	q'atíƛ'
Shaman	ilekq'ón
Seldovia people	ágidáknódana
Alders	koŋgaiyá
Cottonwood	esníh
Mountain	té·le·
Rain	eɬkón
Snow	nžáh
Spruce	ćwála
Wind	káníɬčíyi

Endnotes

[1] Svetlana G. Fedorova, *The Russian Population in Alaska and California, Late 18th Century — 1867*, trans. and ed. Richard A. Pierce and Alton S. Donnelly (Kingston, ON: Limestone Press, 1973) 145.
[2] Richard Pierce, letter to the author, 4 Dec. 1993.
[3] William H. Dall, *Alaska and Its Resources* (London: Sampson Low, Son & Marston, 1870) 430.
[4] P.A. Tikhmenev, *A History of the Russian American Company,* trans. and ed. Richard A. Pierce and Alton S. Donnelly, 2 vols. (Kingston, ON: Limestone Press, 1979) 2: 416.
[5] Tikhmenev 198-199.
[6] Records of the Russian Orthodox Greek Catholic Church of North America, Diocese of Alaska, trans. Katherine Arndt, microfilm #139 reel 199, Alaskan Russian Church Archives, U of Alaska Fairbanks.
[7] James Kari, personal communication, Apr. 1993.
[8] Donald J. Orth, *Dictionary of Alaska Place Names*, Geological Survey Professional Paper 567, (Washington: GPO, 1967) 26.
[9] Ivan Petroff, *Report on the Population, Industries, and Resources of Alaska*, (n.p., 1880) 29.
[10] Carolyn E. Reed, "Community Response to the Alaska Native Claims Settlement Act: Seldovia, Alaska," diss., U. of Calgary, 1979, 21.
[11] Orth 1068-1069.
[12] Petroff 29.
[13] Petroff 162.
[14] Petroff 26.

Endnotes (cont.)

[15] Petroff 137.
[16] Petroff 162.
[17] Frederica de Laguna, *The Archaeology of Cook Inlet,* 2nd Ed. (Anchorage: Alaska Historical Society, 1975) 15.
[18] Reed 22.
[19] Reed 21.
[20] Reed 21.
[21] Johan Adrian Jacobsen, *Alaskan Voyage, 1881-1883, An Expedition to the Northwest Coast of America,* trans. Erna Gunther (Chicago: U. of Chicago Press, 1977) 86.
[22] Jacobsen 99.
[23] Jacobsen 195.
[24] Cornelius Osgood, *The Ethnography of the Tanaina,* Yale University Publications in Anthropology, Number 16, (New Haven: reprinted by Human Relations Area Files P, 1976) 215.
[25] Elsa Pedersen, "Seldovia", *Alaska Sportsman,* July 1958: 8.
[26] Dede Higman, personal communication, 1993.
[27] Wolfgang Haberland, letters to the author, Apr. 1993, June 1993.
[28] Jacobsen 197.
[29] Jacobsen 200.
[30] Archives of the Alaska Commercial Co., Box 168, U. of Alaska Fairbanks.
[31] Cook Inlet Native Association, *Cook Inlet Region Inventory of Native Historic Sites and Cemetaries,* (n.p.: Cook Inlet Region, Inc., 1975) 14.
[32] Nick Elxnit, personal interview, 1988.
[33] Cook Inlet Native Assoc. 15.
[34] Osgood 19.
[35] Osgood 19.
[36] Osgood 22.
[37] Osgood, reprinted with permission of Human Relations Area Files Press, Yale U, 22.
[38] Osgood 26.
[39] Osgood 28.
[40] Osgood 29.
[41] Osgood 31-37.
[42] Osgood 37-38.
[43] Osgood 40-41.
[44] Osgood 41.
[45] Osgood 45.
[46] Osgood 46-52.
[47] Osgood 51-54.
[48] Orth 104.
[49] Osgood 211.
[50] Osgood 55-59.
[51] Osgood 212.
[52] Osgood 67-70.
[53] Osgood 70-72.
[54] Osgood 73-75.
[55] Osgood 75-108.
[56] Osgood 109-113.
[57] Osgood 116-123.
[58] Osgood 123-126.
[59] Osgood 214.
[60] Osgood 136-138.
[61] Osgood 147-160.
[62] Osgood 160-163.
[63] Osgood 163-165.
[64] Osgood 166.
[65] Osgood 172.
[66] Alice Cushing Lipke, *Under the Aurora,* (Los Angeles:Suttonhouse, 1938) 215-216. See Author's Note, p. 30.
[67] Lipke 198-199, 214.
[68] Osgood, reprinted with permission of Human Relations Area Files Press, Yale U, 185.
[69] Osgood, reprinted with permission of Human Relations Area Files Press, Yale U, 185-186.
[70] Osgood, reprinted with permission of Human Relations Area Files Press, Yale U, 188.
[71] Osgood, reprinted with permission of Human Relations Area Files Press, Yale U, 208-218.

RUSSIAN CULTURE AND INFLUENCE

The Role of the Russian Orthodox Church in the Lives of 19th and Early 20th Century Seldovians

The arrival of the Russians in Cook Inlet in the late 18th century was not looked upon kindly by the indigenous people. The Tanaina and Inuit were in general peaceful nations, save for the isolated territorial disputes amongst themselves. They were grossly unprepared, however, for the submission demanded of them by the early Russian fur traders. They responded hostilely to the Russian bid for supremacy, and there are numerous accounts of battles fought between Russians and natives. Unfortunately, the smallpox epidemic of 1838 undoubtedly did much to undermine the resolve of the native people. With their numbers so drastically diminished by disease and death, it is reasonable to assume that their ability to fight was hampered. As they came under the increasing influence of the Russian fur-trading economy, their own aboriginal economy was fatally weakened.[1]

Although the United States purchased the territory of Alaska from Russia in 1867, it was several decades before American influence supplanted that of the Russians. Missionaries from the Russian Orthodox Church had devoted nearly a century of work to Alaska, and their activities did not cease with the purchase.

The Russian American Company was sold to Hutchinson and Kohl in the year following the purchase of Alaska, and it became the Alaska Commercial Company. The Western Fur and Trading Company, operating in Seldovia some fifteen years after the purchase, began as a Russian-owned company as well.

Current photograph of Seldovia's Russian Orthodox Church. View looking to the East.
Photo by Tom Glover © 1997

Orthodox Church Provides Seldovia Census

By the commencement of Seldovia's recorded history (1875), the intermingling of Russian and native cultures had already taken place. Seldovia was the "marriage" of a fur trading post owned by a Russian company and a Tanaina/Kaniagmiut village.

In Russian Orthodox Church records, Seldovia appears as a separate settlement for the first time in 1880 (in the confessional records) with two male surnames listed. By 1881, it was listed in the annual description of the Kenai parish, and was shown as having an Orthodox prayer house.[2] According to church records the population was as follows:

```
1881 .......... 35 male and 29 female Kenaitsy
1882 .......... 37 male and 29 female Kenaitsy
1883 .......... 39 male and 30 female Kenaitsy
```

It is interesting to note that the 1881 Orthodox Church "census" is in contradiction to that of Ivan Petroff, taken one year earlier, in which he lists the inhabitants as Inuit and Creole (part native and part Russian).

The following table lists the names and ages of some of the early Seldovia residents as revealed by the church records:

1875	Nal'tun, Mikhail (39), wife Anna (32), daughters Daria (11) and Agafia (9)
1876	Nal'tun, Mikhail and daughter Agafia
	Nil'tliusha, Stepan (22), came from Skilak to Seldovia
1877	Berestov, Nikolai (21), Creole, came from Ninilchik to Seldovia
	Nal'tun, Mikhail and daughter Agafia (listed under the village of Chkitukskoe, but shown as being in Seldovia, similar to 1875 listing)
	Lup (22) and Makar (26), shown as orphans with no last names
	Nil'tliusha, Stepan
	Tagina, Merkurii (44), widower, shown as being the toyon or head of the village of Kandazinskoe (just north of the mouth of Kenai River[3])

In 1880, more names were listed, but still represented apparently only two male surnames. Upon baptism into the Orthodox Church, an individual's native name was customarily used as his new last name, and he was given a Christian first name. Thus a family being baptized could end up with numerous last names in the first generation post-baptism.[4]

The names from the church confessional record for 1881 are also included here (on page 73), simply for the record they provide of people living in Seldovia at that time. It should be noted that prior to Katherine Arndt's translation of these records, this "partial census" was in the realm of undiscovered historical information.

Partial List of Seldovia Residents in 1880 According to Russian Orthodox Church Records

Akal'khov, Paraskovia—female, (26), "skipped communion"

Tylgyl'na, Evdokia—female, (28), sister of above

Mokiiu, Evgenia—female, (13), illegitimate daughter of Evdokia

Mokiiu, Evdokia—female, (7), illegitimate daughter of Evdokia

Mokiiu, Marina—female, (4), illegitimate daughter of Evdokia

Eliukal', Ivan—male, (38)

Anka or Akka, Irina—female, (36), wife of Ivan

Eliukal', Matvei—male, (7), son of Ivan and Irina

Eliukal', Stefan—male, (3), son of Ivan & Irina
Zakhar—male, (9), listed with above family but unknown if related

Elena—female, (37), wife of Beliaev (no surname), who is not listed

Nadezhda—female, (5), daughter of above

Feodor—male, (1), son of above

Kirilov, Nikolai—male, (36), listed as having moved from Ninilchik to Seldovia

Chainitno, Maria—female, (28), wife of above, (spelling of surname in question)

Byl'nytunutil', Nikolai—male, (30), brother of Maria

Aleksandrov, Ivan—male, " still in Kasilof "

Seldovia Residents in 1881
According to Russian Orthodox Church Records
"Sel'devskoe settlement"

Tagina, Merkurii—-male, (48), widower, (he was shown as toyon of Kandazinskoe in 1877)
Nal'tun, Mikhail—-male, (45), (from Seldovia's "first family"; his first wife and the children from that union have either passed on or live with another family or in another village)
Nugutak, Anna—-female, (47), second wife of Mikhail
    Efim—-male, (19), son of Anna
    Grigorii—-male, (13), son of Anna
    Feodor—-male, (9), son of Anna
Nil'tliulna, Stepan—-male, (27)
Tukhigil'na, Evdokiia—-female, (23), wife of above, shown as deceased
Kilikta or Kilikhta, Vorfolomei—-male, (34)
    Paraskov'ia—-female, (19), sister of above
Ukhita, Ol'ga—-female, (42), wife of Vorfolomei
Kchikigniush, Konstantin—-male, (12), brother of Ol'ga
    Ivan—-male, (21), Ol'ga's child from her 1st marriage
    Akilina—-female, (16), ditto above
    Dariia—-female, (13), ditto above
    Anastasiia—-female, (11), ditto above
    Ananii—-male, (9), ditto above
    Vasilii—-male, (3), ditto above
    Ivan—-male, (2), ditto above
Khnukhital'na, Ol'ga—-female, (51), widow
    Mark—-male, (19), son of Ol'ga
    Samuil, male, (14), son of Ol'ga
Tugitigal'na, Nadezhda—-female, (62), widow
Chudykh, Nikolai—-male, (24), her married son
    Nastas'ia—-female, (10), grandchild
    Marfa—-female, (9), grandchild
    Paraskoviia—-female, (7), grandchild
    Anna—-female, (5), grandchild
Chil'tanik, Stepan—-male, (20)
Chitunil'ia, Matrona—-female, (28), sister of above
Ytyga or Ytycha, Feodor—-male, (34)
Filipova, Liubov'—-female, (34), Creole, wife of above
    Ol'ga—-female, (10), daughter
        Konstantin—-male, (4), ward of the family
Tazzyn, Ivan—-male, (44)

Maiuknak, Feodor—-male, (50)
    Varvara—female, (32), " a Kenaika"
    Nikolai—male, (13), son
    Vasilii—male, (11), son
    Mikhail—male, (8), son
Chanatak, Nadezhda—female, (40), sister of Feodor
    Grigorii—male, (13), illegitimate son
    Agaf'ia—female, (11), illegitimate daughter
Kanshaiak, Mokii—male, (31)
Tiigil'na, Evdokiia—female, (28), wife of above
    Evgeniia—female, (13), daughter
    Evdokiia—female, (7), daughter
    Marina—female, (4), daughter
Akal'khak, Paraskoviia—female, (26), sister to E.Tiigil'na
Eliukal', Ivan—-male, (38)
Anka, Irina—female, (36), wife of Ivan
    Matvei—-male, (7), son
    Stefan—male, (3), son
    Andrei—male, (1), son
    Zakhar—male, (9), their ward
Nukuchish, Nikolai Kirilov—-male, (36)
Chainitna, Mariia—female, (28), deceased wife of above
    Agripina—female, aka Anna, (10), sister of Mariia
Byl'nitukutyl', Nikolai—-male, (30)
Achagak, Ol'ga—female, (18), wife of above
    Natal'ia—female, (4 mos), daughter
Niani, Aleksei—-male, (48)
    Nadezhda—female, (41), wife of above
    Nikifor—male, (17), son
    Vasilii—male, (11), son
    Kuz'ma—female, (8), daughter
Paraskoviia—female, (23), no surname, but listed as having married Chudykh
    Vlasii—male, (6), her illegitimate son

A look at the ages and relationships of some of the individuals on the above list suggests several things about the early native culture in Seldovia. Nikolai Chudykh (left hand column) had his first child at 14, and Evdokiia Tiigil'na (right hand column) bore her first at age 15. This would indicate an early emergence into adulthood, which is fairly consistent with ethnographer Osgood's data, although he notes that the <u>typical</u> age of a woman at her marriage is between 17 and 25 years of age.[5] If Paraskoviia (right hand column) was the mother of Nikolai Chudyhk's children, then she would have begun bearing at age 13. Women continued to have children throughout their childbearing years, as evidenced by several women giving birth at 38. Although there is no data to reflect infant mortality, it is likely that the diseases introduced at the time of European contact still took their toll.

The family unit was obviously flexible, the household extending to include "wards," children from other marriages, and siblings of the spouses. Because there were so few resident priests in Alaska, and because priestly visits to a village might only occur once a year (or less often in some of the most remote areas), the Orthodox Church made allowances for a couple who got together and had a child without being married. As long as that couple married one another when a traveling priest finally made it to their village, any children born before the union was formalized were considered legitimate. If, however, the couple who produced the child failed to marry each other in an Orthodox ceremony at their earliest opportunity, the child was listed by the church as illegitimate.[6]

Travel Journals of the Russian Orthodox Priests

In the early 1880's, while it is likely that Orthodox clergy from the Kenai parish visited Seldovia, little direct mention is made of the village. All of the clergy assigned to the Kenai parish kept journals of their travels. These served to document expenses, record vital statistics, and mark the progress made in missionary work, and they became the basis for later reports to the bishop. In the travel journals are detailed pictures of life in the villages, although these accounts are often colored by the prejudices of the writer.

In 1885, Hieromonk Nikita of the Kenai parish submitted a report to the Alaska Ecclesiastical Consistory. The report listed his expenses in paying and providing food for men from Seldovia who rowed to Kenai to pick him up, and then took him to Alexandrovsky (English Bay/Nanwalek), then returned him to Kenai. According to his report, the chief of Seldovia and five men comprised the rowing crew, who faced a trip between Kenai and Kachemak Bay of over a hundred miles. For their labors, they were paid $2.00 per man for a one-way trip, not including the initial Seldovia-to-Kenai leg. Thus for rowing over three hundred miles each man received $4.00. They were fed by Hieromonk Nikita during the trip, for they did not bring their own food, choosing instead to rely on the resources of the passenger. He bought 1 1/2 sacks of white flour, 6 lbs. tea, 25 lbs. gray sugar, 30 lbs. pilot bread, 10 lbs. salted meat, dry fish and fresh fish, tobacco, yeast, lard, gunpowder and gunshot for the round trip, all for slightly less than $25.00. The Consistory had recently reduced the travel allowance for priests from $100 to $50, and Hieromonk Nikita complained about this in his report, pointing out that the wages paid to the rowers were not commensurate with the time and effort expended.[7]

Sailing ships ride at anchor in 1892 in Seldovia Bay in what is today the small boat harbor. While one might be the ship that brought the photographer, one may also be there on business for one of the commercial companies. Around the turn of the century, sailing ships sometimes arrived in Seldovia bringing "outsiders," men on their way to the Interior gold fields. Russian priests worried that these transient fortune hunters would corrupt the local villagers with alcohol.
Photo courtesy of the National Archives, # 22-FFA-451.

The only other mention of Seldovia by Nikita came a year earlier, when he reported that an influenza epidemic had swept through Kenai, Ninilchik, Seldovia, and Alexandrovsky, claiming the lives of most of the children under two years of age. Nikita noted that the people had already suffered "inundation" because of the eruption of Chernabura volcano that year (today known as the Mt. Augustine volcano, located across Cook Inlet from Kachemak Bay), so it is apparent that some degree of flooding was experienced from this event.[8]

After Hieromonk Nikita left the Kenai parish, there was a period of about ten years during which little seems to have been written about the outlying villages. For part of this time, Alexander Yaroshevich served as priest at Kenai, but there is little translated material to indicate that he visited the missions in his parish. Seldovia is next mentioned in an 1895 petition from the Kenai Indians to the district judge. They complain about their local Alaska Commercial Co. agent, Alec Ryan, and his disregard for their efforts to lead sober and Christian lives. They describe Ryan as a tyrant, and note that that year he had at gunpoint forced another man (an American) out of his store, and then out of Kenai altogether. The man fled on foot through winter snows to Seldovia, but succumbed to a cold shortly after his arrival and died. The Kenai people held Ryan fully responsible for this death.[9]

By 1896, the Kenai parish was being served by the youthful Father John Bortnovsky. Seminary educated in Russia, he came to Alaska in 1888 at the age of 17 and served in Kodiak, Sitka, and Juneau before being transferred to Kenai.[10] Bortnovsky's travel journals and articles he wrote for the *Russian Orthodox American Messenger*, as well as his letters to his superiors, give the most complete picture of 19th century life in Seldovia we have. The following passages are excerpted from his journals contained in the Alaska Church Collection at the University of Alaska at Fairbanks.

Bortnovsky left Kenai in a bidarka on the 29th of July in 1896 to begin a visitation of the villages in the southern part of his parish.

> *We arrived at Seldovia at midnight (July 30). All the people of the village were sleeping soundly, but after they heard the shots of our rowers, they immediately came to life and replied with ceaseless shooting. On the beach we were met by a crowd of people and by the two storekeepers of the trading companies. This time I accepted the hospitality of Mr. Bloch, the storekeeper of the Alaska Commercial Company, who invited me to visit him long ago.* [11]

After a side trip to Alexandrovsky village, Bortnovsky returned to Seldovia around the 2nd of August, and wrote:

> *The Indians of Seldovia, like the Aleuts of Alexandrovsky, live by hunting sea otter. This summer they caught fifty otters: such luck seldom happens. The actual number is much larger as some of the hunters have not yet returned. According to the last count, the population of Seldovia is 103 (62 male and 41 female). To this number should be added seven newly born babies (6 male and 1 female)....*

> *The storekeeper of the Alaska Commercial Company is not very popular: all the otters caught this summer were sold to Mr. Schmidt, the storekeeper of the Northern Alaska Trading Company, which donated a 76-pound bell to the chapel and helped to repair the chapel by supplying all materials at very reasonable prices....* [12]

It seems odd that Bortnovsky would accept the hospitality of Adam Bloch, and then write that he was an unpopular man. The natives' preference for the rival trading company to Bloch's could simply be attributed to the possibility that the Northern Alaska Trading Company offered them a better price for their furs, or perhaps charged less for the goods it stocked in its store. However, a look at Bortnovsky's personal correspondence reveals that Adam Bloch had fallen in love with a married Aleut woman named Marina, and she with him. It appeared as though Bloch, in his powerful position in the settlement, had stolen Marina from her husband. Bortnovsky felt compelled to report this situation in a special letter to his superiors; nothing, however, was ever done. Even Bloch's supervisors in the Alaska Commercial Company administration refused to enter into the private life of one of their employees.[13] Eventually, the situation cured itself, Marina presumably returning to her husband and Adam marrying Elisaveta Balyshev in 1900. [14]

Four years after he first mentions Bloch, it becomes evident from Bortnovsky's journals that Seldovia had assimilated the new couple and that everyone had forgotten Adam Bloch's apparent indiscretions. This was undoubtedly due in large part to Bloch's philanthropic gestures to the community:

August 27, 1900

....Six couples were married, including Adam Block who was mentioned in one of my earlier diaries. Now I want to say a few more words about him in connection with the recent epidemic of influenza, or grippe. In some villages, especially in Seldevoye many people were struck down by this disease. And so, at that time of stress when nobody could or wanted to help with even such simple things as hot water and firewood, Adam Block showed kindness and generosity. And although Block himself was not well, he made the rounds of all those in need of help, or sent his children to see what needed to be done to supply them with medicines, cooked food, fuel and other necessities, all out of the goodness of his heart. And those who died were given a decent burial.

The Seldovians themselves know all this very well and say that had it not been for Mr. Block there would have been a lot more suffering and death in the village.

Needless to say this show of kindness was rare in Alaska. To add to his other qualities, Mr. Block has done a lot for the church. For example, he bought half of all the paints for the whole church, and he also contributed his own effort, and paid half the price of the carpet on the altar. [15]

Adam Bloch pauses in a Seldovia doorway. Bloch was an Alaska Commercial Company agent in Seldovia, and one of the community's first philanthropists. Photo courtesy of Ted Anderson, from the Ralph and Juanita Anderson Collection.

The flu epidemic raged through Seldovia and Alexandrovsky in the spring and early summer of 1900, every few days claiming the life of another native. Alexandrovsky lost eleven people; Seldovia lost nineteen. [16]

Seldovia was well thought of by the Russian Orthodox clergy. Unlike some of the other villages in the area, its residents did not seem to as readily fall victim to alcoholism and apathy. It is likely that Mr. Bloch and Mr. Schmidt, agents of the two trading companies in Seldovia, had much to do with the sober lifestyle of the villagers, as they controlled much of the flow of goods in and out of town. In Kenai, as noted earlier, and in Alexandrovsky, this was not the case, and the trading company agents at these villages did much to contribute to the delinquency of the villagers. [17]

Bortnovsky in 1896 writes a glowing report of the natives at Seldovia:

August 31, 1896—Saturday

At 6 a.m. we continued our journey. Weather is excellent and we row fast. At 6:30 p.m. we are close to Seldovia, we hear the ringing of the bell for vespers. "Evening bell, evening bell, so many thoughts you bring with you." Our rowers began to work with more force. They gave a signal shot. We arrived just in time and celebrated the vespers solemnly and joyfully. The chapel was packed with people. I delivered a brief speech of greeting.

The people sang very well. The readers at the church were all local self-taught children. It is evident that the people thirst for education. I consider it necessary to supply them at least with books, the more so that some of the local men kindly offer to teach the illiterate as much as they themselves know. The main difficulty is, then, to provide the necessary textbooks and school supplies to them....

Sept. 1, Sunday— -At 9 a.m.: Hours and Matins. The congregation sang very well.... It is a pleasure for me to note here that the government customs officer is now stationed at Seldovia to see that the new arrivals, who call themselves American citizens, do not corrupt the Kenai natives with alcoholic beverages. It is a very encouraging thing. [18]

The new arrivals to whom Bortnovsky referred were probably prospectors on their way north to the newfound gold fields in Hope and Sunrise, and up the Knik and Sushitna (Susitna) Rivers to points in the Interior. In the late 1890's and during the first years of the twentieth century, Seldovia was a point of transfer for fortune seekers from the Lower 48. Ships from the Alaska Commercial Co. and Northern Alaskan Trading Co. fleets called here, discharging passengers to transfer to smaller vessels for the trip up the Inlet. In 1898, a Lowman and Hanford Co. map (published in Seattle) identified the recent Alaskan gold discoveries, and showed "Saldovia" as a

In this May 7th, 1906 photograph, the unpainted front tower of the Russian Orthodox Church suggests that it may have been recently built. The native homes, or barabaras, are clustered near the church at the right while the buildings housing the newer arrivals and their businesses are just visible behind the crest of the hill at left. Photo courtesy of the Alaska State Library, Early Prints Collection, #01-323.

"port of entry."[19] For more on Seldovia's role as a customs and shipping center, see the chapter "Fur and Fin."

Bortnovsky spent the first few days of September 1896 setting up a church brotherhood organization, and laying plans for a school. Kenai had for some years had a fraternal brotherhood, whose purposes were to maintain the church and school and cemetery, to help the poor members of the congregation, and to promote spirituality and sobriety. To join, one simply had to be between the ages of 18 and 50, to be a good practicing Orthodox Christian, and to abstain from alcohol, bad language, and rowdy behavior.[20] Bortnovsky's efforts resulted in a Seldovia brotherhood of 27 members, with $44.75 on hand in dues.[21]

Regarding the school, Bortnovsky had very specific instructions:

By 1909 the front tower of the church was complete and painted to match the rest of the structure, as shown in this August 9th photograph by D. F. Higgins.
Photo courtesy of the U.S. Geological Survey.

In regard to the school, the following resolutions were made:

1. To start immediately the building of an appropriate house for school use. This is to be done by all the residents, members, and nonmembers of the brotherhood.

2. The logs must be provided free by common effort of the residents; the work on the building itself is also to be donated. Only the boards, nails, windows, and finishing materials may be purchased with brotherhood funds.

3. The duty of teaching Russian and Slavic reading is laid on John Telenok and Churchman Nicholas Bai is to teach God's law and prayers. The storekeeper of the Alaska Commercial Company, Adam Bloch, has expressed a desire to teach English and arithmetic free.[22]

Bortnovsky next visited Seldovia in the spring of 1897. Although he generally could only visit each of the villages once a year, he decided to move up his annual fall visit to Seldovia, as explained in his journal excerpt below:

April 1897

As the Indians of Seldovia and Alexandrovsky leave their villages to hunt sea otter soon after Easter and as some of them often lose their lives during the hunting season, I decided to visit these villages earlier than usual.

[There is a footnote here which reads: "The Orthodox Church requires that members should have holy communion at least once a year. When somebody's occupation endangers his life, it is advisable for him to partake of communion oftener, in order to be always prepared for a Christian death."]

Thursday April 3...Arrived at Seldovia at midnight. Found everybody well and everything in good order. With the exception of one baby, there had been no deaths at Seldovia during the winter. The people said that it was for the first time in their lives that they had had such a low mortality. Why? I think, first, because of God's grace, and second, because the

The Russian Orthodox Church and the influx of gold seekers from the United States and Europe had a profound effect on the native way of life in Seldovia and throughout Alaska. Note the transition from thatch roofed barabara to shingle roofed log cabin, with its (Aleut) native occupants replete in Western style of dress. Photo courtesy of the Alaska State Library, Early Prints Collection, # 01-3954.

people of this village have become much more temperate and do not poison themselves with all kinds of brewed trash. I notice a considerable improvement in their condition: they have become more active; they have built a number of new, comfortable homes; cleanliness and care are noticeable everywhere. Next fall they plan to build nine houses.

4, Friday — 6, Palm Sunday. Inspection of church books, funds, visits, divine services, brotherhood meeting.

The brotherhood requested me to send them for the next school year, a man from Kenai who could teach more efficiently. They promised to pay him $5 a month by voluntary contribution....

At the conclusion of the meeting I advised the Seldovia brotherhood to have their meetings every month except during the months when they are away hunting; to obey the brotherhood laws; not to brew beer or any alcoholic drinks; in a word, to be brothers not only in name but in actions....

Immediately after the closing of the brotherhood meeting, a meeting of all the residents of the village was called for the election of a new assistant to the chief. After deliberation, an Indian of the village, Akaky Kanitak, a careful, temperate, and active man, was elected to the position. The newly-elected was immediately led to the church, where he took an oath in the presence of all who attended the meeting and then everyone participated in prayers. [23]

It is disappointing that Bortnovsky did not mention here the name of the Seldovia chief whom Mr. Kanitak would be assisting. It would not be too many more years before white settlers flooded Seldovia and the power of the traditional chief and council form of government would slowly be usurped by the newcomers. Just three years after this journal entry, the 1900 census shows Adam Bloch and John Wall Smith (perhaps the "Mr. Schmidt" of Bortnovsky's writing?) as two of the first white settlers. Both are listed as merchants. Smith was single, and Bloch was a widower with four daughters living with him, one of whom was herself a widow with a young son and daughter. (The census was conducted in May, prior to Bloch's August wedding to Elisaveta.) [24]

That the Orthodox priests honored the traditional native form of government was evident in Bortnovsky's involvement with the election of a new chief's assistant. Bloch and Smith enjoyed powerful positions of their own as merchants, and probably found it to their benefit to recognize and support the native power structure too. However, as the number of white settlers increased and as the economic emphasis shifted away from sea otter hunting, the balance of power was altered.

Things really began to change in the first decade of the twentieth century. Thanks to the gold rushes in Nome and the Yukon, Alaska had emerged from the obscurity of being some far distant territory to become a household word in the United States. The 1910 census is written testimony to the dramatic social change that must have been taking place in Seldovia. People from all over the world were streaming to Alaska and settling the territory. Seldovia had thirty new men from places as far flung as China, Germany, and the Scandinavian countries. In addition, another eight men are listed at census time as having been discharged from a ship at Seward, bound for Seldovia.[25] Most of these newcomers would make Seldovia their permanent home, marrying local native women or daughters of other settlers and raising families. In this decade the social fabric of Seldovia was changed forever. Never again would the village chief rule with the absolute authority he once had.

This page from a Russian school book was found at Seldovia's St. Nicholas Orthodox Church. Its title is New Complete Alphabet of Russian Writing *published in Moscow in 1881. Translation by Dr. R.A. Pierce of the University of Alaska Fairbanks. Courtesy of Janet Klein and the Seldovia Village Tribe.*

A resumption of the study of Bortnovsky's travel journals from 1897 gives a look at the beginnings of formal education in Seldovia:

> *Inspection of brotherhood books and funds:*
> *Income* *$79.00*
> *Expenses: school house* *7.00*
> *Relief* *6.00*
> *Teacher's salary* .. *15.00* ... *28.00*
> *($4 a month)*
> *Cash on hand* *$51.00*
>
> *The subjects taught at the Seldovia school this winter were: God's law, Russian and English languages — God's law and Russian in the morning and English in the afternoon. School hours: 8 to 3. Enrollment: 11 (3 girls and 8 boys). The beginning is encouraging. I am very glad that the inhabitants now understand the usefulness of school. In time it will be possible to organize the Seldovia school more efficiently and thereby promote the religious and moral progress of the community.* [26]

The growth of the Orthodox Church school in Seldovia was sporadic at best, for although the villagers might have understood the importance of education, it became clear that it was not always a priority to them. In a society still firmly rooted in the hunter-gatherer tradition, the benefits of education were admittedly not very apparent.

The discussion of education in this chapter ends with the closing of the Orthodox Church school around 1906. The story of post-Orthodox education in Seldovia is a study in human relations between the native villagers and the incoming settlers. The road to a truly blended culture was not without bumps. For more on this subject, see the chapter "Life in Old Seldovia".

Father Bortnovsky's travel journals began being published in the *Russian Orthodox American Messenger*, a semimonthly periodical, in 1898. In that year, he noted with sadness the alarming economic decline that was gripping Seldovia. His choice of travelling companions in the following excerpt is curious, if the reader will recall the story of the evil tyrant Mr. Ryan from the Alaska Commercial Co. station at Kenai. Could this be the same man who accompanies the good father? If so, how was he

Frontispiece from the Russian Orthodox American Messenger.

received at Seldovia, where the victim of his cruelty died just three years earlier?

> On March 23, 1898, I left for Seldevoye, in the company of Mr. Ryan, for my pastoral duties. We stopped over at Kassilov where we stayed until midnight in anticipation of low tide, and arrived in Seldevoye about 8 a.m. next morning in time for the celebration of the mass for the Annunciation. The local chapel was filled to overflowing. There I also spent some time talking to a local church official (prichetnik) and the toyon who told me that the economic position of the local population in Seldevoye was getting worse. The company stores had stopped selling on credit. To ensure that these stores would exist without much financial loss to themselves or to the companies, the storekeepers made the local Kenaians do more hunting than usual. That did not do the Kenaians much good because the pelts were bought at very low prices and were paid for not in money but in commodities from the company stores. That also hurt the income of the chapel and the finances of the local Theodosievskoye Brotherhood. The long and frequent hunting trips prevented the residents of Seldevoye from starting the building of a new school. In fact the funds were so low that the old school was closed possibly for the whole winter. I felt heavy heart as I listened to all that sad news. So I decided to spend the winter of the next year in Seldovia and myself attend to the school affairs, all the more so as I found it easy to watch what was going on in Alexandrovsk, a village a short distance from Seldevaya, which suffered greatly at the hands of the same companies as did Seldevaya. I must add here that in Seldevaya there were many children of school age, and it was very disconcerting to see them loitering in the streets. Only the more assiduous of them have not abandoned their studies. [27]

Bortnovsky lists the services performed over the next few days, commenting on the fine singing of the congregation, and the good work performed by prichetnik Nicholai Bayu and sexton Zachari Balashev. He notes the addition of two new bells in the fall of 1897, making a total of three in the church steeple, and of a new fireplace built at the same time. Nine babies had been born since his last visit, and one woman had died. On March 29th, Palm Sunday, in lieu of palm fronds, local pussy willows were gathered and consecrated, and distributed to the parishioners. That afternoon, the priest took the cross and holy water and made the rounds of the villagers' homes, blessing each one.

Prichetnik Bayu made a spectacular donation that evening at a meeting of the brotherhood. He gave his house and the land on which it stood to the church, so that the school might have a place to continue holding classes. In return, the villagers agreed to help him build a new house, using materials he had already procured and stored for this purpose. [28]

In 1899 Archimandrite Anatolii Kamenskii toured the Kenai parish, among others, and found himself stuck at Seldovia awaiting transport up the Inlet:

> Packetboats do not come into Kenai Bay further upstream than Seldevoye and Kagikmak this year. The mail is ferried across the bay by boat. The small steamship, called Perry, is not a very reliable craft, and I wasted much time waiting for it in order to get to Kenai. It was another ship, the Dora, which ferries miners and goods for the company, that I boarded with a huge sense of relief and that took me to Kasilov. [29]

From the Archimandrite's report, we get a sense of why the sober brotherhood (temperance society) in Seldovia was such a pet project of Father Bortnovsky:

> The village of Seldevoye is within easy reach of Alexandrovskoye, about 15 miles away. It is by far the most populous place, and is visited by Americans much more often than any other villages here. This is why there is a lot more debauchery and drunkenness in Seldevoye than anywhere else in this region. Besides there are practically no people who could read or write. Father Ioann (John Bortnovsky) hopes that by his own presence he will put a halt to drunkenness, and will teach the people Christian morals and the Christian way of life. He is particularly anxious to meet and work with Seldovia's prichetnik, Nikolai Bayu. [30]

The Archimandrite placed the blame for importing vodka into Seldovia on the shoulders of the "local Chinese working at the fish cannery." This is a curious statement, as no Chinese show up in the 1900 census for Seldovia. (One possible explanation for this is that the Chinese tended to be seasonal workers and may not have been present when the census was taken.) Furthermore, the earliest record of a cannery in Seldovia is not until 1911. (For more about Seldovia's first cannery, see the salmon fishing discussion in the chapter "Fur and Fin", page 99.) What is known is that as early as 1897, the employees of the coal mining operation on the Homer Spit were selling alcohol to the Seldovia natives. [31]

Despite the best efforts of the Orthodox clergy, the scourge of alcoholism continued to plague Seldovia. In March of 1901, Father Bortnovsky was called upon to deal with a tragic alcohol-related situation:

> *Also that day the parishioners discussed another rather ticklish business. An American, Hans Sivertsen, had got two Kenaian women drunk on whiskey. They were joined by a young Kenaian, Pavel Bayu, aged 18. The orgy took place in the house of one local Kenaian, the husband of one of the two Kenaian women (who at that time was away). There was no light in the room and the doors were locked. When the door was forced open and the lights put on, Pavel Bayu was found dead, one of the Kenaian women was blind drunk. The other woman was not so badly intoxicated but was very scared. Unfortunately, those who entered the house did not notice immediately that Pavel Bayu was dead but thought he was fast asleep or was unconscious from alcohol. So what they did first thing was to take the children of the intoxicated Kenaian woman out of the room. It was only at 11 p.m. that they noticed that Pavel was actually dead with bruises on his neck, chin, and temple. The woman who was less drunk insisted that he had been killed by Hans the American. These are the doings of the local civilizers who boast about their education.* [32]

Perhaps the real tragedy here is that the "civilized" American, Mr. Sivertsen, was not promptly brought to justice. This passage is of value in that it points out the tough transition from tribal society to the white man's world. The Orthodox clergy wrung their hands at what they called the weak-willed and immoral nature of their native parishioners. Their paternalistic, albeit kindly and patient, attitude toward their native flock at times precluded a real understanding of the growing pains the native society throughout Alaska was experiencing during this period. Under-staffing also frustrated the clergy; it was difficult to compete in influence with men who could exploit and corrupt the natives when the priests were only able to visit a village several times a year.

In the Interior of Alaska not too many years later, Episcopal Archdeacon Hudson Stuck encountered the same terrible abuse of alcohol among the Indians there, and was forced to address the same issues of morality. He took the rather enlightened view that because traditional Indian culture did not share the white man's moral code to begin with, Indians who had intercourse outside the bounds of their "marital" relationships were simply living in harmony with their culture's standards. Conversely, Rev. Stuck had nothing but contempt for the white men who committed adultery with native women, for he felt that such men were behaving in an *immoral* way, in *opposition* to their culture's standards. His point was that to be unmoral and be true to your cultural code of ethics was far more honorable than to be immoral and a hypocrite. Stuck made his travel narrative, *Ten Thousand Miles With a Dog Sled*, a lectern from which he publicly pleaded for a halt to the corruption of Alaska natives with alcohol. [33]

In 1899, Orthodox Bishop Tikhon stopped in Seldovia one night on his way to Kenai. The ship he was on called here to discharge mail and provisions for the trading company stores. The Bishop went ashore and climbed the hill to the church, where he was surrounded and accompanied by villagers, despite the late hour.

> *We experienced a tremendous feeling of elation as we left the chapel. The beautiful peaceful night, the melodious carillion filled the air as the archbishop walked through the village surrounded by a host of people who had not seen a bishop since the days of the Russian Company. All that filled us with nostalgia for our beloved native Russia....* [34]

Several months later, Father Bortnovsky visited Seldovia again, and gives this report about the growing community:

> *The weather was fine and we had no trouble reaching Seldevoye, a postal station which, owing to its geographical position, is beginning to play an important role in the Kenai bay area. It is open to navigation in all seasons and is central to all traffic in this part of Alaska. The Seldovians had a bad winter and spent much of the time roaming the mountains in search of food. Significantly, in those lean days they stayed away from alcohol, and lived in peace with one another.* [35]

He noted that the chapel looked unkept and neglected, but that the people sang well, and because they were all fluent in Russian, did not require a translator when he conducted services.

This pre-1906 photograph looks toward the mouth of Seldovia Bay with homes of the recent settlers in the foreground. Note that the Russian Orthodox Church on the hill does not yet include the front steeple. Photo courtesy of the Anchorage Museum of History and Art, #B67.1.50

This pre-1909 photograph was taken from near the church on the hill, looking toward Lookout Point (with Point Naskowhak at far left) and Kachemak Bay beyond. Dories hauled out on the beach have begun to replace the native bidarkis or kayaks. Photo courtesy of the Anchorage Museum of History and Art, Tom O'Dale Collection, # B90.3.19

The following March, Bortnovsky arrived in Seldovia under grey, drizzly skies:

> *The Seldovians I met seemed happy to see me again after my long absence. On my part I found the village quiet and peaceful as usual. Nothing terribly wrong except for the old sin—cohabitation—which nobody could do anything about. Except for two weak oldsters there were no sick people here. This past winter the Seldovians lived better than before, especially starting with January when whoever wanted to could work at the local coal-mining company. [The coal mine was in Homer.] Luckily the employment manager McPorson did his utmost to help the local natives and provided the residents of Seldovia and Alexandrovskoye with jobs that kept them busy from January through February.* [36]

Despite Seldovia's newfound prosperity, Bortnovsky was distressed that the chapel still looked ill-kept, and he called upon the brotherhood to take better care of it. He felt that their priorities were skewed, for he saw dresses worth *"five and even more dollars"* on the wives, while the men explained that poverty prevented them from keeping up chapel maintenance. Bortnovsky gave them until Easter to fix up the chapel, or, he threatened, he would come to Seldovia no more.

Moreover, the parish till was short nearly 25 dollars. The neglectful church elder was held responsible, and was thereupon replaced with Vassili Bayu, *"a man known for his honesty, sober behavior, and zeal for good works."* The brotherhood pitched in to replace the shortfall, deciding that every man of the 37 present who worked in the *"Kachikmak coal pits"* would tithe 10 cents from every dollar earned. [37]

With the promise of money coming in, the brotherhood decided to spend *"11 dollars for ill brethren, $4.85 for the poor, (and) $4.25 for the burial of a brother."* Bortnovsky then reviewed the school students, and found that although the recitation and reading of prayers in Russian and Slavonic, and the singing were quite good, performance in all other subjects was generally poor. That year, the school operated from September (1899) through March (1900), with a break at Christmas. School ran from 8:30 a.m. to noon with an average of 22 students in attendance. They were taught "The Law of Our Lord," Russian and Slavonic Languages, English, Arithmetic, and Singing by Alexander Demidov. [38]

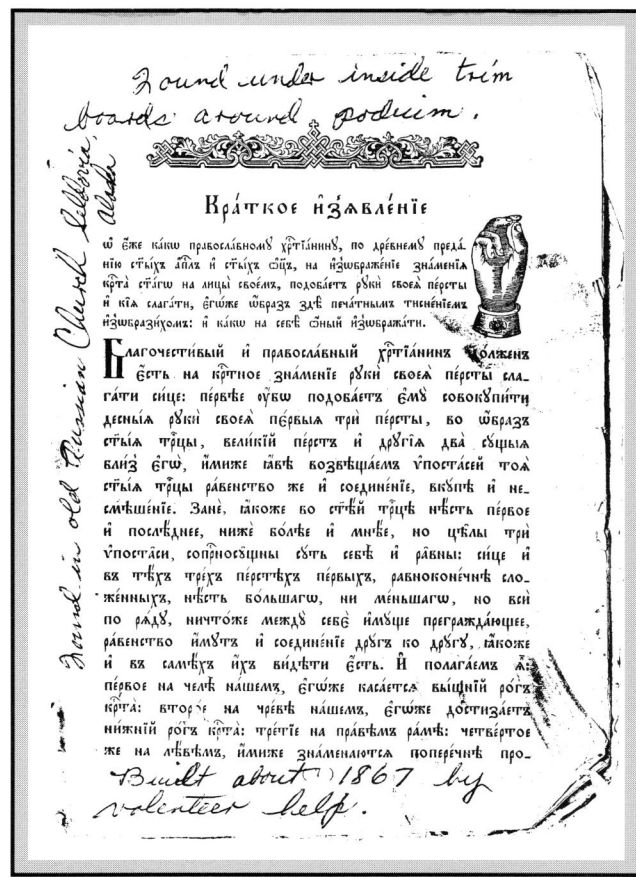

This page from a Russian text was found at the base of the podium in Seldovia's St. Nicholas Orthodox Church. The handwritten note that indicates the church was built in 1867 is inaccurate. There apparently was a log church closer to the beach that predated St. Nicholas, but its exact location and date of construction have not been established. Courtesy of the Seldovia Village Tribe Museum.

Mr. Demidov attributed the students' poor performance to lack of textbooks and truancy. However, in a later visit, the village toyon confessed to the Father that Demidov was a lousy teacher. While it is true that many adolescents missed school in order to help with hunting and fishing for their families, and while it was true that textbooks were in short supply, the toyon complained that Demidov was "work-shy" and did not "do enough to get the children interested in classwork." [39] By 1904, Mr. Demidov had been replaced by Nicholas Fomin, a lay reader in the church, and the maternal grandfather of current Seldovian Nick Elxnit and his sister, the late Dora Ursin of Washington state. Mr. Fomin was paid 15 dollars a month. [40]

By August of 1900, it appeared that Father Bortnovsky's lecture regarding upkeep of the chapel had had a positive affect. He found the building freshly painted and carpeted, with a new covering for the lectern (analoi), a new step at the front door, and boards lining the inside of the cupola. A good half of these renovations were made possible because of the generosity of Adam Bloch. Perhaps the priest put in a good word for the Seldovia parish, for later that year, the Bishop granted them $367 dollars for wedding crowns and $10 for building decoration. [41] From Bortnovsky's comments about the brotherhood meeting he attended, we learn the name of the village chief, or toyon, for his widow is mentioned as succeeding him as chairman of the brotherhood. The chief of Seldovia was Theodor Berestov (spelled Berrystoff in the 1900 census), who in May of 1900 was 50 years old. A small notation on the census confirms that he was in fact "Chief", but unfortunately, he was to die in the next several months from influenza. The epidemic hung like a dark cloud over Seldovia that spring and early summer, killing 24 people, some of them infants. [42]

In March 1901, Father Bortnovsky boarded a bidarky at Kenai for another visit to Seldovia. At Anchor Point, his party met up with five bidarkys from Seldovia that were full of sea otter hunters. They had had no luck, however, and so joined with Bortnovsky to return to the village. Other than the

Exterior of Seldovia's St. Nicholas Russian Orthodox Church. In this early twentieth-century photograph, the church looks well-kept. Photo courtesy of the University of Alaska Fairbanks, Archives of the Alaska and Polar Regions Dept., George Talmadge Collection, acc.# 74-16-19

Officers from a visiting ship pose in front of St. Nicholas Orthodox Church. Photo courtesy of the Alaska State Library, Taber Collection, #PCA 19-41.

Hans Sivertsen affair and the problems with the school teacher's alleged poor performance, he found everything well in Seldovia. He spent nearly the entire month of March in Seldovia, the latter part of his stay due to high winds on the bay which prevented his departure. [43]

Bortnovsky returned to Seldovia in May 1901, but it was not until April of the next year that he wrote more about the village in his journals. Even then he recorded mostly vital statistics, such as one baptism, last rites, two weddings, and one funeral. He visited the parishioners' homes with Holy Water and cross, and conducted several services in the chapel. [44]

In 1903 or 1904, Bishop Innokentii accompanied Father Bortnovsky on a tour of the southern Kenai parish, running into rough weather enroute to Seldovia. Bortnovsky's journals paint an allegorical picture of the holy man's seasickness.

7. Monday. At 7 a.m. His Eminence and his party arrived in Seldevoye. All the way to the village our boat sailed against a strong wind and His Eminence lay on top deck, seasick most of the trip, gasping for fresh air. It was heartbreaking to watch the sufferings of God's own saintly servant. But the stormy sea knew no mercy. "It is the same in man's life. All is storm and disquiet, but the time will come when he will finally arrive in a haven of peace. And happy must be he who can hold the helm firmly in his hands and head the ship of life towards the blessed haven." [45]

This early twentieth-century photograph shows the church interior with the ikonostas (a partition made of ikons) which separates the sanctuary from the main body of the church. Photo courtesy of the Anchorage Museum of History and Art, Case and Draper Collection, #B77.18.25

The bishop must have recovered quickly once he reached dry land, for he held a service, visited the cemetery, and then held an all-night vigil in the chapel, in honor of St. Nicholas, *"the heavenly guardian of the Seldevoye chapel."* Psalm reader Nikolai Fomin assisted at the service. At the close of his visit, the bishop instructed Seldovians to build a new porch (papert) and belltower on the chapel. Ivan Alexandrov, a Creole villager, translated the bishop's words into *"the local dialect."* The bishop departed Seldovia on the steamship *Bertha*, to ringing church bells and a rifle salute. [46] The Bishop returned to Seldovia briefly in 1905 and was pleased to note that Seldovians had contributed money and labor to build the new belltower he had requested on his previous visit. [47]

By 1905, the Orthodox Church may have been ready to move out of the education business. Qualified teachers were hard to find, for they had to be proficient in several languages, knowledgeable in the Orthodox faith, and willing to work in cramped quarters with few materials, little pay, and a student body which, due to its hunter-gatherer culture, was regularly truant. The U.S. Dept. of Education, in response to Bishop Innokentii's call for a public school in Seldovia, wrote him in 1905 that it was willing to appoint a teacher in Seldovia who was of the Orthodox faith, but they couldn't readily find someone to fill the slot. The Department required people of *"sufficient training and experience,"* first and foremost, and so they imported a teacher for Seldovia, a *Mr. Herbert Farros*, who would begin the next school year.[48]

When Bortnovsky next writes of Seldovia, in 1906, we learn nothing of Mr. Farros, nor if he even made it here to teach. (It would appear that Miss Della Borst was sent in place of Mr. Farros. Her rocky tenure is described further on page 165.) The priest is more concerned at this writing about the alcohol situation in Seldovia, which he noted was due to the steamer *Tyoonik* bringing liquor into the village. He urged Seldovians to join the Kenaian Temperance Society, and by the close of his visit, 47 of them had done so, some becoming members for life. A list of their names follows. Bortnovsky noted that the purser of the steamship *Neptune* had collected money from local "Americans" for paint, and had himself spruced up the interior and exterior of the chapel.[49] About the same time, the interior was *"oil-painted with decorations."*[50]

> **Membership of the
> Saint Nicholas Temperance Society
> in the village of Seldevoye — 1906**
>
> **MEN**
>
> Matvei Tolchek, Grigori Vakka, Efim Sokolov, Amdrei Tochek, Nikolai Tolchek, Matvei Lyuku, Fyodor Gusev, Sevirian Shunakhak, Alexei Berestov, Grigori Kalana, Nikolai Chanyi, Semion Slatin, Philip Berestov, Timofei Balashov, Mikhail Balashov, Nikolai Papochka, Ivan Yakovlev, Stepan Tolchek, Konstantin Lyuku, Ivan Alexandrov, Anisim Alexandrov, Fyodor Balashov, Konstantin Berestov, Pyotr Unoskio, Maxim Kanshvayak, Alexii Kavyak
>
> **WOMEN**
>
> Melania Tolchek, Daria Lyuku, Amma Slatin, Amma Kanitake, Anna Yegorova, Marina Chunkhna, Paraskeva Unoski, Mavrda Lyuku, Anna Kaviak, Lyubov Berestova, Matriona Yakovleva, Maria Merkurieva, Yelena Berestova, Anisia Balasheva, Yevdokia Merkurieva, Matriona Kanshvayak

Father John Bortnovsky left his duties as dean of the Kenai mission in 1907, and returned to Russia, where he hoped to give his children a better education.[51] He was replaced by Deacon Pavel (Paul) Shadura, who came from Kodiak to Seldovia on the steamer *Dora* in June of 1907 to be ordained to the priesthood at Kenai. His Aleut wife, from Unga, and his children settled with him at Kenai. Bishop Innokentii accompanied Shadura from Seldovia up to Kenai, and the new dean got his first taste of inlet travel.

> ....on board a small ship *Tonquin*. Unfortunately, this flimsy craft developed one technical fault after another, which gave us an uncomfortable feeling that we might get stuck or abandoned in the middle of nowhere. Only the captain, Charlie Brown, a gregarious Russian-speaking Finn, was in a cheerful mood and was cracking jokes at the expense of the poor *Tonquin* ('this great ship makes two miles forward for every three miles back'). The night we spent on the ship was not the pleasantest one by any means. Pavel Shadura and I were awakened by myriad voracious bedbugs. I was later told that the other passengers (my companions) had the same experience.[52]

St. Nicholas Orthodox Church

Seldovia's landmark, the present St. Nicholas Orthodox Church, was built in 1891.

St. Nicholas, the patron saint of this church, was the Bishop of the city of Myra in the province of Lycia around 300 A.D. He is noted for his generosity and good will, and his fervent dedication to teaching the Gospel. He is also known as the protector of seagoing vessels.[53] How fitting then that the church high on its hill is one of the first things fishermen see as they return home, and one of the last city landmarks to fade from sight as they head out to sea.

Father Pavel Shadura, ordained in 1907 at Kenai, served the Kenai Peninsula, including Seldovia, for many years. Photo courtesy of Ted Anderson from the Ralph and Juanita Anderson Collection.

An earlier church, built of logs, is said by local tradition to have existed down the hill and near the beach, but its location and date of erection have never been established. In the 1890 U.S. Census, Robert Porter's comments tend to confirm that the first church here was built of logs: "The settlements of Seldovia and Alexandrovsk have small chapels built of logs, one of the residents in each serving as reader, and once or twice during the year the priest from Kenai visits these localities." [54]

From the travel journals of the clergy, we know that it was not until 1905 that the tall belltower at the front of the church was added. [55] Other than that addition, St. Nicholas church has remained largely unchanged over the years. By the 1970's it had fallen into an alarming state of disrepair. The Orthodox congregation had dwindled since the early 1900's, and the building was feeling its age. No small amount of money was needed to effect the major structural renovation now required. Former state senator Clem Tillion of Halibut Cove came to the rescue, and was instrumental in securing a $127,000 state grant to renovate the church. This, together with fund-raising efforts conducted by a local restoration committee, funded the project. [56]

During the initial stages of the work, it was discovered that the church had been built on a foundation of logs. These were replaced with a new concrete foundation. [57]

Several color schemes had been used to decorate the interior of the church: green and yellow and white,

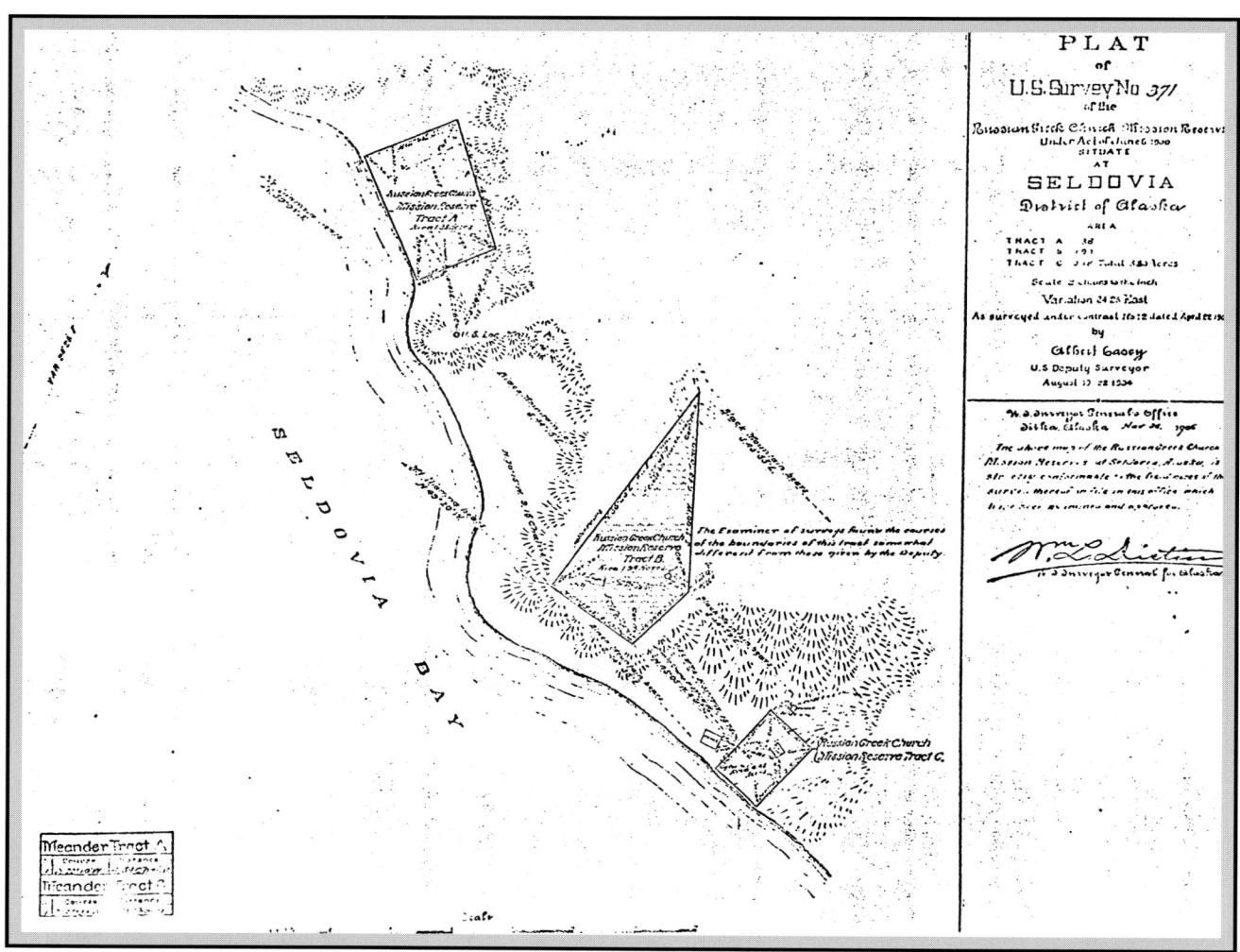

This 1906 survey of Orthodox Church holdings in Seldovia shows a plot at the lower right of the map which may well have been the original chapel site. It is situated roughly where the clinic and community building stand today. The present church property is shown in the middle as an elongated diamond-shaped tract. The parcel shown at the upper left on the map was the original Orthodox cemetery, located at the base of the cliff at what today is the northeasternmost end of Main Street. Map courtesy of the Seldovia Village Tribe.

Distinctive orthodox crosses mark the gravesites at Seldovia's original Russian Orthodox cemetery. Moved as a result of flooding after the 1964 earthquake, the cemetery sat roughly where the city's boat storage yard is located today. Photo courtesy of the Alaska State Library, Early Prints Collection, #01-3953.

and blue and grey and white. School books from 1904 and 1906, one in Russian and one in English, were found when the building was dismantled. A frontispiece dated 1881 was found as well.

In 1981, St. Nicholas Orthodox Church was reconsecrated by the Bishop, and was made a National Historic Site. In recent years, the church has been open sporadically to visitors during the summer months. Today, the church is under the authority of the Anchorage diocese, and a priest visits the small congregation about once a year.

The basic design of an Orthodox Christian church carries theological significance. The log churches built in rural Russia, and later in Russian America, were erected without sophisticated tools or materials or skilled laborers, yet they still contain architectural elements laid out in the Old Testament. [58]

The use of circles or octagons, as in St. Nicholas' octagonal bell tower, symbolizes that the Holy Church is eternal, never-ending, having existed before the creation, and having no identifiable beginning nor end. The sanctuary of the church faces East, signifying the direction of the origin of the true faith and because the coming of Christ is typified by the rising of the sun. The oblong shape of the building represents that the church is an ark for its members and that their belief in Christ saves them from the stormy seas of life. Inside, ikons (Greek for "picture") adorn the interior of St. Nicholas. Their purpose is to stimulate devotion and to teach about the meaning of Church rites. Some of St. Nicholas' ikons date from the nineteenth century. An ikonostas (a partition made of ikons) separates the sanctuary from the main body of the church. This partition symbolizes the faith of Christians, since they must accept as truth many things that cannot be seen with the eye. [59] The distinctive Orthodox cross is known as the Slavonic cross and signifies the victory of Christ over his death. The topmost horizontal bar represents the inscribed board, and the bottom slanted bar a footrest. [60]

The Russian Orthodox cemetery was originally laid out just above the beach in a grassy field at the base of a cliff. (Today this site would be at the south end of the city's Main Street boat storage yard.) Simple white wooden orthodox crosses marked the resting places of the early faithful. The earliest burial was probably in the 1880's; however no documentation is available to prove this. After the 1964 Good Friday Earthquake, the cemetery began flooding at the high tides, and eventually was moved to higher ground in another part of town. For more on this, see the chapter "The Earthquake and Urban Renewal."

Russian Orthodox Celebrations and Observances

The weddings which took place in St. Nicholas Church were beautiful to behold, and due to the length of the ceremony could also be a marathon in physical endurance. Late Seldovia resident Emma Josefson remembered that weddings lasted nearly two hours, with the wedding party and guests standing the entire time. That churchgoers stood was not at all unusual in the Orthodox Church services, where chairs were reserved only for the very old and the infirm. Sitting, kneeling, and prostration of the body were felt to be acts of penitence and were reserved for confession. The remainder of the time in church was for joyful celebration and fellowship, and standing was considered to be the only appropriate posture to reflect such joy. [61]

What we might term the "best man" and the "maid or matron of honor" were represented in the Orthodox wedding. Their roles were to hold wedding crowns over the heads of the bride and groom for the entire ceremony. Nick Elxnit remembers them held above the heads for a much shorter time, perhaps only half an hour. Crowns could be made of gold or brass, adorned with jewels or beads. In 1900, the Right Reverend Tikhon granted the Seldovia chapel $367 to be used for wedding crowns.[62] Nick also recalls that guests could purchase candles for 10 cents, and would typically light them and hold them during the service. Candles also surrounded the ikons.

Although weddings were generally held only in the church building and only to marry communicants of the Orthodox Church, exceptions during the "frontier years" did take place. Notable and colorful is the story of Juanita Anderson, who was married to Ralph Anderson on Seldovia Bay at midnight on February 5, 1917.

Ralph and Juanita wished to be married, but Juanita did not care to married by a U.S. Commissioner in a civil ceremony. There being no resident priest of any denomination at Seldovia, the couple had planned to go to Seward. The steamship *Admiral Evans* had just docked at Seldovia, and so to secure passage on it, Ralph and Juanita rowed from town over to the only pier, that of J.A. Herbert at Schooner Beach.

Aboard the vessel was a black robed Russian priest, Father Gerasim Shmaltz, who was enroute to Kodiak from Russia. He spoke no English, but the Seldovia postmistress did, and she was meeting the incoming

The S. S. Admiral Evans, owned by the Pacific Steamship Company, served as an impromptu wedding chapel in 1917 for Seldovians Ralph and Juanita Anderson. Photo courtesy of Ted Anderson from the Ralph and Juanita Anderson Collection.

steamer. Ralph and Juanita waited for her to interpret their request, and the priest responded that he'd be happy to marry them. Juanita wasn't dressed for the occasion, so she and Ralph rowed back to town where she donned a white corduroy skating costume and an ermine stole and muff. As she and Ralph rowed back out to the pier, a full moon shone brightly on the newfallen snow: a lovely night to be married.

Father Gerasim Shmaltz, when he was aboard the S.S. Admiral Evans *bound for Kodiak, married Ralph and Juanita Anderson at midnight on February 5/6, 1917, during a layover in Seldovia. Photo courtesy of Ted Anderson from the Ralph and Juanita Anderson Collection.*

Many gas boats were clustered around the steamer, some of them bringing the first barrels of salted herring from Halibut Cove to be shipped from this area. Everyone stopped their activities and clustered on the afterdeck of the steamer to witness this unique wedding. Juanita had hoped the postmistress would interpret the Russian spoken service for them, but perhaps in the excitement the ceremony began before it was discovered she had returned to town. Although Juanita and Ralph couldn't understand a word of the service, they knew it was over and that they were married when the priest held up the cross about his neck for them to kiss. Ralph would tease Juanita later that she had no idea of what she had promised in her marriage vows.

After the ceremony, all the guests were invited by Captain Charles Glascock into the ship's dining room, where the steward had laid out a fine feast. [63] Juanita's son, Ted, remembers his mother saying that after the wedding, a procession of dories honored the newlyweds by parading all around the bay. Ralph and Juanita were in the lead dory, and were periodically saluted with rifle shots.

Easter was a happy celebration, after a strictly observed Lenten season which lasted seven weeks. At the end of Holy Week, Easter service began around ten o'clock Saturday evening and continued through the night, ending about three a.m. on Easter Sunday. Communicants brought food to the church for an Easter morning breakfast, where it was blessed by the priest. Traditional fare included pirok, bleenee, colored eggs, and the rich and savory cheese pacha. The crown of the feast was a mushroom shaped bread, studded with fruit, and frosted and decorated, called "kulich." [64] Former Seldovian Jim Busey remembers that during Easter week, the bells in the Orthodox Church rang almost continuously. All the children were invited up to help ring them.[65]

Undoubtedly the highlight of the Orthodox year was the celebration of Christmas and the New Year. Because it follows the Christian Ecclesiastical calendar, based on the Julian calendar, the Orthodox Church celebrates Christmas, the feast of the Nativity, on January 7th. An all night vigil was held on Nativity eve, the 6th, with feasting and services the next day. Gifts were not exchanged until New Year's, so as not to detract from the meaning of the Christmas celebration.

On January 6th, and continuing for three days, the congregation observed the custom of "starring," an element of the celebration that is still performed in Seldovia. A large seven pointed star of shiny, glittery material was made and affixed to a pole. The star was fashioned to accommodate a lit candle, and an axle, so as the celebrants walked the whole affair turned. The star bearer led a group of parishioners around the village, singing beautiful Orthodox Christmas hymns and chants as they progressed from house to house. Just as in the Christmas caroling tradition, those who went starring were typically invited in to various homes for refreshment.[66] According to Nick Elxnit, sweets such as fruit pies and turnovers were handed out to the children. He likens it to Halloween today, when children traipse about town with bags full of goodies. Some folks gave out money to help support the church, and still others slipped a nip or two to the singers during Prohibition. [67]

For a week of consecutive nights after Christmas, feasting and dancing took place, and continued into the wee hours of the morning. Celebrants wore a different costume or mask each night, so as to conceal their identity. Great effort was put into the costumes, which ranged from comic to frightening to lovely. In the 1930's, a native string orchestra played music at Joe Hill's dance hall, and the entire community, native and nonnative, Orthodox and others, all filled the room to capacity.

Former Seldovian Alice Lipke, in her 1938 novel *Under the Aurora*, provided a dramatic account of this annual dance that was part celebration, and part ritual:

> Soon the hall was packed, then the masqueraders entered. Everyone was fascinated by their funny capers, but more so by the strange costumes. Each tried to outdo the other. Men dressed as women and women dressed as men. Natives were dressed in designs at once repulsive, and yet curious. Vitka was there. He was a sight to behold. True he had on a loin cloth, but with the exception of that one item, he was naked. Over his body had been smeared some sticky substance, and over this had been applied feathers! On his head was a headdress made of feathers and worn with a peculiar looking band, binding it tightly about his forehead. Eileen was reminded of a similar looking headdress belonging to the regalia of an Aztec ceremonial dance. She had seen the headdress in a museum together with orbes of feathers and other paraphenalia of the Aztecs and again she wondered where the ideas originated that Alaskan natives use in their ceremonials.
>
> Some of the natives relied upon painting the face entirely over for disguise. Others bound their features in cloth, even their necks, and on the arms were stockings so that even the hands could be disguised.
>
> Some were costumed as rabbits and some as birds. The natives were ingenious in their choice of original costumes. Dried grasses and seaweed came in as adjuncts of decoration. They were chagrined if their efforts at disguise had been in vain. One huge native painted his cheeks a bright vermillion with house paint. Later the skin became terribly blistered and did not heal for some time....
>
> The New Year would appear with the banishment of the Old Year. The part was generally taken by a young man, dressed in white. About his head would be a narrow band of red, around which were Russian words in letters of gold. He would make a speech wishing all the people health and plenty, prosperity and goodwill.
>
> Everyone was on the que vive. Excitement was in the air. Each one looked expectantly at the others about him. Truly a motley crowd. The oil lamps cast queer shadows. The lamps rattled in their hangings from the movement of many dancing feet. Seven nights the dancing had been going on, but tonight, the night so full of mystery, there was a sense of unseen forces at work, a sensing of something entering into one's life that had not been there before. One cannot witness the thrilling ceremonial of this night of all others in the life of the Alaskan native without experiencing something never to be forgotten, entirely new in his life and not to be lightly laid aside....
>
> Each year, it is said, will be the last of these ceremonials. The whites, intent upon enjoying the holiday according to their own accepted desire for a good time, have entirely lost sight of the fact that this is the time of the natives' own holiday. It belongs entirely to them. During these days of preparation for feasting and dancing they have been happily carrying out the traditions that belong to them alone as a race.
>
> It was now eleven-thirty and the dance was in full swing. The outer door suddenly opened, and from without came an old couple dressed in rags, the man leaning upon a crooked staff. He represented the Old Year and was groaning loudly, while his wife supported his failing strength with her own. The old couple circled slowly around the hall. Suddenly the door again opened, and two imps of Satan came in, dressed entirely in black. They had two horns upon their heads. A spike at the end of the tail protruded from behind, rattling as it dragged upon the floor.
>
> They came rushing in, looking about among the dancers for the Old Year. At sight of the two

imps the dancers retreated to the far corner of the dance hall. Women cringed and caught their breath as they clasped their youngsters to them.

They stood upon the benches out of the way of the two imps, who were searching with the barbed poles used in trying to find the Old Year and which they thrust under skirts and benches and any other likely place where the Old Year might have hidden himself. At last the barbs on the poles catch into his rags. He is hauled out from beneath the skirts of his old wife who vainly tries to shield him from these onslaughts. They dragged him out from among the dancers and threw him upon the floor where he lay, whimpering with fear. The old wife rushed out and rescued him, helping him back to a place of concealment.

Away ran the devils, and the dance went on merrily. The time was nearly over, and the Old Year started to dance with each woman present, brown or white.

Quickly he grabbed first one of the women and then another. It was considered good luck to have the Old Year turn once around with you at his death dance. At last he was through. He was growing faint. He was seen to be painfully and slowly making his last weary round of the hall.

The circle of faces about him, so very real in this ceremony, showed fear, terror, and even repugnance, so horrible did he look in his ragged garments. His dress was tattered beyond description; old sacking was wrapped about his feet and legs, and a mantle of coarse cloth thrown about his shoulders. There was no regret or pity in the eyes of the onlookers as the Old Year slowly circled the room; but, rather, a shrinking horror shone in face and eye, for he represented a day that was done, a time forgotten, to be done away with—speedily and surely—put away—forever. The New Year, untrammeled by the binding fetters of the Old Year, entered in the midst of the onlookers with a spring of joy. There was a new dawn, the beginning of a new era of prosperity; Good Luck. Perhaps. At any rate a New Year separate and apart from the Old.

Thus the Old Year swung around for a last round of the hall. He fell to his knees and clutched his stout staff for support, as vainly he tried to rise. A shrill whistle resounded in the room. Children screamed and hid behind mothers' skirts, as two figures raced madly in from the outer air through the open door once more, bringing cold draughts with them that chilled to the marrow the blood of the Whites.

This was chicanery—certainly mystery of some sort. The figures swiftly advanced with their long pike staffs, the cruel sharp prongs held firmly in front of them, as they cast about, looking for the Old Year, to clutch and tear and bruise.

The two figures were dressed entirely in black from head to foot in skintight garments, with two large pointed ears, two horns on their heads, and slits for the eyes. Were they human?

They failed to find the Old Year, who by now had rolled under one of the settees on which children were standing and before which grown-ups were making a brave effort of protection for the tattered figure, so vainly trying to evade his fate of annihilation....

After clawing aside the skirts of the women and giving a series of bloodcurdling yells, the maddening sound of the whistles resounded through the hall, and once more the two figures swiftly rushed out into the freezing cold from whence they had come.

Again the music struck up; a merry fox-trot. Groups of people gradually formed upon the dance floor. Couples halfheartedly commenced to dance. The Old Year painfully rescued himself from under the settee; and covered with dust and grime, he raised himself to his feet.

He was now bent double. His back was like a round sack of meal. Covered with sackcloth and inadequate garments, he stumbled on for a last round. Valiantly, he pulled his rags closer about him, as they appeared ready to fall from his body. Hark! The damming whistles! The door slams back with a loud crash. Faces grow white!

The two devils are shrieking with glee, as swiftly they advance on the Old Year, fairly in the clutches of their cruel spikes. Drums beat as tom-toms....There was a hush. The hush of Doom. The two devils were dragging the Old Year across the dance hall floor. The prongs of the staves bit cruelly into garments and cringing flesh. A tearing and rending sound was heard of cloth being torn, as the Old Year was dragged to the open door. He moaned, groaned and cried feebly. But the imps of Satan were bearing him out—inexorably to his doom!

Midnight struck—God!! What a noise! The shrill whistles of the two devils, as they reached out their arms to carry the Old Year—the shrieks of the children—the sobs of the women—the exclamations of the natives...

Cymbals clashed—drums beat loudly, rolling their booming tones through the night air—tom-toms! Yes! A hundred tom-toms come to life, and above all, the solemn tolling of the church bells.

The last strokes died away in defiance, as with another clash of cymbals—a roll of drums—the two devils literally threw the Old Year outward to the beach, pursuing him over the snow and icy sand.

He was caught up by willing hands and thrown into the icy waters of Seldovia Bay.

Somewhere a woman screamed.

One—two—three—four—five—six—seven—eight—nine—ten—eleven—twelve! The Old Year was dead— The New Year was Born! [68]

SELDOVIA HERALD - January 1931

Russian Christmas festivities concluded with a dance the night of the 14th, last Wednesday, being the 5th consecutive affair of that kind. While they all were enjoyable enough, the masquerade ball given the night of Tuesday, the 13th, was particularly gay and was the most largely attended of any. The music was gay and rollicking, the dancers, masked and otherwise responded gaily to the lilting tunes. The spectators seemed to get as much fun out of the affair as the rest of them, and formed a ringside circle to get a better eyeful of the fantastically dressed and altogether joyous crowd. Toward midnight after the unmasking, the judges Mrs. M. E. Shortley, Dr. J.J. Jenson and Allan Petersen, took the center of the floor, and the dancers promenaded about them in a grand march. First prize was awarded Mrs. Helen Torgramson and Mrs. S. Halvorson, representing Raggedy Ann and Raggedy Andy. Mrs. Grace Olson and Miss Emma Korsnes, in Mexican costume won second prize, while third prize went to Miss Margaret MacKenzie and Fred O'Neil, "Knights of the Bath." Miss Elizabeth Korsnes, the winsome shepherdess carried off fourth, and fifth went to Mrs. Alice McMeekan and Mrs. Agnes Elsos, all dolled up as rabbits with fluffy costumes, long ears and everything. Marshal Milo Hubert completely disguised in a hard boiled hat, was given the prize as the best comic. The prize winners were not the only ones quaintly, attractively masked. They were all good and all the evening was glorious.

Endnotes

[1] Cornelius Osgood, *The Ethnography of the Tanaina,* Yale University Publications in Anthropology, Number 16, (New Haven: reprinted by Human Relations Area Files P, 1976) 190.

[2] Records of the Russian Orthodox Greek Catholic Church of North America, Diocese of Alaska, trans. Katherine Arndt, microfilm #139 reel 199, Alaskan Russian Church Archives: U of Alaska Fairbanks.

[3] James Kari, letter to the author, Apr. 1993.

[4] Katherine Arndt, letter to the author, 15 Apr. 1993.

[5] Osgood 162-165.

[6] Katherine Arndt, letter to the author, 14 July 1994.

[7] Joan B. Townsend, "Journals of Nineteenth Century Russian Priests to the Tanaina: Cook Inlet, Alaska," *Arctic Anthropology,* XI.1 (1974):14.

[8] Townsend 13.

[9] Townsend 15.

[10] Alaska Church Collection, Box 74, U of Alaska Fairbanks, 208.

[11] Church Collection, Box 488, 73.

[12] Church Collection, Box 488, 74.

[13] The Alaskan Russian Church Archives, microfilm D301 reel 203, Alaska Division of State Libraries and Museums. Bortnovskii's letter to Rev. Antonii was translated by Sergei Chulaki for this book.

[14] Woodrow Johansen, *The Family History of Adam Bloch (self-pub., 1986).* This was loaned to the author by the John Gruber family of Seldovia.

[15] *Russian Orthodox American Messenger,* 5(1901) 365-366. Note: Some articles in the *Messenger* are in Russian, others are in English. Those which are in Russian were translated by Sergei Chulaki for this book.

[16] Adam Bloch, letters to Goss, 26 May 1900, 16 June 1900, Alaska Commercial Co. correspondance, *The Family History of Adam Bloch.*

[17] Church Collection, Box 488, 73.

[18] Church Collection, Box 488, 76.

[19] Rare Map Collection, U of Alaska Fairbanks, # G4370/1898/581.

[20] Church Archives, microfilm D263, reel 181.

[21] Church Collection, Box 488, 77.

[22] Church Collection, Box 488, 76.

[23] Church Collection, Box 488, 79-80.

[24] Twelfth Census of the United States, U.S. Dept. of Commerce, Bureau of the Census, 1900.

[25] Thirteenth Census of the United States, U.S. Dept. of Commerce, Bureau of the Census, 1910.

[26] Church Collection, Box 488, 80.

[27] *Messenger,* 3 (1898): 513.

[28] *Messenger,* 3 (1898): 513.

[29] *Messenger,* 3 (1899): 93.

[30] *Messenger,* 3 (1899): 93.

[31] Bloch, letter to Washburn, 14 June 1897, *The Family History of Adam Bloch.*

[32] *Messenger,* 6 (1902): 223.

[33] Hudson Stuck, *Ten Thousand Miles With a Dog Sled,* (Prescott,AZ: Wolfe, 1988) 354.

[34] *Messenger,* 3 (1899): 545-546.

[35] *Messenger,* 3 (1899): 625.

[36] *Messenger,* 5 (1901): 275.

[37] *Messenger,* 5 (1901): 275.

[38] *Messenger,* 5 (1901): 301-302.

[39] *Messenger,* 6 (1902): 223.

[40] *Messenger,* 9 (1905) 106.

[41] *Messenger,* 4 (1900): 439-440.

[42] *Messenger,* 5 (1901): 365-366.

[43] *Messenger,* 6 (1902): 223.

[44] *Messenger,* 7 (1903): 200-201.

[45] *Messenger,* 8 (1904): 333-334.

[46] *Messenger,* 8 (1904): 333-334.

[47] *Messenger,* 10 (1906): 274 and 277.

[48] *Messenger,* 9 (1905): 130-131.

[49] *Messenger,* 11 (1907): 205.

[50] *Messenger,* 11 (1907): 163.

Endnotes (cont.)

[51] *Messenger,* 11 (1907): 279.

[52] *Messenger,* 12 (1908): 82.

[53] Rev. Father George Pletnikoff, untitled photocopy pamphlet (Seldovia: n.p., June 1983).

[54] Robert Porter, *Report on Population and Resources of Alaska at the Eleventh Census: 1890,* (Washington: GPO, 1893) 182.

[55] *Messenger,* 10 (1906) 274, 277.

[56] Mary Ford, "State Grant will Rescue Russian Orthodox Church," *Peninsula Clarion* 5 June 1981: 20-21.

[57] Sam Combs, Project Architect, letter to the author, Feb. 1992.

[58] Fern Wallace, *The Flame of the Candle* (Chilliwack, BC: Sts. Kyril and Methody Soc., 1974) 15.

[59] Wallace 15-16.

[60] The Fellowship of Orthodox Stewards, *About Being Orthodox* (S. Deerfield, MA: Channing L. Bete, 1984).

[61] Wallace 19.

[62] *Messenger* 21(1900): 439-440.

[63] Juanita Anderson, taped interview by Laura Hendricks, Pratt Museum, Homer, 13 Oct. 1983.

[64] Elsa Pedersen, "Seldovia," *The Alaska Sportsman,* July 1958: 6; Wallace 18.

[65] Nick Elxnit, personal interview, 1992.

[66] Pedersen 6; Wallace 18.

[67] Elxnit, 1992.

[68] Alice Cushing Lipke, *Under the Aurora,* (Los Angeles: Suttonhouse, 1938) 243-249; Author's note: I stumbled across this book while on a research trip to Juneau. The book is long out of print, but a signed copy of it was waiting, seemingly just for me, in a rare book store there. I made numerous phone calls to try and locate the publishing house to seek permission to reprint Lipke's account of the New Year's celebration. I was unable to find Suttonhouse, nor anyone who knew what publisher might have bought its rights. A search for Lipke heirs was equally unproductive.

FUR AND FIN

The Evolution of Commerce in Seldovia: A Look at Fur Farming, Commercial Fishing, Mining, Logging, and Tourism, Spanning Nearly 100 Years

Seldovia's "Furst" Industry

As discussed in the chapter "Seldovia's Modern Beginnings" (page 51), the first company known to operate in Seldovia was the Western Fur Company. It was headquartered in San Francisco, as was its rival, the Alaska Commercial Company. A search of California historical repositories turned up nothing in the way of Western Fur Company archives, thus little is known about its operation in Seldovia except for the 1881—1883 station inventories summarized in the chapter "Seldovia's Modern Beginnings." These came from the University of Alaska at Fairbanks, boxed together with early Alaska Commercial Company records. They were most probably the documents on hand in the stations when the Alaska Commercial Company took over the Western Fur Company in 1883, after the latter lost a quarter of a million dollars. While the two companies were operating, competition for furs ensured that native hunters were paid a reasonable price. However, by 1883, with only the Alaska Commercial Company in operation, the price paid for a good sea otter pelt in Seldovia had fallen from $112 to $35. [1]

By the 1890's another company, the Northern Alaska Commercial Company, had taken up business in Seldovia, the monopoly was broken, and prices paid for sea otter pelts jumped again. As shown by the records below, the price paid in 1897 was $125. This high figure probably also reflected a scarcity of sea otters due to decades of ruthless over-hunting during the tenure of the Russians.

These Seldovia trading station 1894 cash disbursement sheets from the Alaska Commercial Company archives (residing at the University of Alaska Fairbanks) give a picture of the sort of fur harvest that was taking place just before the turn of the century.

OCTOBER 1894	
1 moose hide [2nd word illegible]	20.00
Traps—English Bay	3.00
[Illegible]	2.00
2 mink	1.50
1 martin	2.50
Bringing bydarki from English Bay	2.25
Labor on Bydarki	3.00
2 paddles [illegible]	1.50
1 mink	.75
Scrubbing house and store	.75
A. Bloch	2.50
Cash on Hand	<u>118.90</u>
	156.65

NOVEMBER 1894	
[Illegible]	3.40
1 mink	.75
1 martin	2.50
1 sheeps horns	12.00
3 mink @ 2.25, 1 martin @ 2.50	4.75
1 lynx	2.50
2 land otter	12.00
4 martin	10.00
2 mink	1.50
2 sheeps horns	24.00
[Illegible]	2.60
Cash on Hand	<u>108.70</u>
	184.70

Cash Disbursement Sheets from the Alaska Commercial Company

FEBRUARY 1895

Traps [?]—English Bay	3.00
—kachehekmak	5.00
1 martin	2.50
1 rifle	25.00
1 bydarki frame	7.00
Sewing softak [illegible] on bydarki	8.00
1 wolverine @3.00, 1 martin	5.50
Cash on hand	<u>116.10</u>
	172.10

DECEMBER 1897

[Illegible]	5.90
2 mink, 1 lynx	1.80
1 martin	1.50
1 mink	.40
12 mink	4.80
2 martin	3.00
1 lynx	1.00
1 red fox	1.00
11 land otter	33.00
1 mink	.40
1 wolverine	1.50
1 lynx	1.00
1 sea otter	125.00
A. Bloch	2.75
Cash on Hand	<u>227.80</u>
	411.85

[The post recorded 257.80 in sales for this month. Notable is the $125.00 paid for a sea otter pelt. Its singular appearance in these records indicates the scarcity of and the continuing demand for these furs.]

NOVEMBER 1897

[Illegible]	6.10
1 black bear, 1 mink	10.40
2 mink	.80
5 mink @ 2.00, 1 land otter @ 2.50	4.50
4 mink	1.60
1 black bear	10.00
7 land otter	21.00
9 mink	3.60
1 wolverine	1.50
1 martin	1.50
5 lynx	5.00
1 land otter @ 3.00, 4 mink @ 1.60	4.60
9 martin	13.50
1 mink, 1 martin	1.90
1 beaver	2.50
A. Bloch	4.60
Cash on hand	<u>154.05</u>
	244.75

[In November, $97.90 in sales were recorded. On the 22nd of the month, a trapper delivered his fur cache (beginning on the list with 1 black bear and ending 5 entries later with 5 lynx) and spent all of it the same day at the trading post on supplies: some $43.10 worth.]

Cash Disbursement Sheets from the Alaska Commercial Company

Adam Bloch (spelled Block in some early records) came from an Alaska Commercial Company position at Attu to serve as its agent in Seldovia. John Wall Smith had worked for the Alaska Commercial Company in Douglas for sixteen years before coming to Seldovia to run the trading station for the rival company, the Northern Alaska Commercial Company.[2] Letters sent from the Seldovia station to Alaska Commercial Company district headquarters in Kodiak are a testament to the hardships of a life dependent upon a dying resource.

The record of Bloch's correspondence with Kodiak begins in 1896. How long he was here as the Alaska Commercial Company agent prior to that year is unclear. John Wall Smith and the Northern Alaska Commercial Company were also in Seldovia that year. The rivalry between the two storekeepers was never-ending, although some years later Smith would look after Bloch when both were out of work and Bloch was injured from a wood-chopping accident.[3] At his disposal Bloch had a fleet of somewhere around twelve bydarkis (also spelled bidarkis, and also known as kayaks) manned with natives from Seldovia and English Bay. As reports of sea otter came in, Bloch would respond by sending hunting parties to Anchor Point, Nuka Bay, and the Pye Islands. Most often though, bidarkis were dispatched to the "Bering Isld." which may refer to the Barren Island group in lower Cook Inlet. By 1897, the English Bay store had been abandoned[4] although the natives there continued to hunt for the Seldovia Alaska Commercial Company station.

Occasionally, Bloch would send a hunting party out to an island or bay with provisions for several weeks or months so that travel time to and from Seldovia was kept to a minimum. With periods of stormy weather sometimes lasting nearly a month preventing travel over the open ocean, this was a wise move. In 1898, the Seldovia and English Bay hunters brought in six sea otter but by 1899 there was nothing, and Bloch wrote of his frustration. In 1900 the news of one sea otter spotted in the Pye Islands prompted a response of eight bidarkis rushing to the scene, but all for naught.[5] The sea otter population had been effectively obliterated by years of hunting pressure.

Just as the supply of wild furs in the area was dwindling, the news that gold could be found up Cook Inlet was reaching the ears of fortune-hunters Outside. Seldovia's nineteenth century fur industry all but ended as local men turned from trapping to join the multitude in seeking their fortunes, or else going into business serving the incoming prospectors. The transition was not a smooth one, however; the winter of 1901-02 was a particularly hard one. The trading companies had all but closed down their stations here by that time, and there was no food to be had. Bloch and Smith were trying to convince Alaska Commercial Company district headquarters in Kodiak to set them up in business as independent merchants. In the meantime, however, everyone faced a lean winter. Many of the native hunters were at work in the coal mines at Homer, and thus had money to spend, but without provisions to spend it on, they too went hungry.

The story of the big commercial companies in Seldovia ends with Smith leaving in 1902 to take the job of storekeeper at the new cannery in Snug Harbor, and Bloch taking advantage of the influx of gold seekers to set up his own mercantile, buying provisions as an independent merchant through the Alaska Commercial Company station in Kodiak.[6]

Adam Bloch and his combination mercantile and post office. Photo courtesy of the Pratt Museum, #HM-81-16-1

Fur: Trapping and Hunting Give Way to Farming

Although the 1890 census was destroyed by fire, one could expect that of the 99 residents on hand in Seldovia at the time, a larger percentage than in 1900 were listed as hunters. In the 1900 census, nearly one third of the population made their living by hunting and fishing. (46 out of 149) No distinction is made between those who hunted for subsistence and those who hunted and trapped for skins. By 1910, the population had increased to 173, but the number of people shown as hunters had dropped to around 36. [7]

The hunting and trapping of wild animals to obtain furs for sale to the trading posts remained a small piece of the economic pie until the 1920's. It was during this decade that the practice of live-trapping wild fox and breeding them in pens or on islands became popular. Fox-farming had taken root on the south shore of Kachemak Bay as early as 1900 when U.S. Ritchie planted blue fox on Yukon and Hesketh Islands, [8] and in lower Cook Inlet on Elizabeth Island where other individuals planted fox and then abandoned them a few years later. [9]

F.W. Williamson, in his 1925 article "Farming Silver-Black Foxes," claims that about 1909 Joe Filardeau and John Herbert established themselves in a fox farm at the head of Kachemak Bay.[10] However, the U.S. Dept. of Commerce "Report on the Fur and Fishing Industries in Alaska" for the year 1917 states that Filardeau, of Seldovia, began fox farming in 1915 with a single pair of foxes. [11] Filardeau doesn't show up in Seldovia for the 1910 census, and Herbert is shown not as a fox farmer, but a merchant. However, by 1920, the census reports both men earning their livings as fox farmers. [12]

In November of 1917, Filardeau and Herbert entered into a partnership, building eight pens for a stock that was expected to increase to ten breeding pairs of silver-gray foxes by the next year. Fildardeau had noticed that in July a litter of five kits was not as active as usual, and so he gathered "herbs of all varieties and [gave] them to the animals in the hope that they would contain something of benefit to the foxes." [13] When this remedy didn't work, Filardeau dug grassy sod and offered it. The roots were eaten with relish by the kits and their energy returned almost immediately. This hit-or-miss approach to feeding and caring for the animals was not unique. The raising of foxes was still experimental, and breeders often shared tips. Filardeau fed his animals sun-cured salmon, and porcupine meat. Because of a lack of wild rabbit, he raised his own to supplement the foxes' diet. [14]

At about this same time, the Sholin brothers of Homer trapped silver-gray foxes in the Caribou Hills and began a ranch in 1915 with three breeding pairs. They went on to become the most successful fox farmers in the area, and their success was largely responsible for the establishment of other fur farms around Kachemak Bay.[15]

J.A. Herbert left his partnership with Filardeau and started his own blue fox farm on Passage Island. The term "blue fox" refers to a color phase of the arctic fox.[16] Unlike his former partner, Herbert allowed his stock to roam freely over the island. He employed natives from Port Graham to hunt food for the foxes and to help him prepare it. Rabbits at 25 cents and porcupine at 50 cents each were sold to Herbert. These, together with fish heads from the local cannery, were tossed into a giant kettle fashioned from one half of a 55-gallon drum and cooked into a mush for the foxes. Herberts' employees rowed to work each day from Port Graham Village to the island. When a litter was due to be born, the female was confined to a pen and no employees nor visitors allowed near. Fox tended to be nervous around strangers, especially during breeding season. If upset, they could kill or injure their young. [17]

By 1919, Herbert's Passage Island ranch numbered 25 breeding pairs. They produced about 100 kits, but only 23 survived to maturity, the rest being carried away by eagles. Predation from eagles and ravens was a tremendous problem, especially for those farmers who let their stock free-roam over an island. [18] Ravens were apparently the most dreaded predator, for they were crafty. A Chugach Island farmer reported seeing a flock of birds, led by the patriarch, descend upon a young fox. While one bird seized the fox by the side of the head and held on, the others pecked away at the spine, which soon paralyzed the animal so that he became easy prey. This farmer also noted that a raven, upon spotting a large fox, would entice an eagle to the prey and wait for it to make the kill. Then, it is presumed, a flock of ravens would appear and drive the eagle away from the carcass. [19] Weather could also take its toll on the young kits, as evidenced by a Seldovia farmer, who, one unseasonably wet and cold spring, lost all but 11 of his young foxes. [20]

Blue fox were typically more prone to predation since they were island-reared and free-roaming. Black and silver-gray fox, reared in pens, were presumably more protected. It was reported that pen-raised fox became quite tame, and fond of their caretakers. The job of feeding pen-raised fox was certainly more labor intensive, as they relied upon their caretakers for all nourishment. Island-reared blue fox were free to forage the beaches, and apparently relished mussels and other shellfish. [21]

Island-reared fox were fed meat and fish by their caretakers, with supplements of eggs and milk at breeding time. Pen-reared fox ate everything including porcupine, rabbit, ducks, fish, cereal, whale and seal meat and oil, along with the requisite dairy products during breeding season.

The matter of procuring food for one's stock could be a full time job in itself. The abundance of fish and game in the Kachemak Bay area was a big reason why fox farming was successful here. Nonetheless, the labor and equipment required to find, kill, and cook this bounty were still considerable. A typical fox ranch would include a smokehouse, food storage shed, cook shack, pens to house the stock (with special quarters for breeders, pregnant females, and sick fox), caretakers' quarters, and sheds for pelting (killing) and storing the skins. [22] Since most farms were far removed from Seldovia or any other settlement, a workshop, skiff, dock, and various other outbuildings were in order to make the operation wholly self-sufficient. An advertisement for a fox farm for sale listed these components: "6 pair blues, 16 pair silvers, 22 large pens, 4 pelting pens, feed house, 30 gallon cooker, guard wire around ranch, coal stocked for year, power boat, 23 foot coal dory, punt, carpenter shop, material for three more pens." [23]

By 1920, the south shore of Kachemak Bay was dotted with fox farms. The census that year showed Seldovians Tollak Ollestad (Yukon Island) and J.A. Herbert (Passage Island) engaged in island fox farming. Young James Cleghorn was listed as a laborer on a fox farm. The census for "South Shore Kitchamack Bay" listed four trappers, eleven men who raised fox at home, and three island fox farmers.[24] Most of these men were, had been, or would later be Seldovia residents.

Shortly after the census was taken, Keith McCullough, a former Forest Service employee, brought his wife to Seldovia and took up blue fox farming on three islands. He built a large house with a furnace and spent $2100 on breeding stock: eight females and six males. In 1921, McCullough made $3150 selling young fox (some just six months old) as breeders. In 1922, he sold $900 worth of breeding stock, and by 1923, McCullough had made a successful attempt at raising the blue fox in pens. At this point, McCullough was receiving an average of $100 apiece for his skins on the New York market, and the majority of the pelts were from fox less than eight months old. McCullough had certainly found the secret formula, for he was making a handsome profit for his efforts. [25]

> **Trapper, public domain:** Charles Coach, Stephan Dolchuck, John A. (Jack) Fields, and Gabriel Luco
>
> **Fox farmer, home or homestead:** Harry A. Leonhardt (Bear Cove), Charles A. Patterson (Bear Cove), Andrew Lundgren, Hilmer Olsen (Bradley River), William H. Gibbon, Joseph Filardeau, Anisim Alexandroff, Julius Christianson, Timothy Balashoff, Nathan P. White, Thomas Lucanon
>
> **Fox farmer, island:** William McKeon, James Cleghorn Sr., P. Olson (Cohen Island)
>
> [In later years, Seldovians T.L. Loyd, Frank Raby, Dr. Isam F. Burgin, Louie Huber, Ed Dwyer, Anton Johansen, Elizabeth R. Herbert, William Maitland, J.C. Wallen, Anton Nelson, Ero Walli, and others added their names to the roster of Kachemak Bay fox farmers.][26]

By 1925, McCullough was shipping breeding pairs Outside, and had moved to Seattle to open a brokerage for Alaskan farmers who wanted to sell breeding stock to Lower 48 fox farmers. [27] He became president of Alaska Western Fox Corp., with member farms in Cook Inlet and Maine. In the fall of 1925, Keith McCullough visited Kachemak Bay and took 85 breeding pairs of silver gray and blue fox Outside on the steamer. Within days he was bound for the east coast, to visit his Maine concerns, and then on to Europe, where he planned to take 70 pairs of his fox to establish farms in Sweden and Finland.[28]

Dr. Isam F. Burgin was another successful farmer on the south shore of Kachemak Bay. Burgin, a physician for 20 years in Delta, Colorado, came to Seldovia in 1916, in search of a lifestyle that would benefit his health more than that of being an office-bound doctor. He eventually took up fox farming and by 1924 had interests in three island and two mainland fox farms, including operations on Hesketh Island and in Bear Cove. [29] The Hesketh Island farm was one of the two largest in the area, numbering nearly 250 animals. On Yukon Island, Tollack Ollestad had a blue fox farm of similar size. [30] It was reported at the time, that Burgin fed his stock to the tune of 200 lbs per day.[31]

In the 1920's, fox farming reached its peak here. Eighty-seven licensed farmers operated in Cook Inlet, with the heaviest concentration on Kachemak Bay.[33] Kachemak Bay was gaining a reputation for superior pelts and breeding stock. By November of 1923, seventy pairs of breeding fox had been shipped from the Seldovia area to other farmers across Alaska and the Lower 48. This was more than were shipped from any other part of Alaska.[34] Around the territory, fur farmers' organizations were forming in response to poaching problems, the need for better legislation governing the industry, and in an effort to market cooperatively.[35] In Seldovia, the Cooks Inlet Blue and Black Fox Farmers Association of Alaska was formed in 1924, listing 52 members by the following year.[36] Dr. Isam F. Burgin was elected president, Harry Inhart vice-president, Ralph Anderson secretary, and Andy Sholin treasurer. The group listed its main objective as the raising of blue foxes in captivity (pens). Heretofore, blues were mainly raised free on island ranches, but the new organization earned a reputation for showing that they could indeed be successfully raised in pens.[37]

From THE ALASKA WEEKLY
A List of Kachemak Bay Fox Farmers in 1924[32]

Olson & Lindgrun		36 silvers
J.A. (Jack) Fields		4 silvers
Sholin Brothers		56 silvers
Johnson & Johnson		28 silvers
Nate White	8 blues	12 silvers
Dan Peterson		12 silvers
Frank Sanderburg		12 silvers
Julius Christensen		20 silvers
Berglund, Pollack, & Berglund	6 silvers	200 blues
Dan Morris		20 blues
L.A. Dunning		22 blues
Allen Peterson		16 blues
Anton Johansen		100 blues
Tallock Ollstadt		250 blues
Pete Olsen		200 blues
Matt Yuth		18 blues
T. Lloyd		16 blues
R.B. Barnes		4 blues
Keith McCullough		30 blues

Author's Note: Names are spelled as they appeared in the newspaper.

FUR OF A SILKY TEXTURE AND SUPERIOR QUALITY

The Cooks Inlet District has long been noted for its ideal climatic conditions for the production of all kinds of fur.

We feel safe in the statement that nowhere on earth can better Silver, Blue and Black Foxes, and Marten and Mink be raised.

**All of These Animals Are Being Farmed in This District
This Association Invites Your Correspondence**

List of Our Farmers Furnished on Request

COOKS INLET BLUE AND BLACK FOX FARMERS ASSOCIATION OF ALASKA

Tollak Ollestad, President   T. Llloyd, V. Pres   Andrew Sholin, Treasurer
C. L. Vickers, Secretary

SELDOVIA   ALASKA

This ad for the Seldovia-based Fox Farmers Association appeared from 1925 through 1927 in The Fur Farmer Magazine. *Courtesy of the Homer Public Library, Billy Jo Kaho papers, and Janet Klein*

In 1925, Mr. A.A. Bass, publisher of *Fur Farmer Magazine*, visited fox farms in the Seldovia district. He reported that at Yakolof (Jakolof) Bay, Tollak Ollestad was raising blue fox in pens, and had 50 fine pups. Two of his litters had in them eleven pups each. Matt Yuth's Pioneer Blue Fox Ranch was across Seldovia Bay from town, and half a mile from that at T. W. Lloyd's Teton ranch, there was a huge litter of twelve pups. [38]

During the winter of 1927/28, J. A. Herbert suffered severe frostbite to his feet while working on his island fox farm. For some reason he did not seek medical treatment for the injury, or perhaps whatever initial treatment he received was ineffective. By August, his wife Elizabeth was compelled to take the 68-year old fox farmer to Seward for medical treatment. Gangrene and blood poisoning had set in, and Herbert was fading fast. They caught the steamer *Admiral Evans* for Seward, and were but two hours from docking there when Herbert died. His body was returned for burial to Seldovia, his reported home for the last 35 years. [39]

This ad for T. W. Lloyd's blue fox breeding stock appeared in a 1927 issue of The Fur Farmer Magazine.

The following *Seldovia Herald* and *Westward Alaskan* articles give a closer look at some other fox farming entrepreneurs:

SELDOVIA HERALD
May 31, 1930

Joe and Bill Christian, who came in from their Martin River fox farm the other day, report increase of eight litters of silver and five of blue foxes, with the prospect of 11 more to come. They are well pleased with the outlook, the young stock being robust and full of pep. The Christians plan to enlarge their plant in the way of adding pelting and dry sheds, and will lay in stocks of materials for the work within a short time.

[The Christian brothers shortly thereafter sold their farm for around $6000 to Gardo Webb and Seldovian Steve Zawistowski.]

SELDOVIA HERALD
Music Turns Fox Catcher

Music Romanoff started out the other night to catch the silver gray fox running at large about Seldovia, provided himself with a box trap for the purpose. And the next morning was sure he had the truant. So he lugged the sprung trap from one end of the town to the other, got a flash light from R.C. Morris to take a peep at his prize, and discovered a perfectly good black cat crouched in the box. So Music quit right there, went industriously to work playing his harmonica.

SELDOVIA HERALD
Unknown Fox, Golden Red, Brought in by Tony Martin, Veteran Trapper
March 26, 1932

Displaying, among other fur, an unusual and attractive fox—something between a red and a cross— Tony Martin has returned from his trap line along Fox River, head of Kachemak bay. He made small catch, the usual thing it appears, this season, but the few pieces are of fine size and excellently shaded. A lynx, probably six feet long; deep fur, velvety soft. Six black male mink, bigger than average, and as much alike as the proverbial peas in a pod. A collection of ermine, extra large. And then, there is the fox— golden red and brown; glintingly silver tipped, long and silky, with breast of deeper gold, velvet black ears and feet. Martin in all his trapping and woods experience had never seen anything like it. The fur has caused a sensation in Seldovia, and it is expected will cause interest wherever shown. The scarcity of fur-bearing animals, Martin maintains, is due to depletion of the rabbit crop, and as rabbit bands increase so will fur bearers develop. Rabbits, chief fur food, are beginning to come back, the trapper said. The little animals are quite observable, with signs everywhere. Sheep and moose, said Martin, fared excellently during the winter. A lot of snow, but it was dry and there was sufficient wind to blow it about, exposing foraging areas. He was unable to count as many game animals as formerly, but offers no arbitrary reason for this. And in view of the great numbers seen heretofore, the present paucity made an unfavorable impression. As with the fur bearers though, the veteran trapper regards the next few years as an adjustment period, and believes that with proper supervision return to normal conditions will be accomplished.

SELDOVIA HERALD
Milo Hulbert Takes Fox Island
June 11, 1932

Hesketh Island, located in Kachemak bay, and considered by observing men to be an island particularly well adapted to fox farming, has been transferred by sale of lease and holdings, from Ed. Dwyer to Milo Hulbert, deputy U.S. marshal, both of Seldovia. Mr. Dwyer, the recent purchaser of the Blue Fox Cafe, is getting the place shaped up for his business, and expects to be joined shortly by his wife. Milo Hulbert, new owner of the island, has faith in Seldovia and surrounding districts as attended by his varied holdings. Up to the time of his island buy, his latest and most conspicuous purchase was taking over the Colberg hall and saltery, standing on opposite sides of the boardwalk. In this purchase he first bought the half interest from Dr. Frank Burgin. Later when John Colberg visited Seldovia from Cordova, just prior to the opening of the fishing season over there, his half was assumed. Hesketh island is well stocked with blue foxes. Besides the old stock the island is now populated with approximately 90 pups. All animals have been carefully cared for and are in prime condition. They show a remarkable docility, and two litters that have taken up adjoining quarters under the house frolic about Mrs. Dwyer when she steps from the door. These two families, it is interesting to note, get along in perfect amity, the joint offspring of 19 youngsters and the parents living as one peaceful group. Besides a very excellent and in many respects modern residence building, the Dwyer properties embrace a completely equipped one line semi-hand cannery. It was always Mr. Dwyer's intention to go into the canning business along lines of novelty pack choice halibut cuts, minced cod, and the samples he turned out carry proof of success that might have been his had he ventured out. Mr. Hulbert will establish a competent man upon his new properties and in the fall, may engage in a little clam packing on his own...

SELDOVIA HERALD
Tailless Fox Brings Highest Price

A check for $401, being the net returns on the sale of a single silver fox fur, has been received by Mrs. R.J. Herbert, of Seldovia, from the London fur sales. This was the highest price paid for any single fox at the sale, the nearest competitor being 22 English pounds less. An odd circumstance in connection with this amazing sale, was that the fox was tailless, the animal having lost its tail in infancy through some misunderstanding or other with its mother. The fox is purported to have been five or six years old, and was whelped, raised and pelted on Mrs. Herbert's fox farm on Entrance Island.

THE WESTWARD ALASKAN
John Dudas Wins Award For
Fine Furs - Receives $200
Prize For Best Shipment

Two Hundred dollars and an embossed certificate of award greeted John Dudas, trapper of Kachemak Bay, when he called for his mail on one of his semiannual visits to the Seldovia Post Office. The award was that given annually by Sears, Roebuck, & Company for the most ably prepared shipment received by their fur department during the year. Dudas placed first with two mink and three weasel pelts caught in dry set steel traps at the head of Kachemak Bay. Dudas entertained friends in Seldovia before returning to his trap lines.

In addition to fox, enterprising Seldovians tried their hand at raising other fur bearing creatures. A.F. Piper began a skunk farm here in 1919 with eight animals he had shipped up from Outside.[40] There is no detailed record of his success at this venture, although it would appear that he or some successor was still at it in 1922 as there is note of a license issued for skunk farming that year.[41] Also issued in 1922 was a license for raising marten and another for raising mink.[42]

Frank Raby was probably the first person in Seldovia to attempt the raising of mink, which he did from 1923 through 1926.[43] The man who received the most press for his mink farming, however, was J.J. Sparrow in 1930. In May of 1930, Sparrow, a barber on the Seldovia boardwalk, opened a mink ranch across the walk from his barbershop. His silent partner was Matt Issacson. The men had no experience raising mink, but undaunted, procured four breeding pair and by the end of the month had produced kits.[44]

By September, each breeding pair had produced six kittens, and the operation now boasted 32 animals, each with its own pen. Mink have a reputation for being timid, and many eyebrows in the community were raised when Sparrow first proposed to raise them in the midst of a busy community.

SELDOVIA HERALD
Escaped Minks Coaxed Back to Wire Enclosure
Sept. 19, 1931

Neighborhood chickens scrambled for higher roosting retreats Friday night when two young mink, escaped from their quarters of the Sidewalk Mink Farm, roamed about light hearted and free. They probably wanted to give the new boardwalk the double O, as they confined their activities mainly to the thoroughfare, but they also poked inquisitively about nearby henneries but there were no causalities. A little coaxing by the owner, J.J. Sparrow, and an inviting display of choice cuts of porcupine brought safe return of the little fur bearers. An unsuspected enlargement of a wire mesh, caused by the breaking of a single strand, caused all the trouble.

In this 1930's photograph, Winnie Zawistowski, Carl Neilsen, and Steve Zawistowski display the tools and the rewards of a season's work. Photo courtesy of the Jack and Susan B. English Collection.

Frank Wells and Steve Zawistowski display pelts. Photo courtesy of the Jack and Susan B. English Collection.

There's Gold up the Inlet!

At the turn of the century, Seldovia faced a decline in the number of fur bearing animals, and in subsequent years might well have died out as a settlement and fur-trading post had not it received an economic shot in the arm. The event in history that really put Seldovia on the map was the discovery of gold along Turnagain Arm, and north in the Yentna and McKinley districts.

As word of new strikes reached the Lower 48 states, fortune seekers by the thousands crowded the Seattle docks. Men too young or too uncertain to head north during the Yukon and Nome gold rushes in the 1890's now leapt at the chance to claim their own stake. Ocean steamers brought prospectors from all over the world to Alaska.

Most of those bound for the North and interior mining districts were discharged at Seward. There, they faced a long overland trek—hundreds of miles through wild country and imposing mountains—dragging with them all the tools and

Surprisingly though, Sparrow's minks grew not only healthy dark rich coats, but came to be "tame as house-cats," allowing visitors to pet them. [45]

July 1931 found Sparrow well into his second year as a mink farmer, with 100 healthy, friendly little animals. [46] As the Depression gripped the country, it is likely that he pelted off his stock, although no record remains to substantiate this.

With the Depression in 1932 came a drop in the demand for and the price paid for furs of all kinds. Although several farmers continued into the 1940's, most men "pelted off" their entire stock and got out of the business altogether. [47]

A few Seldovians continued to run traplines in the 1940's for seasonal income, among them John Colberg and Clayton Riter at Port Dick, Tony Martin and Fred Hoy near Iliamna, and Billy Carlough and Ronnie Mars. [48]

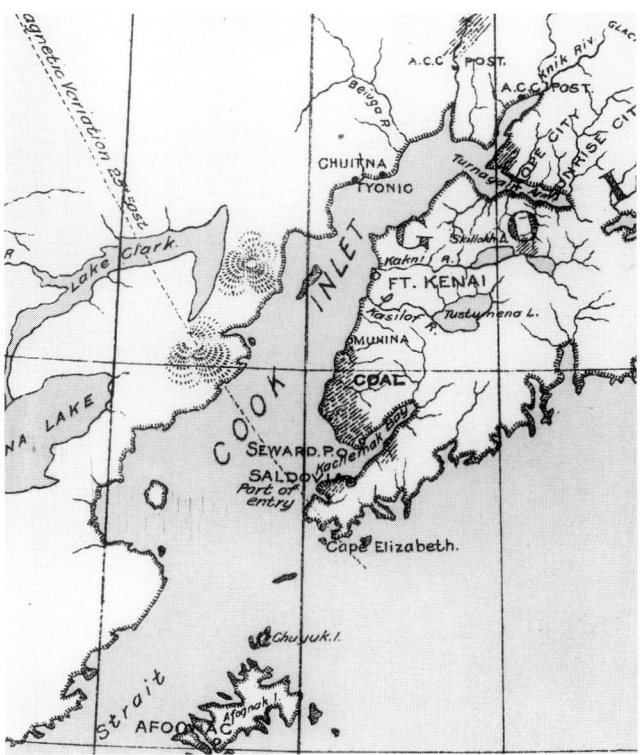

As shown by this 1898 Lowman and Hanford Co. map, "Saldovia" was a port of entry for the upper inlet and interior gold fields before the turn of the century. However, this recognition did not appear to have had a significant economic impact on Seldovia until about 1905. Courtesy of the University of Alaska Fairbanks, Rare Map Collection #G4370/1898/581

supplies needed to live in the harsh north and look for gold. Or, they could board a smaller steamer traveling west to Seldovia. From there, passage on an inlet steamer could be secured and finally, a riverboat engaged to take the prospector and his outfit up the Yentna or Susitna Rivers. This water route drastically shortened the grueling journey by land, and became a popular option for those who could afford it.

Because of its southerly location, Seldovia was one of the few Cook Inlet ports to remain open to navigation through the winter. While the inlet north of Anchor Point and Ninilchik became locked in ice each winter, the southern portion didn't freeze over. This permitted year-round travel between Seldovia and the outside world.

Although the Alaska Commercial Company stations at Seldovia and elsewhere on the inlet readily made the change from supplying trappers to outfitting prospectors, and although the company steamships hustled to carry the latest wave of fortune seekers, it was an independent entrepreneur who positioned himself to take the best advantage of this new traffic up Cook Inlet. As early as 1905, Captain Perl D. Blodgett ran prospectors and their supplies from Seldovia up the inlet on the steamer *Seldovia*.[49]

In 1905, it quickly became evident that there was more traffic than one man and one boat could handle. The Seward Commercial Company operated briefly between Seldovia and Hope, Sunrise, Tionic (now spelled Tyonek) and Knik, with the *S.S. Neptune*.[50] Depending on the weather, boats could usually navigate the upper inlet from mid-May through mid-October before pack ice shut them down for the winter.

Ocean steamers from the Alaska Commercial Company and Northwest Steamship Company discharged hundreds of tons of freight at a time in Seldovia, and because there was no dock, each barrel, box and odd parcel had to be transloaded onto smaller boats which could land on the beach. From these smaller boats, everything was unloaded by hand and carried up the beach to dry land. This process all happened in reverse when the time came to load the smaller inlet steamers with their cargo for the various ports to the north. By October of 1905, Seldovia's waterfront was so choked with freight there was doubt it could all be moved north before ice formed on the inlet. Seventeen head of cattle that

Prior to 1906, vessels bringing gold rush freight and passengers to Seldovia had to anchor and offload onto small dories that came alongside. These dories were rowed to the beach and emptied, and the freight carried above the tideline to wait for smaller inlet vessels. Photo courtesy of the Anchorage Museum of History and Art, O. G. Herning Collection, #B75.134.109

were shipped from Seward to Seldovia were brought back to Seward when it became unlikely that a boat could carry them to Turnagain Arm before winter. In Seward, they were combined with another 35 head who were also waiting to go to Turnagain via Seldovia, and the whole lot had to be driven overland from Seward to Turnagain. [51]

During the spring of 1906, Captain Blodgett had built at Seldovia a new steamer 48' long with a 10' beam and a draft of 3½'. The boat's carrying capacity would be 10 tons and it would be powered by a 15-horse gasoline engine. With this he planned to extend his service from the inlet to the gold creeks. Blodgett would not be the only person to build such a boat at Seldovia, and hence a small side industry was born, helping the economy all the more. [52]

Captain Blodgett's company, the Cook Inlet Transportation Co., in March 1906 leased a brand new California built, 97' steamer, the *Toledo*. This steamer would cover much the same run as the *Tyonic*. Now, in addition to the gold mining traffic, railroad construction brought business to Seldovia, and to Blodgett's inlet boats. Construction of the 85-mile rail route from the head of Turnagain Arm to the head of Knik Arm required the transport of hundreds of men and thousands of tons of supplies. New boats were needed to keep up with the demand. Blodgett planned to add still more boats to the run.[53] To do this, he turned to Captain E.A. Swift, owner of the steamer *Neptune*. Under the banner of the Cook

In this April 27, 1906 photograph, men whipsaw lumber on the beach in Seldovia. This could well be the lumber that would build Captain Blodgett's new steamer. Photo courtesy of the Pratt Museum, # HM-79-13-13

Three years later, in 1909, Seldovia's human-powered sawmill was still operating, as shown in this August 21st photograph by D. F. Higgins. Photo courtesy of the U.S. Geological Survey, U. S. Grant Collection #247

J. A. Herbert's pier, built in 1906, allowed ocean steamers to tie up and offload, a vast improvement over the cumbersome practice of offloading at anchor into dories. The pilings for this pier were driven by hand. Photo courtesy of the University of Alaska Fairbanks, Alaska and Polar Regions Archives, George Talmadge Collection, # 74-18-18

Inlet Transportation Co., Swift met ocean steamers at Seldovia, and carried men, livestock, and freight north to inlet ports. Swift bought a second, smaller steamer, the *Caswell*, and stationed it at Fire Island, off Anchorage. Passengers and freight from the *Neptune* were transferred at Fire Island to the *Caswell*, which carried them up the Shushetna (Susitna) River to the McKinley gold district. [54] Among other notable feats, the *Neptune/Caswell* combination transported nearly 10 thousand sheep and 80 Montana prospectors upriver to the Yentna district to establish a new town. [55]

Blodgett had a knack for joining together with other sea captains and river boat men, pulling them and their vessels under the umbrella of his Cook Inlet Transportation Co., and creating what must have been a very profitable monopoly. His ad from the June 9, 1906 issue of the *Seward Weekly Gateway* illustrates the company's far-reaching operations:

The Cook Inlet Transportation Co. sells tickets and forwards freight from Seward, via Seldovia, to all Cook Inlet points and all points on the Susitna and Yentna Rivers, via river steamers Minx, and Yentna and the Woolsey Transportation Co., and pack trains on the Susitna and Yentna Rivers. Steamer Toledo will call at Seward, Eyak, Valdez, Latouche, Seldovia, and Knik weekly after June 1st. [56]

By July, the freight traffic on the inlet had exceeded all precedent, Blodgett's company having moved over 2000 tons of freight from Seldovia to the upper inlet ports since navigation opened in early April. The tonnage included Alaska Commercial Company freight, supplies for other trading posts at Knik, Tyonik, and Susitna Station, and for Crow Creek Mining Co. on Turnagain Arm. The railroad construction also contributed to the vast amounts of material moving through Seldovia.[57]

Seldovia's new-found importance might have been short-lived had it not been for local merchant J.A. Herbert. Without a dock at which to land the ocean steamers, Seldovia was doomed to the slow, labor-intensive method of lightering freight to shore in smaller boats. Herbert saw that a dock could greatly enhance the efficiency of waterfront operations and help ensure Seldovia's continued growth as a shipping center. In the spring of 1906, he began construction on a dock just up Seldovia Bay from town, where deep water was found close to shore. Today we would refer to his dock site as being on the back side of Backer's Island, at Schooner Beach.

The popular S. S. Dora ran for many years between Seldovia and other south-central Alaska ports. Seldovia elder Nick Elxnit's late sister Dora Ursin was born November 2, 1905 aboard the S.S. Dora near Iliamna. Her mother, grateful to the crew, named the infant in honor of the ship. Photo courtesy of the Jack and Susan B. English Collection.

Herbert hired local natives to drive the pilings for the dock. It was done by hand, unlike most later docks which employed steam- or gas-powered pile drivers. Fifteen men and a long rope were required to pull the hammer up to a height sufficient to drive the piles. It was a slow but effective operation, and once set, the pilings were as good as stone.[58] The stubs of quite a number of them can still be seen sticking up from the beach today.

When completed, Herbert's dock protruded 300' out from shore, and was t-shaped so that ocean steamers could tie up at its outermost end. On the dock was built a 200'-long warehouse for storing cargo while it awaited transport to its final destination.[59] One of the ships to call at the new dock was the *S.S. Saratoga*, which when she came here in October of 1906, was the largest passenger ship ever on this run. At 283' with a gross tonnage of nearly 3000 tons, the Saratoga proved that Herbert's dock had opened up a new era in shipping for Seldovia.[60]

When winter set in that year, Seldovia was still choked with freight waiting to be shipped north. The inlet steamer *Tyonic* made her last run of the season at the end of October, leaving the trading posts at Tyonic and Susitna Station woefully understocked to meet the winter trade. All of their merchandise was stored at Seldovia for the winter, save for 40 barrels of bottled beer slated for Knik, which for some unknown reason were returned to Seward to spend the winter.[61] By March, settlers at Knik were out of supplies and in danger of starving. A man named George Palmer set out for Seldovia in a boat, weaving through the dangerous ice-filled inlet, in a brave attempt to secure food. The success of his mission is unknown.[62]

In the spring of 1907, vessel traffic to Seldovia began gearing up for another busy summer season. Steamships such as the *Bertha*, the *Dora*, the *Portland*, the *Saratoga*, the *Yucatan*, the *Santa Clara*, the *Santa Ana*, and the *Pennsylvania* called here regularly, sometimes so crowded that men slept on the open deck. Many of the ships and smaller boats running in and out of Seldovia were powered by steam generated from coal. With its proximity to the coal seams of Homer

The crew of the S. S. Dora in 1905-1906: Captain Z. S. Moore is seated. Identifiable from their insignia are, at far left, the chief engineer, second from left, the 2nd officer, and at far right, the chief steward. Photo courtesy of the Alaska State Library, Clyda Schott Greely Collection, # PCA 66-833

and the coal mine at Port Graham, Seldovia gained yet another spin-off industry in the supplying of coal to the steamships. More on Seldovia's role in area coal mining can be found later in this chapter.

The fall of 1907 caught Blodgett in the same predicament as the year before, and trading stations to the north were again facing winter with a shortage of supplies. Captain Blodgett pushed his luck and ran up through early November, only to have his steamer *Tyonic* get trapped in the ice on Turnagain Arm. Perhaps tiring of the frantic pace, and probably all the more wealthy for the business, Captain Blodgett announced in January 1909 that he was selling his Cook Inlet Transportation Co. fleet to the Alaska Commercial Company. Included in the deal was his trading station at Seldovia. [63]

Following Blodgett's announcement, the Alaska Commercial Company made one of its own. It would locate a new inlet station at Port Graham, citing the deep water and protected harbor. [64] The ready supply of coal there no doubt also influenced the decision. While this was undoubtedly a blow for Seldovia, the Alaska Commercial Company steamers still called here, as did vessels from other steamship lines. Thus there was still a demand for smaller vessels to transport freight and passengers to upper inlet ports. With the absence of the Cook Inlet Transportation Co. from Seldovia, other operators and vessels stepped in. One such firm was the partnership of James Ward and Tom O'Dale, who operated the *Swan*. [65] Among other jobs, they hauled the U.S. Mail from Seldovia to Homer, Kasilof, Kenai, Tyonic, Knik, Hope, Sunrise, and Girdwood. They took over the contract for $2400 a year from the Alaska Commercial Company. [66]

Merchant J.A. Herbert may have decided that with the closing of the Cook Inlet Transportation Co. and the decision of the Alaska Commercial Company to locate elsewhere, the role of Seldovia in area shipping was headed for a downturn. The following year (1908) he sold his dock to William G. Whorf, owner of the Port Graham coal mine. In December 1910, Whorf announced that he intended to establish a cannery at Herbert's old dock in the spring. Seldovia's fish processing industry was thus born.

In 1911, William G. Whorf started the Seldovia Salmon Co., which under various names and owners continued to operate for many years and opened to the door to Seldovia's biggest and most sustained economic boom ever. More about this first cannery can be found later in this chapter in the section on salmon fishing.

In this pre-1914 photograph, a small inlet steamer chugs into Seldovia Bay. Photo courtesy of the Anchorage Museum of History and Art, Thwaites Collection, #B90.3.14

> Seldovian Nick Elxnit remembers his arrival here as a young boy in 1913. He and his family fled to Seldovia from Kodiak following the eruption of Katmai volcano in 1912. He traveled on the steamship *Bertha* and landed at the dock of the Seldovia Salmon Company. From there, his family paid 50 cents a person to be rowed around the point and into town. [67]

With the only wharf in Seldovia doing double duty as both salmon cannery and cargo dock, there now was justification to build another. In 1917 Ralph V. Anderson built a dock and warehouse on Seldovia Bay at the north end of the village. Readers will remember from the chapter "Russian Culture and Influence". Ralph Anderson's wedding to Juanita at midnight on the afterdeck of a steamship. Now, instead of being merely a transhipment post for freight and passengers, Seldovia was becoming a destination. A growing fishing industry drew people to settle here, and brought in countless seasonal workers.

In an essay written for this book, Ralph Anderson's son, Ted, describes the many services performed by the Anderson Dock Company:

> Anderson Dock Company acted as agent for the Pacific Steamship Company from January 1918 until May 1933. During this period Seldovia became the principal distribution point for all freight destined to Cook Inlet settlements: Kenai, Kasilof, Homer, Illiamna, Snug Harbor, Port Graham, Halibut Cove, Knik, Ninilchik, and to some extent Anchorage. The freight that was discharged in Seldovia at the Anderson Dock from large ships was then transhipped on smaller vessels to the various outports...The salmon and herring packed in Seldovia and to some extent from outports was usually loaded aboard the ships as general cargo was being discharged. This resulted in revenue for the Anderson Dock Company from both inbound and outbound cargo.
>
> The large ships from Seattle that called regularly at Seldovia carrying passengers, cargo, and mail from 1918 through May 1933 were as follows:
>
> S.S. Admiral Watson   S.S. Admiral Evans
> S.S. Admiral Sansome   S.S. Admiral Farragut
>
> The smaller vessels [such as] S.S. Dora, S.S. Starr, and M.S. Fern carried passengers, cargo and mail from Seward to Seldovia and points West to Unalaska.
>
> In 1927 Ralph Anderson was able to convince the Standard Oil Company of California to install tanks on the hill behind the dock and pipelines to the dock for selling gasoline, diesel, distillate and kerosene to all the canneries and vessels in the Cook Inlet area, including Anchorage. [Nick Elxnit notes that the land where the oil tanks were built and still stand was sold to the Andersons by a native with the distinctive nickname of "Contrary Gus". He was also known as "Gloomy Gus".] Practically all of the fishing vessels and cannery tenders were powered by gas engines, some of which could burn distillate that was cheaper than gasoline at that time. Anderson Dock Company was the agent for Standard Oil and received commissions from the products sold. The M.S. Alaska Standard delivered the product to Seldovia from Point Wells, Washington. There were many products such as lube oil, greases, [and] cases containing two five gallon cans of various petroleum products including aviation gasoline that were stored in the warehouse at the head of the dock. [Nick Elxnit recalls working around 1920 on the Anderson Dock, doing longshore work for 6 bits an hour. Freight was moved on four-wheeled hand trucks.]
>
> In May of 1933 the Pacific Steamship Company discontinued operating ships to Alaska and the Anderson Dock Company then became agent for the Alaska Steamship Company. From May of 1933 through September 1947 the large ships from Seattle calling at Seldovia were as follows:
>
> S.S. Lakina   S.S. Oduna   S.S. Derbley   S.S. Cordova
> S.S. Depere   S.S. Denali   S.S. Northwestern
>
> The smaller vessels, M.S. Discoverer, M.S. Kasilof, M.S. Princess Pat, [and] M.S. Monterey carried passengers, freight and mail from Seward and Seldovia to the various Cook Inlet communities.
>
> The Anderson Dock Company was managed and operated by Ralph Anderson until his death in December 1937... beginning [then], Juanita Anderson became the sole owner of the dock and managed it until she sold it to Admiral Carl (Squeaky) Anderson in September 1947. The dock was completely rebuilt about 1939 and specially treated pilings were used instead of the local pilings that had to be replaced regularly. [Ted Anderson recalls the terrible problems experienced with torredo worms, which burrowed into the pilings with such enthusiasm that the pilings soon weakened.] Alaska Seldovia Packers sold the dock and warehouses to Earl Herr about 1949, after which it was sold to John (Dutch) Grootof. [He] in turn sold it to Urban Renewal after the big earthquake. [68]

The S. S. Cordova approaches the Anderson Dock in Seldovia Bay. Photo courtesy of Ted Anderson from the Ralph and Juanita Anderson Collection.

The S. S. Depere dwarfs the Anderson Dock. It discharged general cargo and took on canned salmon. Photo courtesy of Ted Anderson from the Ralph and Juanita Anderson Collection.

Ralph V. Anderson and his dog "Smoky". Photo courtesy of Ted Anderson from the Ralph and Juanita Anderson Collection.

A birds-eye of view of the general cargo aboard a ship berthed at the Anderson Dock. Photo courtesy of William Wakeland, #19G16

On the beach lie local trees, peeled and with their ends shaped in preparation for being driven into the ground as pier pilings. Ralph Anderson's gas boat, the Onyx, sits just offshore. Photo courtesy of Ted Anderson from the Ralph and Juanita Anderson Collection.

Dr. Frederica de Laguna recalls of her time in Seldovia: "Everyone was apt to gather at the Ocean Dock to greet the fortnightly arrival of the steamer, bringing mail, cargo, and new faces from 'Outside'". In this January 1941 photograph, well-wishers watch as a woman boards the S. S. Cordova at the Anderson Dock. Photo courtesy of the Anchorage Museum of History and Art, #B.1.4.40.81

SELDOVIA HERALD
May 17, 1930

New Rates and Service Scheduled by Princess Pat. The M.S. Princess Pat has brought out a new schedule of rates and service applicable to both passengers and freight as follows:

PASSENGER RATES

Anchorage — Seldovia	$12.50
Anchorage — Ninilchik	10.00
Anchorage — Kenai	7.50
Anchorage — Kusilof	7.50
Anchorage — Kustatan	7.50
Anchorage — Illiamna	20.00
Seldovia — Ninilchik	5.00
Seldovia — Kusilof	7.50
Seldovia — Kenai	7.50
Seldovia — Kustatan	7.50
Seldovia — Anchorage	12.50
Seldovia — Illiamna	15.00
Children under 12— one half fare	

The M.S. *Princess Pat*, owned and captained by Tom Perry, was put on the mail run between Seldovia, Iliamna, and Anchorage with points in between in 1926. She was 65' long, with a beam of 13 feet, and a draft of 6' 4". She traveled with an average speed of nine knots, and could carry 21 passengers and 26 tons of cargo. Built in Wrangell in 1919 of cypress planks with a white oak frame, her cost new was $21,800. Perry bought her for $8,200, and together with his crew of two (engineer and deck hand), traveled the inlet. On the 5th and 20th of each month, the *Pat* left her home port of Seldovia for Anchorage. On the 15th of each month, she headed for Iliamna.[69]

Certain ships and their captains and crews became familiar fixtures in Seldovia, and were often entertained in local homes if their vessels had to lay over here. Ted Anderson recalls that Captain Ben Asplin of the *S.S. Denali* was very popular. Ted's father, Ralph, was known to invite visiting captains up to the house for a game of poker and a bit of local moonshine during Prohibition. (For more on local bootlegging, and Ralph's "poker parlor," see the chapter "Life in Old Seldovia.")

Archaeologist de Laguna remembers clearly her last night in Seldovia, in 1932, because of the kindness of one steamship captain:

SELDOVIA HERALD
December 31, 1932

Discoverer Takes Death Plunge in Ice-Filled Inlet, Crew Barely Escaping

The M.S. Discoverer, a 75-HP [illegible] semi-diesel, owned and operated by Heinie Berger, of Kasilof, is reported a total loss, having sunk amidst ice floes, six miles off Ninilchik, midnight of Monday the [illegible]. The boat was on her up-bound trip, discharge of freight having been made at Ninilchik. A quantity of cargo was aboard for Kenai, regarded as probably the final stop. The crew of four men—Heinie Berger, Captain; Jack Wilkensen, Engineer; Oscar Wick, Deckman; Fred Bergmen, Assistant; had a hard time getting to shore. Seizing a few blankets, personal belongings, and some oil, they put off in a life boat, reached the raging surf at 3:30 in the morning. There they abandoned the boat, struggling through the frigid water to the beach. Oil-soaked blankets served as fuel for the fire they obtained only after a struggle with damp matches. After a thawing fest the men struck out for Kasilof, walking the entire distance of 23 [illegible] miles. Later they reached Anchorage by plane. Further details of the disaster are lacking. The Discoverer was a popular carrier, and traveling from Seward to Seldovia and Anchorage, touching all intermediate points, was looked upon as an old friend, and its sinking is regarded more as a personal than a mere property loss.

Charley Sharp planned a magnificent farewell party for our final evening in Seldovia, for we were to leave that night on the steamship. To make room, Charley had all the counters in the store pushed back to the walls, and a trestle table set up for the feast of salmon we were to enjoy. Then there was to be a dance to which about all the townspeople were invited. Alas, the steamer arrived several hours early! And her skipper wished to conduct his business in Seldovia with dispatch and be on his way. That would have spoiled everything. We all begged him to delay the sailing until the scheduled hour, and after refusing several times, he yielded when Charley invited him and his whole crew and the passengers to the party. I don't remember how many came, but the captain himself spent the evening with his old friend, Mr. Anderson, the shipping agent for whom the Ocean Dock was named.[70]

When a favorite ship met with trouble, it was as if an old friend had been lost. People came to trust the abilities of certain captains, and were loyal to them with their business. In 1932 the *M.S. Discoverer* sank

SELDOVIA HERALD
January 28, 1933

Heinie Berger Boat Staunch, Pleasing New 200-HP Craft to Take Place of Discoverer on Inlet Run

Not finding Outside just what he wanted in the way of a boat, Captain Heinie Berger has placed orders for the building of a new one—a motor vessel 75 feet long, powered by a 200 hp Engine. Construction work will be rushed, it being Captain Berger's intention to be on the Inlet run by the end of March. This information has come from Seattle by letter, no further details being given. Before leaving for Seattle the owner of the late Discoverer announced that he was determined to return with a boat in which Seward and the Inlet would take pride and that if he could not be suited in a used boat he would have a new one built to meet requirements. So local friends of "Heinie" are looking forward to something spiffy in the boat line when the new ship is put on the run.

Two unidentified women and a child enjoy the sun on Anderson Dock in 1935. The Alaska Year Round (AYR) cannery is at left.

Looking down at the Anderson Dock, Seldovia, 1935. Both photos courtesy of Ted Anderson from the Ralph and Juanita Anderson Collection.

in the ice-filled inlet. Owner and Captain Heinie Berger was quick to build a replacement. Berger's new boat was delivered to its Seldovia fans at 7 PM on April 7, 1933, and dominated the front page of the next day's *Seldovia Herald*. It was 76' long with a 19' beam, and 17 berths. The new *Discoverer* was capable of making 12½ knots.

A three month Seattle dock workers' strike in the fall of 1946 froze northbound shipping and reminded Seldovia how dependent it was on its sea-link with the outside world. Homer and Seldovia were running dangerously low on food, medical supplies, and livestock feed. Eliza Colberg closed the Seldovia Bakery when she ran out of yeast and could procure no more. Finally, in December, the first of several relief ships arrived, bringing wares for the local stores. Soon after, the strike ended and the normal shipping schedule resumed. [71]

With the construction in 1956 of the Sterling Highway between Homer and Anchorage, and with increased air travel from the Lower 48, the era of the steamship in Alaska was coming to a close. Most inlet ports could now be supplied more quickly and cheaply by road or by air, and Seldovia's role as a major South-central Alaskan shipping hub was finished. Although the Alaska Marine Highway added Seldovia to its route system about 1962, the Anderson Dock saw less and less use. In the 1960's, a new and larger city-owned dock was built slightly north of the Anderson Dock. For many years, the old Anderson Dock was a marine aviary, a haven for Seldovia's resident flock of great blue herons and for resting seabirds of all kinds. This was a great job for the dock in its elderly years, for it was so tumble-down it could no longer support foot or vessel traffic of any kind. The constant ebb and flow of the tide and the fury of winter storms finally took their toll of the old relic, loosening and pulling free its planks and beams, which then presented a hazard to navigation and neighboring docks. In 1994, the Anderson Dock was torn down.

Herring

The herring fishery in Alaska during the early twentieth century was a classic example of conservation measures enacted "too little, too late," leading to the subsequent ruination of a commercial fishery. Prior to 1900, the herring must have been thick in Kachemak Bay - especially in 1849 when Teben'kov's Captain Archimandritov named Seldovia Bay after the fish.

As early in the twentieth century as 1913, the industry was faced with periodic lean years, when the herring run was light in number or size of fish. Voices were raised in concern for the future of the fishery, citing ruthless fishing practices and the use of herring for fertilizer and oil, but these individuals were largely dismissed as alarmists. As a matter of fact, the popular opinion was that the native subsistence practice of gathering herring eggs for food did more to damage the runs than the use of adult fish for fertilizer. There was even a call to prohibit this traditional fishery, while people continued to disregard the possibility of controls on the commercial sector.[72]

Commercial halibut fishermen, concerned about maintaining a supply of herring for bait purposes, were particularly against the use of herring in manufacturing oil and fertilizer. There was advocacy for employing gillnets rather than purse seines in the harvest of herring for salting. The gillnets would capture only the larger fish which were required for the salt market and allow the smaller fish to pass through unharmed. This stood in contrast to the purse seine, which captured all sizes of herring, requiring that the smaller fish be discarded later as waste. Despite these forward-thinking recommendations, little was done to curtail the waste.[73]

Several economic factors both in the Lower 48 and on the world market conspired to suddenly make Alaskan brine-salted and pickled herring an attractive and in-demand commodity. In 1912, freight rates for barrels of herring dropped by 20% on shipments eastward from the West Coast. For the first time, this enabled Alaskan fishermen to compete with imported herring from Scotland. The market was particular however, demanding fish of uniform size, with fat, thick bellies, and requiring perfect curing and packing practices. Barrels of 450 to 550 fish commanded optimum prices, and although smaller fish could increase the per-barrel quantity, the price decreased accordingly. Hence, the impetus to pack only the "cream of the crop," was set in place, leading to the inevitable waste of smaller fish at the cannery.[74]

By 1918, World War I thwarted the usual imports of herring from Scotland and led to the active development of the fishery in Alaska.[75] The herring boom brought people into Seldovia as nothing had

The herring fleet at Seldovia in 1922. Photo courtesy of the Pratt Museum, #HM-79-13-11

done before. The growth of the population and its prosperity are looked upon fondly by old-timers as Seldovia's gold rush.[76] Little data is readily available about the herring fishery in Seldovia prior to 1919, although small scale processing of herring was taking place. In 1915, Ralph V. Anderson and J.D. Nordyke smoked herring for the New York and European markets.[77] In 1919, some of the first figures for a herring processor on the bay were reported, coming from Teets Fish Co., who packed 900 barrels of Norway-style herring that year.[78] By 1924, the *Pacific Fisherman's Yearbook* was disclosing that Cook Inlet herring, while large in size, were noted for having a coarse-textured flesh. This, when taken together with the fact that they were customarily packed in the winter when they were full of milt and roe, contributed to their lukewarm reception in the market. It was found that if herring were caught before reaching their spawning grounds in Halibut Cove, they were generally in better shape. Although more of the herring waste was utilized than in previous years, there still were no conservation rules in place.[79]

The herring runs in 1923 and 1924 were very poor, so the supply decreased and yet the market demand remained high. This drove up prices and led to the acceptance of poorer quality fish in the marketplace. The *Pacific Fisherman* of 1925 reported that in the first few months of 1924 the market was stocked with and dealing in Cook Inlet herring, which had historically been in less demand (one would presume due to their coarse texture). Once that was sold out, the fresh herring from more desirable fishing districts commanded the high price of $30 per barrel. When the Cook Inlet winter pack of herring hit the market, it thus moved very slowly. That December in the inlet was a very cold month resulting in frost-bitten fish, which didn't cure as well and hence were more prone to spoilage.[80]

Despite the sluggish sale of Cook Inlet winter-packed herring, the spring run of 1924 boasted large fish of good quality. In this turbulent business climate, the number of herring processors in the area began slowly to increase. Many companies were very small, others quite temporary. Nonetheless, they all contributed to the local economy and took away a share of the local resource. This pattern of transient "outsiders" harvesting local fish would become more pronounced over the next few years.

In 1924 in Seldovia, the M & M Packing Co. leased part of the old Northwestern Cannery at Schooner Beach, and the Herring Island Packing Co. established itself in Seldovia as well.[81] Although the season started off slowly, Seldovia and Halibut Cove ended up being the hub of activity in the fishery from fall through December of that year, and processors from other districts sent their crews to this area to work.

I ran across a sad but interesting story about the M&M Packing Company while conducting general research for this book. The M&M Packing Company was started in 1924 by two young businessmen, Messrs. McIver and McNab. They had been in operation but a few months when a disastrous fire destroyed their plant in September. Nothing was left untouched by the fire; the four-story living quarters, offices, wharf, and outbuildings all burned. The fire started in the sleeping quarters, in one of the women's rooms. By the time it was discovered the blaze was out of control, and its rapid spread through the old building forced some occupants to jump from the second story. Those on the fourth story were compelled to slide down ropes to safety. The meager insurance policy did not begin to cover the estimated $20,000 in losses. Nonetheless, the following week, Mr. McIver was in Seward seeking material with which to rebuild the facility. The only bright spot in the whole affair was that the plant had just shipped out its first pack of several thousand barrels of salted herring. Had these been sitting on the dock, they too would have been consumed by the fire.[83] The partners somehow managed to finish the season, packing 5,000 barrels of herring.[84] It is unknown whether the M&M partners continued to do business in Seldovia after 1925. Their names are not listed in the *Pacific Fisherman's Yearbook* as salting herring in the years subsequent to 1924, but perhaps they entered into partnership with other entrepreneurs here.

> Mr. McIver was remembered in verse as one of the subjects in "The Old Gang", a poetry column by Pat Cotter, which appeared regularly in *The Alaska Weekly*:
>
> *McIver from Seldovia,*
>   *where he grabs the herring small*
>
> *Is now in fair Seattle,*
>   *to make his winter call*
>
> *To size up all the flappers,*
>   *and take in all the shows*
>
> *And get his optics brimful,*
>   *before he Northward goes.*[82]

The Alaska Fisheries Act in June of 1924 began to place some controls on the herring fishery. Fishermen could no longer use their nets to block off the mouth of a bay or lagoon where herring were trying to spawn. Purse seining was prohibited in Halibut Cove, as was the dumping of offal. This latter practice was condemned, with many blaming it for damaging the fishery. Finally, a season closure in Cook Inlet was called for January 1 through May 31. The Fisheries Commissioner also ordered that the practice of dumping smaller fish and keeping only the larger would stop.[85]

1925 was a very strong season, with a good market and good returns of fish making up for low prices. It was past years' high prices that had encouraged further expansion by processors. Some companies now positioned themselves to operate in more than one district, depending on the size of the runs. Floating processors increased in number, because they could follow the strong returns from one district to another, season to season and year to year, as the fishery continued its erratic fluctuations.[86]

> Seldovia resident Carl Lindstedt reported that in 1925 there was a floating processor in Seldovia Bay, called the *Salvador*. It was actually an old four masted schooner owned by Libby, McNeil, & Libby, and had been retrofitted from a sailing ship to a herring saltry.* Lindstedt worked at the saltry, earning $80 a month, with 50 cents an hour overtime and room and board as well. These were considered big wages.** Mr. Lindstedt came to Seldovia in the mid-1920's at the age of 19. He arrived from Seattle on another four-masted schooner, the *Alice Cook*. He remembered 52 seine boats tied up at the saltry, and four to five thousand people flowing into town during the summer herring run.[87]
>
> *Personal communication to Darlene Crawford, 10/7/87 letter
>
> **Personal interview with Keith Gain, Susan B. English School, 4/27/80

In 1925, Prince William Sound suffered poor returns, so processors flocked to Cook Inlet and other districts where the runs were stronger. North American Fisheries leased a plant in Seldovia for the fall season, and the Imlach Packing Co. took up operating in the building where the M & M Co. finished up business the year before. In 1925, ten companies were shown as packing herring in Seldovia. Processors ranged from S. Sklaroff & Sons, a Philadelphia company, to local fish entrepreneurs like Frank Raby and Ted Nutbeem.[88]

Imports from Scotland were down in 1925 due to a poor season there, so the market was ready to absorb the bulk of the Alaskan herring and to pay a good price. First class Seldovia fish commanded $25 per barrel that fall.[89] Beginning with the 1926 season, the closure in Cook Inlet was lengthened so that the fishery now closed on October 15th and did not reopen until July 14th of the following year. The exception was Halibut Cove, which was permitted to be fished with gillnets up through December.[90]

In 1926 there was a poor return of fish to Cook Inlet and the market was also poor. Prices fell sharply due to inventory carried over from 1925. Processors accordingly curtailed their operations, waiting for better prices. The back inventory was finally moved and the summer pack of Seldovia fish ended up bringing the attractive price of $35 per barrel. Because of the poor late season run in 1926, and the shorter season, prices remained strong.[91] More new firms jumped into the fishery, with B. Bortz taking over Imlach Packing's Seldovia plant. The Crescent Herring Co. and the Latouche Packing Co. added Seldovia to their list of operating sites. Eighteen companies packed herring in Seldovia in 1926. In addition, the following Seldovia residents sold packs of 100 barrels or less to canneries in Halibut Cove: R.V. Anderson, H.L. Dennis, Charlie Engstrom, John Leiren, Ted Nutbeem, and Andrew Ursin. Many of the companies listed as operating in Seldovia that year were firms that sent crews here in the fall and early winter, hoping for a good late season run to supplement their poor showings elsewhere. They were disappointed, however, when the late season Cook Inlet run was below expectations.[92]

Perhaps weary of the up and down nature of the fishery, Pacific Coast processors formed the Pacific Herring Packers Association in 1926. Their mission was to protect and preserve the fishery, promote high operating standards among their members, encourage marketing, etc. Unfortunately, their efforts came too late for the Cook Inlet fishery: its days were numbered.[93]

1927 was another poor year, disappointing the new companies who took up operation in Seldovia, among them the Enterprise Packing Co. and Johnson & Peterson Packing Co. As in previous years, processors pulled out of Prince William Sound after a poor early season, and transferred their activities to Cook Inlet, accounting for some of the twelve companies reported to have done business in Seldovia that year. Axel Anderson and John Colberg were two new local faces in the processing business.[94] Even though this was not a banner year, great numbers of fishermen flocked to Seldovia,

Barrels of salted herring lay dusted by an early snow in front of the old post office in Seldovia in the winter of 1927/28. Photo courtesy of Ted Anderson from the Ralph and Juanita Anderson Collection.

swelling the local population to nearly 1200. Fifty to sixty boats crowded Seldovia Bay, and were rewarded when at the last minute (Oct. 15th) the season was extended for almost another month. Shortly after the announcement of the extension, the fall run of herring began to show in respectable numbers. [95]

Despite the poor initial returns of fish, the market was strong, with high prices paid. Fish brokers had very few good quality imported Scottish herring available and realized that the Alaskan production was down, so for processors it was "their" market. Seldovia fish were reported to have brought $40 per barrel in September of 1927, and only a few dollars less than that earlier in the year.[96]

Fishing was better in 1928, but the same was the case in Scotland. Imports of Scottish herring, with a duty of only one cent per pound, gave stiff competition to Alaskan packed fish. So, even though more fish were packed in Alaska than the year before, profits did not increase accordingly. Other market factors changed the fishery this year as well. For the first time, fish from the Aleutian Islands flooded the market. Fish brokers found they preferred these herring less than those from the tried and true districts, so the inventory sat in Lower 48 warehouses and made the overall market sluggish. In addition, a large U.S. food broker/distributor contracted in advance of the season for almost 90% of the Southeast Alaskan production of herring. Alaskan processors got less money, but felt relieved at having the chore of marketing their pack taken away. The scheme backfired, however, because east coast consumers rebelled at the monopoly of supply and turned instead to Scottish imports. [97]

In 1928, Prince William Sound had one of the poorest seasons yet, resulting in the customary rush to Cook Inlet and other districts. Seldovia in 1928 reached an all-time high of 22 processors (two of the companies operating floating plants). The party was soon to be over, and the fishery changed forever. With the war over, Scotland was again able to export herring to the U.S. Import tariffs were still ridiculously low, and the Alaska Packers lobbied Congress in 1929 to change that. [98] It would not, however, prove to mend a fishery irreparably torn by years of overuse and waste.

The herring resource in Cook Inlet began its crash in 1929, when, despite large numbers of returning fish, very few were of the size and quality required for successful salt-curing. Processors turned to Dutch Harbor and the Aleutian Islands for their fish, virtually abandoning Seldovia. The *Pacific Fisherman's Yearbook* processing report for 1929 shows not one company operating out of Seldovia. What a dramatic change from the previous year! [99]

An added slap in the face was the failure of Congress (bowing to consumer pressure) to increase the tariff on imported herring.[100]

The Anderson Dock in 1929 was busy with the M. S. Princess Pat alongside the M.S. Chacon at the end of the dock, the 65' halibut schooner Decorah in the foreground facing right, and herring seiners in back at right. Photo courtesy of Ted Anderson from the Ralph and Juanita Anderson Collection.

1930 was another poor year for the Cook Inlet run.[101] The herring boom in Seldovia was over. Even by 1932, the arrival of herring at a Seldovia cannery was something of an occasion:

An isolated pack by Cook Inlet Packers was reported in Seldovia for the year 1935, but the run never truly recovered.[102] Today, a small spring run of herring returns to Seldovia Bay where they are gillnetted for personal use, their numbers being too few to enable a commercial fishery.

Seldovia Herald
July 23, 1932

Local Saltery Busy Packing Herring

Seldovians got an old time thrill Monday morning when the M.S. Princess Pat, loaded with herring, docked at the saltery. The fish came from Malina Bay, and were lifted from the pound of the San Marco Fish Co. The trip had been made to Iron Creek with barrels of salt, and to expedite packing, Captain Fred O'Neil brought 150 barrels of the fish to Seldovia. Workers got busy at once and toiled until one o'clock the following morning to complete the job of packing. The Pat will repeat the trip, making other deliveries. The fish are uniform in size, all going into the barrel.

Smelly Seldovia...

Former resident Steve Zawistowski came to Seldovia on July 12, 1930, and his first impression of the town was its terrible smell. Years of dumping herring offal on the beaches below the waterfront canneries had defeated the cleansing effect of the tides. The beaches were fouled with the fishy residue of Seldovia's economic boom. Steve said that when the wind was right you could smell Seldovia as far north as Anchor Point! Here in town, it could make your eyes water. At one point, an effort was made to use the herring offal in the manufacture of fertilizer. Local waste and waste from the cannery at Port Graham were "cooked" in big furnaces and shipped from Seldovia in 100 lb. sacks to the Lower 48. Sadly, though, the deleterious effect on the marine food chain had already taken place.[103]

Pickled Food Herring Packed at Seldovia since 1913
As Reported in *Pacific Fisherman's Yearbook* - Figures shown are in barrels

Year		
1919	Teets Fish Co.	900 bbls.(Norway style)
1924	M & M Packing Co.	2000 bbls. and 2500 half bbls.
	Utopian Fisheries Co.	1137 half bbls.
1925	R.V. Anderson	203 bbls.
	Franklin Packing Co.	(stats for Seldovia are grouped with other villages)
	Imlach Packing Co.	2769 bbls. and 4175 half bbls.
	Jacobsen & Stemland	93 bbls. and 140 half bbls. (incl.Kodiak Island)
	Libby, McNeill & Libby	2184 bbls. and 2029 half bbls.
	Nassau Fish Co. (floating)	2000 bbls.
	North American Fisheries	1924 bbls. and 2608 half bbls.
	Nutbeem, T.	17 bbls.
	Raby, F.	27 bbls.
	S. Sklaroff & Sons	1021 bbls. and 2804 half bbls.
1926	Bortz, B.	2977 bbls. and 2557 half bbls.
	Crescent Herring Co.	353 bbls. and 288 half bbls.
	Culber Bros.	212 bbls. and 51 half bbls.
	Eide & Sutter	200 bbls. and 50 half bbls.
	Everett Pacific Fisheries	898 bbls. and 830 half bbls.
	Franklin Packing Co.	(stats include Port Ashton, Shuyak, and Seldovia)
	Gissberg & Co.	117 bbls. and 6 half bbls.
	Herring Bay Packing Co.	1051 bbls. and 1645 half bbls.
	Latouche Packing Co.	(stats include Latouche and Seldovia)
	Libby, McNeill, & Libby	747 bbls. and 782 half bbls.
	Nassau Fish Co. (floating)	(stats include Kodiak Island and Seldovia)
	North American Fisheries Co. (floating)	(stats include Kodiak Island and Seldovia)
	Opheim & Svendsen	(stats include Shuyak and Seldovia)
	Reese & Buvick	243 bbls. and 146 half bbls.
	Sandvik & Olsen	84 bbls. and 109 half bbls.
	San Juan Fishing & Packing Co.	3599 bbls.
	S.Sklaroff & Sons	1378 bbls. and 1295 half bbls.
	Sundsbye, H.	196 bbls. and 139 half bbls.
	Utopian Fisheries	883 bbls. and 1442 half bbls.

The following Seldovia residents packed less than 100 bbls. each at Halibut Cove:
R.V. Anderson, H.L.Dennis, Charlie Engstrom, John Leiren, Ted Nutbeem, Seward Trading Co., and Andrew Ursin.

Year		
1927	Crescent Herring Co.	(stats include Shuyak Strait and Seldovia)
	Enterprise Packing Co.	(stats include Sawmill Bay, Shuyak St. and Seldovia)
	Everett Pacific Fisheries	215 bbls. and 16 half bbls.
	Feinson, S.	1170 bbls.
	Johnson & Peterson Packing Co.	(stats inlcude Seldovia and Prince William Sound)
	Latouche Packing Co.	(stats inlcude Latouche and Seldovia)
	Libby, McNeill & Libby	400 bbls. and 300 half bbls.
	Nassau Fish Co. (floating)	(stats include Seldovia and other villages)
	North American Fisheries (floating)	(stats include Kodiak Island and Seldovia)
	San Juan Fishing & Packing Co.	971 bbls. and 525 half bbls.
	Shuyak Packing Co.	(stats include Kodiak Island and Seldovia)
	S.Sklaroff & Sons	993 bbls. and 957 half bbls.

The following Seldovia residents packed less than 100 bbls. each at Halibut Cove:
Axel Anderson, John Colberg, and John Lien.

Year		
1928	Aurora Fish Co. (floating)	(stats include Prince William Sound and Seldovia)
	Buvick, D.	121 bbls. and 46 half bbls.
	Collin, C.	81 bbls. and 21 half bbls.
	Colberg, John	73 bbls. and 80 half bbls.
	Enterprise Packing Co.	(stats include Prince William Sound, Seldovia, and Dutch Harbor)
	Feinson, S.	150 bbls. and 49 half bbls.
	Gisberg, E. A.	24 bbls. and 2 half bbls.
	Iverson, Ted	197 bbls. and 62 half bbls.
	Johnson & Peterson	(stats include Prince William Sound, Seldovia, and Dutch Harbor)
	Johnsen, Hjalmar	29 bbls. and 25 half bbls.
	Kodiak Herring Co.	169 bbls. and 762 half bbls.
	Kvarnes, Arthur	26 bbls. and 11 half bbls.
	Martin, Tony	80 bbls. and 25 half bbls.
	Munson, Fred	7 bbls. and 8 half bbls.
	Nassau Fish Co.	323 bbls. and 187 half bbls.
	North Coast Packing Co.	197 bbls. and 62 half bbls.
	Osmond, Sverre	36 bbls.
	Sandvik, E.	121 bbls. and 110 half bbls.
	San Juan Fishing & Packing Co.	1250 bbls. (includes 850 bbls. of bloater stock)
	Shuyak Packing Co.	399 bbls. and 447 half bbls.
	Strand, Henry	16 bbls. and 15 half bbls.
	Utopian Fisheries (floating)	(stats include Prince William Sound, Seldovia, and Dutch Harbor)
1935	Cook Inlet Packers	84 bbls. and 11 half bbls. (Scotch cure)
1940	Washington Fish & Oyster Co.	(took herring from Seldovia to pack in Kodiak Island)

THE PIRATE OF MACDONALD SPIT

This story has less to do with herring and more to do with the dastardly deeds of a tough old man, but herring were what brought him to the area, so it seems fitting to include the story in this section.

MacDonald Spit is a one-mile-long promontory that juts from the western edge of Kasitsna Bay into the waters of Kachemak Bay. It lies about five miles northeast of Seldovia, and today is home to quite a number of seasonal residents. Archaeological evidence suggests that it has a long history of human use, but it was only in this century that it got its name.

The spit was homesteaded in the first decade of the 1900's by Captain MacDonald, who felt that its location was ideal for a herring saltry and who hoped to get rich from such a venture. The captain began his life in Nova Scotia, the son of wealthy and overindulgent parents. They pushed and coaxed him through school and college, and bailed him out of innumerable scrapes. They had aspirations of him becoming a teacher, but he flatly refused. Over their tearful objections, he studied navigation and secured a place on a well-known ship.

MacDonald was headstrong, well-built and handsome, and left a trail of broken hearted women in every port he visited. He was also a schemer, so he came up with a plan to woo a wealthy Boston matron and convince her to buy him his own ship. He was successful in his ploy, and was never found out, for the woman died shortly after he sailed away on his new vessel.

He headed for the South Seas and made a good living stealing lumber from British-owned islands there and selling it in Australia. He bought a newer, larger ship named *The Pass of Bollmaha* with a Filipino crew. He loaded her with a cargo of stolen mahogany and hid to wait for favorable winds. His hiding place was discovered, however, by the British Navy, who had been alerted by the company that owned the lumber. MacDonald made what he thought was a clean getaway, until he turned around and saw that five ships were giving chase!

He sailed for days with the British Navy in pursuit, and he ordered shot a crewman who questioned his judgment in not surrendering. Luck and good winds were with him, and he outsailed his pursuers. In Australia, the mahogany was sold, and MacDonald ordered the ship repainted and renamed. He stole another cargo of lumber in Australia and took it to China, repainting and renaming the ship again. This was to be his pattern, and he made quite a bit of money at it – so much so that he eventually bought the *Glory of the Seas*, built in Boston in 1850 as the sister ship to the *Flying Cloud*, a famous sailing vessel of the day.

MacDonald and the *Glory* made several trips to Alaska, before he settled on Afognak Island. There he married and had a family, and continued his lawless ways. Finally his luck ran out and the law caught up with him. MacDonald was left penniless. With his favorite son, Captain MacDonald moved to Seldovia and built a two-story home of driftwood and scrap lumber on the spit that today bears his name.

The boy succumbed to tuberculosis not long after, and heartbroken, MacDonald probably lost the will to pursue any more moneymaking schemes. Years later, nearing eighty, he saw his health deteriorating and so went to Kodiak, where he committed suicide rather than die a lingering, lonely death. Captain MacDonald enjoyed his reputation as a black-hearted tough old pirate: he preferred a bad reputation to no reputation at all.[104]

The fish scow in the foreground of this 1906 photograph suggests that commercial fishing may have been taking place in Seldovia then. Photo courtesy of the Alaska State Library, PCA 277, Album 8.

Salmon

Even before Seldovia's herring boom, the salmon fishery was quietly and steadily providing a complementary economy. Salmon salting preceded canning by many years, although the first salmon cannery appeared in Cook Inlet at Kenai as early as 1882.[105] The first cannery in Seldovia was reportedly built around 1910,[106] although, as the fish scow in the 1906 photo above suggests, there may have been commercial fishing activity here earlier.

The *Pacific Fisherman* of 1917 reported that in the previous year, the Columbia Salmon plant at Seldovia was taken over by Northwestern Fisheries Co., and proceeded to give a brief history of the cannery:

> The Seldovia plant was built by the Seldovia Salmon Co. in 1911, and after a checkered career finally went into the hands of a receiver in 1915. In the fall of the same year it was sold by order of the court, and the new purchasers, the Lindenberger interests, organized the Columbia Salmon Co. for the purpose of operating it. During the season of 1916 the cannery made a good pack, putting up about 37,000 cases.[107]

Earlier statistics for the Seldovia Salmon Co. are also found in the *Pacific Fisherman*, where the pack of 1913 was reported as 60 cases Kings, 5870 cases Reds, 222 cases Pinks, and 43 cases Chum.[108] In 1914, they packed 976 cases Kings, 6907 cases Reds, 3716 cases Cohoes, and 16,453 cases Pinks.[109]

The going rate for salmon in Seldovia at the time was three cents per fish for silvers, pinks, or king salmon under 25 pounds. A whopping quarter was paid for king salmon weighing over 25 pounds.[110]

The cannery under discussion here, the Seldovia Salmon Co., was located around the corner from the present small boat harbor and behind Backer's Island, along what is today known as Schooner Beach. It was the cannery started by William Whorf, to whom the reader was introduced earlier in this chapter. The site was that of J.A. Herbert's 1906 dock. The pilings from the old pier are still visible, their stubs standing as silent sentinels on the beach. This is the facility that burned in 1924, while leased to the M&M Packing Company.

Fishtrap Method of Salmon Fishing

The early brainchild, and later the bane, of the Cook Inlet salmon fishery was the fish trap. Traps were built on the beach at low tide. Some were fashioned of poles driven by hand into the beach and were generally destroyed by winter storms and icing, necessitating replacement each year. (If taller poles were needed than were trees available, two poles were simply spliced together, the tip of the lowermost lashed to the butt of the uppermost.)

A fisherman's view of the Seldovia Salmon Company dock and facilities. The scow in the foreground with the sign "S.S. Co. No. 4" indicates the company's ownership. The building in the background with the cupola housed cannery workers. Photo courtesy of Ted Anderson from the Ralph and Juanita Anderson Collection.

Other fish traps employed steam-powered pile drivers to set the poles. Poles were generally made of sturdy, straight young spruce. These vertical poles were driven into the beach in a line which formed a 90 degree angle to the coastline. At the head of this line, farthest from the beach, more poles were driven to form a curious sort of double arrow. Wire mesh (or in the first traps, horizontal boards, placed slightly apart from one another so as to allow the thru-flow of water) was strung along the row of poles, which jutted out from the coastline, and then nets were hung at its outer terminus, around the arrow-shaped trap. At high tide the water covered all but the tops of the poles. Migrating salmon, following the coastline home to their spawning streams, encountered the wire (or board) fence and swam away from the beach to avoid it. They followed the fence until it broke for the entrance to the trap. Thinking they had found clear passage, they proceeded forward, and ..... right into the trap! In some traps, the trap area itself went dry, or nearly dry at low tide, and the fish were removed by hand, using one-tined peughs. In other traps, fish were brought to the surface by a series of ropes which operated nets acting as scoops, or brailers.

Seldovian Nick Elxnit remembers going to Tutka and Little Tutka Bays during the winter to cut spruce poles for the hand-driven fish traps. The men camped on their boats by night, and cut trees for poles during the day. The poles they produced had to be at least 32' long, and were generally 6" in diameter at the butt, or bottom end, tapering to 2" in diameter at the top. The hand traps using these poles were deployed primarily north of Anchor Point. [111] By 1917, floating fish traps were common in areas where the bottom was too rocky or otherwise unsuitable for driving pilings. [112]

Moving the Fish

In the 1910's, other methods of fishing included gillnetting from the beach and seining from rowboats. Nets were heavy linen affairs which had to be tanned before every season to prevent them from rotting. They were floated with Spanish corks and hauled by hand. Nick Elxnit notes that power

This next view of the Seldovia Salmon Cannery is taken from a boat approaching the pier. Note the white tents on the beach at right. These most likely provided lodging for an overflow of seasonal workers. Photo courtesy of the Alaska State Library, Thwaites Collection, # PCA 18-138

Workers in a fish trap lift full nets into their boats. Photo courtesy of the Alaska State Library, Case & Draper Collection, # PCA 39-724

Just outside Seldovia Bay, a pile driven fish trap juts out from the shoreline. Photo courtesy of Ted Anderson from the Ralph and Juanita Anderson Collection.

winches and rollers were not in use yet, so a seining operation required several partners to haul in the fish-laden net. [113] Seine nets first began to be used in Southeast Alaska in 1897, and were found to be quite satisfactory in the silty Cook Inlet waters, where fish could not see the mesh in time to avoid it. [114]

Canneries employed larger boats as tenders, whose job it was to collect the fish from the men scattered at traps and in small seine boats up and down Kachemak Bay, and to deliver the same to the cannery. One of Seldovia's first tenders was the *Glovina*, operated by the Seldovia Salmon Co., and built shortly before 1914. [115] At the height of the season, the tenders often could not keep up with the supply of fish being caught. Nick Elxnit remembers that canneries would entice fishermen away from the fishing grounds to deliver their own catch by offering them extra money. Around 1920, he seined in Lower Cook Inlet at Port Dick for pink salmon in August. The going price was 3½ cents per fish, but for bringing their own fish in to the cannery, fishermen like Nick were paid a bonus of 1 cent per fish. [116]

Larger ships, in the 1500 ton class, plied Cook Inlet collecting the packed salmon from the various canneries and transporting them to the Lower 48 fish brokers. In 1914, the *Chas. E. Moody* and the *Star of Russia*, owned by N.W. Fisheries Co. and Alaska Packers' Assn. respectively, operated in the Inlet, along with smaller steamers such as the *Karluk*. [117]

Salted Salmon

Brine-salting salmon, the method employed since the 1880's for preservation of fish on a commercial scale, reached the height of its popularity in 1918 during WWI. After the war, improvements were made in packing facilities and ships were once again readily available to transport the product to market, so the tendency was to can rather than salt. The consumer grew to prefer canned fish and the salt market dwindled. It enjoyed a brief spurt of modest regrowth beginning in 1929, but by 1932 the effects of the Depression hit the salt salmon market. A substantial portion of the 1931 pack was still sitting

Using single-tined peughs, fishermen spear and toss salmon from their boat into the hold of the waiting tender in the foreground. The tender received fish from a number of boats before it headed back to the cannery. Photo courtesy of William Wakeland, #20G4

Salted Salmon Packed at Seldovia since 1913
As Reported in *Pacific Fisherman's Yearbook*
Figures shown are in 200 lb. barrels

1921	Peterson	42 bbls.
1925	Waterbury, R.	18 bbls. (bellies)
1926	Gissberg, E.A.	16 bbls.
	Johansen, Albert	34 bbls. (including bellies)
	Leiren, John	14 bbls.
	Munson, Fred	8 bbls. (bellies)
	Norstad, Axel	172 bbls. (including bellies)
	Sparks, Ralph	3 bbls. (bellies)
	Swanson, Carl	27 bbls.
	Waterbury, R.	8 bbls. (bellies)
	Wik, A. & Co.	12 bbls.
1927	Babis, Wm. J.	13 bbls.
	Dennis, Henry	16 bbls.
	Johansen, Anton	11 bbls.
	Peterson & Beach	35 bbls.
1928	Kodiak Herring Co.	5 bbls.
	Parsons, J.E.	28 bbls.
1930	Perry, T.O.	10 bbls.
1932	Peterson, Dan	5 bbls. (bellies)

in Lower 48 warehouses in 1932, with the result that new production was sharply curtailed.[118] In 1932 the only entity packing salted salmon at Seldovia was Dan Peterson, who put up a meager 5 ea. 200# barrels of bellies.[119] The apex of salmon salting in Seldovia appears to have been in 1926, when nine individuals and firms reported salt packs. The highest pack that year was 172 ea. 200 lb. barrels by Axel Norstad.[120]

Canning Overview

At the cannery, the salmon were offloaded from waiting tenders and scows. In the early years this was a labor intensive event, but eventually mechanized elevators replaced the efforts of men, saving money for the processor and reducing mutilation of the fish. After unloading, the salmon were sorted according to species and conveyors carried them deeper into the cannery for butchering.

Fishing boats pull up to the pier at the Alaska Year Round Cannery in Seldovia. A net brailer bag was lowered to the waiting boat and the fish loaded into it. Photo courtesy of William Wakeland, # 3R8

The full brailer was lifted onto the dock and released into a box where a worker guided the fish into a chute that carried them into the cannery. Photo courtesy of William Wakeland, # 5R2

clean a little over 3000 salmon per hour.[121]

Cans were shipped from the Lower 48 flattened, in order to save space, and thus had to be reformed at the cannery. Before the invention of the can reforming process, canneries either had to have the materials and machines on hand to manufacture their own cans, or else endure the high cost of shipping cases of pre-formed cans from the Lower 48.

The butchered salmon were washed and inspected, and traveled along the conveyor to cutting machines which sliced each fish transversely, the pieces appropriately sized for the cans they were to fill. Yet another machine filled the cans with fish and a measured amount of salt. Automatic weighing machines sent correctly filled cans along one conveyor toward waiting inspectors. Underweight cans were diverted to a second conveyor, which carried them away to be topped off by hand and then sent back for inspection.[122]

In 1904, the "Iron Chink" was invented and it was touted as a great development in the canning process, as it eliminated the need for Chinese laborers to do the job of butchering and cleaning the fish by hand. One operator guided the fish past a blade which cut off its head, and a second operator guided it to a blade which removed its tail. From there, blades removed the fins and sliced open the belly. Entrails were removed with a rotary gutting blade, and the blood along the backbone loosened. The final touches were administered by a hemp rotary cleaning brush and a stream of water. The fish then left the Iron Chink and continued along the processing line. At its optimum, the machine could butcher and

As they moved down the line, salmon fillets were inspected and cleaned as needed by hand. Photo courtesy of William Wakeland, #3R5

133

Cannery workers topped off underfilled cans of salmon by hand. Photo courtesy of William Wakeland, #5R4

Former Seldovian Jim Busey remembers working for 35 cents an hour in the H.H. Malcolm cannery in 1928, at the tender age of twelve. Jim's job was to "patch the cans", that is to top off any underfilled cans with fish. It was a terribly tedious job, and so he informed the foreman that he'd like to try something else. Fine, said the foreman, you may pack the cans into cases. When the foreman came back a bit later to get Jim to patch some more cans, Jim said that he'd rather not do such dull work. Exasperated, the foreman sent him home, and thus ended after three days Jim's first career.

A year later, with a bit more maturity under his belt, Jim hired on at Cook Inlet Packing and continued there for five years. He worked in the storage loft, taking empty cans from boxes and sending them down a chute to the working areas below. By creatively selecting boxes from the stacks, Jim found that he could create a rabbit warren: a very useful place in which a young boy could hide from the foreman![123]

Cans were shipped from the Lower 48 flattened in order to save on shipping costs. They then had to be reformed at the cannery. Photo courtesy of William Wakeland, #1R5

The next step in the process was a machine which applied the top to the can. The first processing lines sent their cans into a heater to complete a vacuum seal. In later years, this was performed by a separate machine with a vacuum chamber. The sealed cans were sent through a washer and then stacked onto iron trays. The trays sat on a car which ran on trolley tracks on the cannery floor. The tracks led into a retort or giant pressure cooker, where the cans of salmon were cooked. Emerging from the retort, they were washed a final time, and then cooled as quickly as possible to stop the cooking action. Some canneries performed their own labeling, but many others relied on specialized Seattle firms to handle this final step, and shipped the cans unlabelled.[124]

Salmon canned by this process appeared in one pound, tall cans. Cans of different shapes and smaller sizes were also produced regularly, but these were packed by hand, and generally represented the higher-priced product.

The Salmon Fishery in the 1920's and 30's

In 1920 the salmon industry faced a tough year. Most of Alaska was feeling the effect of too-intensive fishing in previous years, and the runs of fish returning to spawn were very light. Storms raged all over the coast, and the cost of several essential items increased. The sale of distillate was discontinued and the price of gasoline rose accordingly. Fishermen demanded and received a pre-season advance of 26%. New regulations restricted fishing in and near the mouths of spawning streams, and use of the popular floating fish trap was also curtailed. Fish traps were robbed by "fish pirates," as in past years, and enforcement was inadequate to catch the thieves.[125]

No new players entered the processing arena, save for a number of small operators and some floating canneries. Two of the latter took up business in Seldovia: Arctic Packing Co. and Charles Myers.[126] Nick Elxnit remembers Charlie Myers's floating cannery, which was anchored up Seldovia Bay by Powder Island.[127] On shore, the Northwestern Fisheries plant remained closed.[128]

Recent immigrants from the Scandinavian countries must have questioned the wisdom of their decision to leave their native lands. In Seldovia in 1920, about 70 men made their living as fishermen for the cannery or the saltery, or as deck hands, engineers, or longshoremen. Nearly half of them immigrated from Norway, Sweden, Denmark, and Finland.[129]

> **From a Seldovia Womens Club Program c.1930**
>
> I love Humpback Salmon,
>   Good old Humpback Salmon,
>   Caught by a real Swede fisherman.
>
> I like crabs and shell fish,
>   They sure make a swell dish,
>   I think your hand-packed clams are fine.
>
> I don't like T-bone steaks,
>   cut from a steer from Texas,
>
> But give me fish,
>   and I don't give a darn if I do pay taxes,
>
> I love Humpback Salmon,
>   Good old Humpback Salmon,
>   Caught by a real Swede fisherman

If it seemed like 1920 was a bad year, 1921 proved that things could indeed get worse. Due to the shortage of fish and to ensuing regulations, *Pacific Fisherman* reported that "More salmon canneries lay idle in 1921 than ever before in the history of the industry."[130] With the Northwestern plant still shut down, the only canneries processing salmon at Seldovia were the Seldovia Canning Co. and Charles Myers's floating cannery.

The industry in 1922 recovered from its two-year depression due to improved market conditions and a stronger return of fish. The regulation prohibiting fishing within 500 yards of the mouth of a stream was expanded to apply to all Alaskan waters. In Seldovia, the only business change was a transfer of the Seldovia Canning Co. to the Seldovia Packing Co.[131]

Alaska Year Round Canneries began doing business in Seldovia around 1923, and for that year and the next they packed in conjunction with Cook Inlet Packing Company. In the spring of 1924, Alaska Year Round Canneries built a mile-long pipeline to supply their operation with fresh water. They also installed an "Iron Chink" and a filling machine.[132] By 1925, Cook Inlet Packing Co. had built its own small new cannery here.[133] A company called Bainbridge Fisheries, which had previously been operating in Seldovia, dissolved that same year. It was a predicted "off year" for pinks, and although other areas in the Central Alaska district enjoyed a good pack, the Cook Inlet run was almost nonexistent. Returns of the other species were light,

Waiting for the Salmon

Our nets are mended, in our dories;
Traps are strung along the shore;
Salmon from the chill salt ocean
Seek their birthplace streams once more.

Every knife is honed to brightness,
Each machine is oiled and set;
Steam is building in the boiler–
Floors are freshly cleaned and wet–

Take that cash crop of Alaska!
Fill those miles of gleaming tin–
Friday food for hungry people!
It's time to start the harvest in!

By John C. Frohlicher

Photo courtesy of William Wakeland, #1R6. Poem by John C. Frohlicher, reprinted from The Alaska Book, *with permission from J.G. Ferguson Publishing Company, Chicago.*

but red salmon saved the day, and kept Cook Inlet Packing Co. and Alaska Year Round Packers in business at Seldovia.

In 1926, Cook Inlet pink and red salmon were plentiful, and good weather further helped the fishery. Two new canneries appeared on the scene in Seldovia: Keller & Fjeldahl, two local men, formed a partnership and Mr. Chambers, another local man, began late in the year building a new plant for the 1927 season.[134] The next year, 1927, was reported to be strong for runs of pink and red salmon in Cook Inlet,[135] and encouraged yet another small new cannery, John Wik Co., to locate in Seldovia in 1928.

Selected Salmon Fishery Articles from the *Seldovia Herald*

SELDOVIA HERALD - May 3, 1930

KAMISHAK BAY REGION CLOSED FOR FISHING BALANCE OF SEASON

In order to increase the escapement of reds in the Kamishak Bay region, orders have been handed down closing that area to fishing the balance of the present season. This was the word that reached Seldovia today. The district has been pretty well fished this season [illegible] reds being an early run fish at that point. The loss to fisherman, however, by the closing order is not alarming, so they say, as the run is practically over. Those spoken to take the order philosophically, agreeing that the restriction under the circumstances, and intended as it is for only the balance of this season, is not an unreasonable one. So they are getting their outfits overhauled, taking on supplies and will hit out for other fishing grounds. The [illeg.] boat "Alice" [illeg.] beach is reported to be high boat to date, being [illeg.] with over 8,000 fish.

SELDOVIA HERALD - August 30, 1930

SALVATORE TO BE MADE ONE LINE FLOATING CANNERY

Axle Anderson and Peter Belmont, joint owners of the schooner Salvatore, formerly owned by the Libby, McNeill & Libby company, plan to transform their vessel into a one-line floating cannery, costs and details involving installation of the plant are now being disoussed. While full arrangements have not been worked out, the thought is to dismantle the ship, stripping it of all unnecessary gear and [illegible] to rearrange the housings to accommodate the canning machinery. The barge will be towed to an inlet point to be selected later, but where fish can be obtained without great transport expense. Misters Anderson and Belmont expect to have their cannery in readiness for next season's operations.

SELDOVIA HERALD - Sat., June 28, 1930

AXEL ANDERSON BUYS LIBBY SCHOONER FOR FISH SALTRY

Rumors of impending sale of Libby's four-mast schooner Salvator, lying at anchor off the Northwestern cannery, at Seldovia, evolved this week into the definite announcement that the transfer has been made, the purchaser being Axel Anderson, of this community. Mr. Anderson is in the employ of the Libby interests at Kenai, and being so much gone on the upper inlet on the fishing grounds, could not be reached for a statement. But it is known that the vessel was a salting station when Seldovia is again blessed with herring. While the schooner is stripped of sails, and much of the loose and small gear that go to make up the rigging and general equipment of the type of ship such as the "Salvator," it is stated that the donkey hoist, a 40 horse boiler and gas engine in good condition are included with the sale. The "Salvator" is one of the real old timers, and is said to have sailed into many ports and upon many seas before being moored in Seldovia bay. In former years, the craft was used as a carrier of canned salmon for the Libby concern, taking down the Kenai pack besided the barreled herring. A few years ago a start was made for the annual trip to Seattle, and came nearly ending in disaster when the old ship was be set [sic] by terrific gales before she had fairly gotten underway. Sails were torn to shreds, and it was only by careful [illegible] the vessel managed to get back to Seldovia. Since then she has been riding at anchor in Seldovia bay.

SELDOVIA HERALD - July 4, 1930

MALCOLM CANNERY PACK EXCEEDS THIS TIME LAST SEASON

Delivery of 8,000 reds, [illegible] caught, was made to the Alaska Year Round cannery yesterday by the gas boat "Defiance". This was the biggest single load of fish brought into Seldovia this season, and places the Malcolm cannery well in advance of its pack at this time last year. Pack today is practically all reds and kings, mostly reds. The work-of-caring for the raw fish on hand was begun at 4 o'clock this morning, the intention being to finish up about the middle of the day and allow all hands to get a kick out of the Fourth of July celebration.

SELDOVIA HERALD

REDS MAY OPEN AT $2.25, SEATTLE REPORT

W. A. Estus, of Cook Inlet Packing co., has been advised by wire that it is generally believed that the opening price on tall reds would be $2.25. The information was also offered that one of the large packers had sold a lot of pinks at 85 cents, and that an offer of 80 cents had been made to the Cook Inlet Co. for their few remaining chums.

SELDOVIA HERALD - July 18, 1930

GOOD FISH RUN KEEPS PLANTS BUSY

The delivery of 10,000 trap fish to the Cook Inlet Packing co. immediately following the Fourth of July week, marked the beginning of a run that has kept the local plants fairly busy since. The Port Graham and San Juan plants have also been faring well, it being reported the Fidalgo cannery received 60,000 fish within two days this week. Plants on the upper inlet have been getting fish, it is stated and in the neighborhood of Kustatan, gill net men are reaping a harvest.

FALL SILVER PACK BELIEVED FAIR

— "Standard" high boat with single haul 2500 fish - Four seines on job —

The A. Y. R. Cannery is starting off with a creditable showing in a fall silver pack, four seines are supplying the plant with fish. To date the high boat is the Standard, operated by Martin Hogansen and Olof Hanson, one haul alone netting them 2,500 fish. While the market on canned silvers is not just now a settled factor, H.H. Macolm is not discouraged by the outlook, but believes that adjustment with return to normalcy in price, is sure to come. Silvers, in reality high grade fish, will come into its own, it was gathered. The Alaska Year Round is the only cannery in this section engaged in fall canning.

The Great Depression Weakens the Salmon Fishery

By 1931, in a poor national economy, the market demand was down and processors in response packed fewer fish. Alaska Year Round Canneries (AYR) hung on in Seldovia, as did Cook Inlet Packing Co. The modest flurry of smaller operators from the 1920's dwindled. Throughout the 1930's, this would be the pattern: AYR and Cook Inlet Packing complemented by one or more smaller packers, the players changing year-to-year.

> **SELDOVIA HERALD - June 27, 1931**
>
> ## SELDOVIA REDS FIRST OUTGOING SHIPMENT
>
> The first salmon shipment from this district, was made on the last sailing of the Admiral Evans, a consignment of 500 cases tall reds going forward from the Cook Inlet Packing co. W. A. Estus, head of the company, sees no immediate change in the salmon market as to advance price, but a large movement in pinks last month, and prior sales of reds, have done a lot toward reducing the size of carry over stocks and should go a long way toward creating a more balanced trade for fourthcoming packs. New, or opening prices general observers state may not be expected until the Bristol Bay pack is announced.

In 1931, regulations began gradually reducing the number of fish traps licensed in Alaska and the areas in which they could operate.[136] In 1933, even greater reduction was seen in the number of fish trap licenses issued. From a 1930 peak of 701 traps in operation, the next few years saw that number decrease to just under 400, although some of the traps sat idle due not to regulation but to the economy.[137] The face of the salmon fishery was slowly changing from an industry controlled by large Outside interests to one with greater opportunity for individual fishermen. However, it would not be until Alaska statehood in 1959 that fish traps were altogether banned.

> **SELDOVIA HERALD - August 26, 1931**
>
> ## NEW ASSOCIATION WORKS IN HARMONY WITH BROKERS TO QUICKEN FISH DISTRIBUTION
>
> What cannot escape being of interest to Seldovia fishermen and packers are the stories coming from Seattle regarding the activities of salmon packing interests to stimulate sales of the canned article. The stagnation of salmon sales, especially pinks, has become such a problem that the Northwest Salmon Canners Association has joined forces with the Pacific Canned Salmon Brokers Association in an intensive campaign of advertising calculated to create demand for the product. [illegible] shows some unusual and rather startling figures, in the view of the interests involved. These figures are based on reports from 81 canneries, representing 85 per cent, of the 1929 pack:
>
> | | Cases |
> |---|---|
> | Steel-head | 1,070 |
> | Kings | 32,806 |
> | Sockeyes (Puget Sound) | 25,941 |
> | Alaska Reds | 50,757 |
> | Silvers | 20,555 |
> | Chums | 360,346 |
> | Pinks | 1,009,074 |
> | Total: | 1,600,549 |
>
> The Northwest Salmon Canners Association is a new organization, starting some months ago in Seattle through a sort of get-together movement among smaller packers.

SELDOVIA HERALD - Dec. 12, 1931

NEW RULES TO REDUCE GEAR

— Short season, short nets are reported Inlet features season 1932 —

A reduction of gillnet lengths to two fathoms, a regulated fishing distance of 1000 feet from any trap instead of 600 feet as formerly, with the opening date for the season set for June 25 mark the most radical change as reported for the 1932 fish law as applied to Cook inlet.

— Trap area closed —

That there will be new closed areas established for traps is believed to be true, and the East Foreland district has been maintained as being affected. These fish news items were contained in a letter from W.A. Estus, received by Captain Gene Mason in the last mail. Mr. Estus' information did not come from the printed law, as the 1932 issue was not at that time released. He had been talking with authorities however, and had no doubt but that what he was saying were the facts.

— Salmon seized —

Mr. Estus also mentioned that it had just been broadcasted out of San Francisco that a seizure of 37,000 cases of salmon, accounted impure pack had just been made in Seattle, and that further seizures were expected within a few days. No suggestion was made regarding the ownership of the fish. Local fishermen are much concerned over the reported added gillnet restrictions. Early alarm that such regulations would be made effective for 1932 was lulled to rest by authoritative statements that nothing of the sort was in mind. It is understood that regulations would not be issued in printed form until January 15.

SELDOVIA HERALD - May 21, 1932

REDS PLUNGE TOWARD $1.75, WHILE [illegible] PRODUCT TUMBLES PINKS

The report prediction that red talls would go as low as $1.75 per dozen seems in a fair way of being fulfilled, judging from information received in the last mail by W. A. Estus, head of the Cook Inlet Packing co. Therein reds are quoted $1.80 to $1.90 with little interest being shown on the part of the buyers. Pinks have flopped to .85$ a low level reached when the Japanese article was offered in certain market [illegible] delivered to buyers. At least one Eastern broker predicts that reds will go as low as $1.25 but Western men are not looking under $1.75. Anything might happen to pinks, and no surprise will be felt if the price goes to .75$ F. O. B. Pacific coast points. Following are prices quoted May 4: Pound talls-chum, 80 cents; pink, 50 cents; silver, $1.15; reds, 1.50 [illegible] Half pound flats-pink, 60 cents; silver, 95 cents; red, $1.35; Puget Sound sockeye, $1.50;

The Brokers Association reports sales the last week in April amounting to 22,000 cans leaving the following stocks on hand as of May 1.

Chinooks and Kings, 126,696; Sockeyes and Reds, 502,041; Silver, 152,656; Pink, 1,402,003; Chums, 142,393; Bluebacks, 64; Steelheads, 5,262. [*Author's note: These figures should be taken as approximate since the legibility of this newspaper article on microfilm was poor.*]

Fish prices were a big worry during the Depression. Fishermen and processors could only watch helplessly as despite their best marketing efforts, salmon sales were sluggish and prices continued to fall.

> **SELDOVIA HERALD - August 6, 1932**
>
> ## REDS DROP TO $1.25, WITH COHOES AT 90 CENTS
>
> Low ebb in prices for red salmon has been reached, according to advices just received by W.A. Estus, in which reds were quoted at $1.25 per dozen, kings $1.10, cohoes 90 cents and pinks 75 cents. The appalling figure to Mr. Estus is the $5 per case for red salmon and he is unable to see how he can come out without great loss. The Cook Inlet's next to the last delivery of 18,000 fish was divided between the company's plant and Snug Harbor, the latter having received 12,000, this being the fish stowed in the ship's hold. The deck-load and scow fish were canned in Seldovia.

> **SELDOVIA HERALD - 1932**
>
> ## REDS $1.25
>
> With red talls selling at $1.25, pinks 80 cents, kings $1.00, there is nothing cheering in the immediate salmon outlook in effect, writes W.A. Estus, head of the Cook Inlet Packing Co. But he is laying his plans for 1933 season operations and hopes for better things by the time the pack is up and on Seattle docks.

The years 1936 through 1940 were marked as some of the best production years ever on Cook Inlet, although stormy weather and persistent trouble with labor unions marred the good fortune. Nonetheless, Seldovia's Cook Inlet Packers made some improvements to its fish elevator equipment and installed a new high-speed can filling machine. The Puget and Alaska Canning Co. in Seldovia was replaced by Capt. C.E. Anderson's Kodiak Island Fishing, Trading, and Packing Co. [138]

Working in the Cannery: Elsa Pedersen's Reminiscences

Writer and historian Elsa Pedersen lived in Seldovia during the height of the salmon fishing years. The following narrative about a cannery worker's day is based on her unpublished manuscript *Kachemak Bay Story*, and is used with her permission.

Elsa worked as an assistant bookkeeper for the Seldovia Bay Packing Company, and her days were long but varied. She began before 7 a.m. as she listened to the cannery superintendent call each tender on the radio. The tenders gave reports regarding the number of fish they were bringing in and relayed requests from the fishing boats for groceries and engine parts. Elsa took these requests to the appropriate parties, in person if necessary, as there was no telephone system in town.

At 7:30, breakfast for the cannery workers was announced with a loud horn. Sixty people came running, ate quickly, and left to relax for a few moments before heading back to work. Most employees were local residents, but there was a small bunkhouse for transient workers. A whistle sounded over the town to call employees to work. When an unexpected delivery of fish was brought in, Elsa rode the cannery's bicycle from house to house, rousing the workers. Elsa's day finally ended with the last scheduled radio call, at 8:15 p.m.

The pace at the cannery was leisurely until the first week in July when red salmon began to flood the Inlet. Once full boatloads of salmon began arriving at the dock, everyone operated at full capacity, with little time for anything but work, nourishment, and sleep. Although workers got a 15-minute cookie and coffee break every two hours, they still flocked outside for an unanticipated rest when something went awry with the machinery on the production line and temporarily shut things down. [139]

The Wartime Fishery

Although the United States' official entry into the Second World War did not come until December of 1941, that entire year was marked by frenzied wartime preparations, and these affected the Alaskan salmon industry.

In Britain, already war-torn, demand for canned salmon was high, and the United States government began buying it as well for our own growing armed forces. For the fishing industry, however, the first of many wartime obstacles to production was beginning to be felt.

With the increased demand for government and industrial shipping, many of the vessels that would otherwise have been carrying workers and supplies to Alaska and cases of canned salmon back to the Lower 48, were being sold or leased to the government. Cannery scows, tenders, and fishing boats were also pressed into patriotic service. Seasonal workers became more difficult to find and the labor unions, by combining to increase their bargaining power, didn't help matters. Topping all this was a stormy season in Cook Inlet. One of Seldovia's long time canneries, the Alaska Year Round Cannery, didn't operate, but it did spend the year making substantial physical improvements. It built a new larger dock and a fish house and warehouse, as well as installing a high-speed canning line and two retorts.[140]

In the first year of participation in active fighting, the United States' demand for canned salmon increased all the more, but so did the hardships faced by the industry. The War Shipping Administration took over all transportation in Alaska, so canneries were utterly dependent on the government to move their workers, supplies, and finished product. As the Aleutian Islands became involved in the war, shipping was even further restricted. Canneries had become fairly dependent on radio communications, which now were curtailed. Although unions seemed more cooperative and although many fishermen and cannery workers received draft deferments, canneries were still short-handed, and wages and fish prices rose nearly 30%.[141]

Canneries had to deal with a myriad of government agencies now: two agencies controlled the selling of salmon, a third the price, a fourth and fifth manpower problems, and a sixth arranged delivery of the pack. Ever more agencies and departments became involved, and inter-agency coordination was poor. Cannery owners were scared that they would invest money in pre-season preparations and then be shut down by the war. The government offered insurance policies to canneries, but this concern was not adequately addressed. Fortunately, emergency closures due to the war did not turn out to be a widespread problem.[142]

By 1943, the shortage of manpower, raw materials, and available shipping space on vessels was so pronounced that the government introduced a cannery concentration program. By requiring canneries to pool their resources and produce on a cooperative basis, the goverment was able to reduce the number of workers needed by over 4000 and the northbound freight by 16 tons. This concentration schedule continued in place through 1945, but Seldovia canneries suffered no consolidations because of it.[143]

In 1944, the United States Government was buying around 70% of the canned salmon produced,[144] and Cook Inlet had a pretty good year. Seldovia's Cook Inlet Packing Co. rebuilt its tender, the *Westward*. In a $20,000 improvement program, her length overall was increased to 80'.[145] 1945 was another fairly good year for the Inlet, and the wartime restrictions were eased somewhat. But the issue of Indians' aboriginal fishing rights was being debated in the Interior Department, and other fishing restrictions that had been postponed due to the war were now slated for consideration.[146]

Postwar to Present

The remainder of the 1940's were marked by good fishing years and bad, but all seemed plagued by labor union troubles. In May of 1947, Buckley Douglas, Seldovia agent for the United Fishermen of Alaska, transferred his group's afiliation from the Congress of Industrial Organizations (CIO) to the American Federation of Labor (AFL) and confusion reigned in Cook Inlet fish price negotiations as a result. The National Labor Relations Board (NLRB) stepped in to insist upon an election so that fishermen could "officially" decide which organization they wanted to have represented them in negotiations. The Territorial Labor Department got into the act, deciding to run this election, and the NLRB backed off. Buckley refused to recognize the validity of such an election, and the AFL and the CIO argued over who should be eligible to vote. After nearly a month of haggling, the election which would decide who (the AFL or the CIO) had jurisdiction over the Seldovia fishermen was cancelled by consensus of all parties involved; after all, most of the men who would vote were by this time already on the fishing grounds, having quietly reached price agreements with the local canneries. Squeaky Anderson of Alaska-Seldovia Packers paid the best prices on the Inlet:

> Kings over 12 lbs. 2 dollars . . (up 50 cents from last year)
> Reds and Cohoes . 50 cents . . (up 14 cents from last year)
> Pinks . . . . 12 cents . . (up 2 cents from last year)
> Chums . . . . 16 1/2 cts. . (up 2 1/2 cts. from last year) [147]

Anderson's Seldovia Packers replaced Alaska-Seldovia Packers, and the B&G Cannery operated in Seldovia in 1948. That same year, Alaska Shellfish Co. canned salmon in Seldovia for the first time, and the Alaska Year Round Canneries established its own boat moorings and repair shop in Seattle.[148]

The years 1950 through 1952 were excellent for salmon fishing in the Inlet, but fishing pressure was intense. It was not uncommon for canneries from other districts, such as Kodiak, to carry fish from Cook Inlet back to their own districts to can. Drift gillnetting had increased dramatically from the 1940's. In 1952, 66% of all red salmon in the Inlet were caught by drift boats, with the remainder almost equally split between setnets and fish traps.[149] The industry and the government were so focused on harvesting the salmon that any natural predator of the fish was seen as dangerous competition. Seldovian Fred Elvsaas reports that federal programs designed to curtail salmon predators paid 2 cents per fish tail for Dolly Varden trout (a consumer of salmon eggs), 3 dollars per nose for harbor seals, and 50 cents for a pair of eagle's feet.[150] The rest of the 1950's saw more poor fishing years than good, which was generally attributed to years of overfishing. Despite the poor years, the late fifties saw new players on the Seldovia salmon canning scene, be they only temporary: Everitt & Co., Whitney & Co., and Parks Canning Co.[151]

In 1959, the new State of Alaska prohibited fish traps in all state waters. The Department of the Interior followed suit, banning traps from all federally controlled waters as well. Certain Indian-owned traps around the state were exempted.[152] The 1960's were the last decade for the salmon canning industry in Seldovia, the death knell resounding surely after the 1964 Good Friday Earthquake. For more on the canneries and post-earthquake Urban Renewal, see the chapter, "The Earthquake and Urban Renewal."

It was fortunate for Seldovia that canneries had, decades ago, diversified here, and hence the fisheries for crab, shrimp, halibut, and other bottom fish and the freeze-processing of salmon and other fish extended the life of the fishing industry.

Captain Roy Cole, left, with Lynn Jorgensen, commanded the Bureau of Fisheries vessel, Teal, and was also Fish Commissioner in the Cook Inlet area for many years prior to statehood. Photo courtesy of Ted Anderson from the Ralph and Juanita Anderson Collection.

**Mild Cured Salmon packed at Seldovia since 1913
As Reported in *Pacific Fisherman's Yearbook***

1918	Kachemak Canning & Salting Co.	40 bbls.
1926	Gissberg, E.A.	23 ea. 800 lb. tierces
	Norstad, Axel	8 ea. 800 lb. tierces
	Wik, A. & Co.	73 ea. 800 lb. tierces
1927	Morris, R.C.	5 ea. 800 lb. tierces
1928	Kodiak Herring Co.	12 ea. 800 lb. tierces
1929	Kodiak Herring Co.	9 ea. 800 lb. tierces
1956	Seldovia Bay Packing Co.	81 ea. 825 lb. tierces
1957	Seldovia Bay Packing Co.	42 ea. 825 lb. tierces
1958	Whitney & Co.	336 ea. 825 lb. tierces (kings & silvers)

**Salmon Canned at Seldovia since 1913 - As Reported in *Pacific Fishermans' Yearbook*
Reported in cases (can size generally 1 lb., but some 1/2 lb. are included)**

Year	Cannery	Kings	Reds	Coho	Pink	Chum	Total
1913	Seldovia Salmon Co.		60	5870	222	43	7625
1918	Northwestern Fisheries Co. (statistics include Chignik, Kenai, Orca, Uyak, and Seldovia)						
1920	Arctic Packing Co.		200				200
	Meyers, Chas (floating)	189	1084	1448	712		3699
	(Meyers's statistics include 266 cases of steelhead)						
1921	Arctic Packing Co.		1188				1188
	Seldovia Canning Co.	150	9000	10			9160
1922	Arctic Packing Co.		851				851
	Seldovia Packing Co. (formerly Seldovia Canning Co.)		1402	87		76	1565
1923	Ak Year Round Canneries	12	1941	56		90	2099
	(formerly packed crab meat only, but this year packed salmon jointly with Cook Inlet Packing Co.)						
1924	Ak Year Round Canneries		4728	827	2155	14	7724
	(packed jointly with Cook Inlet Packing Co.)						
1925	Ak Year Round Canneries	113	3000	130	45	56	3344
	Cook Inlet Packing Co.	440	3814	448			4702
1926	Ak Year Round Canneries	582	6565	475	2276	141	10039
	Cook Inlet Packing Co.	442	6146	438	3435	45	10506
	Keller & Fjeldahl (new co.)	242	361	110	133		846
1927	Ak Year Round Canneries	1613	8233	518	2562	85	13011
	Cook Inlet Packing Co.	2352	6064	333	2545	105	11399
	Keller, W.A.	557	248	25			830
1928	Ak Year Round Canneries	759	5095	859	3733	722	11168
	Arctic Packing Co.	3	69	636	576	431	1715
	Cook Inlet Packing Co.	892	3220	487	2185	449	7233
	Keller, W.A.	384	222	58	49		713
	Wik, John (new co.)	78	210	50			338
1929	Ak Year Round Canneries	1057	4800	1264	2662	1369	11152
	Arctic Packing Co.	16	62	190	566	432	1266
	Cook Inlet Packing Co.	382	2253	168	1989	1259	6051
	Wik, John	30	204	36			270
1931	Ak Year Round Canneries	421	2163	2009	3307	16	7916
	Cook Inlet Packing Co.	268	2209	183	1800	71	4531
1932	Ak Year Round Canneries	858	2568	2195	648		6269
	Cook Inlet Packing Co.	760	5684	697	2389		9530
	(CIP statistics include fish from the North Coast Packing Co., Ninilchik, & Kenai River Packing Co., Kenai)						
	Ninilchik Packing Co.	316	400				716
	(canned by Ak Year Round Canneries, Seldovia)						
1933	Ak Year Round Canneries	879	7090	877	1960	75	10881
	Assoc. Fishermen Cook Inlet		1477				1477
	(canned by Ak Year Round Canneries, who also canned for Ninilchik Packing Co. this year)						
	Cook Inlet Packing Co.	936	9610	574	3179	274	14573
1934	Ak Year Round Canneries	551	6801	1694	5694	208	14948
	Puget & Ak Canning Co.	303	3518	483	17827	3722	25853
	(This was a new cannery operating this year.)						
1935	Ak Year Round Canneries	601	2315	1193	2640	469	7218
	Cook Inlet Packing Co.	1276	6033	223	1512	287	9331
	Puget & Ak Canning Co.	45	171	28	12318	3751	16313
1936	Ak Year Round Canneries	434	3571	2030	3721	1140	10896
	Anchor Line Packing Co.	123	358				481
	Cook Inlet Packing Co.	1035	7179	1614	5595	357	15780
	Puget & Ak Canning Co.	513	6356	250	16816	6567	30502
1937	Ak Year Round Canneries	912	3845	1501	2712	146	9116
	Anchor Line Packing Co.	177	253	65			495
	Cook Inlet Packing Co.	1456	4391	238	1483	15	7583
	Puget & Ak Canning Co.	1993	11275	278	9922	4526	27994
1938	Ak Year Round Canneries	900	5222	2235	2242	138	10737
	Cook Inlet Packing Co.	1023	7306	444	3464		12237
	Puget & Ak Canning Co.	1444	19504	1048	7601	4951	34548
1939	Ak Year Round Canneries	502	6839	1947	1325	993	11606
	Cook Inlet Packing Co.	1440	11371	500	171		13482
	Red Mountain Packers Inc.		713		10463	6960	18136
	(formerly operated by Puget & Ak Canning Co.)						
1940	Ak Year Round Canneries	286	3914	2677	6925	248	14050
	Cook Inlet Packing Co.	899	6685	1506	7619	25	16734
	Kodiak Island Fishing,		1834	507	33843	9295	45479
	Trading & Packing Co. (Bought out Red Mtn. Packers.)						
1941	Cook Inlet Packing Co.	943	3492	708	125		5268
	Kodiak Is. F/T/P Co.	73	1535		26295	10444	38347
	(Ak Year Round Canneries transferred its fish this year to General Fish Co. in Anchorage)						
1942	Ak Year Round Canneries	689	2266	3123	6946	982	14006
	Cook Inlet Packing	1293	5678	1947	1447	12	10377
	Kodiak Is. F/T/P Co.		828	4005	22033	22177	49043
1943	Ak Year Round Canneries	4523	6604	2404	13855	1056	28442
	Kodiak Is. F/T/P Co.		465		29609	6432	36506
	Cook Inlet Packing Co.	2615	3780	426	299	27	7147
1944	Ak Year Round Canneries	4917	6299	2246	23695	1657	38814

Salmon Canned at Seldovia since 1913 - As Reported in *Pacific Fishermans' Yearbook*
Reported in cases (can size generally 1 lb., but some 1/2 lb. are included)

Year	Cannery	Kings	Reds	Coho	Pink	Chum	Total
1944 cont...	Cook Inlet Packing Co.	1475	5765	1039	3542		11821
	Kodiak Is. F/T/P Co.		919	127	36616	5733	43395
1945	Ak Year Round Canneries	4564	8568	2209	12884	3884	32109
	Cook Inlet Packing Co.	1310	7650	811	162	28	9961
	Seldovia Packers (formerly Kodiak Is. F/T/P Co.)		647		27749	7398	35794
1946	Ak Year Round Canneries	4168	5124	1937	10339	6951	28519
	Cook Inlet Packing Co.	958	3448	1075	2317		7798
	Seldovia Packers	165	624	40	25604	13944	40377
1947	Ak Seldovia Packers Inc. (formerly Seldovia Packers)	1676	7074	2181	17217	6902	35050
	Ak Year Round Canneries	6286	2428	1273	7793	1242	19022
	Cook Inlet Packing Co.	1824	2655	1208	115	8	5810
1948	Ak Seldovia Packers Inc.	6562	18386	2601	16297	10412	54258
	Alaska Shell Fish Inc.	513	1194	136	683	286	2812
	Ak Year Round Canneries	7929	7983	2385	9868	2962	31127
	B & G Packing Co. (New Co.)		54		130		184
	Cook Inlet Packing Co.	2824	3594	1141	5473	9	13041
1949	Alaska Shell Fish Inc.	417	1898	422	1077	1135	4949
	Ak Year Round Canneries	9857	6698	1867	2278	1876	22576
	Cook Inlet Packing Co.	2488	6931		107	1071	10597
	Seldovia Bay Packing Co. (formerly Ak Seldovia Packers Inc.)	5258	25091	2030	13235	6011	51625
1950	Alaska Shell Fish Inc.	526	4763	717	1472	1625	9103
	Ak Year Round Canneries and General Fish Co.	6563	18921	5436	12907	7891	51718
	Cook Inlet Packing Co.	2632	5633	1007	4895	19	14186
	Seldovia Bay Packing Co.	4745	29367	2392	17573	10926	65003
1952	Alaska Shell Fish Inc.	579	2381	922	4088	2082	10052
	Ak Year Round Canneries and General Fish Co.	2812	9140	1646	14075	4581	32254
	Cook Inlet Packing Co.	764	2915	774	6681		11134
	Seldovia Bay Packing Co.	3804	12366	2226	19044	6197	43637
1953	Alaska Shell Fish Inc.	1651	2486	673	2166	3153	10129
	Ak Year Round Canneries and General Fish Co.	5333	11477	3727	3092	5612	29241
	Cook Inlet Packing Co.	914	2091	561	164		3730
	Seldovia Bay Packing Co.	4954	20629	3127	10599	9761	49070

(Some of the reds and kings shown in the Seldovia Bay Packing Co. figures were actually canned in Cordova under a joint operating agreement with another cannery. Seldovia Bay Packing Co. also operated in arrangement with Pacific American Fisheries this year, and that company brought fish to Seldovia under its own joint operating agreement with Alaska Packers Assoc.)

Year	Cannery	Kings	Reds	Coho	Pink	Chum	Total
1954	Alaska Shell Fish Inc.	863	3081	232	1559	5027	10762
	Ak Year Round Canneries	3941	8748	4987	15156	12039	44871
	Cook Inlet Packing Co.	598	1855	712	8422	20	11607

(The fish of Cook Inlet Packing Co. were canned in Snug Harbor this year.)

	Seldovia Bay Packing Co.	2332	19604	3514	13714	23858	63022

(Figures include Cordova fish as well.)

1955	Alaska Shell Fish Inc.	2023	130	3442	1036		6631

(Some of these fish were canned in the Ak Year Round Canneries plant.)

	Ak Year Round Canneries	1684	7607	2247	7821	3314	22673
	Cook Inlet Packing Co. (canned in Snug Harbor)		1448	2607	390	434	4879
	Seldovia Bay Packing Co.	1951	14696	1680	18357	5937	42621
1956	Alaska Shell Fish Inc.		1315	19	2537	4557	8428

(These fish were canned in the company's Port Williams and Ouzinkie plants.)

	Ak Year Round Canneries	2270	9216	1776	12962	8585	34809
	Cook Inlet Packing Co.	1054	2262	404	7924	9	11653

(These fish were canned in Snug Harbor.)

	Seldovia Bay Packing Co.	816	15330	1407	6515	16046	40114
1957	Ak Year Round Canneries	421	3668	984	1934	12129	19136
	Seldovia Bay Packing Co.	357	6915	724	8864	27358	44218

(Cook Inlet Packing operated this year but is now shown based in Snug Harbor.)

1958	Ak Year Round Canneries	335	1989	1742	18437	8118	30831
	Cook Inlet Packing Co (back in Seldovia this year)	71	930	231	3787	2	5021
	Everitt & Company		57		5643	437	6137
	Parks Canning Co.		62	16	964	532	1574
	Whitney & Company	87	2845	1545	18630	7252	30359
1959	(Ak Year Round Canneries, Cook Inlet Packing Co., and Whitney & Co. are all shown operating out of Port Graham this year. No canneries are listed as processing salmon in Seldovia.)						
1960	Ak Year Round Canneries	2	1230	150	2657	2931	6970
	Cook Inlet Packing Co.		1231	148	2657	2882	6918
	Snug Harbor Packing Co. (also includes Seldovia plant)	10	4107	1689	861	3989	10656
1961	Ak Year Round Canneries	3	3551		3320	1731	8605
	Cook Inlet Packing Co. (Figures shown match those of AYR above: probably a transcription error.)						
	Fidalgo Island Packing Co.		7206	246	6636	3691	17779
1962	Seldovia-Port Graham (consolidation)	152	8375	778	42334	19707	71346
1963	General Fish Co.		6	58	4101	335	4500
	Seldovia-Port Graham (consolidation)	10	10167	1257	4278	15126	30838
1964	Seldovia-Port Graham (consolidation)		7923	2351	41714	46849	98837
1965	Seldovia-Port Graham (consolidation)	7	22859	1299	4648	8598	37411
1966	(No canneries are listed as processing salmon in Seldovia.)						

Shellfish and Mollusks

As early as the 1920's, Seldovia processors were experimenting with and expanding into other seafood fisheries. The harvest of seafood other than salmon and herring could stretch an operating season for a cannery, and could supplement an otherwise poor year.

Crab

Some of the first statistics for an alternative fishery in Seldovia record the canning of crab. *Pacific Fisherman's Yearbook* of 1926 reported that in 1925, the State of California, the primary consumer of Alaska crabmeat, had passed legislation prohibiting the shipment of product into that state. This greatly hurt the Alaskan crab processors, and the only cannery in the state that year to can crab was Alaska Year Round Canneries of Seldovia, which put up 75 cases of king crab in half-pound cans.[153]

Perhaps the coming Depression stifled this new fishery, or perhaps in light of the salmon boom it was discounted as an economically viable industry. In any event, the next report of crab canning at Seldovia doesn't occur until 1937, when the King Crab Co. put up 47 cases. For the next few years, this company produced crab as noted below:

    1937 . . . . . 47 cases
    1938 . . . . . 145 cases
    1939 . . . . . 220 cases
    [in 1939, new regulations prohibited the taking of female crab, and required a minimum shell diameter of 5.5 inches for males]
    1940 . . . . . 100 cases[154]

While this may not seem like an impressive output, it is worth noting the laborious process required to safely can this shellfish.

Crabs were brought live to the cannery, and killed there to ensure maximum freshness. The back shell was removed and the body cut in half. A pressure jet of water was employed to clean away the innards, and then the body halves were steamed for twenty minutes. Workers picked out the meat by hand,

This photograph was given to the author with the inscription: "Three crabs." Actually, the middle character is Gene "Whitey" Wadsworth, Seldovia commercial fisherman and homesteader, posing with two king crabs. Photo courtesy of Gene Wadsworth.

taking care not to shred the leg meat in the process. The meat was then dipped in a preservative solution of dilute acetic acid, then fresh water, and lastly brine. After being pressed and drained to eliminate excess moisture, the meat was hand packed in cans. Can tops were applied and the cans vacuum sealed in a special machine. From here, they were sent to the retorts for a little over an hour of cooking. When done, they were cooled quickly with a fresh water bath, to prevent crystallization of the salt inside.[155]

Because in the early years crab canning was not a widespread Pacific Coast fishery like salmon, it did not enjoy the labor-saving devices and machinery developed for the salmon industry. Many fishermen were undoubtedly not interested in changing their gear over from salmon to crab for such a new and uncertain fishery. Thus it is not surprising that the Seldovia cannery had such a small yield.

During the war years, it does not appear that crab canning was going on in Seldovia, even though the restriction of imports from Japan had cut off the supply of crab from that source and thus had given the American market a boost.[156]

It was not until the 1950's that crab again became a Seldovia fishery. This time, thanks to new technology and declining salmon harvests, crabbing became a real part of Seldovia's economy. The annotated table below (data gathered from *Pacific Fisherman Yearbook* for the years listed) provides an overview of the industry.

Wakefield Fisheries continued to be the main player in the Kachemak Bay crab fishery through the mid-1970's, and was an important part of Seldovia's economic base. In 1973, Wakefield bought $2.2 million worth of crab from area fishermen. By 1975, they were responsible for bringing $5 million into the community, operating year round and employing 14% of the 437 people here. The remainder of the population, it has been noted, were fishermen. [157]

As with other fisheries, the "boom" soon ended. Wakefield sold out and by 1989 the last cannery in Seldovia had closed its doors. Today, tanner crab are taken commercially in a 12-hour season once a year. King crab are no longer present in sufficient numbers to justify a commercial harvest.

Crab Processed at Seldovia, As Reported in *Pacific Fisherman's Yearbook* - 1953 through 1966

Year	Cannery	Method	Output
1953	Parks Canneries	canning	3,385 cases
	(The crabs canned were primarily king crab; after 1953, freezing of crab became a viable alternative to canning.)		
1954	Seldovia Bay Packing Co.	freezing	137,790 lbs.
1957	Tom Lazio Fish Co.	freezing	360,572 lbs.
	(This company, a California concern, put up Dungeness crab.)		
	Seldovia Bay Packing company (king crab)	freezing	45,453 lbs.
1958	Whitney & Company (king crab)	freezing	140,000 lbs.
		canning	3,200 cases

In Kachemak Bay, 1956 and 1957 had been outstanding years for the crab harvest. The health of the fishery experienced a temporary decline over the next several years. In 1959, Wakefield Fisheries leased the Whitney & Co. plant at Seldovia, and prepared to expand its crab operation to this community.

Year	Cannery	Method	Output
1962	Seldovia-Port Graham Consolidation (king crab)	canning	11,292 cases
	Ekren Packing Co. (Dungeness)	canning	22 cases
	Wakefield Fisheries	freezing	(statistics for Seldovia not reported separately)
1963	Seldovia-Port Graham Consolidation	canning	21,000 cases approximate
1964	Seldovia-Port Graham Consolidation	canning	21,647 cases
	Sutterlin & Wendt	canning	80 cases
	Wakefield Fisheries	freezing-meat	645,704 lbs.
		freezing-in shell	450,413 lbs.
	Sutterlin & Wendt	freezing-in shell	2,113 lbs.
1965	Seldovia-Port Graham Consolidation	canning	38,170 cases
	Wakefield Fisheries	freezing-meat	956,598 lbs.
		freezing-in shell	1,055,295 lbs.
1966	Wakefield Fisheries	freezing-meat	800,000 lbs.
		freezing-in shell	627,783 lbs.

Clams

Commercial clamming was an Inlet industry as early as the 1920's, and Seldovians found jobs digging on beaches across Cook Inlet. In 1924, an unknown number of local residents went to work for the Hemrich Packing Co. at Kukak Bay. The company's tender, the *Marathon*, stopped in Seldovia to pick up the new hires on its way to the cannery and settlement at Kukak Bay, on the west side of Shelikof Strait. [158]

In 1932, Gilbert Chambers opened a clam cannery in Seldovia to process the razor clams so plentiful on the western shore of Cook Inlet. That first year his plant packed 3,910 cases of razor clams, in 1/2 lb. flat cans, 8 dozen cans to the case. The *Seldovia Herald* articles on this page detail the logistics of his operation.

SELDOVIA HERALD - Feb. 27, 1932

SELDOVIA CLAM CANNERY TO OPERATE FROM MAY 1

The arrival in Seldovia on the next Seattle steamer of retorts and other canning equipment, sufficient for a pack of from ten to fifteen thousand cases. Employment from May 1 to July 1; from August 12 on into the fall, from 50 to 65 clam diggers, and from 18 to 25 plant workers. Such is the mapped out program of the North Pacific Packing Company; Alaska corporation with offices and clam canning plant at Seldovia. G. M. Chambers, Seldovia merchant, president and chief promoter of the enterprise, came home from Seattle on the Evans last Wednesday. He is enthusiastic about the new business. " The market," said Mr. Chambers, "is practically cleaned up on canned clams. The Seldovia pack will find ready sale, I feel sure. There is special call for half pound flats, which we shall can exclusively. Every clam fan knows the Polly creek razor clam —fat, clean, white. Already I have assurance that the product will be in demand. My business outside has been checking up on canning equipment, and upon that most important angle- the market. I am very glad to have a part in starting this new industry in and for Seldovia, and am assured on all sides of the kind of hearty cooperation that promises success." Mr. Chambers was accompanied by H. H. Malcolm, well known Seldovia salmon canneryman, who has associated himself in the business, and will be the chief operative at the plant. Mr. Malcolm's [illegible] and aspirations are well wrought out in his editorial statement appearing on page 2 of this paper. The first season, it was explained, will be from May 1 to July 1. The second from August 10 on into the fall. The M. S. Princess Pat will be the chief carrier from clam beds to plant. Between times the boat will be on the Anchorage- Seldovia run.

SELDOVIA HERALD - May 28, 1932

THOUSAND CASES CLAMS SHIPPED

First shipment of canned goods of the season went out from Seldovia Wednesday last, when the North Pacific Packing Co. Inc. Made shipment of 1060 cases of half pound clams. Delivery was made to the S.S. Admiral Watson. The new plant has been active since the sixth of the month and since that time approximately 1300 cases of clams have been packed. Between four and five hundred cases, however, were so recently packed that the operation thought best not to make shipment until the goods had entirely cooled from the cook. Due to the small tides clams will not be available for a week or ten days, during which time Superintendent Malcolm and his associates will make a quick overhaul of the plant and improve the plan of operations by remodeling here and there. President G. M. Chambers is well pleased with the outlook, efficiency and dispatch in the conduct of the plant being evidenced in a pure clean pack and he voices the belief that the next shipment will number many more cases than the first outgo.

In 1932, Mr. Chambers paid around 7 cents per pound for razor clams. The price dropped several cents the next year, but ended up at 6 cents per pound.[159] By 1933 the scarcity of razor clams on the Washington coast put Mr. Chambers in an even better market position. Washington clammers were alarmed at the steady decline in the number of clams to be found, and yet harvesting efforts continued as intensely as before, with no conservation measures enacted. Heretofore, the Pacific Coast taking of hard shell, or butter/steamer clams, had been comparatively light, as that product had to compete with hard shell clams from Japan and the Atlantic Coast. This would have put Mr. Chambers's Seldovia clams in high demand, but for the fact that fish brokers still had 1932 stock sitting in their warehouses. They had paid processors a high price for the canned clams and now had difficulty moving them. Clam packing was down sharply all over the Alaska territory, except for Mr. Chambers. In 1933, his North Pacific Packing Co. put up a whopping 9,435 cases of canned clams, far more than any other producer in Alaska, and second in volume in the entire North Pacific. [160]

Although it was for a time very productive, Gilbert Chambers' clam cannery was a short-lived enterprise. Probable over-harvest threw the clam beds into a multi-year period of scant production, discouraging Chambers and other would-be entrepreneurs. The only other notable clam activity in Seldovia was the 1948 pack of 8,107 lbs. of frozen shucked clams by Seldovia Fisheries Co.[161]

Today, a limited commercial harvest of butter and steamer (Pacific Littleneck) clams is taken from Jakolof Bay. This bay is also the site of a new marine industry in this area, the commercial farming of oysters and blue mussels.

Halibut

From the *Pacific Fisherman's Yearbook* it is somewhat difficult to define exactly what year halibut began being delivered to Seldovia docks. Reporting was done by districts, and the villages comprising those districts are not always listed. In general, prior to the widespread use of domestic and commercial freezers in the late 1940's/early 1950's, most of the halibut caught was restricted to the fresh market. Seldovia's distance from major markets precluded this community's involvement in the halibut fishery until use of freezer technology in shipping and in the home became more common.

SELDOVIA HERALD – Saturday, August 13, 1932

SELDOVIA PLANTS REPRESENTED 100 PER CENT IN SHIPMENTS

Salmon, clams, herring make up nice outgoing cargo with forty tons inbound freight – Busy day as Evans takes tonnage

Discharging 40 tons of store freight, and taking on approximately 130 tons of Seldovia products as outgoing shipments, the steamer Admiral Evans spent a busy six hours at the Anderson dock last Wednesday. An interesting detail connected with the outgo, is that every local producing fish and clam plant is represented on the shipper manifest. Besides the usual miscellany plunder, following is the list of cargo-making shipments, together with shippers.

Anderson Mercantile Co., 300 cases red salmon, talls
Chas. H. Sharp, for the account of the Frank Cooper clam cannery, 102 cases clams, talls
Cook Inlet Packing Co., 1446 cases salmon, talls.
North Pacific Packing Co., 581 cases clams, halves.
Alaska Year Round Canneries, 970 cases salmon, talls.
Ninilchic Packing Co., 105 cases salmon, talls.
Chambers & Colwell, 396 [?] full barrels and 37 half barrels herring.

The herring represented three loads of fish brought over from the Kodiak district by the M.S. Princess Pat, fish that belonged to the San Marco Fish Co., an arrangement designed to relieve congestion of fish impounded by the San Marco people. Captain Fred O'Neil, of the Pat, bossed the job of packing and attended to final shipment.

Halibut Freeze Processed at Seldovia During the 1940's and 1950's

Year	Cannery	Number Lbs. Frozen Halibut Produced
1948	Seldovia Fisheries Co.	544,477
1949	Seldovia Fisheries Co.	530,225
1950	Alaska Seldovia Packers	730,442
1951	Alaska Seldovia Packers	534,835
1952	Alaska Seldovia Packers	673,803
1953	Whiz Fish Products	525,000
1954	Seldovia Bay Packing Co.	418,403
1955	Seldovia Bay Packing Co.	684,229
1956	Seldovia Bay Packing Co.	742,683
1957	Seldovia Bay Packing Co.	795,275
1958	Whitney & Co.	700,000

(Data from *Pacific Fisherman Yearbook* for those years listed)

Until recently, halibut was harvested during two 24-hour openings each year, one in the spring and the second in the fall. With the advent of the IFQ, or Individual Fishing Quota System, boats that qualify are given a poundage limit and can fish year round until that limit is reached. Lacking a cannery here, most of the Seldovia fleet currently delivers to Homer.

Shrimp

Shrimp enjoyed a brief heyday in Seldovia. Like halibut, shrimping prior to the 1950's was almost completely limited to the fresh trade. Around 1958, the U.S. market "discovered" Kachemak Bay shrimp: Side Stripe and Coon Stripe. Larger than their Pacific Coast cousins, these delicacies were said to taste like lobster, and sold for $10 a case.[162]

In 1958, Whitney & Co. in Seldovia was one of only three canneries in Alaska to process shrimp, putting up 2,500 cases.[163] They were joined the next year by Sutterlin & Wendt, a Washington State firm who processed in the Whitney plant. By 1961, Sutterlin & Wendt were the only processors in Seldovia canning shrimp, which they continued to do until 1964. This was the year of their peak output, 25,860 cases, and it was also the year of the great Alaska earthquake.[164] Sutterlin & Wendt left Seldovia then, and the fishery never regained its strength. Too few shrimp remain today to support a commercial harvest.

A good halibut catch literally covered the floor of a Seldovia cannery. Photo courtesy of William Wakeland, #19G21

Diversified Catch Today

Because the harvesting of all marine food resources is so tightly controlled now, fishermen have been forced to diversify. Very few fishermen can afford to limit themselves to catching only one species.

In the Seldovia fleet, the larger boats may begin the year fishing tanner crab. Then it's a change of gear to fish for grey cod and then a wait until spring, when boats start to fill their quotas for black cod and halibut. By late June, tendering for salmon begins, which lasts into August. A tender's job is to stand by in a productive salmon fishing area to receive deliveries of fish from the smaller boats. A tender also serves as floating gas station, grocery store, ice depot, and post office for the small boat crews, many of whom spend several months on the fishing grounds. In September, boats may continue fishing for halibut if they didn't fill their annual quota during the spring. After September, it's time off for the remainder of the year, unless the captain decides to fish for crab in the Bering Sea or seine for bait herring in November. [165]

Some smaller Seldovia boats also fish crab, grey and black cod, and halibut. Instead of spending the summer tendering, however, they may seine or drift-fish for salmon, or seine for herring. Still other local fishermen fish for salmon from skiffs, using setnets which are located on or near shore.

Because of Seldovia's good harbor and proximity to the fishing grounds, many salmon drift-net boats from other communities make Seldovia their home port for the busy salmon fishing months of June and July. Drift-net fishing for salmon in the Cook Inlet opens several days each week during these months, and fishermen return to Seldovia on the "off" days to mend gear and rest up for the next fishing period.

Mining Around Seldovia

Since before the turn of the century, mining has been an "on-again/off-again" sort of industry for Seldovia. Beginning in 1899, mining activity provided sporadic employment for Seldovians, but in all cases, such activity has been short-lived.

The Russians were aware of a sizable coal deposit near Port Graham prior to 1786, when it was described by the English explorer, Nathaniel Portlock. It was not until the 1850's, however, that they made regular use of coal in their Russian American Company steamers. This requirement for coal led to the development in 1855 of a mining operation at Port Graham, staffed by Russians under the leadership of Finnish mining engineer Enoch Hjalmar Furuhjelm. Initially the coal was mined in an open pit, but that was soon replaced by vertical shafts. By 1859 a village of 20 dwellings, shops, and a church had grown around the mine. However, by 1865 the Port Graham coal was costing more to mine than it could be sold for, as competition had driven the market price down. The Russian American Company moved some of the buildings and equipment away from the Port Graham site, and abandoned the rest. [166]

The next coal venture began in 1888, when the Alaska Coal Company dug a tunnel and began mining operations near Homer.[167] Over the next decade, several coal mining firms established themselves and operated for a time in Homer, and it was one of these that provided Seldovians with some of their first employment in the industry. In January of 1899, a Mr. McPorson hired a number of Seldovians for two months to work along the Homer shore. [168] He was the personnel manager for an unidentified Homer-based coal company. Less than a year later, the Cook Inlet Coal Fields Co. incorporated and began working in the area. [169]

Around the turn of the century, prospector William G. Whorf landed his small boat at Port Graham late in the summer and was walking the beach when he found coal. When he asked the local Indians where it came from, they showed him the deposit which had been abandoned by the Russians 35 years before. As this was exactly the kind of mining opportunity he'd spent nearly a decade looking for, Mr. Whorf was terribly excited. (Whorf came to Alaska about 1893.[170]) Bidding his wife adieu, he left her and their six-month old infant with the Indians, and rushed off to another site, presumably up the Inlet, where they had cached all their worldly goods and provisions. Winter must have come early and cruelly that year, for Whorf got weathered in and was unable to return to his ever-patient wife until the following April!

He promptly staked a 160 acre claim, only to find that because the land in Alaska wasn't surveyed, the coal land laws did not apply here. He waited until 1904, when the law changed and allowed him to hire his own government surveyor. This he did, and the surveyor ran the survey lines due north, south, east, and west, as called for in the new legislation. Unfortunately, the land office to which Whorf submitted his claim found some technical fault with the survey, and required him to hire yet another man and do it all over again. The second surveyor, in trying to both comply with the law <u>and</u> placate the fussy land office, cut Whorf's claim down to 65 acres, which by this time, he felt darned lucky to get. [171]

Whorf divided his time between Port Graham and Seldovia, and did his best to make a go of coal mining. He employed local men, paying them $1.00 to $2.50 a day. [172] In June of 1907, he traveled to Seattle to try to convince the steamship companies to haul his coal to Seward to his customers there, but for some reason they refused. At this point, the mine was producing 30 tons of coal a day, employing a coal-fired steam-driven hoist to lift the product up out of the mine shaft and a pump to discharge the sea water that crept in. The mine was capable of producing three times what it did, lamented Whorf, if only there were a way to get it to the people in Seward who wanted it. Nonetheless, Whorf had a ready market in supplying his product to coal-powered steamers and canneries around Cook Inlet. His coal was even sold as far away as Nome, to the Pacific Coal Storage Co. [173]

Whorf experienced more government difficulty with his claim. He paid $10 an acre and filed the necessary papers but his final patent was slow in coming. Not even a 26-day round trip to Juneau to personally expedite the matter had any effect. [174] It wasn't until 1913 that Whorf received his patent. [175]

SEWARD WEEKLY GATEWAY
April 27, 1907

INLET COAL TO GO TO NOME

W.G. Whorf Contracts Output of Port Graham Mine to Pacific Cold Storage

"Nome will take most of the output of the Port Graham coal mine this summer. The Pacific Coal Storage Company has contracted to take the output for its operations at Nome and will send steamers from there to get it. W.G. Whorf, owner of the mine, came up from Seattle on the Pennsylvania to go to Seldovia. He states that he expects the mine to yield from 7000 to 10,000 tons this summer and that nearly all of this will be taken to Nome. He says he could have made contracts for several hundred thousand tons this year as the fuel famine in the states is getting worse and the big consumers are much perplexed to get their needed supplies. The first run from the mine will be taken by the San Juan Fish Company for the plant which it will install at Kenai, the material for which is now coming on the bark Amelia."

As related earlier in this chapter, Whorf was the same entrepreneur who in 1911 started Seldovia's first cannery, and then later lost it to the bank. By 1920, at age 74, Whorf had grown weary of the frustrations of running a business, and he had retired to Seldovia. In the fall of 1922, Whorf became ill enough to require hospitalization in Anchorage. Soon after, he journeyed to Seattle for treatment and died there February 2, 1923 at age 77. [176]

A curious story regarding Mrs. Whorf came to light during my research for this book. While viewing microfilm of the Seward Weekly Gateway, I stumbled across this article:

June 16, 1906 – "The steamer Bertha brought an old Russian cannon to Seward, a present to the town from Mrs. W.G. Whorf of Seldovia. Only the gun remains, very rusty, the carriage having disappeared long ago. A government report says the cannon is known to have been in the neighborhood of Seldovia in 1716. It is about three feet long and of about 4-inch bore. The inside of the rim is larger."

Upon reading "in the neighborhood of Seldovia in 1716", my jaw dropped, for this was a reference to Seldovia nearly 200 years before any other I had seen previously. My excitement was short-lived when I realized that surely this was a misprint; certainly the newspaper had meant 1816, or even 1786.

On a lark, I called the city of Seward and was given the name of their local museum curator and historical society member. I phoned Mr. Lee Poleske, and after identifying myself as a writer of a Seldovia history book, said "I'm sure this will seem like a silly question, but do you still have a cannon some lady from Seldovia gave your city eighty-seven years ago?" To my great surprise, Mr. Poleske informed me that indeed the cannon was still in Seward, and he shared with me some of its colorful history:

After arriving in Seward, the cannon was placed by a downtown flag pole. After some time, it was moved to a small park in front of the railroad depot. When the park was enlarged in the 1930's, the cannon disappeared, only to reappear some thirty years later. In 1967, to mark the celebration of the Alaska Purchase, a wooden carriage was made for the wayward cannon, perhaps in hopes it would stay put. In the early 1970's the cannon was displayed in front of Seward City Hall. On Halloween night, 1974, mysterious persons removed the cannon from City Hall, right from under the nose of the neighboring Police Department. One week later, the cannon was deposited on the front porch of the Seward City Manager. Shortly thereafter, the cannon with a passion for traveling found its permanent home, safely ensconced in the Seward museum. [177]

A museum patron with a penchant for old artillery cleared up some of the cloudiness surrounding the origin of the cannon. He believed that, based on its markings, the cannon was of British origin, manufactured in Scotland sometime in the late eighteenth or early nineteenth century for the Royal Navy. He felt that it was used as a bow gun on a small boat assigned to a frigate. It would have protected landing parties from hostile action on shore. [178]

Aside from employment with area coal-mining firms, the Kachemak resource provided extra income for a number of Seldovia men. Coal was the primary domestic heating fuel for many years here, most all of it carried from Homer. While a small amount of coal can be found on the south shore beaches east of Seldovia, it is only around Homer that it is found on the beach in abundance. Seldovians commonly journeyed across the bay to fill their skiffs with a good supply of the black stuff, and some enterprising men made a business out of supplying homes, businesses, and cannery boilers here.

Around 1915, the going rate for coal was around $5.00 a ton. A good quantity was required to heat a building for the year: the school house at the time consumed nearly 20 tons of coal during the school year.[179] In 1921, the Seldovia schoolchildren were recognized statewide for their efforts in carrying 30 tons of coal from its landing place on the beach up to the schoolhouse and caching it in the coal shed. They were commended for saving money that would otherwise have had to be spent on labor to deliver it.[180]

Dr. Frederica de Laguna remembers:

Many establishments burned low-grade coal. This coal, really lignite, was mined or dug out of the partially solidified clay beds that formed the north shore of Kachemak Bay, or could be picked up in chunks along the beaches below the cliffs. When damp, these chunks were easy to handle, but the lignite checked and disintegrated when allowed to dry out, so for this reason, the people using it stored their supplies in bins built among the pilings that supported their buildings or docks, so that the

Seldovians Archie Keller, Gene Mason, and Nick Kelly (with a fourth unidentified man) comb the beaches north of Homer at Happy Valley for coal. This coal would be used back in Seldovia to fire the boilers at the Cook Inlet Packing Company. The photograph dates from 1933. Photo courtesy of Ted Anderson from the Ralph and Juanita Anderson Collection.

THE SELDOVIA HERALD
December 2, 1932

BAD WEATHER KEEPS BACK COAL DEALERS

Coal merchants have been wary of the coal coast the past two weeks, but taking advantage of storm rifts offered chances to run over and back between blows. Some of the boats are being laid up. Bert Hansen finds that his carrier needs caulking, and a general overhaul may follow. Captain Lars Sagen, of the *Pilot*, is considering only one more trip. Axel Ursin, it is reported, may continue deliveries throughout the winter. Ursin is operating the Lawrence Dunning craft, *Seward*. The reduced prices of coal together with the hazard of boat loss do not combine to make business inviting.

tides might keep it damp. This fuel, I noticed, burned with a sulfurous odor, producing as much ash as what had been consumed.[181]

Eventually, heating oil supplanted coal as the heating fuel of choice in Seldovia. The article at left speaks of the inconvenience, and sometimes danger of having to rely on a fuel source across the bay. The paradox of coal gathering is that it is the stormy winter season which wrests the chunks loose from their underwater seams, and thrusts them upon the beach. It is this same season which is the most hazardous for navigation.

Chrome Mining

Seven miles to the southeast of Seldovia, Red Mountain holds a sizable deposit of chrome ore. It is unique to the Kenai Peninsula save for a deposit south of Seldovia, near Port Chatham. The partnership of Whitney & Lass in 1917 and 1918 mined the Port Chatham site, and held 14 of the 49 claims filed on Red Mountain.[182]

Due to the onset of World War I, the Red Mountain claims sat idle. The *Seldovia Herald* of August 2, 1930, details a renewed interest in the resource.

A coal dealer prepares to unload coal from his scow to a customer on the Seldovia boardwalk during the late 1920's. Photo courtesy of the Alaska State Library, Taber Collection, #PCA 19-37

> **THE SELDOVIA HERALD**
> **August 2, 1930**
>
> ## CHROME IRON ORE SAMPLES SOUGHT BY EXPERTS IN SELDOVIA DISTRICT
>
> Red Mountain Scene of Activities for Next Few Weeks, With Opening Mines in View
>
> The Whitney & Lass chrome iron ore properties, located on Red Mountain, 15 miles from Seldovia, will undergo thorough inspection within the next few weeks [illeg.]. J.R. Van Fleet, mining engineer expert with the Electro Metallurgical Co. in Santa Barbara, California, and F.A. Rapp, Santa Cruz, will go over the prospects and take out samples. Mr. Van Fleet is accompanied by his young son, J.R. Van Fleet Jr. The party is stopping at the Shortley Hotel. Chris Spellum has been engaged to throw up a camp for the party, and he headed a group that left for Red Mountain Friday last. They will be followed shortly by the mining experts. The properties were prospected in 1918, enough work done to assure heavy deposits, and the plan at that time was to undertake mining on a commercial scale, but upset conditions brought on by the war compelled temporary abandonment of the work. The same interests also control properties at Port Graham, and 2000 tons of the ore was mined and shipped from there in 1917 and 1918. The output proved to be high-grade stuff, but foreign competition and war price deflation stepped in and operations ceased. It was explained that chromite is beginning to be more and more recognized as an important alloy in steel composition possessing a rust defying quality not commonly possessed by corresponding [illeg.] minerals. Particularly in demand by automobile manufacturers, it was started by the Ford company making exclusive use of chrome in headlight rims and door edgings. The Pacific coast does not lack deposits, Turkey supplies the world with a lot, but the United States fills most of its requirements from Africa. Mr. Van Fleet said that it was too early to say just what might be done with the local mines; but further demonstration will be undertaken to open up the mines.

Perhaps put off by the Great Depression, no one engaged in commercial mining at Red Mountain before the Second World War. In 1942-1944, Red Mountain was finally mined, yielding over 6,000 tons of chrome ore. The yield averaged 42% pure Cr_2O_3.[183] Over 50 men were employed by the Alaska Chrome Co., which established buildings and bunkhouses on the site.[184]

Red Mountain lay idle again until 1952 or 53, when miner and entrepreneur Mike Seiler came from the Seattle area to prospect along its slopes. Seiler drilled and took core samples from various points on the mountain. At a place some distance from the site of the former Alaska Chrome Co., he found what appeared to be a rich deposit consisting of 70 – 90% chrome ore. After surveying the deposit and its perimeters, Seiler staked his claim.

On his return Outside, Seiler won government contracts to buy the ore and lined up nearly one million dollars from investors to build a mill. Back in Alaska, he began blasting into the mountainside to build a shaft. The floor of the shaft sat on the bottom of the deposit, and over the next few years, the shaft grew to penetrate the mountain to a depth of almost 300 feet. Seiler's Kenai Chrome Co. built its own buildings, bunkhouse and mess hall 150 yards from the shaft entrance. Some of these buildings, high on the mountain slope, still stand.

A twisting road made the precarious climb from Jakolof Bay to the Red Mountain mine, 3500' above sea level. Due to heavy winter snows, the mine operated only seasonally. In May, the arduous work of clearing snow from the road began, and by June the long days of sunlight had melted the snow-pack at the mine enough to permit operations to begin.

A crew of 12 men ran the Kenai Chrome Co. operation, together with Mike Seiler and his brother. Four mining engineers worked inside the shaft, and, because of the hazardous conditions, they were the only workers allowed inside. These blasting wizards drilled and positioned dynamite such that the ore, when blown, would fall conveniently for loading into a mine cart. The cart sat on tracks and was powered by an air motor. It was known as an air-jenny, although the Red Mountain men called it the poop-a-leena. When the cart was loaded, an air compressor filled an attached tank with 80 – 90 lbs. of pressure. To propel the cart out of the mine, air was slowly let out of the tank, thus running a motor, which turned the cart's wheels. The escaping air sounded a distinctive "poop-poop-poop" as it pushed the motor, hence the nickname. Red Harrington had the dubious honor of being known as the "poop-a-leena operator."

Red Harrington and the "poop-a-leena" cart in 1955 at the Kenai Chrome Company operation at Red Mountain, near Seldovia. This cart, powered by compressed air, was used to move ore out of the mine. Photo courtesy of John Child.

Once outside of the shaft, the cart full of ore was dumped onto a grate. The "fines", or those pieces less than 2 or 3 inches in diameter, fell through the grate into a hopper. The larger chunks were sent to a second hopper where they were held awaiting transport by truck to a crushing mill at Jakolof Bay. The "fines" were processed on-site by a method designed by John Child of Homer. From the "fines" hopper, the smaller pieces of ore dropped onto a conveyor belt where they were washed with high pressure streams of water. Water came from a small lake on the ridge top, and was gravity fed down to the mine. Two pickers worked the belt, sorting the ore from the rubble that traveled down its course.

At six p.m., the end of a 12-hour workday, the men sat down in the mess hall to dinner, ably prepared by the cook and his helper. Regular camp rations were often supplemented by freshly-killed ptarmigan and spruce hen, and occasionally by king crab and fish from the sea below. During dinner, the charges set in the shaft earlier in the day would be scheduled to go off, and the men ate accompanied by a succession of small explosions. The crew signed on for the full season, working until snow began to fall in late September. Sundays were free days, and some workers took advantage of a landing strip on the Red Mountain valley floor to summon a plane and visit

*Joe Hodel and Mike Seiler work sorting ore on a conveyor belt at the Kenai Chrome Company's Red Mountain operation.
Photo courtesy of John Child.*

their families in Homer or Seldovia. Only a footpath existed between Jakolof Bay and Seldovia (The Jakolof Bay Road was not built until the mid-1960's), and so mail and supplies were brought by boat to Jakolof or by plane to the mountain valley.

Because of the long hours of hard work, washing up and eating were about the extent of the afterhours recreation at the mine. No liquor was allowed in camp because of the dangerous nature of the work. Seiler permitted the men to go into town on the Fourth of July, but had to suspend the privilege after several years of having a few hands go "AWOL" in the aftermath of the celebration. John Child remembers one of the few onsite diversions was watching a pair of wolverines scavenge in the mine company's garbage dump.

Mike Burke and Mike Seiler at the Kenai Chrome Company's operation on the side of Red Mountain, 1955. Photo courtesy of John Child.

A fleet of four trucks ran all day long up and down the winding road, carrying ore to a storage hopper on Kachemak Bay. The storage hopper released its load down a vertical shaft cut into the rock cliff of the shoreline. The shaft met up with a tunnel, whose mouth opened onto a pier. Several times during the season, ships (usually recycled WWII vessels) called at the pier to load the ore and carry it Outside. Ford F8 trucks and GMC 10-wheeled GI carriers hauled 5-ton loads of ore from the mountain down to sea level. At 300 lbs. per cubic foot, the chrome ore quickly filled each truck to capacity. Overloading was not an option, for even hauling 5-ton loads wore down the braking systems on the vehicles. Each truck had a water-cooling system for its brakes to prevent their overheating on the long slow trip down the mountain. Even so, brakes had to be replaced often. Engines were put in low gear for the downhill trip, but couldn't be relied upon alone to control the descent, for they too would overheat and fail under the strain. John Child recalls that on more than one occasion, brakes would fail and the drivers were forced to leap from their careening trucks to save their lives.[185]

The Kenai Chrome Co. operated through 1957, extracting over 21,000 tons of high-grade ore before it shut down. The closure was due to the federal government reneging on its agreement to purchase all of the Red Mountain product it had promised to, citing the availability of cheaper ore in Turkey. Left holding several thousand tons of ore, Mike Seiler brought suit against the government and was in part successful. Nonetheless, he was still compelled to sell off his equipment and abandon the operation. In recent years, a new, more economical method for processing ore has been developed, and interest in the Red Mountain deposit has been reawakened.[186]

Harvesting Trees

As noted in the section on shipping in Seldovia, the gold rush helped birth a new cottage industry: boat building. Although the construction of larger vessels here was limited to the first decade of so of the twentieth century, fishing and pleasure skiffs continue to be built by various artisans to the present day. A walk along Seldovia's Otterbahn trail reveals curious vertical slabs cut from a number of the great old spruce. This phenomenon is repeated all around Seldovia Bay, both along forgotten footpaths and in the deep woods. The slabs have been cut over the decades by various boatbuilders for "boat knees". The boat builder looked for a tree with just the right bend where the base of the trunk curved out to the root. This natural curve was used to create a frame to join the sides and bottom of the boat.[187]

One of the first tales of logging in Seldovia comes from longtime resident Nick Elxnit. Nick recalls a local horse who, around 1913, became somewhat famous about town for her independent antics. Kayuse was a mare owned by Rofey Bowen and his

Unidentified men build a seine skiff in Seldovia in 1949. The craft of boatbuilding is still practiced on Seldovia Bay today. Photo courtesy of the Pratt Museum, #HM-86-48-4

family, and she enjoyed free run of the town. Rofey got a job logging at the head of Tutka Bay, and decided to put Kayuse to work for her keep. He loaded her onto a scow and transported her to Tutka Bay, where she was pressed into service pulling 12 to 14' logs from the woods onto the tidal flats. After several days of this working for a living, Kayuse decided she'd had enough and ran off. Rofey was angry, and a little sad too, for the horse would certainly starve to death if she were not first done in by wolves or a bear. Long-faced, he returned to Seldovia at the end of the logging job, and made it known that he would never see dear Kayuse again. Two weeks later, guess who sauntered into town, hardly the worse for her trek, but Kayuse. Nick reports that everyone got a good laugh at Rofey's expense.[188]

In the mid-1920's, remembers Nick, there was a sawmill in operation on Powder Island, owned by partners Lawrence Dunning and Archie Keller. The mill was powered by a steam boiler, which was fed with slabs of wood discarded from the operation. Nick spent the summers of 1924 and 1925 working at the Powder Island sawmill. He received $90 per month plus meals for working six eight-hour days a week. He notes that lumber (dimension not specified) sold for $25 per thousand board feet, and tongue-and-groove sold for $40 per thousand board feet. One June, the crew had just banked the fire to keep it going while they took their lunch break. Sparks from the roaring fire sailed up onto the wood shaked roof and caught it on fire. The sawmill was supplied with fresh water, but the flow was too scant to do much good fire-fighting, and flames claimed the building, thus ending the career of the Powder Island sawmill.[189]

Sometime before 1931, a man named George Perault (spelling uncertain) built and operated a sawmill in Seldovia. Upon his death, it was purchased by Nels Svedlund. Subsequent owners included Martin Peterson, Zenas Beach, Bill Murphy, Casey Patton, Red Calhoun, and Clair Heiner.[190]

In 1975, the Seldovia Native Association (SNA) sold logging rights to some of its Seldovia Bay land to Robertson & Sons, who cut 5 million feet of Sitka spruce. In 1977 and 1978, Tim Spradlin logged 6 million feet on SNA land. In conjunction with Spradlin's operation, "Buzz" Moore set up a sawmill to mill non-export-quality logs. For a short time, he also ran a mill that produced house-quality logs.[191] Today, several entrepreneurs operate small sawmills

> **THE SELDOVIA HERALD**
> **May 16, 1931**
>
> ## SVEDLUND BUYS SELDOVIA MILL
>
> **Young Gas Skipper Plans Operating Next Year**
>
> Nels G. Svedlund made purchase of the sawmill owned by the late George Perault [?-spelling; illegible], at administrator's sale conducted at the office of the U.S. Commissioner W.A. Vinal Wednesday the 13th. There were no competitive bids. The holdings consist of a sawmill, dwelling, house, site, etc. Mr. Svedlund is employed by the Port Graham cannery as skipper on one of the larger tenders. Mrs. Svedlund, teacher of the Port Graham school, is a local visitor at this time, and stated upon inquiry that Mr. Svedlund hoped to be in position to operate the mill next year if conditions look favorable.

> **THE SELDOVIA HERALD**
> **April 15, 1933**
>
> ## SELDOVIA SAWMILL GOING FULL BLAST
>
> **Log Delivery Follows Mill Overhaul, Setting Wheels in Motion**
>
> Lumber is beginning to pile up at the plant of Seldovia Lumber Co. William Murphy and Alfred Gherke, proprietors, a delivery of 101 logs marking resumption of operations. The mill is now in excellent condition, every part of the machinery having been overhauled with painstaking care. And a new log deck and roofed over lumber platforms make for storage space and convenience. An arresting feature of the improvements is the battery of fir piling on the slough side of the mill, reinforcing the structure's foundation at a bracing angle. The logging crew expects to make delivery of approximately 200,000 feet, the major portion of which is in the water at Sadie Cove. A fair portion of the timber will be turned into clear boat lumber, for which ready sale is anticipated.

> **THE SELDOVIA HERALD**
> **June 11, 1932**
>
> ## SAWMILL MEN TO FINISH GAS BOAT
>
> Wm. Murphy and his son-in-law Alfred Gherke, proprietors of the Seldovia mill, have taken over the job of completing the gas boat begun by Zenas Beach. Mr. Beach launched the completed hull shortly before he started out fishing. The boat will be installed with a seven h.p. gas engine, one that Gherke brought up from Seattle a year ago. It is the intention of the millmen to use the boat both as a log getter and in fishing, engaging in the latter work when logs and orders are scarce.
>
> While the mill at the present time is not pressed with business, no complaint is offered because of lack of activities. Only recently the Snug Harbor Packing Co. took delivery of 5,000 feet while the Libby cannery has bought a generous quantity of trap materials since the opening of the season's work. Homer has come in for a number of nice orders, while local deliveries in small quantities have been the general order of things. But the operators feel that if they can do a little extra side work with their boat to help out the old bank account they would be that much better off, and hope to have the boat in readiness for business when the fishing season begins.

providing local lumber, and a log home builder uses local trees to craft everything from log outhouses to fine homes.

Tourism

Seldovia's natural resources have been tapped, one by one. Some, such as fur-bearing animals, herring, crab, and shrimp, have been harvested to the extent that the resource has yet to rebound. Others, like trees and minerals, await only a change in the world market before they will undoubtedly be harvested again.

The logs in the foreground were floated up the Seldovia Slough to the sawmill, where they await hoisting into the building. This photograph dates from the 1950's. Photo courtesy of William Wakeland, #16G28

By the late 1950's or early 1960's, the sawmill on the slough had fallen into disrepair. A heavy snowfall collapsed the roof. Some time later, the fallen building was burned. This photograph shows water cooling the charred debris. Photo courtesy of Jan Cevene.

In this May 1951 photograph, Gene Wadsworth's F.V. Sea Scout tows logs to the sawmill. Photo courtesy of Gene Wadsworth.

One resource which has not been "used up" is Seldovia's natural beauty and isolation from the crowds of humanity: its drawing card for tourism. Seldovia is not overdeveloped nor has it thus far been recklessly developed, and with great care and wisdom, perhaps it can remain that way. At present, visitors arrive in Seldovia on one of several tour boats from Homer, or on one of several bush air carriers from Homer or Anchorage. Sport-fishing for halibut and salmon are popular pursuits, as are kayaking, biking, hiking, and, in the winter, cross-country skiing. A number of tourist-related businesses have established themselves here in response to the visitor industry, among them bed and breakfasts, hotels and lodges, water taxis, gift shops, a wild berry jam manufacturer, restaurants, and guides offering everything from bicycle and kayak rental to guided tours to hunting and fishing charters.

It is interesting to note that the lure of Seldovia is nothing new. Even in the 1930's visitors were journeying here in sufficient numbers to prompt this editorial in the December 26, 1931 edition of the *Seldovia Herald*.

SELDOVIA HERALD - December 26, 1931

Tourists (and may their tribe increase) are expected to flock into Alaska in ever-increasing numbers next season, numerous conventions scheduled for Seattle being regarded as probable reason for anticipating more sight-seeing travelers than would otherwise head northward. Much is being made over this, and in some circles, it is felt that all worries are over, and that life generally will be nothing less than one long sweet song. But listen; unless something substantial can be shown those tourists, so that out of it capital can be interested to invest, or more important still, unless homeseekers can be attracted enough to come and see and be conquered, then will benefits derived be as fleeting as the tourists themselves. Alaskans have banked a great deal on tourist travel. Too much. For be it understood that a solid, industrious citizenry is a powerful factor in the maintenance of real and lasting prosperity. May many tourists come. Accord them welcome. Make them feel so much at home that Alaska will become home, indeed, if not to some of them or to their friends, then to a lot of their permanent dollars.

Endnotes

[1] Johan Adrian Jacobsen,"Glossary of Place Names," *Alaskan Voyage, 1881-1883: An Expedition to the Northwest Coast of America*, trans. Erna Gunther (Chicago: U. of Chicago P, 1977).
[2] *Investigation of the Fur Seal and Other Fisheries of Alaska* (Washington: GPO, 1889)325-326.
[3] John Wall Smith, letter to Goss, 5 Nov. 1901, Alaska Commercial Co. archives, U of Alaska Fairbanks; also in Woodrow Johansen, *A Family History of Adam Bloch* (self-pub., 1986).
[4] Adam Bloch, letter to Washburn, 22 Sept., 1897, *Family History of Adam Bloch*.
[5] Bloch, letters, 1896-1903, *Family History*.
[6] Bloch, letter to Goss, 7 Oct. 1901, *Family History*.
[7] Twelfth Census of the United States, U.S. Dept of Commerce, Bureau of the Census, 1900; Thirteenth Census of the United States, U.S. Dept. of Commerce, Bureau of the Census, 1910.
[8] Lone Janson, *Those Alaska Blues*, Alaska Historical Commission Studies in History, #168, 5.
[9] R. V. Anderson, "Fox Farming in Cook Inlet District," *Pathfinder of Alaska*, June 1922: 6.
[10] F.W. Williamson, "Farming Silver-Black Foxes," *Pathfinder*, Oct. 1925: 6.
[11] Ward T. Bower and Henry D. Aller, *Alaska Fisheries and Fur Industries in 1917*, Bureau of Fisheries Doc. No. 847, U.S. Dept of Commerce (Washington: GPO, 1918) 62.
[12] Fourteenth Census of the United States, U.S. Dept of Commerce, Bureau of the Census, 1920.
[13] Bower and Aller, *Fisheries and Fur 1917* 62.
[14] Ward T. Bower, *Alaska Fisheries and Fur Industries in 1918*, Bureau of Fisheries Doc. No. 872, U. S. Dept. of Commerce (Washington: GPO, 1919) 73.
[15] John R. Huston, "A Geographical Analysis of the Fur Farming Industry in Alaska," diss. U. of California, 1962, 71-74.
[16] Janet Klein, *A History of Kachemak Bay, the Country, the Communities* (Homer: Homer Society of Natural History, 1981) 57.
[17] Janson 6.
[18] Ward T. Bower, *Alaska Fisheries and Fur Industries in 1919*, Bureau of Fisheries Doc. No. 891, U. S. Dept. of Commerce (Washington: GPO, 1920) 67.
[19] "Raven More Deadly Than Eagle, Says Fox Man," *Seldovia Herald* 28 May 1932.
[20] *Alaska Weekly*, 18 July 1924: 7.
[21] R. V. Anderson 6-7.
[22] Klein 58.
[23] *Seldovia Herald* 16 Aug. 1930.
[24] Fourteenth Census.
[25] *Alaska Weekly* 13 Apr. 1923: 8.
[26] Fourteenth Census; Huston 72.
[27] *Alaska Weekly* 23 Jan. 1925: 8.
[28] *Alaska Weekly* 6 Nov. 1925: 1; 20 Nov., 1925: 3.
[29] "Doctor Now Foxfarmer," *Alaska Weekly*, 18 Jan. 1924: 5.
[30] *Alaska Weekly* 30 May 1924: 3; "Fox Farming on Cook Inlet,"18 July 1924: 7.
[31] *Alaska Weekly* 30 May 1924: 3; 18 July 1924: 7.
[32] *Alaska Weekly* 30 May 1924: 3; 18 July 1924: 7.
[33] Klein 61.
[34] *Alaska Weekly* 30 Nov. 1923: 6.
[35] Janson 4; Klein 61.
[36] Huston 81; *Pathfinder* Sept. 1924: 13.
[37] Huston 81; *Pathfinder* Sept. 1924: 13.
[38] *Alaska Weekly 21 Aug. 1925: 3*.
[39] "Seldovia Man Called to Rest," *Alaska Weekly 31 Aug. 1928: 1*.
[40] Bower, *Fisheries and Fur 1919* 68.
[41] *Pathfinder* December 1923: 17.
[42] *Pathfinder* December 1923: 17.
[43] Huston 72.
[44] *Seldovia Herald* 17 May 1930: 31 May, 1930: 2; 27 Sept 1930:5.
[45] *Seldovia Herald* 17 May 1930: 31 May, 1930: 2; 27 Sept 1930:5.
[46] *Seldovia Herald* 11 July 1931.
[47] Klein: 61.
[48] *Frontiersman* [Seldovia] 23 Nov. 1946: 1.
[49] *Daily Gateway* [Seward] 7 Aug. 1905: 1.
[50] *Seward Gateway* 2 Sept. 1905: 4.
[51] *Seward Weekly Gateway* 7 Oct. 1905: 4.
[52] *Seward Weekly Gateway* 20 Jan. 1906: 1; 19 May 1906: 1.
[53] *Seward Weekly Gateway* 3 Mar. 1906: 1.
[54] *Seward Weekly Gateway* 31 Mar. 1906: 1.
[55] *Seward Weekly Gateway* 21 Apr. 1906: 1.
[56] *Seward Weekly Gateway* 9 June 1906: 3.
[57] *Seward Weekly Gateway* 7 July 1906: 1.
[58] *Seward Weekly Gateway* 7 July 1906: 1.
[59] *Seward Weekly Gateway* 7 July 1906: 1.
[60] *Seward Weekly Gateway* 27 Oct. 1906: 1.

Endnotes (cont.)

[61] *Seward Weekly Gateway* 10 Nov. 1906: 3.
[62] *Seward Weekly Gateway* 30 Mar. 1907: 2.
[63] *Seward Weekly Gateway* 23 Jan. 1909: 2.
[64] *Seward Weekly Gateway* 13 Feb. 1909: 2; 27 Feb. 1909: 2.
[65] *Seward Weekly Gateway* 20 Nov. 1909: 3.
[66] *Seward Weekly Gateway* 04 Dec. 1909: 4.
[67] Nick Elxnit, personal interview, 1992.
[68] T. W. Anderson, "Anderson Dock," unpublished essay written for this book, 27 Mar. 1991.
[69] *Alaska Weekly* 30 Apr. 1926: 7.
[70] Frederica de Laguna, "Impressions of Seldovia in the Nineteen Thirties," unpublished essay written for this book, 1993: 6.
[71] *Frontiersman* 20 Nov. 1946: 1; 30 Nov. 1946; 4 Dec. 1946: 1; 14 Dec. 1946: 4.
[72] *Pacific Fisherman Yearbook* 1914: 66.
[73] *Pacific Fisherman Yearbook* 1914: 66.
[74] *Pacific Fisherman Yearbook* 1914: 66.
[75] *Pacific Fisherman Yearbook* 1929: 145.
[76] Elsa Pedersen, "Seldovia," *Alaska Sportsman* July 1949: 33.
[77] T. W. Anderson, "Ralph Anderson," unpublished essay written for this book 27 Mar., 1991.
[78] *Pacific Fisherman Yearbook* 1920: 132.
[79] *Pacific Fisherman Yearbook* 1924: 104.
[80] *Pacific Fisherman Yearbook* 1925: 136-143.
[81] *Pacific Fisherman Yearbook* 1925: 136-143.
[82] *Alaska Weekly* 13 Feb. 1925: 7
[83] *Alaska Weekly* 29 Aug. 1924: 3; 12 Sept. 1924: 6; 17 Oct. 1924: 6.
[84] *Alaska Weekly* 13 Feb. 1925: 4.
[85] *Pacific Fisherman Yearbook* 1925: 140; 143
[86] *Pacific Fisherman Yearbook* 1926: 142
[87] Catherine Brickey, "Seldovia: From Boom Town to Modern Village," *HEA Ruralite* Oct. 1977: 4.
[88] *Pacific Fisherman Yearbook* 1926: 142.
[89] *Pacific Fisherman Yearbook* 1926: 148.
[90] *Pacific Fisherman Yearbook* 1926: 150.
[91] *Pacific Fisherman Yearbook* 1927: 200.
[92] *Pacific Fisherman Yearbook* 1926: 196-200.
[93] *Pacific Fisherman Yearbook* 1927: 202.
[94] *Pacific Fisherman Yearbook* 1928: 178; 180.
[95] *Alaska Weekly* 4 Nov. 1927: 7.
[96] *Alaska Weekly* 4 Nov. 1927: 180.
[97] *Pacific Fisherman Yearbook* 1929: 143;145.
[98] *Pacific Fisherman Yearbook* 1929: 145; 147.
[99] *Pacific Fisherman Yearbook* 1930: 192.
[100] *Pacific Fisherman Yearbook* 1930: 192.
[101] *Pacific Fisherman Yearbook* 1931: 213.
[102] *Pacific Fisherman Yearbook* 1936: 219.
[103] Steve Zawistowski, personal interview, 29 Mar. 1989.
[104] Katherine Bayou, "The Tough Old Pirate," *Alaska Sportsman* May 1944: 16.
[105] Laurence Freeburn ed., *The Silver Years of the Alaska Canned Salmon Industry* (Anchorage: Alaska Northwest, 1976) 22.
[106] "Old King Crab and the Seldovians Talk Oil," *Seventy Six* [Union Oil] May/June 1975: 25-29.
[107] *Pacific Fisherman Yearbook* 1917: 16.
[108] *Pacific Fisherman Yearbook* 1914: 38.
[109] *Pacific Fisherman Yearbook* 1915: 38.
[110] George Kosmos, *Alaska Sourdough Stories,* ed. Mary Lou Patton (Seattle: Seal & West, 1956) 9.
[111] Elxnit, personal interview, 1989.
[112] Freeburn 92.
[113] Elxnit 1989.
[114] Freeburn 33.
[115] *Pacific Fisherman Yearbook* 1914: 22.
[116] Elxnit 1989.
[117] Freeburn 139.
[118] *Pacific Fisherman Yearbook* 1933: 183.
[119] *Pacific Fisherman Yearbook* 1933: 183.
[120] *Pacific Fisherman Yearbook* 1927: 194.
[121] Freeburn 56.
[122] *Pacific Fisherman Yearbook* 1936: 15-20.
[123] Jim Busey, personal interview, 27 Apr. 1993.
[124] *Pacific Fisherman Yearbook* 1936: 15-20.
[125] *Pacific Fisherman Yearbook* 1921.
[126] *Pacific Fisherman Yearbook* 1921.

Endnotes (cont.)

[127] Elxnit 1989.
[128] *Pacific Fisherman Yearbook* 1921: 33.
[129] Fourteenth Census
[130] *Pacific Fisherman Yearbook* 1922: 35.
[131] *Pacific Fisherman Yearbook* 1923: 37.
[132] *Alaska Weekly* 30 May 1924: 6.
[133] *Pacific Fisherman Yearbook* 1926: 52.
[134] *Pacific Fisherman Yearbook* 1927: 72; 76.
[135] *Pacific Fisherman Yearbook* 1928: 66.
[136] *Pacific Fisherman Yearbook* 1932: 54.
[137] *Pacific Fisherman Yearbook* 1934: 45.
[138] *Pacific Fisherman Yearbook* 1941: 57.
[139] Pedersen, "Kachemak Bay Story," unpublished ts. ,Pratt Museum, Homer, 77-79.
[140] *Pacific Fisherman Yearbook* 1942: 59.
[141] *Pacific Fisherman Yearbook* 1943: 71.
[142] *Pacific Fisherman Yearbook* 1943: 71; 113.
[143] *Pacific Fisherman Yearbook* 1944: 45; 47; 49.
[144] *Pacific Fisherman Yearbook* 1945: 68.
[145] *Pacific Fisherman Yearbook* 1945: 111.
[146] *Pacific Fisherman Yearbook* 1946: 81.
[147] *Frontiersman* 29 May 1947.
[148] *Pacific Fisherman Yearbook* 1949: 107; 127.
[149] *Pacific Fisherman Yearbook* 1953: 111.
[150] Fred Elvsaas, personal communication, 1989.
[151] *Pacific Fisherman Yearbook* 1959: 101.
[152] *Pacific Fisherman Yearbook* 1960: 61.
[153] *Pacific Fisherman Yearbook* 1926: 116.
[154] *Pacific Fisherman Yearbook*, 1938: 210; 1939; 1940; 1941: 275.
[155] *Pacific Fisherman Yearbook* 1938: 210.
[156] *Pacific Fisherman Yearbook* 1945: 72.
[157] "Old King Crab" 25-29.
[158] *Alaska Weekly*, 12 Sept. 1924: 6.
[159] *Pacific Fisherman Yearbook* 1934: 148.
[160] *Pacific Fisherman Yearbook* 1934: 148.
[161] *Pacific Fisherman Yearbook* 1949: 227.
[162] *Pacific Fisherman Yearbook* 1959: 177-178.
[163] *Pacific Fisherman Yearbook* 1959: 177-178.
[164] *Pacific Fisherman Yearbook* 1965: 165.
[165] Alison "Pixie" Jones, personal communication, 1994.
[166] "Coal Village Site, Alaska, National Register of Historic Places Nomination Form, National Park Service, 1977.
[167] William Healey Dall, "The Coal Rush," *The Cook Inlet Collection: Two Hundred Years of Selected Alaskan History* ed. Morgan Sherwood (Anchorage: Alaska Northwest, 1974) 121.
[168] *Russian Orthodox American Messenger* Dec. 1899: 625.
[169] Klein 41.
[170] *Pathfinder* March 1923: 16.
[171] *Seward Weekly Gateway* 19 Mar. 1910: 3.
[172] Jenny Lee Giles, "The Coal Mining Operation," unpub. paper, Susan B. English School, Seldovia.
[173] *Seward Weekly Gateway* 15 June 1907:1; 24 Aug. 1907: 1.
[174] *Seward Weekly Gateway* 19 Mar. 1910: 3.
[175] Giles.
[176] *Pathfinder* Mar. 1923: 16.
[177] Lee Poleske, letter to the author, 10 Nov. 1993.
[178] Robert H. Wright, letter to Lee Poleske, 20 July, 1986.
[179] "Treasurer's Annual Report, 1915-1916," Seldovia School, Jack English Collection.
[180] "Alaska School News," *Alaska School Bulletin* [Juneau] Dec. 1921: 3.
[181] De Laguna, "Impressions."
[182] Mary J. Barry, *A History of Mining on the Kenai Peninsula* (Anchorage: Alaska Northwest, 1973) 179.
[183] Klein 18.
[184] John Child, personal interview, 17 May 1994; Klein 18.
[185] Child.
[186] Child.
[187] John Gardner, *The Dory Book* (Camden, ME: International Marine, n.d.) 68.
[188] Elxnit, 1989.
[189] Elxnit, 1989.
[190] Fred Elvsaas, personal communication, 1997.
[191] Elvsaas, 1997.

LIFE IN OLD SELDOVIA

Schooling, Mail Delivery, Bootlegging and More, in this Boardwalk Community

Life in old Seldovia was colorful and bustling. I had more fun gathering reminiscences and materials for this chapter than for the rest of the book. Here is where we hear stories of how human nature shone, how disappointments were poignant, and where tales of long-ago conflicts and tragedy become uncomfortably close. Those ups and downs of daily life still happen in Seldovia, as they do in any small town. It is, however, more graceful to write those stories whose featured characters are long gone from this place, rather than those stories which are still unfolding.

Seldovia School Days

As noted in the chapter "Russian Culture and Influence," it was in 1905 that Russian Orthodox Bishop Innokentii wrote to Washington, asking the government to establish a public school in Seldovia. It is unclear just who the first teacher was here, or what year they started. The last Russian Orthodox teacher seems to have been Nicholai Fomin, who taught in 1904-05. Sometime around 1906 or 1907, it would seem that the teacher was either Mr. Herbert Farros (according to the Bureau of Education's plans), or Mr. Nash (according to a 1983 interview with Juanita Anderson).

The first teacher to provide substantive records on Seldovia is Miss Della Borst. Her letters and reports to the Bureau of Education, Department of the Interior, speak of her frustration in her Seldovia teaching position. The school was a Bureau of Indian Affairs sponsored school. Intended primarily for the education of Native children, it was open to the white children who lived here as a minority, there being no school for them. To someone from an Outside city, the way of life in a native village was so foreign that it required a person of special understanding and spirit. Miss Borst made it through the winter, but by March 1908 had had enough. She wrote to her superiors, asking for a raise or a transfer to a school closer to Seattle and "civilization." In addition, she complained that a proposed saloon in the town would add to the general degradation.[1]

She wrote in April of the difficulty of teaching children who left school as soon as they were old enough to work, and of the truancy sanctioned by the Russian priest, who gave "numerous holidays."[2] Miss Borst may have failed to realize that in the traditional native culture, children entered the adult world soon after puberty, so it was not surprising they left school to work. Much of the population of Seldovia was transient, according to Miss Borst, and this did little to set an example to the students as to the value of education. The children spoke Russian, and very few knew enough English to be able to understand their teacher. Although she had isolated successes in teaching basket-making and drawing, by and large her pupils were not progressing well in their studies. Miss Borst saw the power-brokers in town as the white men or foreigners who were married to native women, and who for the most part were liquor dealers. She had little use for them or for their code of ethics.[3] Miss Borst's superiors back in Washington, perhaps themselves unfamiliar with life in the Alaskan bush, and being very far away, were not of much help in assuaging her frustrations.

So, in May 1908, Miss Borst ran away. She was reported as a passenger on the *S.S. Dora*, leaving Seldovia to return to her home in Boston.[4] She got as far as Seward:

SEWARD WEEKLY GATEWAY
May 23, 1908

RETURNED TO HER POST

"Miss Della Borst, who got 'cold feet' in Seldovia and started for her home in Boston, came as far as Seward, and after spending a few days in this town in communication with congenial spirits she felt so much better that she concluded to return to her post and complete the term's work in the school in which she was the teacher. Miss Borst returned to Seldovia on the *Northwestern*."

165

This early photograph of Seldovia schoolchildren probably dates from between 1910 and 1915. Photo courtesy of Ted Anderson from the Ralph and Juanita Anderson Collection.

I had to chuckle when I found this article. We all want to run away from life sometimes: how dramatic to do so on a steamship!

Needless to say, Miss Borst did not opt to endure another year on the frontier, and so for the 1908-09 school year, Mr. Evans from Seattle was hired at $90 a month. A new school had just been built in Seldovia, complete with living quarters for the teacher and his wife.[5] When the school was built, the materials for its construction were lightered from the steamer to shore via small dories and a scow, and were discharged at high tide. The contractor, in an apparent effort to save money, neglected to carry them very far above the tideline before he began building. Thus at extreme high water, the ocean lapped at the front steps.[6]

The first floor measured 22' x 56'[7] and featured one school room and an entry hall, as well as a kitchen and small living area for the teacher. The second floor housed two bedrooms. Three outhouses stood behind the school in a filled-in bog: one for boys, one for girls, and one for the teacher.

Mr. Evans, too, only lasted a year, and by October 1909, Miss Amelia McMicheal was in place here as teacher. Her June 1910 report on her previous year's work reflects sincere concern for the local Seldovians, and an ingenious approach to teaching the English language and customs to people of another culture.[8] Although the school building was new, Miss McMicheal noted that storage facilities inside were nonexistent so that everything was piled upon her desk. The problem was solved with the construction of cupboards. Not so easy to remedy was the condition of the school grounds:

> The school is without doubt situated in the most undesirable place in Seldovia. On the north is a swamp, a receptacle for old cans, logs, and trash in general. On the east is the overflow from the swamp. A temporary ditch was dug by the nurse and large boys, which carried away the surface water for a while, but the rain soon broke the banks and the water resumed possession of the whole back yard again.

> On the south is the beach and carpenter's shop, which formerly was a barn housing twelve horses. While the east side is taken up by a cowpen, chicken pen, and pig sty. All these inconveniences were here long before the school was ever thought of being built, and why the present site was chosen instead of one of the many beautiful places in which the village abounds is a mystery beyond solving.[9]

1910 was the year in which the Alaska School Service started a rural sanitation program. For many centuries, the indigenous peoples of Alaska had been surviving just fine without the white man's standards of cleanliness. Before European, Russian, and American explorers and settlers sailed in bringing disease and vermin, the native program of hygiene served their needs beautifully. Unfortunately, once tuberculosis was introduced here, spitting on the floor became taboo, for it spread the sickness. Unwashed bodies and hair became hosts to lice. And, with ever more people crowding into Seldovia, the practice of throwing trash on the ground or into gullies created a breeding ground for disease.

The school program, headed in this region by Dr. Joseph Romig, employed trained nurses to spend time in each village, teaching personal and home sanitation to children and their parents.[10] On December 6th, 1910, Miss Ada Van Vranken arrived here as Seldovia's designated sanitation nurse.[11] This relieved Miss McMicheal of the burden, and as she noted:

> The swamp must be drained and the ground leveled before any gardening can be done or even the work of sanitation carried on to any great extent in the village, as it is no worse for the natives to have truck and trash in their yards than for the teacher to live that way. These people watch the teacher and do things just about as she does them. To prove this, one cold Friday the schoolroom was scrubbed with snow; the next day in making the weekly visit to the homes seven out of the eight houses visited had been scrubbed with snow.[12]

Miss Van Vranken worked with the children teaching personal hygiene, and then worked with their parents to show them how to disinfect and ventilate their homes. She gave spitting cups to the TB patients, and in the spring rolled up her sleeves and cleaned the yards of trash. Teacher and nurse worked together, Miss McMicheal making a game out of Friday hair-washing day such that the children, in a competitive spirit, tried to best one another in their cleanliness. She also rewarded them by having the best-groomed child of the week lead the twice-daily exercise sessions on the beach. The children became so proud of their new skills that they joined the two women in making a cleanup raid on a woman's trash-filled yard and burning the debris. The occupant was furious at first, accusing the do-gooders of making "too much smell" with their fire. However, when all was done, she was so impressed with the result that she told all her friends, and soon trash fires were being built all over the village.[13]

When the Bureau of Indian Affairs schools were set up, the teachers were charged with instructing students in the manual arts as well as the "three R's." Native pupils were to be taught the art of handling wooden boats, modern methods for curing and tanning skins, and agriculture, among other things.[14] It was this last category, agriculture, that dumfounded Miss McMicheal:

> The only place we have for a garden is the aforesaid swamp, and even if we would get some few plants to grow on the hillside the cows and pigs would eat them as our grounds are not fenced and the stock run at will over them. In fact, I do not understand how school gardening can possibly be a success here, as school closes usually May 31st, and the teacher leaves for some other school for the summer and every native goes up the bay to fish and hunt or to work in the fisheries.[15]

Miss McMicheal recommended that a man with knowledge of land clearing and soil preparation, familiarity with tools, and experience with agriculture in far northern climes be employed to handle this area of education.

With her other subjects, Miss McMicheal enjoyed much more success. At the beginning of her tenure, very few children spoke English. Those who could speak and read simply mimicked their teacher and had no idea of what they were saying. Unlike those before her, Miss McMicheal turned the learning of English into an interactive exercise. Instead of reading aloud sentences from a book, the children were made to turn these sentences into questions and ask them of a fellow student, who then had to make a response. Whispering during classes was even tolerated, as long as it was done in English. Those slipping into Russian or their native tongue had to sit under the desk for a spell; the children called it "Indian jail." It took time, but her method seemed to work, for eventually she heard English being used on the beach at playtime. In hindsight, it is unfortunate that the school did not make a formal effort to preserve the native tongue, for by the 1930's there were very few speakers of the Seldovia dialect left.

Miss McMicheal solved the problem of truancy by going and collecting the truant herself. Children and parents quickly realized that unless there was a good reason for a child to be absent, he was to be in school. One problem Miss McMicheal could not solve was the general destitution. Game had not yet rebounded from the devastation of the Russian fur-trading years, and many would have starved had it not been for the willingness of the local storekeeper, J.A. Herbert, to carry them through the winter. He knew that once their summer employment began he would be paid back. However, this spending of one's summer earnings to pay off past debts did little to prevent the same destitution from occurring again the next winter.[16]

University of Washington civil engineering student Juanita Anderson in 1912. She would go on to open the third Nelson school in Alaska, at Seldovia, on October 5, 1914. Photo courtesy of Ted Anderson from the Ralph and Juanita Anderson Collection.

A woman named Isabelle Gilman replaced Miss McMicheal, and taught here from 1912 through 1914. It was she who witnessed the measles epidemic that plagued those years, claiming over thirty people.[17] However Nick Elxnit, who arrived in Seldovia in 1913 with his parents, remembers being taught that year by a Mr. Nash, who lived at the schoolhouse with his wife and young son. It would appear that Miss Borst's tutelage in basket-making carried on after her departure, for Nick recalls that Thursdays were in part devoted to basket-making. The educational value of this activity was never very clear to Nick![18]

While Seldovia was working out the bugs in its new school, a U.S. Senator from Minnesota was becoming indoctrinated in the difficulties of educating children in Alaska. Senator Knute Nelson had been in Nome during the Gold Rush and had learned that white children who lived outside of incorporated towns had no school of their own. They were welcome to attend the Bureau of Indian Affairs schools, but, already knowing English, were out of place as far as the general curriculum was concerned.

Senator Nelson introduced into Congress a bill which would provide for the establishment of schools for white children outside of incorporated towns. These schools became known by the tongue-twisting moniker of "The Knute Nelson Schools For White Children Outside of Incorporated Towns." Thankfully, that awkward title was at some point reduced to simply, "The Nelson Schools."

Juanita Anderson titled this photo: "Father, just a little corner of my garden." She is shown just outside the Seldovia schoolhouse, c.1916. Photo courtesy of the Anchorage Museum of History and Art, #B90.3.5

Seldovia schoolhouse c. 1916. Photo courtesy of the Anchorage Museum of History and Art, #B91.9.137

Governor Hogatt was ruling the territory at this time, and he asked Juanita Anderson's mother to teach at Unga, the first Nelson school established under this Act. Alyce Anderson started up the second Nelson school, at Ninilchik, and it was here that daughter Juanita made the connection that led her to Seldovia.

Juanita was a civil engineering student at the University of Washington. While she was visiting her mother in Ninilchik, it was learned that Miss Gilman was ill and wouldn't be able to return to Seldovia. It was too late in the season to bring a teacher up from Outside. Annie Christensen of Seldovia, upon hearing that Juanita had some university training, journeyed north to Ninilchik to offer her the job. Over her mother's objections, Juanita hopped on the gas-boat with Annie and departed for Seldovia to open the third Nelson school on October 5, 1914.[19]

Juanita arrived to discover that the head of the Bureau of Indian Affairs schools in this region was stripping the schoolhouse in order to outfit a school at Knik. He only left the desks and the blackboard because there wasn't enough room on the boat. So, without books, Juanita began her teaching career instructing pupils through the fifth grade level. She gathered up newspapers and magazines to use as textbooks. She also did a lot of talking -- so much so that she soon lost her voice. By January a

By 1930, additions had been built onto the school, and the boardwalk ran in front of it. Photo courtesy of Ted Anderson from the Ralph and Juanita Anderson Collection.

In the foreground of this photograph, two cultures side by side are illustrated by the Seldovia schoolhouse at left, and the native barabara-like dwelling at right. Photo courtesy of the Alaska State Library, Clyda Schott Greely Collection, PCA 66-278

replacement teacher had arrived on the steamer, as well as a supply of school books and materials, and Juanita left to finish her degree.

Juanita returned to teach the next year at a salary of $150 a month,[20] and made Seldovia her home. Her marriage to Ralph and the birth of two sons precluded an extended teaching career, but she did teach again in the early 1920's. During this time, the school population grew to over 70 children ranging in age from 5 to 21.[21] This meant more teachers, the leasing of the old Russian log schoolroom, the conversion of the teachers' quarters into classrooms, and the building of several additions onto the main school building.[22]

Late Seldovian Nellie Pilskog recalled being taught by Jettret Stryker Peterson: "We'd do excercises first. Then the teacher would check our hands, ears, and neck for dirt and head cooties. Then we'd do school work."[23] Jettie Stryker was a childhood friend of Juanita Anderson, and had spent some time in Seldovia visiting Juanita during her first teaching stint. Around 1918, Juanita was asked to teach again, and accepted, only to discover she was pregnant. So Jettie came to Alaska and filled in for her. It became apparent that two teachers would be required to handle the growing school population, and so Allen

Jettie and Allen Peterson and their children Peggy and Jimmy, in 1925. Photo courtesy of Ted Anderson from the Ralph and Juanita Anderson Collection.

Jettie Stryker, childhood friend of Juanita Anderson, came to Seldovia to teach while Juanita began a family. Miss Stryker married fellow teacher Allen Peterson, and the couple taught and raised their own family here. Photo courtesy of Ted Anderson from the Ralph and Juanita Anderson Collection.

Peterson, back from WWI, was hired to be Jettie's assistant. Jettie and Allen married in 1919 and taught for three years. They then left the profession to try their hand at fox farming. By this time, Juanita was finished having children, and so came back to teach until 1925.

By the mid-1930's, the school population had so outgrown its original building that a new structure was built on the hill behind the fuel storage tanks. This building served Seldovians until the construction of the present school in the 1960's. All that remains of the 1930's era school are photographs such as the one below, and the wide concrete steps on the hillside, now much overgrown with grass.

From its first years until now, the school in Seldovia has always been one of the focal points of community social life. In 1915, a new maple floor was installed in the school house, and the desks were mounted on 2x4's so they could be moved aside for dancing. As the Russian Orthodox Sabbath was observed from six p.m. Saturday through six p.m. Sunday, dances were usually held on Sunday nights.[24] Seldovia writer Alice Lipke said of Seldovia in the 1920's : "People in Seldovia like children; they do yet. This village is a children's paradise."[25] That statement is still pretty true today. Not only parents, but oldsters and single folk turn out faithfully to pay and partake at countless fundraising school dinners. One can dine on tacos assembled by tiny second grade hands to help fund their class trip to Homer, or enjoy Oriental food supplemented by band and choral music, and local adult musical talent. (The latter function served to send the children to Nenana for a band workshop.) Basketball games have the power to draw out the entire community, even on the darkest, coldest winter nights.

A larger school was built about 1936 up the hill from the waterfront, and behind the fuel storage tanks. This building was demolished in the 1960's to make way for the construction of the current school shop building, but the old steps set into the hillside can still be seen. Photo courtesy of Ted Anderson from the Ralph and Juanita Anderson Collection.

Seldovia schoolchildren, 1915. Photo courtesy of Ted Anderson from the Ralph and Juanita Anderson Collection.

Teacher Jettie Peterson enjoys an outing with Seldovia schoolgirls in 1929. Photo courtesy of Ted Anderson from the Ralph and Juanita Anderson Collection.

The crowning school social event of the year is the Christmas program, which is capped by the arrival of Santa Claus, who hands out a goody-filled stocking to every child present.

As I write this, the Anchorage television stations boast of a plan in the school system there to eliminate overcrowding by bussing kindergarten children to a nearby high school. Parents of the tiny students were concerned that their children might be corrupted by the teenagers, and exposed to knives, guns, and drug use. Happy was everyone when this proved to be far from the case. The high school students took the little ones under their wing, and everyone was enriched by the experience. Had they only looked to Seldovia, they would have seen that this mingling of all ages has worked well here since the turn of the century. The Susan B. English (named for Adam Bloch's daughter Susan) School here today has separate classrooms for grades Kindergarten through Twelve, but all students share a common gym, lunch room, swimming pool and locker room, outdoor playground, library, and art room. Between classes and after school, all sizes of scholars can be seen racing around the building, and there is a tolerance and affection among the older students for their underclassmen that is seldom seen in larger schools.

Special Delivery: Seldovia's Post Office

The Post Office in Seldovia was established in 1898. John Wall Smith, agent for the Northern Commercial Company, was appointed Postmaster on Sept. 10th of that year.[26] This is the "Mr. Schmidt of the Northern Alaska Trading Company" referred to by Russian priest John Bortnovsky as being the person to donate the bell to the local chapel. He served until 1902, when he gave up both his trading company position and his job as Postmaster to James Cleghorn. The two businesses were operated from the same building, and the Northern Commercial Company steamships brought the mail. In 1905, Adam Bloch, agent for the Alaska Commercial Company, was appointed Postmaster, probably because around this time the steamships of the Alaska Commercial Company took over the duty of carrying the U.S. Mail.[27] The earliest photographs of the Seldovia Post Office were taken during Mr. Bloch's tenure, which lasted until his death in 1915.

In 1906, the mail was delivered to Seward by steamers coming up from Outside. The Alaska Commercial Company steamer, *Dora*, brought mail once a month from Seward to Nushagak, stopping at

Postmaster Adam Bloch and the Seldovia Post Office, 1907. Photo courtesy of the Jack and Susan B. English Collection.

Mail clerk John Thwaites, from the S. S. Dora, took many of the early photographs of Seldovia. Here Mr. Thwaites enjoys a respite from work on board the ship. Photo courtesy of the Alaska State Library, Thwaites Collection, PCA 18-50

Seldovia, Homer, Kodiak, Uyak, Karluk, Coal Bay, Chignik, Unga, Sand Point, Cold Harbor, Petkafsky, Sarechief, and Scotch Cap.[28] The Homer Post Office, opened to accomodate the coal trade on the Spit, closed in 1907, so that port-of-call was eliminated from the list and the Homer mail was distributed from Seldovia.[29]

During the Gold Rush years, Seldovia's Post Office was often as crowded with mail as the waterfront and dock were with freight. The *Dora* made one especially crowded trip, when 139 sacks of mail were carried from Seward, destined for ports from Seldovia to Nushagak. The mail clerk, John Thwaites, had difficulty finding room for it all, and was forced to shift everything about when the time came to unload.[30] (It was Thwaites, by the way, whom we have to thank for many of the early photographs of Seldovia.)

Up until 1909, the Alaska Commercial Company vessels also held the contract for delivering mail from Seldovia to waypoints on Cook Inlet. In December of 1909, James Ward and Thomas O'Dale took over the contract from the Alaska Commercial Company for $2400 a year. On the 5th and the 15th of each month, they picked up mail from steamers calling at Seldovia and carried it north. The route included Homer, Kasilof, Kenai, Tyonic, Knik, Hope, Sunrise, and Girdwood.[31]

Merchant J.A. Herbert filled in as Postmaster after Adam Bloch's death, and then in January of 1916 Bloch's daughter Annie Christensen took over the job. She served for five years, and was succeeded by a string of short-timers: Eugene Bogart, Juanita Anderson, and Milo Hulbert. The latter resigned to accept the position of U.S. Deputy Marshal, and Susan Bloch, another of Adam's daughters, was appointed on June 12, 1925.[32]

Miss Susan Bloch, who in a year would become Susan B. English, was Seldovia's career Postmistress. Operating for the next forty-three years from the same building as had her father, Mrs. English witnessed the greatest growth in the role of the Seldovia Post Office.

By the 1920s, Seldovia had blossomed with people and a booming fishing economy, necessitating once-weekly mail delivery from Seward. Seldovia's mail distribution responsibilities grew to include Anchorage and Iliamna. Heinie Berger's popular *M.S. Discoverer* was one of the boats that carried mail to the northern Inlet ports.[33]

Homesteaders living around Kachemak Bay had no regular way of sending or receiving mail if they were

---

OFFICE NO. 05605   FOURTH CLASS

United States Post Office

SUSAN E. ENGLISH, POSTMASTER

SELDOVIA, ALASKA

Susan B. English (not "E." as shown in the above letterhead) was Seldovia's postmistress for 43 years. Courtesy of the Gruber family.

For many years, Susan Bloch English was Seldovia's Postmistress. Using the same building as had her father just after the turn of the century, Mrs. English and her husband Jack also operated the Seldovia News Stand. This 1954 photo is courtesy of the Jack and Susan B. English Collection.

not on the route of villages served by Seldovia vessels, so Mrs. English set aside a mailpouch for each small settlement and accumulated the letters, packages, and magazines due them. Whenever someone from the wilderness came to Seldovia (and she could judge him reliable), Mrs. English sent him off with the appropriate bag to its eager consignees. As Mrs. English was also the volunteer librarian, she could be counted upon to include in the mailbag a package of books on loan, knowing that eventually they would find their way back to Seldovia.[34]

Patience and tenacity were necessary virtues for early postal patrons. Bad weather could delay mail for weeks, even months. In the 1930's Iliamna residents once waited six months for their Sears & Roebuck and Montgomery Ward winter clothing and supply orders to be filled. The holdup was due not to stockroom malaise but to mail "lost" under a driftwood log on the beach near Iliamna Bay. Captain Nate White failed to return one fall from his last Seldovia to Iliamna freight and mail run of the season. In the spring, Seldovia boatman Jack Fields made a trip there, and found the mail safe and sound in two pouches on the beach. The contents were sent on their way by Mrs. English and the grateful Iliamna residents received their by now much-needed purchases.[35] In *The Alaska Weekly*, a reference is made to a mail boat bound from Iliamna that wrecked and left its mail on the beach there in October 1925. This mail too was salvaged, and a registered letter that had been destined for Seattle finally made it there in May of 1926![36]

With the advent of air service from the Lower 48 the use of steamers to carry mail to Seward was discontinued. Mail instead moved by air to Anchorage. When the Seward and Sterling Highways were built in the late 1950s, linking Anchorage to Homer, Seldovia ceased to be a distribution point for Inlet communities. Our mail came then, and now, from Homer, first by boat, and, beginning in 1961, by bush plane. Through the stormy winter months, flying is severely curtailed and it is not uncommon for Seldovians to receive mail only once or twice a week.

After the 1964 earthquake, the Post Office moved into temporary quarters while Urban Renewal was busy rearranging the waterfront. By 1968, the Post Office had been relocated to its present site. Susan B. English retired from her career in 1974 and passed away in 1986, leaving an empty spot in the community with her passing.[37]

Even today, the Seldovia Post Office is a social magnet for the community. Many local folks are seldom seen out and about, except for their daily pilgrimages to the Post Office. Our mail arrives on a plane around eleven o'clock, weather and space permitting. By noon, folks begin to congregate at the Post Office, with great anticipation at the thought of a mail order parcel arriving, or the mail box holding a letter from a faraway loved one. Much time can be idled away here, reading the public information bulletin boards—one for City business, one for school announcements, and one a free-for-all of meeting notices, items for sale, pleas to help find lost pets or bicycles, letters from former residents to be shared with the community, and flyers touting the Friday night specials at the local restaurants. At Christmas, a special bulletin board is dedicated to Christmas cards, and it is here that Seldovians tack up their Christmas greetings to the community. The Postmistress receives similar cards from former Seldovians who just wish to be remembered or to say hello, and these go on the board as well. Many issues of world and local significance are discussed and chewed over by small groups of people, both inside the Post Office and in the sunshine on its front step.

Law and (dis)Order in Early Seldovia

Prior to the turn of the century, the task of sorting out disputes generally fell to the commercial company agents. Misdeeds done by church members might be referred to the Orthodox priest on his visit. Until "outsiders" began flowing through Seldovia, bringing liquor with them, things were fairly calm.

The first decade of the twentieth century was a lawless time in much of Alaska, and Seldovia was no exception. Great numbers of gold-field-bound transients descended upon the quiet community, spreading corruption in their wake. Seldovia had no law enforcement or court system of its own, and thus matters requiring a judge were referred to Seward. Witnesses, victims, and the accused journeyed to Seward by steamship, and the convicted served their jail time there.

This 1905 murder made front page headlines in the *Seward Daily Gateway* of October 12th. Those involved were former Seldovians.

(See article at right) Like others living along the south shore of Kachemak Bay, Murray and Fisk should have been regular visitors to Seldovia to pick up their mail and restock their larder. When they were not heard from for six months, friends in Seldovia became anxious and Mr. Whorf headed up the search party that found Fisk. During Hildreth's investigation of the case, it was learned that Murray

---

Seward Daily Gateway - October 12, 1905

With the mark of a rifle ball on the back of the vertebrae the skeleton of Jim Fisk was found a few days ago at Halibut Bay. In the cabin occupied by himself and John Murray, his prospecting partner, were found a bloody knife and razor and other indications of a sanguine struggle. Murray is missing but in the cabin was found a package of letters written by him but not mailed, whose text indicate that he was stark mad. Both men were well known on the inlet where they had worked for several years. They left Seldovia last February with a large outfit to go to Halibut bay to work mining property there. Neither has since been seen alive. Fisk's skeleton, destitute of flesh, was found by natives a few days ago. It was recognized by the clothing. William Whorf of Seldovia accompanied the natives who found Fisk's remains to the scene and identified it by the clothing and by letters found in the cabin. The letters came to Judge Hildreth [in Seward] on the *Portland*.

In the letters written by Murray he states that he and Fisk had agreed to die. To Joseph S. Lewis of Victoria, B.C. he wrote, "Give my best regards to wife, son, and daughter. I am about to die in a few seconds." Then follows a long rambling statement which is plainly the product of an unhinged mind. It is socialistic in tone, critical of religion and kingcraft, showing that the writer had brooded over topics of that nature.

The letter which was most homicidal in tone was probably the last written, as it was not enclosed in an envelope. It read as follows: "Halibut Cove Alaska 16-2-1905 Dear Brother by a strange mystery I happen to be stokes in my past life and my partner Jim Fisk we also found out the purpose of life why there is such a strife in this world between races and individuals we allso know who is and what is god so we have agreed that my partner fiske should kill me today at 5 o'clock and he is to be killed after me by some agency. all this is for wrongs committed in our past lives and also for the sake of humanity me and fisk represent the men in all its countries cruel strifes against not only men but women we have agreed to wipe out all the scores of out of

...continued...

our past lives in a sane and friendly way so that in doing this we forgive one another as well as we forgive all our enemies we also ask to be forgiven and forgive to be forgiven. kinly regards to all mankind and to all its earthly creatures I know that my mother is dead she has been here for some time my mother represents womankind for all the cruelties suffered from men."

While the possibility of murder is a feature of the case, and Judge Wickersham last night instructed Assistant United States Attorney Clegg and Commissioner Hildreth to make a searching investigation, it is thought more probable that Murray while insane killed Fisk and then made away with himself either by drowning or by going far into the interior and shooting himself. The bloodstained knife and razor and marks of blood on the cabin furniture are proof of a struggle there. Fisk's body was found a few steps away. It is thought probable that Murray assaulted him in the cabin with a knife: that Fisk escaped and ran and Murray then shot him in the back.

Fisk is known to have had $700 when he left Seldovia. Murray also had money but none was found in the cabin or in Fisk's clothing. But for the crazy letters left by Murray circumstances would point to murder and robbery. These letters are addressed to men and women in various coast cities, including one to the Portugese "cost counselor," San Leandro, California. Murray's real name was John M. Moreira. He signs this to some of the letters he wrote, and among his other papers is a certificate of naturalization which he took out in Oakland, California, January 28, 1905, a few days before he came north. All his letters are dated the second month of 1905, but that is evidently a mistake as in two of them he speaks of having arrived at Halibut bay "the 24th of last month," which would be January. But he was naturalized in California four days later...and was in Seldovia in February. The letters were doubtless written in March.

Murray and Fisk had worked together two or three years at different places around the Inlet. Last year they worked for James O. Buzard at Hope. They were industrious men and saved money. Murder and suicide by an insane man seems to be the only theory that fits the case."

had been spotted in California after the time of the murder. He disappeared though, and it was not until 1909 that he was found again, this time in Honolulu, Hawaii, where he was running a very successful drug store.[38] Although an effort was made to extradite him to Alaska to stand trial, it is not known if the law was successful in doing so.

In looking through Jack English's collection of papers with him some years ago, I came across depositions from a case even more compelling than that of Murray and Fisk; a case that must have been one of the biggest stories of the day in Southcentral Alaska. This was the case of Valentine, Fuller, and Kares. While undertaking later research, I found the story was followed closely by the *Seward Weekly Gateway*, and subsequently discovered related photographs in the Anchorage Museum of History and Art.

In late March of 1909, three men made an ill-fated hunting trip on Kachemak Bay. They had been waiting at Seldovia for the Cook Inlet icepack to break so they could continue their journey north to the Interior gold fields. To pass the time, they decided to undertake a brief hunting trip up Kachemak Bay from Seldovia. Jack Kares, from Cordova, and the elderly Mr. W. D. Valentine, a recent Colorado emigree, were joined by Mr. Elli Fuller, a young man whose origins were unknown.

On March 24th, the three left Seldovia and reached Lone Island (presumably an island east of Seldovia, on the south shore of Kachemak Bay) in the late afternoon. The wind was rising, so they camped there for the night. Twenty-four hours later, the seas were calm enough to attempt a crossing to the Homer Spit. Only a small cloud to the westward threatened bad weather.

"Do you think we should attempt the crossing?" Kares asked the young Fuller. "If **you** think so," came the reply. "Well, all right," exclaimed Kares, "Spit on your hands and go to it." By this he meant for them all to get a good grip on the oars, and be ready to row. When they had ventured about a mile and a half into the bay, the wind picked up sharply from the west. Fuller looked to Kares for direction, and Kares replied, "Run for shore as quick as God will let us." The wind increased as they rowed, forcing them to run before it. This meant that they veered east of their intended destination. (Author's note: I've made several violent crossings from these islands to the Homer Spit and can vouch that a west wind blows exactly crossways to the optimal route.) The sea rose quickly, threatening to swamp the dory. Kares threw a sack of flour overboard and yelled to Fuller to ditch the bedding. The young fellow replied, "Better drown than freeze to death!" Kares hollered at him to follow orders and bail, since he didn't seem to be doing a good job of rowing.[39]

In a snowy gale, the trio finally landed an hour before dark at China Poot Bay on a spit that protected a lagoon from the rough waters of Kachemak Bay. Kares hiked up the spit and determined that it did indeed connect with the mainland. He instructed Fuller to unload the boat and bring it around into the lagoon, but the young man refused. Old Valentine was near dead from the cold, he said, and they ought to simply turn the dory over where it lay and make a shelter immediately. Once the shelter was erected, the two put Valentine underneath and wrapped him in the tent, for they could not make it stretch far enough over the dory to provide a windbreak. Kares tried to gather firewood, but could only scavenge a few small sticks. So, cold and tired, they huddled together under the dory. Kares had misgivings about their location, but was unsuccessful in motivating his exhausted companions.[40]

At four a.m., Kares was awakened by the rising tide washing under him. He jumped up and hollered, "For God's sake, boys, let's get everything and get it over in the lagoon!" The boat had righted itself on the tide, and Valentine and Fuller were inside, freezing under wet blankets. Kares alone was left to fight the surf and the cakes of floating ice. At last he got the dory around the spit to the lagoon, but by this time it was full of water and his companions were hypothermic. He landed on the east side of the lagoon and bailed the boat as best he could. Advising his companions to keep moving, he ran into the woods to find boughs for a fire, only to discover that his matches were wet. Five minutes' walk from the boat, he found a cabin and rushed back to tell his companions.[41]

Kares, his own feet bare and frozen, told Valentine and Fuller to cheer up and follow him to the cabin. "Take him (Fuller)," Valentine croaked, "as I am too weak and pretty nearly dead." So Kares dragged the semi-conscious Fuller up the beach, expending the last of his energy. Moments later, Fuller died in his arms.

Kares knew that he himself might not survive if he had to go back for Valentine and carry him too, so he went on to the cabin alone. It was the home of some natives who were out when he arrived, but who returned shortly thereafter. They brought the lone survivor to Seldovia, and Kares was dispatched on the steamer *Bertha* to the nearest doctor, who announced upon examining him that he would surely have to amputate several toes, if not whole feet.[42]

These events were tragic and created a compelling story, but they were only part of the whole affair. As the nearest settlement, Seldovia became involved in the aftermath of the tragedy. Jack Kares was brought

Tom O'Dale and Sydney Laurence (two middle figures) with two unidentified men in front of the U. S. Commissioner's office on the Seldovia waterfront, c.1910. Photo courtesy of the Anchorage Museum of History and Art, # B91.9.134

here by Henry China Poot, the native who shared the name of the bay on which he lived. It was in fact Poot's cabin into which Kares stumbled. As China Poot came up the lagoon on his way home, he spied the body of Valentine sprawled on the beach with eagles picking at its face. He fired a shot from his rifle, which roused Jack Kares to come crawling out of the cabin, whereupon he told China Poot the story.[43] China Poot was paid $5.00 for his services to bring Kares to Seldovia, and his receipt was signed by Adam Bloch and the painter, Sydney Laurence.[44] The latter was setting aside his artistic pursuits for a few years to search the Cook Inlet streams and beaches for gold.

A group of prospectors appointed themselves to take Jack Kares's deposition, this miners' inquest including Seldovians R.G. Doherty, R.B. Barnes, Tom O'Dale, Samuel May, and Sydney Laurence.[45] After listening to Kares's story, the men decided that Valentine and Fuller had indeed died of exposure, rather than foul play or neglect, and they exonerated Jack Kares from all blame in the matter.

The next order of business was to go and retrieve the bodies of the deceased from China Poot's cabin. Tom O'Dale was paid $40 to boat up the bay and bring back Valentine and Fuller. Captain Blodgett supplied the lumber for the coffins at a cost of $8.50, and from merchant J.A. Herbert was purchased the hardware. James Linder was given $8.00 to build the coffins, and Miss Mimi Blodgett, for $5.00, supplied and sewed the black cloth linings. Several unidentified native men received $7.50 for digging the graves, and Adam Bloch was paid $20.00 for orchestrating the whole procedure.[46]

Next came the job of inventorying everything down to the last handkerchief found on the bodies of the two men. Both men carried personal effects and a little over $50 apiece in cash.[47] Undoubtedly many things were lost overboard in the surf. Sold at auction were all the items found with the men, and those things that they had left behind in Seldovia: tools and camping equipment mostly. Two gold watches belonging to Elli Fuller were listed as "not for sale."[48]

On April 14th, Adam Bloch wrote to Seward to Judge J.L. Reed, the U.S. Commissioner in charge of law enforcement here. Dutifully he related the steps taken in handling the estates of Valentine and Fuller, and enclosed receipts and accountings for everything. He noted that he was holding cash and two gold watches, and awaiting further instruction. Mr. Bloch couldn't find any relatives for Mr. Fuller, but on the person of Mr. Valentine, he found a Grand Junction, Colorado, address. In April, he wrote to Mrs. Valentine to inform her that she was a widow.

The citizens of Seldovia turn out to pay their respects to Valentine and Fuller, who lie on the beach in their coffins awaiting burial. Photo courtesy of the Anchorage Museum of History and Art, #B91.9.135

Shortly thereafter, he received this impassioned reply:

> Dear Sir, I received your letter of April the 1st telling me of my darling husband's death. Now as a broken hearted wife, I ask you to please tell me all the particulars and all about it, and I would like to have all his belongings sent to me, his beds and tool chest and two guns, all his clothes. If there [isn't] money enough to send them let me know what it will cost. I would thank you very kindly if you will inform me if his body can be sent here. If not, what kind of a place is his dear body buried in. Do you know if he had made any requests for pity of a broken hearted wife and family. Please tell me all you can. I must have his things if possible.
>
> Very kindly,
>
> Mrs. Mattie Valentine [49]

It appears as though Bloch sent the widow about $12 in cash and five packages of effects. In a May 31st letter, she again beseeched him to send everything belonging to her late husband, and she advised that she was dispatching a gentlemen to retrieve her husband's body. Thus far, it sounded like the voice of a truly grief-stricken widow. However....enter, stage right, the cashier of The Bank of Meeker, Colorado: Mr. A. C. Moulton. On April 27, 1909, he wrote Adam Bloch to advise that he had just been appointed administrator of the affairs of W.D. Valentine. Mr. Moulton had read Bloch's initial letter to the widow, and rushed to inform him that Mr. Valentine had divorced her over a year ago. A grandmother, Mrs. Valentine had allegedly "conducted herself in such a way with a young man that her husband had to divorce her." Mr. Valentine, normally a hearty man, able to withstand much physical stress, had in Mr. Moulton's opinion, lost heart after divorcing his wife and lost the will to live. Thus, Mrs. Valentine had no claim on the estate, especially since her late husband had been heavily in debt to others.[50] It was too late now, of course, to retrieve those items sent to Mrs. Valentine. Adam Bloch must have been groaning in frustration at this point, and to top it all, this icy editorial appeared in the *Seward Weekly Gateway* on May 29, 1909:

> **SEWARD WEEKLY GATEWAY**
> **May 29, 1909:**
>
> "Some curious people would like to know what became of the effects of Valentine and Fuller, the two men who died from exposure and exhaustion in Cook Inlet some two months ago. They are known to have left three gold watches, rifles, dories, and overcoat worth $30, and a sum of money said to be $100. There are some people in Seldovia who could probably answer this question if they were so disposed. And they probably will answer it."

This is the last we hear of the Valentine and Fuller case. It is reasonable to assume that after Mr. Bloch satisfied those peevish persons in Seward, the whole matter blew over. The bodies of Fuller, and perhaps Valentine, lie somewhere in Seldovia in peaceful slumber.

While the saga of Valentine and Fuller was unfurling, Mrs. Mercer, a career troublemaker from Seward, was taking advantage of attentions turned elsewhere. She allegedly stole $100 worth of lumber from merchant J.A. Herbert and took over his hotel, holding him at bay with a gun. Unknown was her motivation for such acts, but by the time a marshal could be dispatched from Seward to investigate, the case had fallen apart. The court in Seward later dismissed the case against her for lack of evidence.[51]

Later that year, Herbert himself went before the court in Seward to answer charges of bootlegging, brought against him by John A. Sanburn, a watchman aboard the barkentine *Amelia*. Sanburn stated that he had purchased a bottle of liquor from Herbert for $2.[52] Why he then turned and accused Herbert of selling liquor without a license is a mystery. Perhaps the stuff was no good!

Capping off the lawless year of 1909 was a knife fight at the end of December. Captain Albert Filmore was having a party and the liquor was flowing freely. Two guests, Captain Andrew Johnson and a man named Duffy, fell to arguing and then exchanged blows, Captain Johnson apparently the aggressor. Duffy pulled a knife and stabbed Johnson twice: once in the chest and once in the right shoulder. There was no physician in Seldovia so Miss Van Vranken, the sanitation nurse, was summoned. She dressed the wounds and sewed them up, and was credited with saving Johnson's life.[53]

By the time a team of Seward lawmen reached Seldovia, over a month had passed. Now it was revealed that the knife wielding guest was not Duffy, but an elderly gentleman named Mr. Markle. Because Capt. Johnson was identified as the aggressor, attacking Markle without provocation, no charges were filed in the case. This certainly differed from the original story, and it was becoming evident that Seldovia needed its own law enforcement official.[54]

Finally, in October 1910, Seldovia got its first judge: G. W. Kuppler was appointed U.S. Commissioner of Seldovia.[55] After him followed other commissioners, such as Ralph Anderson, Sid Bettman, and G.M. Chambers, as well as those appointed to serve as U.S. Marshals. For many years, the commissioner was paid out of the fees he collected for his services. Finally, in 1947, a bill was introduced in the territorial legislature to pay commissioners a salary, ranging from $2400 to $5000 a year.[56]

Gilbert M. Chambers owned the mercantile Chambers and Caldwell, operated a clam cannery, and was one of Seldovia's U. S. Commissioners. Photo courtesy of Ted Anderson from the Ralph and Juanita Anderson Collection.

Major crimes in Seldovia were the exception, there being mostly "garden variety" disturbances such as public drunkenness and brawls to straighten out. Sometimes, matters left alone resolved themselves, as in the case of Charles Corser and Robert Hawes. The two men together owned and operated the coal oil steamer, *Yentna*, on the upper reaches of the river of the same name. Some disagreement in 1906 found the men chasing one another up and down the beach on the Seldovia waterfront, wielding knife and gun. They ran, yelling and brandishing, until they wore themselves out. Weapons put aside and exercise having cleared their heads, they commenced to iron out their business differences in a more civilized fashion![57]

By the 1920s, Seldovia had a jail, but designed to hold only a prisoner or two. U.S. Marshal Jimmy Hill, upholding the Fisheries Law in place at the time, one day arrested forty fishermen. Obligingly, they slept that night on the jail floor and elsewhere about the building, both in and outside of the cells, until things could be sorted out.[58]

Jim Busey recalls: "When we came, Milo Hulbert was the U.S. Marshal. He would let his prisoners leave the jail during the day to find work or take care of personal needs; but I well recall that he warned them that if they didn't return by 9 p.m., he'd lock them out."[59]

Lawrence Dunning Jr. remembers his father describing how the U.S. Marshal here in the 1920s exercised his law enforcement powers. Apparently some of the habitual drunkards were also some of the town's most talented musicians. If they happened to be in jail on the weekend when a big dance was planned, the marshal would let them out to provide the music for the event![60]

Jimmy Hill, and after him Milo Hulbert, traveled as far as Kenai to uphold the law. Through the 1920's, it was not uncommon for the Seldovia marshal to be called away to investigate a death in Kenai, or to escort a lawbreaker to trial in Anchorage.[61]

The Alaska territory was divided into judicial districts, and Seldovia fell into the Third Judicial District. Periodically, through the 1940's, the district court judge arrived here once a year on a steamship or Coast Guard cutter to hold floating court before moving on to another coastal community.[62] From 1910 through 1915, the floating court made its rounds each summer. In 1926, the practice was resumed, the ship starting at Naknek and proceeding on to Dillingham, Unalaska, Sanak, Belkofsky, Unga, Kodiak, and ending in Seldovia about three weeks later. Judge Ritchie presided over the court, which sailed complete with a district attorney and a district clerk. During the summer of 1926, a schoolteacher enroute to his job served as court reporter.[63]

When Seldovia incorporated as a city in 1945, part of the impetus to do so was to gain more local control of the law enforcement system. The flyer on page 183 was circulated by the Committee for Incorporation.[64]

In the 1940's, a former private home was converted to Seldovia's jail. Pieces of water pipe were cut to the size of the windows, and each end flattened. The pieces of pipe were laid vertically across the window and the flattened ends were nailed to the frame. Escape was apparently not difficult. Photo courtesy of the Jack and Susan B. English Collection.

Raise Yer Jug: Bootlegging in Seldovia

The years "1928-1933 were among the last prohibition years, [Prohibition was in place from 1918 through 1933] and Seldovia was renowned as a center of bootlegging. According to one report of the Internal Revenue Service... amidst a population of about 370 people there were at that time no less than 39 bootleggers... more than one for each ten people, including children. Some of the stuff that was consumed was pretty unhealthy... people would drink all winter, then show up at the R.C. Morris store with a complaint and a request for medicine, saying that for some reason their stomachs didn't feel too good. After big parties, some people had to be conveyed in wheelbarrows to their homes... Once some poor fellow was tipped over by his only slightly more sober wheelbarrow-pusher friend, but fortunately fell only a short distance to the sand beach near the Estes Cannery." [65]

Former Seldovian Jim Busey, who wrote the previous paragraph, recalls the wrath of the IRS. He and the son of George Baltazar, the barber, were upstairs in the Baltazar home. The barber, like many residents at the time, made moonshine on the side to supplement his income. As the boys played, they heard a crash from down below and then the smashing of glass. The IRS had stormed the house and was destroying the still. Quietly, young Jim sneaked out the window and ran home.[66]

Some of the most unlikely folks operated stills. Jim remembers the Russian priest, Father Sarikovicoff, helped to support his large family by bootlegging. He also was in heavy debt to Frank Raby, who was having trouble collecting payment. One day, Frank spied the IRS boat steaming into Seldovia Bay. He ran and told the Father, and together they moved the still into a back room at Frank's store. That's where it stayed, the debt considered settled.[67] Frank later moved this still, or one similar, to his property at Raby's Spit on the west side of Seldovia Bay.[68]

Supporting one's family was a not uncommon reason to engage in bootlegging. A woman blessed with many children made homebrew, and fed and clothed her family with the proceeds. Most small time bootleggers did not practice the craft to get rich or to corrupt their neighbors, but simply to support themselves during lean economic times.[69] Nick Elxnit reports that moonshine went for as much as $20 a gallon, or $3 a pint.[70]

Seemingly innocuous ads in the newspaper touting "soft drinks for sale" were oftentimes coded messages advising those in the know that bootleg liquor was also sold under the counter.

VOTE

FOR A "NEW DEAL" IN SELDOVIA
THE LAW IS YOUR FRIEND   ITS MISUSE YOUR ENEMY

After Election on May 1st, Your City Council will appoint a Chief of Police and Police Judge from Seldovia Residents. These men will be Your SERVANTS AND NOT RULERS. They are appointed for a term of ONE YEAR and may for cause, be removed at any time—They are not appointed for Life. To aid in Good Government, Local Ordinances will be drawn, consistent with the laws of Alaska—no new laws will be made. Your Local Court will prosecute and not persecute.

Long jail sentences are a thing of the past. It has been proved that a small fine will accomplish more. "It is not the severity of punishment that deters crime, it is the surety."

Our problems are no worse than those of other unincorporated areas, except during the summer and when a Steamer is in. Somehow, Seldovia has the name of being an Open Town where anything goes—and usually does. It is this situation that must be curbed and it is this Class of Fines that will pay our Police Dept.

No one wants a Blue Law in Seldovia but during the Summer and when a Boat is in, we must have Law and Order in public places. The streets must be a safe and decent place for women and girls to walk on without being insulted, when the Boat is in. Our local drinkers are in the main, Gentlemen, and we now have the opportunity to make Gentlemen out of the strangers within our gates.

Police Departments are practically self-supporting everywhere so there is little worry for taxpayers here. Fines will be substituted for jail terms and all that will be needed is an overnight Jail for Misdemeanors—Felony cases will go to the Commissioner. Fines will be collected from those who are broke, when they have money. BUT as has been said before, our trouble lies with the Outsiders and not local residents.

EQUAL RIGHTS TO ALL PERSONS WILL BE THE COURT'S ORDER. Native and white, rich and poor will all get the same fair and square deal. If for no other reason, every man and woman in Seldovia should—VOTE FOR INCORPORATION. DON'T MISS THIS CHANCE.

A VOTE FOR INCORPORATION IS A VOTE FOR JUSTICE AND A NEW DEAL.

NOTE: Nothing contained herein is to be taken as criticism of the U.S.Commissioner or U.S.Marshal, who are handicapped by Federal Laws and Orders—within a Town.

Establishments which at various times allegedly subscribed to this practice were Baltazar's Barber Shop, Joe Hill's Place, The Owl Cardroom, and the Seldovia House Hotel. Other individuals simply sold out of their homes.[71]

U. S. Deputy Marshal Jimmy Hill met his end in the fall of 1924 while trying to bring several bootleggers to justice.[72] Hill, jail guard Milo Hulbert, and a man named Jacobsen made their way to the head of the Seldovia Slough to the home of William Brooks, a suspected bootlegger. Upon arrival at Brooks's home, Hill and his assistants found Brooks together with three other suspects. The four men were placed under arrest without incident, and Hulbert was dispatched to escort three of them to the Seldovia jail. Hill and Jacobsen stayed behind to try to locate a still believed to be on the property. Brooks was apparently left unguarded. The lawmen were inspecting a tent behind Brooks's residence when the bootlegger came out of his house and began shooting into the tent with a Remington 35mm automatic. Hill and Jacobsen ran out of the tent, and Brooks shot Hill in the back, killing him instantly. William Brooks then went into his house, put the gun to his head, and committed suicide.[73] Here was the very tragic side of bootlegging. Both Hill and Brooks left behind wives and children, who together with the community were stunned at this violence. Jimmy Hill was given an Anchorage funeral by his old friends at the American Legion and the Elks.[74] Milo Hulbert became the next U.S. Deputy Marshal.

Prohibition forced those wishing to have a drink, even occasionally, to be creative about concealing their imbibing. In the author's own home, (the old R.V. Anderson home), the dining room was the site of such surreptitious merrymaking. Between 1925 and 1935, a group of Seldovia men formed the Ace-In-The-Hole Poker Club. They met once a month from fall through spring, and played stud and draw poker. The homemade liquor of Seldovia is said to have had an excellent reputation in the Kachemak Bay area. Usually one of the members was able to bring a jug of home-brewed whiskey so each member could have a drink or two.

After the game was over, the men would have a "mug up," a term borrowed from the maritime industries where hands would duck inside the ship's cabin for a hot drink and a bite to eat. The poker club mug-up consisted of a hot dish of chili and beans, and sandwiches made of chopped garlic and homemade mayonnaise. It is not known for sure if the purpose of such fragrant fare was to deceive the local marshal should he be encountered later in the evening, or to avoid detection by the wives waiting at home.

The founding members of this illustrious group included Axel Anderson, Allen Peterson, Nig Lippincott, Ralph Anderson, Ed Jensen, Gilbert Chambers, Jack Tansy, Adam Lipke, and Bill Maitland. When they were in town, Lynn Jorgensen, Bill Studdart, and Jack English were included, as were the captains and engineers of whichever steamship might be in port. [75]

The club even had its civic side, evidenced in 1933 when Jack English, at a public meeting, volunteered the group to seek out a plot for a city cemetery. The matter had been raised by Juanita Anderson, who felt that the community should find a place for burials which would avoid trespassing on Russian Church cemetery ground. The public must have had faith in the group's ability to perform away from the poker table, for they voted unanimously to have the club undertake the task. [76]

In the late 1920s and early 1930s, R.V. Anderson was also a member of a group called "Pirates of the Cove." These were men of Seldovia and Halibut Cove who were affiliated with the herring fishery, which was prospering at the time. Jack Tansy and Ed Jensen, too, were members of this mysterious club, as well as Lynn Jorgensen, John Emil, and Bill Studdart. Ted Anderson doesn't recall the primary purpose of his father's club, but does note that the members would get together for a drink or two. They even had

The R.V. Anderson home (in the background on the hill and surrounded by fence posts) housed the unofficial Ace-in-the-Hole Poker Club during Prohibition. This 1926 photo is courtesy of Ted Anderson, from the Ralph and Juanita Anderson Collection.

William Studdart, shown here in Seldovia in August 1917 with his fresh-baked pies, was in charge of the Cook Inlet District for the Bureau of Fisheries. By 1925 he worked for the North American Fisheries Company as manager of the floating salmon processor, the Rosamond.[77] When in Seldovia, he was also a member of the Ace-in-the-Hole Poker Club. Photo courtesy of the U. S. Geological Survey, J. B. Mertie Collection, #651

a special "Pirates of the Cove" pin made, one of which Ted was given by his father.[78]

Ted also recalls an amusing story about a Seldovia Bay bootlegger named Dan Place. The year was around 1930. Milo Hulbert was the Deputy Marshal, and he lived above the jail in a building built on pilings over the beach. Dan Place made beer up the bay, in the bight behind Nordyke Island (today known as Powder Island). Across the bay, T. W. Lloyd made moonshine. The revenue service had heard about these two "entrepreneurs" and came to Seldovia to investigate. Ted feels that had the revenue service not caught wind of the operations, Marshal Hulbert would probably have let the two men go on about their business. Hulbert figured that if they made a raid on Dan Place, the revenue agent would be satisfied, and T. W. Lloyd could be left undisturbed. So that's just what they did. Dan Place had apparently been tipped off that they were coming, and had put all his beer profits in coffee cans and buried them on the beach. Through a misunderstanding with his partner, some of the cans got hastily dug up at the last moment and thrown into the bay, but apparently Place was able to retrieve most all of them later. Hulbert and the agent arrived in a huge dory. They filled the dory full of beer bottles, all of which had a good inch of yeast in their bottoms. They paraded back into Seldovia, and to show the agent and the town that he was doing his job, Hulbert dropped all the beer, bottle by bottle, off the deck of his place and onto the beach below. Ted Anderson recalls that the resulting foamy mess was spectacular.[79]

On the Boardwalk

Prior to the 1920s and the herring boom, Seldovians traveled from one end of town to the other by boat at high tide and on the beach when the tide was low. The terrain of pre-earthquake Seldovia was that of foothills sloping directly into the ocean, or ending abruptly in small cliffs and rock promontories. Flat land on which to lay out the town was nonexistent. Homes perched on the hillsides, reserving the waterfront for business activity. For those not caring to row, a series of winding footpaths were worn into the hillside. They did not provide an expeditious route, however, nor an easy means of moving heavy barrels of salted herring and other freight.

Since most of the business activity was in one way or another marine-oriented, most of the business community was built along the waterfront. During the gold rush, livings were made hauling freight, loading and unloading it, and serving the transients who stopped here on their way north. As the gold rush gave way to the herring rush, the economy continued to center around the waterfront with its docks and canneries.

The first boardwalk in Seldovia was built during the herring boom years, the 1920s. It was a four-foot-wide walkway with planks laid perpendicular to the direction of travel. Intended for foot traffic only, it grew from Joe Hill's Dance Hall on the Seldovia Slough along the waterfront to the general vicinity of the present city dock. Jim Busey recalls that it was in place when his family arrived here in 1928, and had been in use for several years.[80]

At low tide, Seldovians walked from building to building along the beach. Photo courtesy of the Jack and Susan B. English Collection.

At high tide, the sea came right up to the doorsteps of waterfront buildings. Travel from one part of town to another had to be achieved either by rowboat or else by a series of paths slightly inland. Photo by F.H. Moffet, U.S.G.S. Photographic Library, 1904.

In this late 1920s photograph, a wooden walkway connects beachfront buildings. Photo courtesy of the Alaska State Library, Taber Collection, PCA 19-36

As the fishing industry grew, the need for a means of moving freight back and forth through town increased. The little four-foot-wide boardwalk could not accommodate a hand truck laden with barrels or crates. In the spring of 1930, a delegation of territorial legislators came to Seldovia for a visit and promised their constituents they would push for an appropriation to build Seldovia a roadway. After all, they noted, the territory collected taxes from Seldovians so it was reasonable for the residents to expect help with a roadway in return. They cautioned, however, that existing law did not provide for road-building within a community, but rather focused on building roads leading out from communities, linking one with another. They also couldn't guarantee that unearmarked money would be available. But, in the manner of politicians, they assured Seldovians that they were solidly behind the idea and couldn't imagine that Seldovia would go roadless much longer. [81]

The rug was pulled out from underneath the eagerly waiting community in 1931 when the highway engineer wrote to U. S. Commissioner W. A. Vinal and advised him that Seldovia's road project would not happen. Over-projection of revenues was cited as one reason, and the large number of projects the territory had already committed itself to was another. [82]

Seldovia was crushed, but not defeated. Juanita Anderson wrote a contest-winning limerick which voiced the feelings of the whole town:

*OUR PLANS FOR THE SIDEWALK LOOK JAMMED
AND HOPES FOR THE FUTURE SEEM SLAMMED...
WHILE WE CANNOT REJOICE,
WE CAN SHOUT WITH ONE VOICE
THE BEACH IS STILL AT OUR COMMAND!* [83]

By August 21, 1931, Seldovians had taken matters into their own hands. A community meeting was called at 8:45 p.m. at Joe Hill's Hall. Mr. W. A. Estus, superintendent of the Cook Inlet Packing Company, called the meeting to order and acted as chairman. He explained that their purpose that evening was to discuss how they as a community could build a new boardwalk. He had drawn up some rough plans, which called for a boardwalk 8 feet wide and about 3,000 feet in length.

As folks discussed the matter, it was found that only two buildings would need to be moved in order to accommodate the wider walk. The vote was unanimous to go ahead with the project. Juanita Anderson moved to transfer the more than $500 that had been raised for a new play-shed to the boardwalk construction fund, and the gathering voted to do so. Mr. Estus was named superintendent of the sidewalk construction. After the meeting, the audience was invited to step forward and sign a pledge sheet to donate money, pilings, or labor to the project. That evening alone, $1024 was secured. [84]

Work was begun on August 28th. On top of the $537.60 in community funds that was diverted to the project, money came in from 55 Seldovia citizens and businesses. Contributions ranged from 7¢ to $250. The canneries provided much in the way of labor and materials in return for consideration on their property taxes for that year. In total, over $2700 was raised and used to purchase lumber and spikes. A little over 80,000 feet of lumber was cut by Mr. Murphy's saw mill on the Slough. The pilings were donated, as was the labor of over 90 local men. It was calculated that the total cost of the boardwalk, finished October 11th after some 3039 feet, was $5399.78. What an accomplishment! [85]

Some of the boardwalk builders are still living or are represented by their descendants in Seldovia today: Mike Balishoff, Simon Josefson, Matt Yuth, Nick Elxnit, Russel Waterbury, Adam Cleghorn, Charles Lund, and Nick Sarakoff, to name but a few. [86]

A well-attended dance at Joe Hill's Hall, featuring an orchestra, celebrated the completion of the boardwalk. Speeches were made, and Mr. Estus was presented with a gold watch. He later wrote his thoughts and his thanks:

Mr. W. A. Estus, Cook Inlet Packing Company superintendent, volunteered to lead the fundraising and construction of a new boardwalk for Seldovia in 1931. Photo courtesy of Ted Anderson from the Ralph and Juanita Anderson Collection.

CONTRIBUTIONS TO THE SELDOVIA BOARDWALK

D.T. Mitchell 5.00	A.W. Lipke 50.00	J.F. Johnson 5.00
W.A. Keller 11.30	R.V. Anderson 169.00	G.M. Chambers 210.00
S. Stoffer 10.00	M.E. Shortley 25.00	Ed Danielson 25.00
J.A. Coburn 25.00	T.W. Lloyd 52.95	John Roe 25.00
Martin Jensen 2.00	L.A. Dunning 25.00	R.D. Simpson 40.00
W.L. Lippincott 10.05	Cook Inlet Packing 125.00	E.M. Johnson 10.00
J.E. Dwyer 10.00	James Hart 5.00	Wm. Nielson 2.00
P. Pedersen 5.00	Chas. H. Sharp 250.00	Joe Hill 30.00
Whitney & Lass 10.00	Jack Smith 25.00	E.F. Jensen 40.00
Jack English 25.00	R.C. Morris 60.00	Antone Nelson 5.00
Mrs. A. Nelson 5.00	Mrs. James Stryker 5.00	F.H. Burgin 20.00
George Baltazor 10.00	Pete Bellman 25.00	H.S. Young 50.00
Jack Tansey 20.00	Shorty Robinson 5.00	Ladies Dance 120.30
AK Year Round Can . . . 100.00	Linder's Orchestra 41.00	Milo Hulbert 145.00
Mrs. J.A. Herbert 10.00	N. Coast Pkg. Co. 25.00	Frank Raby 40.25
M/M T. Nutbeem 25.00	Al Burglin 5.00	Sanger Estus 07
Tom Stephenson 15.00	Murphy Mill 15.00	J.T. Hansen 5.00
Play Shed Fund 537.60	Fred M. O'Neill 20.00	Chas. Sword 4.00
Fulmor Estate 35.00	C.B. Peterson 70.00	

Our sidewalk (the one the territory did not build) is completed and entirely paid for; and as superintendent of the job I want to thank everyone that took part and helped me in the financing and building of the walk, and aided and cooperated with each other in its construction. Personally I am happy that the job is done; glad that Seldovia now has a substantial thoroughfare of which we can all be proud. I treasure the kind expressions because of any part I may have had in the building of the walk; prize more than words can say the handsome watch that you, my neighbors, have given me, and the friendly spirit that prompted its giving. The spirit of harmony and good will shown both in the preliminaries and during the actual time of construction would be unusual anywhere, deserves special recognition and speaks volumes for Seldovia's future prosperity.[87]

The Seldovia Herald ran an editorial praising the cooperation shown by community members in completing the project:

Seldovia Herald - Editorial

"The boardwalk... is an accomplished fact.... Seldovia quit asking anybody and everybody to build a walk, took off its composite coat, and went to work. We owe nobody outside of Seldovia, either in dollars, praise, or votes, for any part of the walk. Every board laid down; every supporting brace; each timber; every firmly driven nail; every bit of expended effort—Seldovia dollars; Seldovia volunteer labor...the fruits of cooperative effort have been clearly shown. Petty differences forgotten, personal feelings laid aside; shoulder chips brushed cleanly off. Citizens buckling in, and with their own dollars, and with their own strength of arm and of purpose building their own boardwalk. Keep that picture before you, Seldovians. We have learned our lesson—the difference between bickerings, gossip, spiteful thoughts, cheapening quarrels; and the broad expanse of cooperative, hearty fellowship." [88]

The school children wrote to Mr. Estus, and he sent them this amusing reply:

"Dear Children; I was very much pleased with the word I received from you, saying that you liked the new sidewalk, and what pleased me most was your promise that every one of you would help to keep it clean and that you would not write on the railing. I have been watching so far and I have noticed that you are not marking it up, and now I am going to leave you. I am going to Seattle on the next EVANS [steamship] and when I come back here about the first of April I feel sure that I will find that you have kept your promise to me all Winter long. And when I come home I will bring some paint and we will paint the railing...."[89]

It was a big occasion when, the following year (1932), an automobile was brought to Seldovia on its way up the Inlet for work on a clam beach. The obliging steamship captain fired it up and took everyone for a ride. It was the first time a vehicle had been driven

Seldovia Herald - June 4, 1932

SELDOVIANS TAKE AUTO JOY RIDES

Seldovia youngsters had a grand and glorious time last Tuesday when Captain Fred O'Neill cranked up the North Pacific Packing Co.'s trusty Ford and gave them a series of joy rides practically the length of the 8-foot boardwalk. Being the first time in the history of the community that an automobile was driven through the town was in itself something to stir the pulses, and the antics of the passengers and the manifest interest that the driver got out of the performance added to the general jubilation. The car, a light truck, was brought down from Anchorage by the Princess Pat for use on the clam beaches, and was discharged on the Chambers and Colwell dock to be picked up when the boat returned from its trip to Seward and Cordova. And Captain O'Neill took advantage of this to show the kids a good time. The only difficulty experienced was in alternating the passengers for when they once got a taste of the thrill of auto travel it proved a man sized job to pry them loose for another consignment of clamoring hitchhikers. [90]

through town. Another vehicle had been transloaded here the year before, but folks had had to be content then with just being driven up and down the dock.

Dr. Frederica de Laguna remembers: "In addition to life lived in the open, or above boardwalk, so to speak, there were the activities on the lower level, dependent, of course, on the stage of the tide. In Kachemak Bay country one goes by the U.S. Coast and Geodetic Survey's three sacred revelations: the Chart, the Coast Pilot, and the Tide Book. These inform us that 'The diurnal range of tide is about 18 feet at Seldovia.' This is a range that must be seen to be understood.

"Only at the northeastern (or outer) end of town, was there enough water (22 feet) at the lowest low tide to permit ocean steamers to use the 'Ocean Dock.' Near here was also the dock for the cannery tenders that needed to come and go at all hours. But elsewhere along the boardwalk, docks could be used only when the tide was in. For a good part of the day, therefore, the beach was exposed, while small boats were anchored out in or up the bay, or tied up securely to a piling, awaiting the release of the tide. Not only did every dock have a ladder leading down, and every warehouse or store a hoist to move cargo to and from the beach, but almost every house in the upper end of town had steps that gave access to the shingle.

"Naturally, it was here that small children and dogs gathered when there was nothing interesting going on elsewhere. Catching fish (or trying to do so), dabbling in ponds left by the tide, and superintending the comings and goings of small boats were among the occupations pursued by the young, who could recognize each boat by the sound of its engine. Above, meanwhile, their elders went about their several businesses, greeting each other as they passed on the boardwalk, stopping sometimes to pass on the latest news or to argue hotly about it." [91]

Over the years, Seldovia became known as "The Boardwalk City," famous for its picturesque community which grew up around the wooden walkway. The very nature of the boardwalk itself fostered an intimate community atmosphere. Said late Seldovian Bill Hopkins, "You just didn't pass people on the walk without taking time to lean against its rail and inquire about each other's latest family happenings."[92] Seldovia retained this moniker until the 1964 Good Friday Earthquake. For more on what happened in Seldovia and how it affected the boardwalk, see the chapter "The Earthquake and Urban Renewal."

The goings-on beneath the boardwalk could be every bit as interesting as life above. This 1932 photo is courtesy of Dr. Frederica de Laguna.

A view of the boardwalk at the north end of Seldovia. The old Russian Orthodox cemetery is on the right. Photo courtesy of Ted Anderson from the Ralph and Juanita Anderson Collection.

Business on the Boardwalk

Perhaps the best-known, most well-liked business on the entire waterfront was Joe Hill's Hall. "Joe Hill, a black man, was probably the finest man in town, and was highly respected by everyone," wrote Jim Busey. In testimony to his pure heart and character, Joe carried the distinction of being known as "the whitest man in all Seldovia." When Jim and his parents came to Seldovia in 1928, Joe ran a pool hall and barber shop. After a fire destroyed the business, he relocated to a larger building at the mouth of the Seldovia Slough. Joe's second location "included the same facilities as previously, plus a large dance hall that was used for [a] city auditorium, dance hall, school graduations, and other important public events. Joe was especially liked because of his high standards of personal conduct. Contrary to the more usual practice in Seldovia, he did not drink; and he was well informed, an interesting and literate person, who played an important role among numbers of admiring people, young and old."[93] From the Russian Christmas masquerade dances to basket socials benefitting one cause or another to plays put on and performed by the Seldovia Women's Club, Joe Hill's Hall played host to most social events in town. Perhaps a more important role played by Joe Hill was a quiet one: that of local philanthropist. Stories still circulate about how Joe financially carried more than one fishing family through a hard winter, or financed a boat for others. Seldovian Albert Wilson recalls being taken care of by Joe Hill. Circumstances prevented his staying at home for a period as a child, and so he went to live with Joe, who fixed him breakfast each morning and bustled him off to school.[94] After Prohibition, Joe added a tavern to his multifaceted hall, but it was said he permitted no misconduct there. The tavern and dance hall were separate from one another, so that youngsters could enjoy a dance while some of their elders whiled away the evening in the tavern.[95] The tavern business created employment for a number of local boys. In the winter, Joe provided big-toothed saws with which ice could be cut from Susan Lake. The boys hauled the cut ice to Joe's on a sled and stacked it, and then covered it with sawdust. Joe paid them $5.00 a ton, and used the ice to cool his beer through the warmer months. A typical winter's store of ice was as much as 23 tons.[96]

Joe was known for not picking up things off his floor. Instead, like most buildings along the boardwalk, his had a trap door through which debris was swept onto the beach. Included in Joe's debris were half gallon and gallon wine jugs. Children picked these up off the beach and sold them back to Joe for a quarter apiece. This was a smart move on Joe's part, for the youngsters generally turned right around and handed back the money as entrance to the latest moving picture show.[97] The beach below Joe's was also a favorite place for children to scavenge for money—change mostly, but on rare occasion a greenback. He neglected to sort this out from the end-of-an-evening rubbish on the floor, so out onto the beach it was swept![98] Joe Hill showed movies twice a week, with phonograph or live piano music

Many talented Seldovia musicians provided entertainment for the community through the long winter months. Before the introduction of television, dances and other social gatherings brought folks together at Joe Hill's or one of the other halls in town. In this photo (from left to right), Hank Kroll Sr., Mervin Brun, and Oren Dimond pick a few tunes. Photo courtesy of William Wakeland, #22G9

realized he had found the receptacle for Joe's used razor blades! An insignificant treasure to be sure, but still somehow proof for us 1990s folk that this great man did indeed exist.

On December 3, 1940, Joe Hill faced a second fire, and his famous dance hall/pool hall/movie theatre/tavern/barbershop burned to the ground. Joe later built and operated the Polar Bar until retiring to Philadelphia. There he spent the last years of his life involved in the Civil Rights movement.

There were as many as three grocery stores operating in Seldovia at a time, and at least that many general mercantiles. Dr. Frederica de Laguna remembers doing business with Charley Sharp's Cash Store when she was conducting an archaeological excavation near here in the early 1930s: "Charley Sharp ran his store on the unusual assumption that it was as much his business to promote the health of his fellow citizens as to make a profit. For this reason, he regularly ordered fresh lettuce from Outside, and as regularly sold the same at 25 cents a head. From him we naturally purchased all our supplies: canned goods, dried fruit, eggs by the crate (a dozen dozen), sugar, salt, pepper, flour, syrup, matches, toilet paper (most of which was used for packing delicate objects that we excavated), paper bags to hold the animal bones from each square and level excavated, pilot biscuit by the wooden box, and Danish rye bread in great round disks, jams, peanut butter, eating chocolate, oatmeal, cookies (of which we never bought enough), gasoline and oil for our outboard motor. We even bought planks and two-by-fours to make flooring for our tents. Probably our skiff was rented from Charley. We could take only those perishables that we could consume before they

preceding the picture. He ran the whole operation himself, and still took time to lecture young people who came in for a haircut. In fact, it is said that with Joe trying to tend bar and oversee the pool hall while running the barbershop, a haircut could take the better part of a leisurely afternoon. Several years ago, a friend of mine was mucking about in the slough below the site where Joe Hill's used to stand. To his delight, he found a china barber pole, about 6" high and still bearing its red and white striping. It was hollow, with a good-sized slot in the top. We

The 1940 fire that consumed Joe Hill's Hall lit up the December night. Photo courtesy of Jan Cevene.

spoiled...My diary reminds me that it took a whole day for Charley to put up our first month's order, and since it had to be loaded aboard Steve's boat at low tide, Charley had to lower everything by rope and pulley from the back of his store to the beach."[99] Charley Sharp came to Alaska in 1910 and to Seldovia in 1917. He spent his summers fishing and ran a coal drayage business in the winter. In 1929 he opened his store, and ran it for seventeen years. Ill health forced Charley to sell the store in 1946 (to Oren Dimond) and he left Seldovia to seek medical treatment at the Mayo Clinic in Minnesota.[100] Dr. de Laguna also remembers a memorable night spent at another boardwalk business—the Seldovia House: "The Seldovia House was the caravansary where we always stayed when we were in town. It was set at an angle to the boardwalk, and consisted of two floors.

shampoo—both sorely needed. There were two double rooms overlooking the water that we usually occupied: my mother and I in one, the young men in the other. In addition, there was a large room with several beds that served as a dormitory for single men. Since the walls of the establishment were not soundproof, we could not help overhearing a conversation between two men in the dormitory—or rather a discourse by one of them. He was evidently rather drunk: 'You see that bed,' he said. 'I was gonna sleep in that bed, but with liquor (moonshine) two dollars a quart, and that bed cost one dollar, I gotta sleep out on the God dammed grass!' "[101]

Five years after Dr. de Laguna visited the Seldovia House Hotel, its proprietors opened the Alaska Bar across the boardwalk. The new establishment served hamburgers

The community gathers on the Fourth of July in 1920 in front of the Seldovia House Hotel. Photo courtesy of the Jack and Susan B. English Collection.

The proprietress...was certainly used to having her guests appear at almost any hour of the day or night. In 1931, after we had spent a month digging at Cottonwood Creek, Steve Zawistowski moved us to Yukon Island, leaving Wally and Ed to establish a camp, while he brought me into town to get another month's supplies, and to meet my mother who was coming up by steamer to join us for the second half of the summer. Since Steve's boat moved at a majestic pace and had an idiosyncratic motor that required periodic doses of seal oil to prevent stalling, we did not arrive in Seldovia until two a.m. Nevertheless, my hostess willingly fired up the heater so I could have water for a good bath and

and chili, beer and wine, and offered a cardroom.[102]

In the early 1920s, Adam and Alice Lipke arrived in Seldovia from McGrath. They were a young married couple, hot for adventure, who had come to Alaska in 1916 and mushed to the Interior. They ended up in McGrath and had been living there until a flood inundated the town. Faced with rebuilding or leaving, they took the opportunity to relocate to Seldovia. On their first day here, they were surprised to find school teacher Allen Peterson, whom they had known in the Interior before he came to Seldovia.[103]

Adam Lipke's home and wireless station. Photo courtesy of Ted Anderson from the Ralph and Juanita Anderson Collection.

Adam Lipke and Boscoe on the boardwalk in Seldovia. Photo courtesy of Ted Anderson from the Ralph and Juanita Anderson Collection.

Adam purchased the apparatus to set up his own telegraph, or wireless station in Seldovia. His timing was excellent, for the herring boom was bearing down upon the town and the need was burgeoning for contact with the outside world. Soon packers and many others brought him their business. Alice Lipke was feeling a bit lost with her husband so involved in his new business, so she resolved to open one of her own. She had noticed that among the inventory of the two general stores in Seldovia, there were not many things for women and children and so she bought a good stock of coats and shoes, dresses and children's clothing. She purchased a small building on the boardwalk next to the wireless station and opened Lipke's Dress Shop. The store continued in operation under the proprietorship of Adam Lipke's second wife, Tyndall.

Lipke's clothing store on the boardwalk specialized in outfitting women and children. Flanking Lipke's are The House of O'Brien Hotel, the Linwood Bar Blue Room, and the Surf Club. Photo courtesy of William Wakeland, #445

The Frontiersman
April 2, 1947

Mr. and Mrs. Buckley Douglas opened an ice cream and soda fountain in the Seldovia Beachcomber Hotel. The new business featured chrome and leather stools, fluorescent lights, and a juke box. It also boasted a soft ice cream machine and a soft drink dispenser [apparently the first of its kind in Alaska]. All these accouterments gave the new business that modern, metropolitan touch.

Read All About It!... In the Seldovia Herald

In 1930, Seldovia decided it had stories to tell, opinions to share, and important events to report. In this year Seldovia's first newspaper made its debut. This badge of Seldovia's growing sophistication was made possible by the expertise of M. Lester Busey. Mr. Busey had for some years worked for the *Portland Oregonian*, but it was a bookkeeping position with the R.C. Morris General Store that brought him to Seldovia in 1928. Busey lasted two years before the newspaperman in his blood turned his focus away from the bookkeeping profession.

Busey acquired a 10' x 15' Chandler and Price foot-treadle printing press with a supply of handset type, and thus the *Seldovia Herald* was born. Lester's wife, Mary Louise, was an accomplished musician and a piano teacher by profession, but she and their young son Jim pitched in to work as typesetters and printer's devils. The 10 cent weekly paper seldom numbered more than six pages, but Jim recalls that hand-setting the type was a dreary job.

Dreary as it may have been to produce, the *Seldovia Herald* provided the maturing community with a link to news of the outside world, a chance to read about its own events and happenings, and a forum in which the many businesses could advertise and sell their wares and services. To an historian, the *Seldovia Herald* provides an invaluable record of everyday life here in bygone days.

The *Herald* ceased publication in 1933, when Lester Busey moved his family to Seward and accepted a job as editor of the *Seward Gateway*. Less than 10 years later, he was in Anchorage working for the *Anchorage Times*. By 1946, Mr. Busey had joined a group of forward thinking men to become one of the founders of the *Anchorage Daily News*, a paper that is still in publication today.[104]

In addition to her career teaching piano, Mary Louise Busey was a poet. Her work ranged from the thoughtful to the entertaining. Two examples of her writing, both with relevance to Seldovia, are reprinted here with the kind permission of her son Jim, from her 1957 book *Many Moods*.

ENUPEAK

A man who had journeyed from Cairo to Nome,
With Alaska his newly adopted home—
Had traversed the earth and had pondered much
And with human traits kept in ready touch;
Learned the ways of the Turk and the ways of the Greek—
Why the Eskimo calls himself "Enupeak",
Which means a "real human being"!
Heard the Yank thank the gods for his brains and his cheek,
Learned the Roman, though strutting and chesty, was meek
And modest and shrinking compared with the case
Of the "pureblooded Nazi–of super-man race;"
Found the Negro's "po' white trash" despising the black;
While the man in the mansion looked down on the shack
That sheltered the "real human being."
But the stars scan our planet from Capetown to Nome
And all the four corners from cellar to dome,
In search for the humans so rare and unique
That they never imagine themselves "Enupeak",
As they probe far beneath the mere color of skin
And judge by the heart that is beating within,
Just who is the "real human being."

AN ALASKA IDYL

Old Farmer Jones was a skeptic,
Sallow and lean and dyspeptic;
Food his folks would suggest
didn't seem to digest,
and at times he had fits epileptic.
Came a friend from Seldovia, Alaska—
Farmer Jones took occasion to ask her:
"How's the 'ice chest' up there?
Do you have the same fare
That has brought my poor stomach disaster?"
Said she: "We have salmon delicious
And herring so fat and nutritious;
To say nothing of clams,
Sheep ribs and moose hams—
Even goose tongues for diet ambitious."
With a look all keenly ecstatic,
Farmer Jones made gesture dramatic:
"I'm going," said he,
"To the land of the free
And forsake all my ills so erratic."
O'er Seldovia's mountains majestic,
With rifle and shot-gun so zestic,
He now goes with a grin—
And a vast double chin
Speaks of nutriment wholly digestic.
All the diet so drab and so drastic,
He has left for the tidbits Alaskic—
He could eat a whole bear
And he spurns all hot air
About "Seward's Ice Chest," fantastic.

The Seldovia Herald
A COOK INLET ENTERPRISE

Vol. 2--No. 32   Seldovia, Alaska, January 14-19, 1933.   Price, 10 Cents.

Harrington Choice At Group Meeting

Committee Named to Submit Preference--Shortley As Commissioner

C. W. Harrington for deputy marshal.

M. E. Shortley for U. S. Commissioner.

Such was the sense, in the form of a rising vote, of a meeting at Joe Hill's hall Wednesday night. The meeting was called to order by Emil Sandvik, who thereafter acted as chairman.

The vote in both cases was practically unanimous.

A committee of three--R. C. Morris, James Hart, M. E. Shortley--was appointed to make report of the proceedings of the meeting to Democrats in high place.

The point was made that a permanent committee of contact with the Democratic central committee should be formed and a motion bestowing such authority upon the reportorial committee was offered, but it did not come to a vote.

Japanese Put Chinese to Flight, Taking Base

CHINCHOW, Manchuria, Jan. 18.--Green infantrymen of the imperial Japanese army today held the Yunganpu base of Generyl Cheng Kie Ling, while Japanese airplanes dropped bombs on Cheng's retreating volunteer troops.

The Japanese occupied the base at 11 A. M. yesterday without conflict. Cheng's troops retired to the mountains.

Report has it that John Rustgaard, retiring attorney general, plans to take up residence in Paris. Questioned on this point, he merely says that he is going abroad.

But it is reported that he is selling his personal effects and has listed his home for sale; and the story persists that he is going abroad to stay.

Russian Christmas Festival Proves Week Solid Enjoyment, With Dances Nightly

With six nights turned over to entertaining shows and gay dances, another Russian Christmas has passed into local history. And although the festival started off as a very impromptu affair, it turned out to be just one good time after another.

Beginning Tuesday evening, the 10th, with an hour and a half of songs, folk dances, Russian and Hawaiin music played by an inspiring band of string instruments, the big show carried on throughout the ensuing week. There was an interchange of the Milo and Hill halls.

The opening show had many features to commend it. The string band, composed of a dozen performers on mandolins, banjos, guitars and one violin, was particularly good.

A violin solo, "The Flower Song," played by Bob King, accompanied on the piano by Ted Nutbeem, popular restaurant man, got such hearty applause and thunderous calls for "more, more," that the performers were obliged to respond by repeating the number. The offering lost none of its novel effect by the pre-statement of Mr. Nutbeem that as a piano player he

(Turn to Page 6)

Seldovians Lucky, Thinks Mrs. Lipke

"Seldovians cannot realize how lucky they are just to be Seldovians!"

Such is the expressed view of Mrs. Adam Lipke, just returned from a four and half months visit to the outside, most of the time being spent in Los Angeles. She found San Francisco in better shape than other coast cities.

Abject poverty, with a fearful let-down of pride and loss of possessions is everywhere seen. The depression, in other words, is still on in full blast, according to Mrs. Lipke.

Her trip, personally, was enjoyable and profitable; but she finds it a great relief to be home again, far from the stress and strain of the battle for existence.

At Juneau Mrs. Lipke talked with territorial and party leaders, getting their viewpoints on administrative angles. She reports their attitude of willingness to do the right thing for the Cook inlet district, and invited opinions and requests from local citizenry.

Demo Leaders Strive Against Hoover

WASHINGTON, Jan. 13.-- House Democratic leaders today speeded action to block President Hoover's plan for reorganization of the government, when the rules committee reported a special rule to insure consideration of the Cochran resolution nullifying the reorganization plans.

Seldovia Miss Regains Health, Says Letter

A letter and a photograph, both radiating health and buoyant spirits--these are the treasured Christmas presents received in a late mail by Mr. and Mrs. T. W. Lloyd from their daughter Charlotte, at Elmo, Washington.

After three years under hospital care, Miss Charlotte writes, and is pictured, as being practically cured. She and her parents expect an early discharge from the Oakhurst sanitarium.

It is not definitely known regarding a Seldovia return, but that matter will be decided upon later.

Charlotte had stopped with her married sister while attending school in Aberdeen, Washington. Lung trouble developing, the young girl was hurried to the sanitarium, where she has been ever since. She was visited first by her father, and next by Mrs. Lloyd, the latter remaining by her daughter until signs of real danger had passed.

Petition Would Retire O'Malley

Locals Sign Paper To Boost Paul In High Federal Fishing Post

A petition calling for the removal of Henry O'Malley as fish commissioner, and replacing him with William L. Paul, of Ketchikan, has been received in Seldovia. Copies of the petition have been circulated generally, and, like the one on local exhibition, are reported to carry a generous number of signatures.

The petition, addressed to President-elect Roosevelt, recites that O'Malley's indifference to the appeals and suggestions of fishermen, totally unfits him for the office that he holds, and dwells briefly upon the close contact of Paul with real fishing needs.

For public convenience the petition is on file at the Seldovia Cash Store; and parties interested are asked to call and check it over.

New Attorney General Pleased With Seldovia

James S. Truitt is grateful to the people of Seldovia for their support of his candidacy for the office of attorney-general, and in a letter to this paper has this to say:

"I trust that you will extend my thanks and appeciation to the citizens of Seldovia and vicinity for their support, and for the hospitality extended me while in their little city. I like the little place; have always liked it since my first visit there many years ago, and it certainly did me good to see the improvements made there and to note the civic interest manifest in their town and community."

Judge Truitt adds that he will be leaving for Juneau late in January or very early in February; and he expresses a wish and willingness to be of service to Seldovia "in matters warranting," whenever the need for such service may arise.

The Seattle Fur Exchange

Sales
EVERY MONTH OF THE YEAR

1933 Auction Sale Dates

January	24	May 16	September 26
February	21	June 20	October 24
March	21	July 25	November 21
April	18	August 29	December 21

Special Sales Held on Request of Shippers

Advances will be made as usual when requested. Transferred by telegraph if desired.

The Seattle Fur Exchange has always demonstrated to the satisfaction of all their shippers that it can and does sell furs in a manner superior to anyone else. Our monthly auction sales are recognized by buyers of raw furs as the best source from which to provide the world markets with their requirements of fine Alaska furs.

The Seattle Fur Exchange
1008 Western Avenue   Seattle, U. S. A.

H. S. YOUNG
Cash and Carry

Infants Long Sleeve Outing Flannel Slips	45 Cts.
Rayon Rubber Panties	45 Cts.
Sleeping Garments	95 Cts.
Crib Blankets	$1.40 $1.65
Bath Robes	$1.50
Rompers	75 Cts. $1--$1.50-$1.65
Rayon Dresses	95 Cts.
Bootees	25 to 75 Cts.
Silk Coats	$3.00

H. S. YOUNG
Dependable Merchandise
Seldovia, Alaska

Brighten the Dark Corners of Your Home!

Paper Flowers for All Occasions

-PRICES REASONABLE-

-Joyce Christensen.

Russian Christmas Festival
(From Page 1)

could deliver a rib-steak—rare, well-done, or medium that will suit the most fastidious.

Andrew Anderson did some high class yodling, while Fred Fitka, Billie Nelson and others captured the house with their unique antics.

Friday night (Russian New Year's Eve) was featured by two devils, the crimson imps dashing in on the mask dance at Hill's hall, flitting about among the dancers in a frantic search for the Old Year. And at midnight they found the decrepit old figure and his tottering, faithful wife—latter well acted by Jack Thape, and the two ancients were roughly seized and rudely tossed into oblivion.

The devil portrayers were Nick Michikoff and Freddie Bowen.

One of the best bits of character acting seen in Seldovia for a long time was the portrayal of 1932 by Freddie Ponchene. Roughly raggedly clad, with drooping shoulders and halting gait the youthful actor performed the part with extraordinary fidelity to detail and circumstance. A bearer of the world's cares and burdens for a fateful season, he surely looked it. Considering that this was Freddie Ponchene's first appearance, and that the public performance had not been preceded by any sort of rehearsal make the portrayal the more interesting.

At the closing dance Sunday night, the following maskers took the prizes:

Mrs. Lawrence Olsen and her brother-in-law, Richard Olsen—best dressed couple.

Mrs. N. Jean McCullagh and Earling Niewejaar—most original couple.

Mrs. Helen Torgramson, Mrs. Annie Lindstedt—best comics.

Mrs. David Bowen-best dressed. Na iji Loco—worst dressed.

T. A. Nuthoem, chief promoter of the festival, had as first aids George Ritchie and Billie Hunter, the latter two directing the program for the initial performance. These three young men and their associates are being thanked by the Seldovia public for having provided and carried through a week of solid enjoyment.

Doings At Homer
(From Page 2)

ilchie is visiting in Homer.

Dog Mushers Derby

Elaborate plans are underway for the holding of a dog carnival under the auspices of the Homer Athletic Club. The day is being planned so there will be an event of interest to both grownups and to the children.

Entrants to the dog derby are Virgo Anderson, Carl Sholin, Frank Brooks, Star Neilsen, Bill Peck, Fred Svedlund and Karl Neilsen. Stubs, gallant charger, racing under the colors of the Sholin kennels, is a five to one favorite.

The second event of the day will be a skiing race. The take-off will be the top of Shafer's hill, with the first one running into the fox pens being proclaimed winner.

These Boardwalk Businesses Advertised In The Seldovia Herald - January 1933

Chambers & Colwell

- Announces -

Now is the time to buy your
Sheep Lined Coat - Mackinaw, or
Overcoat---
25 Per Cent Off!

The Lowest Prices These Coats Have Ever Sold For In Seldovia!

- The House of Standards -

Seldovia Machine & Electric Shop

Prepared at the New Location to do Engine Repair Work and Installation.

Selling Agents for Fairbanks, Morse Lighting Plants and General Motors Radios

Moreover

"We do Anything for Anybody Any Time!"

PHILCO
The World's Best In Radios

- Tone -

Improved Philco Permanent-Magnet Dynamic Speaker
Pentode Power Output.
Tone Control and Static Modifier.
Rubber Floated Tuning Condenser and Radio Chassis.
Balanced Unit Construction

In Philco you get all of the many New Features of modern radio---but of far greater importance is the built-in Philco dependability and quality of performance.

Only Phico, the World's Largest Radio Manufacturer, can give you such performance value with all the latest improvements of radio design

New 1000-Hour, 3-Volt Battery Sets On Hand

For Price and Details of Performance---See

A. Lipke,
Authorized Dealer for Philco

Petersen's

Nice New Line of
Ladies House Dresses--
$1.00 each

We have a nice line of Stamped Goods for Embroidery Work

25 Cts. -- 50 Cts.

Come In
and
See
Us!

"The Little Store With the Big Idea."

Any Building or Repair Work to be Done?

Consult

Albert Linder

Contractor ∴ Builder

Carpentry Work

- Mary Louise Busey -
Piano--Harmony--Ear Training
... First Steps and Advanced Work ...
Thorough Foundation Laid for
Artistic Piano Playing

-Boatmen-
"Oil Up at Seldovia!"

DOCK AND STORAGE FACILITIES

OIL TANKS

OILS AND GREASES

R. V. ANDERSON, Operator

SELDOVIA CASH STORE
- Chas. H. Sharp, owner -

Others	We
Save	Save
Your	Money
Money--	for You!

We Invite You to Drop In to See Us!

The Seldovia House

Seldovia's Hotel of Comfort and Conveniences

- Smokes and Candies in Connection -

... Located for Boats and Business ...

"The Home Away From Home"

---T. W. Lloyd, Prop.

The Seldovia Pool Hall noted "Established in 1920—Here everybody is made welcome at all times." The Owl's ad read "A comfortable card room nook with that home-like feeling." At Ted's Cafe, diners were "made content by home cooking that satisfies." The Green Horse Shoe Lunch Room advertised " With french pastry as our specialty and the welcome that never wears out." Just after the war, in another local paper called *The Frontiersman*, the Seldovia Bakery advertised "wheat or white bread-25 cents a loaf."

Seldovia fathered two other newspapers, both short-lived. The *Westward Alaskan* was published here during 1936. The challenge of engineering the production of a newspaper in a small remote town was evidenced when in October the newspaper ran out of newsprint stock and the steamer bringing the re-supply was delayed. Undaunted, the editors of the paper approached Anderson Mercantile, where Juanita Anderson provided them with wrapping paper. Thus, the October 8th edition of the paper was printed despite the lack of proper materials.

The Frontiersman, edited by Viola Daniels, was published on Wednesdays and Saturdays from November 1946 through September 1947. Subscription rates were 75 cents a month. In addition to publishing numerous articles about local businesses, people, and events, editor Daniels made extensive use of the editorial page to speak to Seldovians about local issues. One of her most oft-repeated themes was the plea to end the practice of dumping garbage and cannery wastes on the beach.

"Together Let us Seek the Heights" —The Seldovia Women's Club

The Seldovia Women's Club was founded in 1933 at the suggestion of Mrs. Leon S. Vincent. She had been corresponding with a representative of the American Federated Women's Clubs, and felt Seldovia would benefit from such an organization. So, one Wednesday evening in February in a meeting room of the community church, a gathering of women enjoyed "an impromptu music program and a delightful service of light refreshments," in addition to discussing the purpose and organization of their new club.[105]

Four days later, the women met again and the constitution and by-laws were hammered out. Then on February 17th, the club adopted its constitution and elected officers in its first official meeting. The purposes of the club were stated as follows:

1. To promote individual effort and friendly cooperation among its members.
2. To encourage intellectual development and progress.
3. To render civic improvement to the community.
4. To promote unity of action in all matters of general concern.

(From Women's Club Papers, Author's coll., gift of the John Gruber family)

The club was open to any woman of Seldovia, but she had to be voted upon and accepted by a two-thirds majority of the members before she could join. Meetings were held monthly on the first Friday, at 7:30 p.m. Annual dues were $1.00 per member.

The club motto was "Together let us seek the heights." Their official flower was the wild rose, and their official colors silver and pink. Charter members of this organization included Mrs. Ralph Anderson, Mrs. Lester Busey, Mrs. Jack English, Mrs. W.W. Maitland, Mrs. Jean McCullagh, Mrs. Erling Nieuwejaar, Mrs. Allen Peterson, Mrs. Mable Shotter, and Mrs. Leon Vincent. The club grew quickly, adding 13 new members in 1934, its second year. Nell Scott, a member during this time, went on to become the first woman elected to the Alaska Territorial Legislature. A Democrat, she was elected in the fall of 1936 to represent Seldovia, Homer, Anchorage, Seward, Palmer, and Wasilla.[106]

After approving minutes and the treasurer's report, the club discussed old and new business and received reports from its various committees. The ladies then opened the program portion of the meeting with a brief prayer and a song sung in unison. Then, depending on the activity scheduled for that month, there might be a paper written by one of the members and presented: "Christmas Customs of Foreign Lands," "Women Who Have Influenced the Life of Lincoln," and "Russia Under the Czars" are but a few examples. One member might offer a book review, followed by a vocal or piano solo, or a dramatic recitation performed by another. In the 1940s, the membership grew more ambitious, performing one act plays and stunts in their monthly programs.

Aside from programs designed to further the intellect of its membership, the club concentrated on local charity and larger philanthropic causes. The Seldovia Women's Club served as the hospital auxiliary, and sponsored the local Girl Scouts and Boy Scouts and 4-H groups for both sexes. A public playground and Christmas stockings full of goodies for every child in town were other projects. In 1946, the Women's Club threw a Christmas party for 135 local children. The ravenous youngsters consumed 15 gallons of ice cream and each carried home a stocking stuffed with 2 popcorn balls, one orange, one apple, half a pound of hard candy, nut crunch, cheese crackers, and mixed nuts.[107] (This tradition has been carried forward, and today the Seldovia Native Association sponsors the arrival of Santa Claus, who comes bearing a laden stocking for every child, toddler, and infant in town.) The Seldovia Women's Club is credited with sponsoring Seldovia's first library, begun by Susan B. English.

Seldovia children c.1928 land on the beach near Hoen's Lagoon for a picnic. The boys pose precariously on a driftwood pile. Photos courtesy of Ted Anderson from the Ralph and Juanita Anderson Collection.

Seldovia Girl Scouts show off their signal flag skills c.1929. By 1933 the newly formed Seldovia Women's Club was sponsoring both the Boy Scouts and the Girl Scouts. Photo courtesy of Ted Anderson from the Ralph and Juanita Anderson Collection.

The club meeting room and library were housed together, and in 1941 the Seldovia Women's Club sponsored a redecorating of the 4,000-volume facility, hanging blue and tan flowered curtains and a blue and black rug.[108]

The women became expert fund-raisers, sponsoring bake sales, dances, basket socials, card parties and the like. The proceeds from these events bought athletic equipment for the school, books for the library, food and clothing for local families down on their luck, and homemade ice-cream parties for the local children. In addition, sizable contributions were made to the March of Dimes, tuberculosis victims, and nursing scholarship programs.

World War II sent the Seldovia Women's Club into a flurry of activity. During the war years, the organization sponsored a local Red Cross chapter, remembered at Christmas the crew of the crash boat stationed here, and, together with the other women's clubs across the territory, helped sponsor a war plane. Through the Red Cross, afghans were knit for the boys overseas. It was also the Seldovia Women's Club who conducted a drive for contributions to the National War Fund. They canvassed Seldovia, and included Portlock, Port Graham, English Bay, and Halibut Cove in an effort that raised $570.75.[109]

The funds were sent to War Relief Fund Territorial Council member Z.J. Loussac of Anchorage in December 1944. He had written to the Seldovia Women's Club, asking for their help in obtaining contributions from this area.

"The NWF [National War Fund] is a sort of nationwide community chest for the major war-related philanthropies, except the American Red Cross.

Among the war organizations for which the NWF collects funds are the famed USO...the War Prisoner's Aid, Refugee Relief Trustees, U.S. Committee for the Care of European Children, United Seaman's Service, and assorted relief societies for Belgium, Britian, China, Czechoslovakia, Denmark, France, Greece, Italy, Luxemburg, Norway, Poland, Holland, Russia, and Yugoslavia." [110]

The Seldovia Women's Club dissolved some years later after an illustrious career of service to the community spanning several decades.

Behind the Scenes: Public Utilities and Services

The first medical man known to have settled in Seldovia was the Colorado physician, Dr. Isam F. Burgin, who arrived in 1916. While he probably practiced medicine here as a sideline, it was fox farming and the opportunity for an outdoor lifestyle that lured him to the area.

In 1918, J.J. Jensen came to Seldovia from Europe via the Klondike. Born in Copenhagen in 1860 to a physician and his wife, Jensen studied medicine as a youth but abandoned it for the glamour of riding the races. He worked as a jockey for a Danish count before coming to America to seek his fortune. Jensen joined the gold-seekers heading north to the Yukon in 1897, but upon arriving in Skagway found an outbreak of spinal meningitis. He pitched in to lend assistance and missed his chance to cross the divide before winter set in. Jensen stayed on in Skagway, and then lived Outside briefly before coming to Seldovia. [111]

Although his medical training had never been completed, "Doc" Jensen was welcomed here and came to be highly regarded for his capabilities in ministering to the sick and injured. He was remembered in Seldovia for his heroic efforts during the flu epidemic of 1919-1920, when he worked day and night, tending the sick until he himself collapsed from exhaustion. [112]

In addition to medicine, Doc Jensen also practiced law in the court of the U.S. Commissioner, and "became front page news in many hotly fought cases."[113] Nick Elxnit remembers Doc Jensen as a lawyer, and auctioneer as well. Nick credits Jensen, as a doctor, with saving his life. In the late 1920s, Nick went across the bay to Homer to load coal and returned home with chills that quickly developed into pneumonia. Although Prohibition was in effect, Doc Jensen procured some moonshine and administered it hot to Nick. He then used a peanut-butter-looking Denver mud poultice slathered on cheesecloth. This he applied to Nick's chest and back, changing it every day for the two weeks he confined Nick to bed. Nick pulled through, and later

This title appeared with the photograph: "As early as 1927, the Fourth [of July] was honored by speeches and games. Doc Jensen gave this speech, with Jack Kendricks seated beside him." Jensen's Seldovia Herald *obituary noted: "Short and stocky, rumpled iron gray hair on a massive head; resonant of voice, ready of speech and wit, Dr. Jensen was a fighting Democrat, making a picturesque figure in Seldovian affairs, leaving a place that none believe will ever again be filled." Photo courtesy of the Jack and Susan B. English Collection*

consulted Doc Jensen for fish poisoning in his hands (infections common to fishermen and cannery workers, caused by bacteria from raw fish entering the body through cuts in the skin), when the Denver mud poultice treatment was successfully applied again. [114]

J.J. Jensen died in Seldovia in 1932 at the age of 72. He was tended in his bed at the Seldovia House Hotel by a newly arrived physician, Dr. Kirby.[115] Dr. Kirby worked here for several years.

During the decades prior to the availability of the Sterling/Seward Highway, people from a number of Inlet communities came to Seldovia for medical treatment or to have their babies. A small hospital was built here in 1940 by H. L. Olmsted and by 1942 was open under the management of the Seventh Day Adventist Church. Dr. Wilson was one of the first physicians to work in the new facility.[116] Several years later, the hospital operated under the jurisdiction of the Seldovia public utilities board.[117] With Seldovia's incorporation as a city in 1945, the management of the facility was given to the Seldovia City Council, in whose hands it remains today. In the 1940s Mrs. Olson, wife of the Methodist minister, was a registered nurse and ran the facility during those times when a doctor was not in residence. The doctors were not paid a salary, but instead took their income from the profits after the expenses of running the hospital were paid.[118]

Dr. Melvin Beltz served Seldovia in the mid 1940s. A public health nurse, Eunice Berglund, had been stationed here and she and a cook were the hospital staff. Illnesses and surgeries of all kinds were treated and performed at the Seldovia hospital, and the sick and injured came from all over Kachemak Bay. In November 1946 the *M/S Hygiene*, a health ship, docked at Seldovia and gave chest x-rays to 271 people as a screening for tuberculosis.[119]

In order to better serve his far-flung patients, Dr. Beltz ordered an airplane shortly after his arrival here, and by the spring of 1947 was flying to Homer every Monday to keep office hours there and to Kenai once every three weeks for the same purpose.[120] When the time came to add another nurse to his staff, the "flying doctor" even flew Outside to personally pick her up. It should be noted that Beltz was also picking up his new airplane as well: a 1947 Piper Supercruiser. The two flew from Sacramento, California to Seldovia.[121] The "flying doctor" was grounded briefly when Frank Bell's dairy cows strolled to the Seldovia airstrip to more closely examine the airplane. The curious bovines did some damage to the rudder and the elevator, and became locally famous when their escapade was reported in

Seldovia's hospital, built in 1940, still stands and today is a private residence. Photo courtesy of Ted Anderson from the Ralph and Juanita Anderson Collection.

The Frontiersman under the headline: "Flying Medico Grounded by Curious Cows."[122]

When the Sterling Highway linking Anchorage, Kenai/Soldotna, and Homer was built, the lower Peninsula communities began building their own medical facilities. Seldovia's hospital now only served locals and folks from homesteads around Kachemak Bay. Attracting and retaining a doctor to serve so few people was hard enough, let alone keeping the hospital outfitted with modern equipment. Elsa Pedersen was one of the people largely responsible for starting the Seldovia Hospital Guild, a fundraising organization dedicated to supporting the hospital and those needing medical care. Their first accomplishment was the purchase of a used x-ray machine for $6000. Contributions came from local businesses and even from some Seattle-based suppliers of fishing gear. The guild also held a number of fundraising events. Encouraged by their first success, the guild went on to raise the money to purchase other needed medical supplies and equipment, a function that they continue to perform to this day.[123]

Dr. Russell Jackson brought his R.N. wife and three children to Seldovia in the summer of 1957. Like most doctors who have served Seldovia, he came not to get rich but rather to escape city life and to practice medicine in a peaceful village setting. A hunting and fishing enthusiast, he was undoubtedly lured by Seldovia's proximity to the bounty of forest and sea as well. Jackson's son, Oly, remembers living in the Seldovia hospital. The doctor's family lived downstairs in a modest 3-bedroom apartment. Three patient rooms, the doctor's office, and the operating room were above. Oly's mother served as nurse and chief hospital cook. Since most patients were short term, they ate whatever the Jacksons happened to be having. People with complicated illnesses or conditions requiring special care and diet were sent to larger hospitals up the Peninsula.[124]

Dr. Jackson was a general practitioner who also had a reputation as a fine surgeon. However, the practice of medicine in a small town often called for rather unorthodox procedures. Oly recalls one such event: There was an old fellow named Bill Smith. He lived where Mickelsons' house is today and he ran a business called Smith's Trading Center. His dear friend and sole companion was a little dog, part dachsound, mostly mutt. The little dog was ailing and it was feared he had a tumor, so the old man brought him in to Dr. Jackson with a plea that he operate to try to save him. Young Oly was pressed into service as the anesthesiologist and Dr. Jackson performed the operation. Unfortunately, the cancer was too widespread and the patient succumbed. The doctor's compassion in trying to help, however, must have been a comfort to the old man.[125]

In 1962 Dr. Cary Whitehead and his wife, also a physician, arrived in Seldovia with their five children. They came from Chatham, Virginia to run the Seldovia Hospital and did so until Cary's tragic death in March 1963. Whitehead and Gary Sheldon, a Seldovia fisherman, were clamming with friends from Kenai on the shore of Seldovia Bay opposite town. As they were returning home, high winds caught and capsized their 14-foot aluminum skiff and all four persons on board were drowned. The bodies of Sheldon and Whitehead were never recovered.[126]

Numerous physicians have lived in Seldovia for short stints over the years. Sometimes, there was no resident doctor, and the community was served by a visiting physician from Homer. Seldovia's present physician, Dr. Larry Reynolds, arrived here in 1974 and witnessed the building of the new clinic in 1980.[127] Although simple emergency procedures can be performed at the clinic, Seldovia no longer has inpatient hospital services and instead relies on Homer. The sick and injured are tended to by a dedicated flock of volunteer emergency medical technicians as well as the doctor until they can be flown to Homer. Dr. Reynolds flies his own plane back and forth several times weekly to tend his patients there. On several occasions, a baby intent on coming into the world has arrived too quickly for the flight to Homer, and thus has had the honor of being born at the clinic here.

Another mark of Seldovia's growing maturity as a community was the development of a water distribution system. Folks had relied on wells and creeks for decades, but with an increasing population and increased pressure on the available groundwater, some sources simply weren't safe any more. In 1939, the Federal Works Projects Administration funded the construction of the first public water system in Seldovia.[128] This is not a topic about which I had intended to write; not, that is, until I stumbled upon the forgotten skeleton of this old system.

It is my habit to hike or run with my dogs almost every day, regardless of weather or season. Late in the fall of 1993, I was hiking the steep dirt road which leads to Seldovia's current reservoir and dam, at an elevation of about 600 feet. We'd had hard frosts and the leaves had long since fallen from the alders. Sound traveled farther without the insulation of summer's green curtain, and half way up the road my ear caught the rushing of a waterfall. I left the road, heading toward the sound, and nearly fell over the bones of a log cabin, all tumbled down and wet with moss. It couldn't have been more than twenty-five feet from the road, and yet in all the times I'd hiked this route, I'd never once glimpsed it!

Thrilled with my discovery, I raced down into town and burst into Seldovia Native Association President Fred Elvsaas's office. "You'll never guess what I found!", I crowed. "No, " replied Fred calmly, "I probably couldn't." When I described the cabin, he told me about Seldovia's first water system. A newspaper article I happened to have on file filled in the gaps, and Jack and Susan B. English's marvelous photo collection provided a shot of the cabin and dam when it was first built.

The original dam was made of logs. After tramping about in the woods, I found it, just up-creek from the old cabin. The dam face must be 20 feet high, and it is still in very good repair. The log work looks perfectly aligned and stout, even now. From this log dam ran wooden water pipe. A number of the old joints of it lie scattered in the ravine below the dam. Each joint of pipe was formed of thin cedar planks, carefully cut so that they formed a rough circle, and held together by wire that ran round it in a spiral. The exterior of the pipe was waterproofed with tar. As the pipe left the dam, it cut across the ravine on a wooden trestle nearly 16 feet high until it reached the road bed. There it descended to the surface and snaked its way down the hill into town.

During the coldest weeks of winter, the pipe usually froze, especially where it was elevated on the trestle. Even though the elevated pipe was packed with moss and further enclosed by a wooden box, it still required frequent thawing. This is where the cabin fit into the picture: it was home each winter to teams of men who volunteered in shifts for dam watch and pipe steam-thawing duty.[129]

Jack English was generally the citizen who recruited the steam-thawing crews, for his wife Susan was (in addition to her jobs as Postmistress and Librarian) the bookkeeper and manager for the Public Utility District.[130] In later years, the system was moved underground and the dam site relocated farther up the hill. Despite new federal regulations requiring the addition of chemicals to safeguard public drinking water, Seldovia still has some of the sweetest-tasting stuff around.

When Nick Elxnit arrived in Seldovia in 1913, light in homes and businesses was provided by kerosene lamps and Coleman gas lamps. By about 1927, Seldovia had its first power plant. It was located just up the Slough from the bridge and next to the sawmill. The plant was operated by Martin Jensen

This c. 1939 photograph is taken from atop the log dam looking down at the wooden pipe that snakes its way across the ravine on an elevated trestle. At the dam-keepers' cabin the pipe left the trestle and continued down into town at ground level. Photo courtesy of the Jack and Susan B. English Collection.

and Mr. Hofsteadt, and ran off a generator which was powered by a one cylinder, 25-40-hp Fairbanks Morse engine. The engine had no muffler, so all over town folks heard the "Boom—Boom—Boom" of the Fairbanks Morse starting up and knew that the electricity would soon be on. In the first few years the engine was shut off at 10 p.m., ending the flow of electric current and signaling any night owls to light their lamps. Not everyone had electricity then, but those who did bought secondhand meters from the plant and installed their own wiring.[131] Later, in the 1940s, the electric plant was known as Seldovia Light and Power and was operated by John Groothof. In 1947, Seldovia Light and Power began the job of installing the first street lights.[132]

Today, Seldovia is served by the Homer Electric Association, a rural electric cooperative. An underwater cable runs from Homer across Kachemak Bay to the south shore, and then from power pole to power pole along the coast into Seldovia. When winter storms descend upon the area, power outages are frequent; the cooperative keeps diesel-fired turbines at the ready here to provide emergency power to Seldovia in the event of a prolonged outage.

It is unknown what sort of fire protection was available to Seldovians until the 1930s. We can assume that bucket brigades probably served most, including the author's own home. While conducting research for this book, I came across an article in the March 28, 1931 edition of the *Seldovia Herald* about the near ruin of the R.V. Anderson home. On Saturday night, Ralph discovered a blaze in the closet of an upstairs bedroom and began battling it with buckets of water while Juanita put out a call for help. Neighbors quickly arrived with buckets, extinguishers, and axes and the fire was subdued. Several years ago while doing a major remodel on the second floor of this building, now our home, we uncovered a section of blackened and charred studs and timbers, the reminder of that near-disastrous evening.

In October 1936, the community purchased a new Pacific pumper unit. The portable fire pump was powered by an Austin engine, and came equipped with several hundred feet of hose. Sea water from the bay provided water for fire fighting, and it was reported that the new rig could reach almost any building in town. Seldovians T.W. Lloyd, Thor Hofstead, and Tom Garner tested the new pumper and easily shot a stream of water over the old schoolhouse. The pumper was assembled on a bright red cart, and a shed to house it was built next to Mr. Lloyd's Seldovia House Hotel. Hofstead was named fire chief at the first meeting of the Seldovia Volunteer Fire Department later that month, and he set about the task of training a large corps of volunteer fire fighters.[133]

That very same year, the new Fire Department planned its first fund-raiser, a New Year's Eve ball.[134] This tradition has been carried on more or less unbroken to today. Each New Year's, the current volunteer corps makes a huge effort to stage a dance and casino night with live music at one of the local bars. The eagerly-awaited cap to the evening is the auctioning of the (locally famous) Oly beer bottle. Since 1957, the Oly bottle has done its duty as a fund-raiser for the department. Its story began at the 1957 ball when the department ran out of items to auction. In the spirit of good fun, a man standing next to auctioneer Jack English was grabbed and auctioned off. It is not known who was the successful bidder, nor what they did with their new "purchase!" Next, Jack grabbed a bottle of Olympia beer from the shelves at the Linwwood Bar and cried, "What am I offered for this bottle of Olympia beer?" No one spoke, so Jack bid $25. At the end of the night, the still-full bottle was tucked away. Some stories have it rattling about in the Linwood's safe for a year, others say it got stuck into the box of Fireman's Ball decorations. In any event, there it was the next year, and again, Jack English held it up for auction at the end of the night. Once again, nobody bid, and Jack put in his $25 dollars to retire the bottle for yet another year. Eventually, the bottle became a tradition, and today it has attained the status of a legend. The bidding starts out with widespread participation and generally ends with the captains of local fishing boats bidding against one another in good-natured rivalry. It seems to matter not if the community has weathered hard economic times that year. When it comes to the Oly bottle auction, pockets seem to deepen and good will abounds. Over the years, the Oly bottle has raised thousands of dollars for the fire department and its charitable outreach, and today the full bottle of Oly resides in its own glass case.[135]

Seldovia did not have telephone service within the community until the 1940s. At this time John Groothof, owner of Seldovia Light and Power, purchased from a Southeast Alaska community a secondhand telephone system. The telephones were wooden wall-mounted affairs that used round cell batteries. The hat was passed among all interested parties to string telephone wire, and each telephone owner was given his or her own Morse code designation in lieu of a telephone number. Telephone privacy was nonexistent under this system, and anyone with a telephone could listen in on any and all calls. Shown below is Seldovia's first "telephone book."[136]

Seldovia's First Telephone Book

NAME	RING PATTERN
Alaska Shell Fish Co.	Long-short-long-short
Anderson Dock Co.	Short-short
Juanita Anderson	Short-short-short-short
Andrew Anderson, Marshal	Short-long
A.Y.R. Canning Co.	Long-long-short-short
Z. Beach	Long-short-long
Beachcomber Hotel	Long-short-short-long
F.L. Bond	Short-long-short-long
Susan English, Post Office	Short-short-short
Nick Elxnit	Short-long-short-short
Torvald Jensen	Short-short-long-short
Ed Jones	Short-short-short-long
Dick Miller	Long-long-long-long
R.C. Morris	Long-long-short
Seldovia Air Service	Long-long-long
Seldovia Bakery	Short-short-long-short-short
Seldovia Hospital	Long-long
Seldovia Hotel, Mrs. Lloyd	Long-short-short
Seldovia Light & Power	Long
Seldovia Packers	Short-short-long-long
Seldovia School	Short-long-long
Seldovia Radio Station	Long-short
Chas. H. Sharp	Short-long-short
Standard Oil Co	Short
H.S. Young	Short-short-long
John L. Wilson	Long-short-short-short

Phone list courtesy of Gerry Willard, Seldovia

Adam Lipke, of the Seldovia telegraph station, installed a radio telephone transmitter in June of 1947, enabling folks to speak directly with parties in Anchorage for the first time. A power surge promptly burned up the receiver unit, but Lipke repaired it and soon Seldovia was linked to the "big city" to the north. [137]

Seldovia's first airline made its maiden flight in 1945, under the command of pilot Dick Miller. Miller's Seldovia Air Service operated a six-passenger double wing Waco on floats. The great expanse of Seldovia Bay served as the airstrip, and the plane, when idle, sat tethered to a dock. [138]

In 1946 Miller operated a Stinson, but in November the plane burned in a mishap at Jakolof Bay while on a surveying job for the chrome mine. Miller had been on the beach measuring rails needed to build a ramp for the plane. The Stinson burned on the beach when its motor burst into flames as the plane backfired on a takeoff. Pilot Miller used a hand extinguisher to fight the fire, but in no time the flames had reached the cabin and ignited the fuel tanks. He was forced to abandon his efforts to save the plane. Dick Miller was unhurt, and returned to Seldovia on Steve Zawistowski's boat. [139]

Earl Herr became Miller's business partner, and together they tried to convince an Anchorage-based air carrier to station an airplane in Seldovia until they could buy a new craft to replace the Stinson. All the planes were in use, however, and none could be spared to service Seldovia. [140] In late 1946, Seldovia's present airstrip was built, but with no wheeled plane in town there was no one to give it a practical test. The City Council put out the request that planes flying over land at the new strip and provide feedback to the community. [141] Mr. Smith of Palmer, formerly of Seldovia, perked up when he heard of Seldovia's dilemma. He flew his own Stinson here, and in so doing became the first person to land on Seldovia's new air strip. It was not yet graded, so the

Seldovia's first airstrip was the great expanse of Seldovia Bay. Here a floatplane sits tethered to a dock. Photo courtesy of William Wakeland, #64K3

surface was rough and rutted. Smith could land with passengers, but the poor surface prevented him from taking off with them. When snow fell, he was able to put skis on his plane and provide both inbound and outbound passenger service.[142]

Herr and Miller had put in an order for a new Seabee float plane, but were being held up waiting for the insurance settlement on the ruined Stinson. Sensing a business opportunity, Merrill Henington flew his Taylorcraft from Texas to Seldovia in the early months of 1947, and set himself up in the air charter business. Noting that with spring breakup the new strip wasn't always navigable, Henington engaged his brother Luther's Seabee so that he could switch to float plane service when poor airstrip conditions prevented wheeled operations.[143]

Scrambling to stay in competition, Herr and Miller hired Harry White of Anchorage and his 4-place Waco biplane on floats.[144] Their Seldovia Air Service was once again airborne, and in May of 1947 their new Seabee finally arrived. Miller was pleased with its performance in the air but found it ill-suited to taxiing on Seldovia's soft sand beaches, and so made plans to build a ramp.[145] That same spring, another small carrier based in Homer began serving Seldovia with a Piper Cub.[146]

Merchant Charley Sharp (left) and pilot Merrill Henington. Henington was one of Seldovia's first commercial pilots in the 1940s. Photo courtesy of Ted Anderson from the Ralph and Juanita Anderson Collection.

Perhaps deciding that the playing field was too crowded and that fishing might prove more lucrative, Merrill Henington suspended his charter service for the summer and went fishing in Chignik instead.[147]

In the 1940s, several harsh winters fell in succession upon Seldovia. The sustained cold temperatures caused thick ice to form on the bay. Near shore, tides piled ice on top of ice in untidy stacks. Ice cakes floated about in the open water, preventing planes from landing. Prior to the construction of the Seldovia landing strip, such icing conditions in the bay made it impossible to operate a float plane. Dick Miller took action and created a wintertime landing strip. The construction technique chosen was quite rudimentary: Miller strapped on his snowshoes and in the swampy area surrounding Susan Lake, stamped out a strip on which he could land his plane on skis. This Herculean effort lasted but one winter, it being too much work to maintain.[148]

In the decades since it was built, the Seldovia airstrip has been lengthened and improved to the 1,845 feet (by 60 feet wide) of packed gravel it is today. With no air traffic control tower or instrument system, the Seldovia airport is rated for VFR flights only. Two bush carriers serve Seldovia from Homer, their "terminals" here small sheds set up along the edge of the airplane parking area. The honor system prevails in this small community: outgoing freight is left along one wall of the shed; incoming is piled against the opposite wall with access to the freight sheds open to all. Rarely has anything ever been disturbed. Quite simply, that would go against the way things are done here.

As with all bush Alaskan flying, weather is the supreme flight commander here. Weather conditions dictate who will fly, and when. Through the stormy winter months, there are often days when, due to blizzard conditions or high winds, no planes fly. Sometimes, stranded passengers scramble to charter a boat to make the crossing. Other times, when both air and sea conditions prevent travel, folks just heave a sigh and resign themselves to waiting for better weather.

Fourth of July:
A Seldovia Celebration

The first record of an Independence Day celebration in Seldovia is a photograph of a crowd gathered in front of the Seldovia House Hotel, with the caption "Fourth of July, Seldovia, about 1920." (See page 193)

Around 1927, the flagpole that stood for years in the yard in front of Adam Bloch's trading store and post office was moved to the schoolhouse where it was preserved and placed in a concrete foundation and dedicated on the 4th of July. Bloch was a very patriotic man, and had flown the American flag every day in front of his store from the 1890s until his death in 1914.

An interesting story about Adam Bloch and his patriotism has been passed down over the years. As a young man, he enlisted and fought in the Civil War. When the Alaska Purchase was announced in June of 1867, Bloch's company was sent to Sitka to begin the United States' occupation of the territory. Former Seldovian Alice Lipke wrote of Bloch's role in the transfer ceremony that took place in Sitka on Oct.18, 1867:

> *Flags were flying from every masthead in the harbor. And on land, every house was decorated with all the panoply of an international event. Russian and American flags fluttered from windows — housetops — flagpoles — an imposing array.*
>
> *That afternoon a curious event happened at the ceremony of transfer, the memory of which still lives in Seldovia. Probably for a century to come, it will not have been forgotten; maybe not then, for it has survived for nearly seventy years.*
>
> *At three-thirty, with a blare of trumpets, a barrage of beating drums, officials of the United States Government, together with citizens and natives, United States troops and Russian soldiers, drew up in front of the castle on Katalan's Rock.*
>
> *The order was given to lower the Russian flag. The firing of guns from the "Ossipee" in salute, resounded through the quiet afternoon air. From the battery on the wharf, the Russians returned the salute to the United States flag, as it was being raised to its pinnacle. The Russian flag caught, as it was being lowered, and clung to the flagpole. A sailor ascended and cut the ropes that held it, and the flag was about to fall to the ground, which would have been an insult to the Russian Government had it been allowed to touch.*
>
> *History tells us that a soldier caught the flag as it was about to fall. We are told, by an eyewitness, that Adam Bloch, who later came to Seldovia to live, and who died in the Alaska he loved, was that soldier. He was close to the spot at the time the flags were being raised and lowered. Seeing the flag about to be flung to the ground, he rushed forward and received the colors in his arms. His quick brain and nimble feet had saved the day.* [149]

For many years after his death, schoolchildren, who had received gifts of warm clothing from the Christmas tree in Adam Bloch's store, placed a flag upon his grave each Fourth of July in honor of his record as soldier and citizen.[150] With the dedication of the flagpole, the wish was made that this flag ceremony and remembrance of Mr. Bloch, his patriotism, and his many local acts of kindness be made on Independence Day in Seldovia for all time to come. Although Seldovia still has a flag-raising ceremony on July 4th, these remembrances are, sadly, no longer a part of the public ceremony.

Independence Day in Seldovia has always been marked by a rousing celebration that attracts visitors from other Inlet communities. In the late 1920s, the roster of festivities might have included games for all ages, with "prizes that were not to be sneezed at."[151] Joe Hill threw a free dance and handed out apples and oranges, and the harbor was full of boats all making noise to rival the crowds on shore.

In 1930, cannery tenders steamed into Seldovia Bay, packed with visitors and with flags flying. From the San Juan Cannery came the P*aradise,* from Port Graham came the C*hacon* and the *Cypress*, and from Portlock and the lower Cook Inlet came the *Delaware* and the *Blanche*. Others came from Homer and Ninilchik. They were treated to a community decorated to the nines with flags, bunting and streamers. A fifteen-voice children's chorus gathered at the open windows of the school house and sang patriotic songs to the crowds gathered outside. The words of "America," "Star Spangled Banner," "Columbia," and "Gem of the Ocean" were accompanied by Mary Louise Busey on the piano, R.C. Morris on the cornet, and Albert Linder on the violin.

Then the games began! Foot races for boys and girls, a sack race for boys, and a three-legged race for men were but a few of the athletic events. Ladies could indulge in a nail-driving contest or an egg race, while boys and men fought one another with pillows. For the brave there was the pie-eating contest or the outboard motor race for boats under 14 feet.[152] Musicians from Port Graham aided the local Filipino orchestra and other local talent in providing free dancing for all.

The Fourth of July more or less coincided with the start of the red salmon run, and in the 1940s the celebration was also a gay sendoff for the fishing fleet. A parade made its way up and down the boardwalk, with cannery hand carts serving as the bases for floats. In addition to games, local organizations took advantage of the crowds to sell food, drink, and souvenirs as fundraising measures. Local fishermen pitted themselves against "outsiders" in a spirited tug-of-war that on occasion turned into a brawl.[153]

Today, Seldovia is famous throughout Alaska for its down-home July Fourth celebration. Visitors stream in by the hundreds, more than quadrupling the local population for this one day. At the airstrip, private planes stand wing-tip to wing-tip, and in the harbor pleasure boats are rafted four deep along the floats. The events of the day change from year to year, but a parade and games can always be counted on. In some years, pigs and beef have been roasted over an open fire, and volunteers serve up the barbecue with a multitude of side dishes. Other years, local gourmet cooks become food vendors for a day, and the visitor can choose from a number of seafood offerings. Log rolling and canoe jousting in the harbor are popular, as are the 5 km race and the softball game between a town team and the sailors from the Homer-based Coast Guard cutter. The greased-pole climb, auctions of baked goods produced by local men, and the dunking tank are other favorites. Festivities are generally capped with a community picnic and fireworks at the Outside Beach.

For many visitors, Seldovia doesn't just celebrate the Fourth of July; it *is* the Fourth of July!

Childhood Scrapbook: Growing up in Seldovia

Despite its isolation and lack of modern entertainment, Seldovia was and still is a big playground for children. Most youngsters who grew up here loved the out-of-doors, and it was the surrounding mountains and sea that made up their play-yard.

Before the advent of modern conveniences, children kept busy with chores: hauling water, firewood, and coal. Through the 1930s, many native children spent a good part of their summers up the bay at the fish camp by the mouth of the Seldovia River. For those left in town, there was summer work in the canneries for the industrious. The real business of children, though, is play, and plenty of time was left for that. Former Seldovian Jim Busey counts fishing, rowing boats, and hiking among his pastimes in the late 1920s and early 1930s.

The businesses about town held endless possibilities for children. When they weren't scuffling around for change on the beach below Joe Hill's Hall, they might sneak past the watchman and climb aboard the old schooner *Salvatore*. Scraps of lumber from the sawmill made fine rafts and crude rowboats for small boys imitating their seagoing fathers.

Nick Elxnit in the 1910s and 1920s made skis from the staves of herring barrels and secured them to his feet with rubber straps. A bit of candle wax applied to the bottom and a good steep hill completed the recipe. A square of moosehide served as a toboggan, carrying a pile of tumbling, laughing children down the slope. [154]

Seldovian Albert Wilson recalls ice skating under the moonlight on the lagoon at the head of the Seldovia Slough, and ice fishing for whiting. He chopped a hole in the ice and set his pole, and then left it while he skated around. A bonfire on the beach warmed cold hands and feet. [155]

In the winter of 1947, Dr. Melvin Beltz and Everd Jones built a ski tow on Frank Raby Hill behind the Beachcomber Hotel. The gas-powered engine carried young skiers from the Yuth residence to the top of the hill in eight seconds.[156]

Today, local children enjoy sledding on the lower part of Reservoir Hill and ice-skating on Lake Susan. The Seldovia Native Association plows and floods its parking lot, providing an informal hockey rink. Summertime finds youngsters fishing for salmon in the Slough and exploring the surrounding woods, beaches, and hills.

Local boys gather for Robert Anderson's birthday party in 1932. Top row, L to R, are Louis Shell, Ralph Anderson, George King, and Robert Anderson. Middle row, L to R, are Ted Anderson, Jimmy Peterson, and Stanley McLane. Bottom row, L to R, are Herchel and George Burgin. Photo courtesy of Ted Anderson from the Ralph and Juanita Anderson Collection.

Axel Anderson looks up from supervising the ice-fishing activities of several youngsters on the ice-covered lagoon at the head of the Seldovia Slough in 1930. Photo courtesy of Ted Anderson from the Ralph and Juanita Anderson Collection.

Steve Zawistowski and "Rosie" Rosenbush wait for a bite on the Seldovia Slough lagoon. Whiting and herring were the typical catch. Photo courtesy of William Wakeland, #56K6

Sunday visitors to the schooner Salvador, which worked out of and later came to rest in Seldovia Bay. This c.1930 photo is courtesy of the Jack and Susan B. English Collection.

In the sunshine of an August afternoon in 1917, two Seldovia girls play with a (chained) black bear cub. Photo courtesy of the U. S. Geological Survey, J. B. Mertie Collection, #660

Endnotes

[1] Alaska Division Chief, Bureau of Education, Dept. of Interior, letter to Della Borst, 21 Mar. 1908, Seldovia Native Assoc. Collection, from National Archives.
[2] Della Borst, letter to Commissioner of Education, 27 Apr. 1908, Seldovia Native Assoc. Collection, from National Archives.
[3] Borst, report to Commissioner of Education, 15 July, 1908, Seldovia Native Assoc. Collection, from the National Archives.
[4] *Seward Weekly Gateway* 16 May 1908: 3.
[5] AK Bureau Chief, letter to E.D. Evans, 16 July 1908, Seldovia Native Assoc. Collection, from National Archives.
[6] Juanita Anderson, letter to Jan Int-Hout, 4 Mar. 1972, Jack English Collection.
[7] Archibald R. Law, Superintendant of Construction [Seldovia], "Plat of School-grounds at Seldovia," ms., 11 July 1908, Jack English Collection.
[8] Amelia McMicheal, report to E. E. Brown, Commissioner of Indian Affairs, Bureau of Education, Alaska Division, 30 June 1910, Seldovia Native Assoc. Collection, from National Archives.
[9] McMicheal.
[10] *Seward Weekly Gateway* 26 February 1910: 1.
[11] McMicheal.
[12] McMicheal.
[13] McMicheal.
[14] *Seward Weekly Gateway* 25 July 1908:2.
[15] McMicheal.
[16] McMicheal.
[17] J. Anderson, letter to Jack and Susan English, 4 Mar. 1972, Jack English Collection.
[18] A.J. Clanahan, *Our Stories, Our Lives* (Anchorage: Cook Inlet Region, 1986) 167.
[19] J. Anderson, letter to Int-Hout; J. Anderson, taped interview with Laura Hendricks, Pratt Museum, Homer, 13 Oct. 1983.
[20] J. Anderson for W.A.Keller, Clerk, "Annual Report of the School Board for the Seldovia School District," 26 July 1915, Jack English Collection.
[21] Gilbert M. Chambers, "School Census, Seldovia School District," 17 Oct. 1921, Jack English Collection.
[22] J. Anderson, letter to Int-Hout.
[23] Catherine Brickey, "The Little Lady From Norway," HEA *Ruralite* Feb. 1977: 17.
[24] J. Anderson, letter to Int-Hout.

Endnotes (cont.)

[25] Alice Cushing Lipke, *Under the Aurora* (Los Angeles: Suttonhouse, 1938) 225. Author's note: I stumbled across this book while on a research trip to Juneau. The book is long out of print, but a signed copy of it was waiting, seemingly just for me, in a rare book store there. I made numerous phone calls to try to locate the publishing house to seek reprint permission. I was unable to find Suttonhouse, nor anyone who knew which publisher might have bought their rights. A search for Lipke heirs was equally unproductive.
[26] Melvin B. Ricks, *Directory of Alaska Post Offices and Post Masters* (Ketchikan: Tongass, 1965) 57.
[27] *Seward Weekly Gateway* 17 Mar. 1906: 4
[28] *Seward Weekly Gateway* 20 Jan. 1906: 1
[29] Janet R. Klein, *A History of Kachemak Bay, the Country, the Communities* (Homer: Homer Soc. of Natural History, 1981) 41.
[30] *Seward Weekly Gateway* 27 July 1907: 1.
[31] *Seward Weekly Gateway* 4 Dec. 1909: 4.
[32] Ricks 57.
[33] Susan B. English, "History of the Seldovia Post Office," unpub. ts., 20 July 1968, Jack English Collection.
[34] Elsa Pedersen, "Kachemak Bay Story," unpub. ts., Pratt Museum, Homer, 16.
[35] S. English.
[36] *Alaska Weekly* 11 June 1926: 1.
[37] Hal Spence, "Englishes Left Behind a Legacy," *Homer News* 7 Sept. 1989: 1; 15.
[38] *Seward Weekly Gateway* 2 Jan. 1909: 1.
[39] Jack Kares, "Deposition to Miners' Inquest," ts., 1 Apr. 1909, Jack English Collection.
[40] Kares.
[41] Kares.
[42] *Seward Weekly Gateway* 17 Apr. 1909: 2; 24 Apr. 1909: 4.
[43] Henry "China" Poot, "Deposition to Miners' Inquest," ts, n.d., Jack English Collection.
[44] Adam Bloch and Sydney Laurence, receipt to China Poot, 5 Apr. 1909, Jack English Collection.
[45] Kares.
[46] Bloch, "Expenses to Bringing the Bodys of WD Valentine and Elli Fuller to Seldovia from China Poots [illeg. word] Kachemak Bay and to Bury Them," ms., n.d., Jack English Collection.
[47] Bloch, untitled inventory ms., n.d., Jack English Collection.
[48] Bloch, "Effects of WD Valentine, Sale at Auction," ms., n.d.; "Fuller Effects, Sale at Auction," ms., n.d., both Jack English Collection.
[49] Mattle Valentine, letter to Adam Bloch, 15 Apr. 1909, Jack English Collection.
[50] A. C. Moulton, letter to Adam Bloch, 27 Apr. 1909, Jack English Collection.
[51] *Seward Weekly Gateway* 1 May 1909: 1; 5 June 1909: 3.
[52] *Seward Weekly Gateway* 20 Nov. 1909: 4
[53] *Seward Weekly Gateway* 29 Jan. 1910: 4.
[54] *Seward Weekly Gateway* 22 Jan. 1910: 1; 26 Feb. 1910: 3.
[55] *Seward Weekly Gateway* 10 Oct. 1910: 2.
[56] *Frontiersman* [Seldovia] 8 Feb. 1947: 6.
[57] *Seward Weekly Gateway* 7 July 1906: 3.
[58] Lipke 192.
[59] Jim Busey, letter to the author, 18 June 1992.
[60] Lawrence Dunning Jr., personal interview, 1991.
[61] *Alaska Weekly* 26 June 1925: 8; 13 Nov. 1925: 8.
[62] *Frontiersman* 5 Mar. 1947.
[63] *Alaska Weekly* 6 Aug. 1926: 7.
[64] "Vote," Committee for Incorporation, 1946, Jack English Collection.
[65] Busey.
[66] Jim and Marian Busey, personal interview, 27 Apr. 1993.
[67] J. & M. Busey.
[68] John Crawford, personal communication.
[69] Crawford.
[70] Elxnit, personal interview, 1989.
[71] Crawford.
[72] Lipke 214.
[73] *Alaska Weekly* 7 Nov. 1924: 1; 14 Nov. 1924: 5.
[74] *Pathfinder* July 1925: 16.
[75] T.W. Anderson, "Ace In The Hole Poker Club, Seldovia," unpub. essay written for this book, 27 Mar. 1991.
[76] *Seldovia Herald* 11 Mar. 1933: 6.
[77] Jimmy Hill Obituary [title illeg.], *Pathfinder* Dec. 1924: 15.
[78] T.W. Anderson, personal interview, 6 June 1994.
[79] T.W. Anderson.
[80] Busey.
[81] *Seldovia Herald* 19 Apr. 1930; 21 June 1930; 19 July 1930: 5.
[82] *Seldovia Herald* 23 May 1931.
[83] *Seldovia Herald* 11 July 1931: 6.
[84] Lester Busey, "Record of the Meeting," ts., 21 Aug. 1931, T.W. Anderson Collection.
[85] "Board Walk, Completed, Accepted as Job Well Done," *Seldovia Herald* 17 Oct. 1931:1; Lester Busey, "Grand Summary: Statement showing all costs, and all contributions relating to the Seldovia sidewalk," ts., n.d., T.W. Anderson Collection.
[86] *Seldovia Herald* 17 Oct. 1931.
[87] *Seldovia Herald* 17 Oct. 1931.

Endnotes (cont.)

[88] *Seldovia Herald* 17 Oct. 1931.
[89] W.A. Estus, letter to Seldovia Schoolchildren, n.d., T.W. Anderson Collection.
[90] *Seldovia Herald* 4 June 1932:5.
[91] Frederica de Laguna, "Impressions of Seldovia in the Nineteen Thirties," unpublished essay written for this book, 1993.
[92] Larry Beck, "Earthquake Changed Beautiful Seldovia," *Anchorage Times* 4 Nov. 1979:8.
[93] Busey.
[94] Clanahan 187.
[95] Pedersen, "Seldovia," *Alaska Sportsman* July 1958: 38.
[96] Elxnit interview.
[97] Clanahan 187.
[98] Clanahan 187.
[99] De Laguna 5.
[100] *Frontiersman* 4 Dec. 1946.
[101] De Laguna 5.
[102] *Western Alaskan* 19 Nov. 1936: 4.
[103] Lipke 169.
[104] Busey, letters to the author, 18 June 1992; 20 July 1992.
[105] *Seldovia Herald* 4 Feb. 1933: 5.
[106] *Westward Alaskan* 9 Sept. 1936: 1; 8 Oct. 1936: 3.
[107] *Frontiersman* 21 Dec. 1946: 5.
[108] *Alaska Daily Press* [Juneau], 4 May 1941: 5.
[109] "Minutes of the Seldovia Women's Club Meetings," unpub., 1941-46, Jack English Collection.
[110] Z.J. Loussac, letter to Juanita Anderson 23 Oct. 1944, Jack English Collection.
[111] *Seldovia Herald* 2 Dec. 1932: 1.
[112] *Seldovia Herald* 2 Dec. 1932: 1.
[113] *Seldovia Herald* 2 Dec. 1932: 1.
[114] Elxnit interview.
[115] *Seldovia Herald* 2 Dec. 1932: 1.
[116] Fred Elvsaas and Larry Reynolds, personal communications, Sept. 1994.
[117] *Frontiersman* 8 Mar. 1947: 1.
[118] Ethan Smith, "Seldovia, Typical Alaskan Town," unpub. ts., 1946/7, loan courtesy of Lynne A. Sinnhuber, Homer.
[119] *Frontiersman* 22 Jan. 1947.
[120] *Frontiersman* 5 Mar. 1947; 26 Mar. 1947: 5.
[121] *Frontiersman* 12 July 1947: 8.
[122] *Frontiersman* 19 Apr. 1947: 6.
[123] Pedersen, "Kachemak Bay" 123.
[124] Kenneth "Oly" Jackson, personal interview, 29 Sept. 1994.
[125] Jackson.
[126] "Ketchikan to Barrow," *Alaska Sportsman* July 1963: 38.
[127] Larry Reynolds, personal communication, Sept. 1994.
[128] Spence 15.
[129] Fred Elvsaas, personal communication, 1993.
[130] Spence 15.
[131] Elxnit interview.
[132] *Frontiersman* 24 Sept. 1947: 1.
[133] *Westward Alaskan* 1 Oct. 1936: 1; 15 Oct. 1936: 1.
[134] Westward Alaskan 22 Oct. 1936: 2.
[135] Sue Hecks, personal communication, 1 Oct. 1994.
[136] Elxnit interview.
[137] *Frontiersman* 21 June 1947: 8.
[138] Mike Miller, personal interview, 16 June 1992.
[139] *Frontiersman* 20 Nov. 1946: 1.
[140] *Frontiersman* 30 Nov. 1946.
[141] *Frontiersman* 4 Dec. 1946: 4.
[142] *Frontiersman* 18 Dec. 1946.
[143] *Frontiersman* 15 Mar. 1947: 3; 16 Apr. 1947: 1.
[144] *Frontiersman* 2 Apr. 1947: 1.
[145] *Frontiersman* 7 May 1947: 8.
[146] *Frontiersman* 2 Apr. 1947: 6.
[147] *Frontiersman* 14 May 1957: 8.
[148] Miller.
[149] Lipke 262-263.
[150] Lipke 257-258.
[151] Lipke 259.
[152] *Seldovia Herald* 28 June 1930: 1; 4 July 1930: 1.
[153] Pedersen, "Kachemak Bay" 79.
[154] Elxnit interview.
[155] Clanahan 187.
[156] *Frontiersman* 1 Feb. 1947.

THE EARTHQUAKE AND URBAN RENEWAL

How the Events of a Single Day Changed the Face of Seldovia and the Lives of its Citizens

On March 27, 1964, massive tectonic plates deep within the earth shifted and collided, setting in motion a natural disaster that would change Seldovia forever.

Many active faults run through Alaska and cause frequent tremors. A July 1964 National Geographic article names four faults involved in the Good Friday earthquake of that year. They are listed as the Lake Clark Fault, the Cook Inlet Fault, The Fairweather Fault, and the Seldovia Fault. Inquiries made to the U.S. Geological Service today show no clear record of a fault named for Seldovia, but do yield maps showing a fault line running from southwest of the Chugach Islands and the Kennedy Entrance, bisecting Koyuktolik Bay, English Bay, Port Graham, and Seldovia Bay, and continuing in a northeasterly direction across Kachemak Bay before turning inland slightly to terminate in the Caribou Hills. There it appears to join forces with a fault line that continues northward toward Anchorage and is today known as the Border Ranges Fault. What was once called the Seldovia Fault crosses Seldovia Bay on roughly the bearing of the current Post Office, runs somewhat along the waterfront to a point behind Lookout Point, continues on through the woods to Seldovia Point, and then goes back to sea again as it crosses Kachemak Bay. [1]

The Good Friday Earthquake (as it became known) began at 5:36 p.m. Its epicenter was about 12 miles beneath Prince William Sound in Port Wells, east of Whittier. Slipping along fault lines, plates of the earth's crust converged with the force of 12,000 Hiroshima-sized atomic bomb explosions. Shock waves traveling thousands of miles per hour caused tremors in an arc 500 miles long. [2]

In Seldovia, the rumbling and trembling began slowly, and at first were dismissed as just another one of the small tremors that are not uncommon in Alaska. When the shaking continued, however, stretching from seconds into terrifying minutes, all doubts as to the gravity of the situation vanished. [3]

Cracks in the ground appeared, snaking their way across roads and through front yards. Seldovian Lou Collier had just returned from a commercial fishing trip to Lituya Bay. He was headed home from the boat harbor and was walking across the wooden Slough bridge when the earthquake hit. "The road bed of the bridge looked like a roller coaster," remembers Lou, "and the trees were moving every which direction at once! Some folks, fearing a tsunami, moved up to the school, which was on higher ground. Others walked up the hill to the dam. My wife and I just stayed put. I wasn't worried about a wave. Fred Elvsaas lived across the street from us on the Slough. He brought all his personal papers up to our place, just in case." [4]

Former Seldovian Elsa Pedersen was helping a friend put together a birthday party when the ground started shaking. She watched the hanging lamp over the dining table swing crazily. She notes that the enormity of the disaster hit them when they turned on the radio and discovered that all of the Anchorage stations had gone off the air. Even on the short wave radio, calls from the other coastal towns were eerily missing. [5]

I met well-known mystery writer Dana Stabenow as I was writing this book. Dana was in town to speak to a women's reading group that was visiting Seldovia. In the course of my conversations with Dana, I learned that she was the young guest of honor at the birthday party Elsa Pedersen was helping to host. Before this, I hadn't known that Dana had once lived in Seldovia and attended school here. Who better than this talented writer to provide an eyewitness account of the earthquake for my book? Many thanks to Dana for recording her compelling story of that terrifying day for this book.

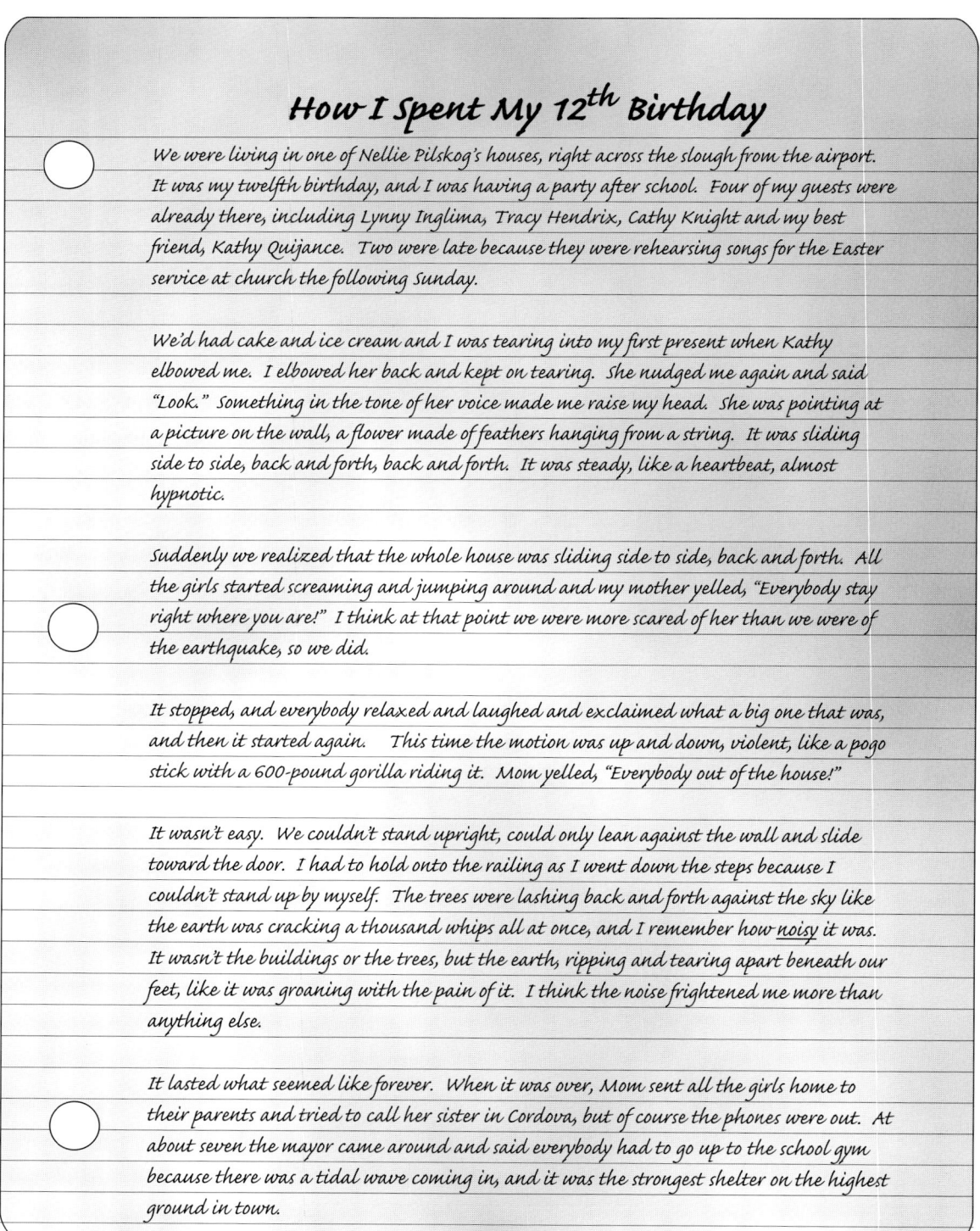

How I Spent My 12th Birthday

We were living in one of Nellie Pilskog's houses, right across the slough from the airport. It was my twelfth birthday, and I was having a party after school. Four of my guests were already there, including Lynny Inglima, Tracy Hendrix, Cathy Knight and my best friend, Kathy Quijance. Two were late because they were rehearsing songs for the Easter service at church the following Sunday.

We'd had cake and ice cream and I was tearing into my first present when Kathy elbowed me. I elbowed her back and kept on tearing. She nudged me again and said "Look." Something in the tone of her voice made me raise my head. She was pointing at a picture on the wall, a flower made of feathers hanging from a string. It was sliding side to side, back and forth, back and forth. It was steady, like a heartbeat, almost hypnotic.

Suddenly we realized that the whole house was sliding side to side, back and forth. All the girls started screaming and jumping around and my mother yelled, "Everybody stay right where you are!" I think at that point we were more scared of her than we were of the earthquake, so we did.

It stopped, and everybody relaxed and laughed and exclaimed what a big one that was, and then it started again. This time the motion was up and down, violent, like a pogo stick with a 600-pound gorilla riding it. Mom yelled, "Everybody out of the house!"

It wasn't easy. We couldn't stand upright, could only lean against the wall and slide toward the door. I had to hold onto the railing as I went down the steps because I couldn't stand up by myself. The trees were lashing back and forth against the sky like the earth was cracking a thousand whips all at once, and I remember how <u>noisy</u> it was. It wasn't the buildings or the trees, but the earth, ripping and tearing apart beneath our feet, like it was groaning with the pain of it. I think the noise frightened me more than anything else.

It lasted what seemed like forever. When it was over, Mom sent all the girls home to their parents and tried to call her sister in Cordova, but of course the phones were out. At about seven the mayor came around and said everybody had to go up to the school gym because there was a tidal wave coming in, and it was the strongest shelter on the highest ground in town.

I asked Mom what a tidal wave was, and she said a big wave of water. "How big?" I said. We'd lived on a boat for five years before moving ashore and I'd seen some pretty big waves, so I wasn't all that worried. "As big as our house?"

"Maybe," she said.

Her tone of voice made me ask, "As big as the town?"

"Maybe," she said.

Then I was scared all over again, too scared to stay inside the gym with everybody else. I went outside with my mom's friend, Maka (Mayjoice Colberg).

I remember standing on the walkway between the school and the gym, holding Maka's hand, staring into the dark and waiting for the wave. After a while we could hear it, a long, low shshshshshshshshshsh. It didn't sound so bad, certainly nowhere near as bad as the earthquake had.

It wasn't until daylight the next day that we could see it had destroyed our brand-new small boat harbor, and it wasn't until April and the spring tides that we realized that the land had dropped five feet. Everyone fifth grade and up was taken out of school to help the grownups fill sandbags at the Outside Beach and stack them on the boardwalk so it wouldn't float away. Later that year, the town had to decide what to do, drive new pilings and jack up the town, or go with the Corps of Engineer's plan to dike and fill.

The worst memory of my childhood is not the earthquake or the tidal wave. No, the worst memory of my childhood is of me standing in front of Inglima's store, the boardwalk ripped up by the roots and scattered around like pick-up-sticks, watching as they dynamited Capp's Hill into a pile of dirt and gravel. I'll never forget it. Sometimes I think I'll never forgive it. I know I'll write about it, someday.

Dana Stabenow
Anchorage 1995

Just after dark the fire whistle warned Seldovians of the impending tsunami, or tidal wave. This was the moment everyone had been dreading. Important papers and treasured belongings were gathered up and moved to higher ground. The townspeople congregated at the school, and in the gym confusion reigned. Babies cried, keyed-up children ran through the crowd bouncing basketballs, and along the edges of the room parents sat quietly, wondering if their homes would be spared.

Men roamed restlessly about the boat harbor, those with small boats helpless to save them. Many of the seine and drift boats were still winterized, their engines drained. Despite the frantic efforts of their skippers, they could not be started. Some of the larger boats had already left the harbor to ride out the wave in the relative safety of deeper, open water.

The tide was low when the earthquake struck, so that when the water began flooding in, it thankfully did not inundate waterfront buildings. In the boat harbor, however, the force of the inrushing water was amplified as it funneled between the rock jetties. The flood tore boats loose with their owners trapped, snapped off pilings, and wrenched apart sections of dock, then pushed them all toward the head of the harbor in a jumbled stew. As boats whirled about, men stood on their decks and tried to fend off huge broken timbers, which could damage the wooden hulls. Water overflowed up the Slough, flooding the banks and the airstrip. Backer's Island and the back side of Schooner Beach formed a big catcher's mitt for boats and debris, and it was on their banks that most of the wreckage was stranded when the flood finally receded. [6]

When daylight dawned on March 28th, relief was evident on the faces of the townspeople. As reports trickled in of the vast devastation in places like Kodiak, Valdez, Seward, and Anchorage, Seldovians realized how they had been spared. True, the boat harbor was a mess, but homes remained standing and the tidal wave had not swept the town into the sea. Amazingly, even with all the havoc wreaked in the harbor by the surging water, there had been no loss of life.

Sandbags are piled along the edges of the boardwalk to try and keep the wooden walkway and the water main from floating away with the tide. They were also used in a vain attempt to stem the flow of seawater into the adjacent buildings. Chuck Hendrix photo, courtesy of Candy Hendrix.

Water Torture

A new calamity, however, lay in store for the unsuspecting town. When high tide came on March 28th, water crept into the homes of several houses built along the boardwalk and the floor of the Polar Bar was covered by nearly a foot of water. Fishing boats were busy combing the harbor, cleaning up floating debris and salvaging any usable pieces to patch together a dock until such time as it could be properly rebuilt. Still, everyone was troubled by the strange action of the tide. [7]

As the days passed, it became clear that the March 28th high tide was not an isolated freak. The lowest spots on the boardwalk were now wet during the high tides. Flooding had not been unknown in the past, but it had been confined to a few instances over the years when the fall "super-high" tides and a particularly bad storm had combined forces. Now, even during a relatively normal 21 foot high tide, the boardwalk and some of its occupants were being inundated. Worried glances were exchanged when folks thought of the 25 foot tides that could be expected with the autumnal equinox. The fall months were also the advent of the stormy season, when huge swells often enter the bay. [8]

Although some people felt that the tides were simply temporarily disturbed as an aftermath of the

Those caught without rubber boots at high tide could only hope to piggy-back a ride from a sympathetic neighbor. In this photograph, the Wakefield Cannery office is at right. Chuck Hendrix photo, courtesy of Candy Hendrix.

Rubber-booted pedestrians try to go about their normal business on the flooded boardwalk. Photo courtesy of the Alaska State Library, U. S. Army Corps of Engineers Collection, # PCA 100-220

Local children and dogs waded about in the floodwater, many of them unaware of its impact on the future of their boardwalk community. Photo courtesy of the Alaska State Library, U. S. Army Corps of Engineers Collection, # PCA 100-221

earthquake, there was a growing realization that the land had subsided nearly four feet and that community action would be required. In May, high tides again flooded the Polar Bar and sent four inches streaming into the ground floor of the Beachcomber Hotel. The Seldovia House was flooded too, although less so than the Beachcomber. [9]

Sandbags were piled up to weigh down the water main that ran along the boardwalk. Businesses resigned themselves to drilling holes in their floors so that the now-regular flooding could drain back out. Merchants moved stock up from the lowermost shelves. One of the canneries even removed metal sheathing from some parts of its buildings so that the water wouldn't push the structures off the very pilings on which they sat, but would instead flow through them.

After a time, even the canine population of Seldovia grew tired of wet feet. "Cocoa," whose master Pete Polson worked at the Wakefield Cannery, waits impatiently at the door to the (sandbagged) Wakefield cafeteria kitchen. The popular dog could always count on a tidbit from the Filipino cooks. Chuck Hendrix photo, courtesy of Candy Hendrix.

Seldovian Mel Molberg shrugs his shoulders in good-natured disbelief as seawater floods into this house. Powerless to stop the regular inundation, folks did the only sensible thing: don rubber boots or waders and move possessions to the second floor. Before long, however, the novelty grew thin, and people worried what would happen when the fall high tides and storm surge combined. Chuck Hendrix photo, courtesy of Candy Hendrix.

During a spring snow storm, Wakefield Cannery employees take a smoking break, standing around in the flood from a high tide. Chuck Hendrix photo, Courtesy of Candy Hendrix

By August, yet another problem had arisen. The road along the Seldovia Slough began to collapse and drop into the water. Weakened by tidal action and increased water levels, the roadbed caved in, dragging with it water pipes and exposing the foundation of a nearby home.[10]

As fall approached, attempts were made to raise some of the most exposed buildings along the boardwalk. The Seldovia-Port Graham Consolidation cannery raised its messhall and office buildings almost two feet. The Polar Bar, Morris and Morris store, and the Beachcomber were also raised. Townsfolk waited for September with concern, and for October and November with outright dread.[11]

Their worst fears were realized in October, when stormy weather and slushy snow joined with high tides and savagely attacked the waterfront. In the Wakefield cannery, a foreman rowed a skiff through the plant. In the Seldovia House Hotel, sea water poured into a bathtub on the ground floor! Buildings were flooded and even the low spots on the back roads near the head of the slough were under water.[12] All in all, nearly 80% of the commercial/industrial activities in the community found themselves threatened by tidal inundation.[13]

Urban Renewal :
To Be or Not To Be
(That was the question.)

During the summer, Kenai Peninsula Borough Assembly chairman Harold Pomery had called fellow assemblyman and Seldovia city councilman Lou Collier to offer his help in securing Urban Renewal assistance for Seldovia. Historically, Seldovia had prided itself on its self-reliance as a community. No project or tragedy, big or small, sent Seldovians whimpering to the government with outstretched hands. This community of fiercely independent fishermen was proud that it took care of its own. Now, however, they faced a bigger problem than ever before: the rebuilding of nearly the entire town. To complicate matters, some folks still maintained that the tides would eventually return to their pre-earthquake level.

Nonetheless, the city council was charged with doing its best for the community and so they agreed to a visit from representatives of the federal Urban Renewal program. Here began the greatest period of controversy in Seldovia's history.[14]

The Army Corps of Engineers had estimated the cost of raising the Seldovia boardwalk to be about $700,000, but this figure did not take into account the cost of raising any of the buildings along it. An Oregon firm was hired to produce a feasibility study for urban renewal in Seldovia. Many of its recommendations and observations were not carried out, perhaps lost in the confusion of the times. The city council in September of 1964 rejected the idea of rehabilitating the boardwalk (that is, raising it). Instead, they looked at the second option presented by the Army Corps of Engineers: to tear down the boardwalk and then build a dike/reinforced waterfront and fill behind it.[15]

Once the city council rejected the idea of rehabilitation, the dilemma became more clear. Should Seldovia agree to allow the Alaska State Housing Authority to buy out all the affected property owners along the boardwalk? Should Seldovia vote to allow the Army Corps of Engineers to tear down the boardwalk and its buildings, replacing them with a new waterfront composed of rock and gravel fill? Powerful arguments were made both by those for and those opposed to the project. The Alaska State Housing Authority representatives lobbied for the project. The canneries, the direct or indirect employers of most Seldovians, made it clear that without this urban renewal project, they could not afford to rebuild and would be forced to move elsewhere.[16] Wakefield Fisheries posted notices around town that if the urban renewal project were accepted by the voters, they'd rebuild here; if it were not, they would move their operations to Port Graham. Other canneries made similar promises, but in the face of declining fish resources in the area, either didn't intend to or couldn't end up keeping those promises. In the end, Wakefield was the only plant to honor its word.[17]

State Senator Clem Tillion and Seldovia civic leader Jack English led the opposition to the project. They were joined by others who faced financial loss from the destruction of the boardwalk and reshaping of the town, and by those who could not imagine Seldovia without its trademark wooden walkway. One city councilperson was torn between public opinion and his own newly-purchased air jacks. He had invested in these devices intending to go into the business of jacking up buildings. If Urban Renewal were given the nod, his investment would be for nought.

The timing of the decision to accept Urban Renewal was critical. The October council elections were drawing near, and the opposition had rounded up candidates who were against the destruction of the boardwalk. The seated council realized that if they intended to resolve the issue they must act immediately, while they still had a majority in favor of Urban Renewal. Although no public vote was required, the council, perhaps in an attempt to

A look at some of the homes and businesses that flooded during the post-earthquake high tides. Photo courtesy of the Alaska State Library, U. S. Army Corps of Engineers Collection, PCA 100-210

The sandbagged boardwalk dries in the sun at low tide. Photo courtesy of the U. S. Geological Survey, Alaska Earthquake Collection, #149

mollify the opposition, decided to take a public opinion poll. A sheet was posted at the city office with two columns—a "yes" column for those favoring the Corp's destroy/dike/fill plan, and a "no" column for those who did not want to see the boardwalk torn down and the waterfront reshaped.

Seldovians trooped into the city office and wrote their names in one column or another. The drawback to this method, of course, was that a person's vote was thus public, and many found themselves lobbied by their friends and convinced to go back to change their votes. So, a secret ballot was arranged and again Seldovians indicated their choices. When the ballots were opened and counted in the city clerk's office, the tally was nearly two to one in favor of the Urban Renewal project. But the opposition cried "Foul play!" and "Rigged election!" for the votes had not been counted in a public forum. In response to these concerns, a second secret ballot vote was conducted, and this time the votes were opened and counted at a special public meeting. When the results matched those of the previous election, the opposition finally conceded defeat.

This did not mean, however, that all opposing voices were silenced, nor that peace and harmony would now reign in Seldovia.[18] To the contrary, the strong opinions held by both sides gave way to bitterness. Elsa Pedersen had been writing a Seldovia column for the *Anchorage Daily Times*, and now found it too difficult to continue with any regularity. No matter what she wrote, someone was bound to be offended by it and vociferous in their displeasure. In a small isolated town like Seldovia, having your lifelong friends and neighbors angry with you could be unbearable.[19] Nearly twenty families and nine businesses, their properties purchased by the Urban Renewal project, left town forever.[20]

It was not only the bitter taste of the changing aesthetics of Seldovia that drove folks away. Accepting Urban Renewal funds carried with it strings: the regulations of modern city living came to Seldovia. This comfortable little town of rambling wooden walkways and weathered old buildings now found itself doused awake with the cold water of zoning laws, building codes, plumbing codes, and electrical codes thrown at it from every direction. State income tax and Kenai Peninsula Borough taxes became a new and unpleasant reality, and pages of building restrictions from the Urban Renewal agencies made the cost of owning a business here increase. People were unused to being told what to do and how to do it. To many, selling their property to the project, taking the money, and leaving for some place simpler and quieter sounded just great.[21]

Prior to the earthquake, as many as five seafood processors (General Fish Co. [salmon], Seldovia/Port Graham Consolidation [salmon and crab], Sutterlin & Wendt [shrimp and crab], Alaska Shellfish Co. [crab], Wakefield Fisheries [crab]) operated in Seldovia, employing nearly 200 people. It is speculation to try to say how many more years those firms would have operated here, for the marine resources on which they depended were declining. After Urban Renewal, however, only Wakefield Fisheries honored its pledge to rebuild in Seldovia, and the labor force dwindled to about 60.[22] The other companies took the money they received for their plants and departed to build elsewhere or to not rebuild at all. Urban Renewal may simply have moved up plant closure decisions that would have eventually been made had the earthquake never taken place.

The Reshaping of Seldovia

Although the vote to accept Urban Renewal came in the fall of 1964, it was a long time before the physical work of the project actually began. The federal government had to write an urban renewal plan and had to buy up all the property which would be in the way of the project bulldozers. To do this, they used the Alaska State Housing Authority (ASHA) as the purchasing agent. When it came to determining property values, the independent appraisers hired by ASHA had their work cut out for them, as many of Seldovia's property lines had been muddied by time and neighborliness. Two appraisals were given for each property slated for destruction, and the average of those appraisals was offered to the property owner. If he didn't agree with the offered price, he was welcome to hire his own appraiser and challenge the ASHA price. The dozen or so families who carried through with this ended up receiving about 25% more for their property than those who had not challenged ASHA's offer.[23] According to Elsa Pedersen, this made many of those who sold out on the first offer bitter toward those who held out for more money.[24]

While ASHA was busy securing property, a flock of government officials descended upon Seldovia. They were followed closely by consulting firms hired to study everything from how the new town should look to the demographic, economic, and social history of the town. Elsa Pedersen recalls that very little communication seemed to flow between survey teams, so that she and others began to feel as though they were answering the same questions over and over again.[25] On top of this, a number of the questions could only be given a speculative answer, and many townspeople stopped taking the whole survey process seriously, regarding the questioners as little more than annoying gnats.

The project at times seemed like a boondoggle for any government employee who had ever entertained the notion of a trip to Alaska. Lou Collier remembers that every other day, it seemed, a different bureaucrat arrived with some new scheme or mission. There were visiting admirals from the Dept. of the Navy, who surveyed Seldovia Bay with an eye toward sinking the hulls of old warships at the entrance so as to break up and dissipate any future tsunamis. There was a retired general with the Civil Defense group who came to Seldovia to argue for relocating the entire community to Port Graham. Great sums of money could be saved, he maintained, by abandoning the destruction and rebuilding of the waterfront and simply moving all the people to Port Graham instead. Fortunately, a gale blew on the day he was to lead a study team by boat to that village, and his illustrious plan went the way of numerous others. Inexperienced in the ways of large-scale government projects, incredulous Seldovians looked about them at the graft and waste and nicknamed the project "Bourbon Renewal."[26]

When the buyout of affected properties was complete and Seldovians had been thoroughly studied and surveyed by all manner of government agencies, the actual work of destroying the boardwalk and its buildings began. In the summer of 1965, Joe Studnick of Anchorage was hired for the job, and he barged his bulldozers across Kachemak Bay to Seldovia.

Scores of families and businesses had to be relocated. Over twenty 55' trailers were brought in for the purpose of temporary housing. Not everyone was eager to move into them, and some folks stayed in their homes until the dozers worked their way down the waterfront to them. These families had sold their property to ASHA, but now found themselves in the curious position of having to pay rent to the federal government to live in what had been until recently their own homes! The rent gathered from these families, and from those who rented the trailers, was put back into the project budget. For some people, the trailers were luxurious quarters compared to their wooden cabins, but for others the three bedroom mobile homes were woefully inadequate. Everyone seemed affected by the emotional upheaval of the move.[27]

The tearing down and destruction of Seldovia's picturesque waterfront buildings made for an emotional time for residents. Jack English titled these May 1966 photos "Pillage, Plunder, and Devastation." Photos courtesy of the Jack and Susan B. English Collection.

Nothing so stirred the emotions of the town as did the relocation of the old Russian Orthodox cemetery. Originally located in a grassy field just above high tide line at the seaward end of town, the cemetery had fallen victim to the post-earthquake flooding that had inundated the rest of Seldovia. With each high tide the grassy field became a sodden swamp. The equinoctal tides and storm surges did further damage by eroding away the earth and exposing some of the graves closest to the sea.

Lavake Renshaw was in Seldovia serving as an intermediary between the Urban Renewal headquarters in San Francisco and the Army Corps of Engineers on site. He had sited a dozen graves exposed by the tidewaters and had located nearly sixty additional gravesites by identifying mounds in the earth. Most of the wooden crosses or simple headstones were gone, and those few that remained were for the most part illegible. There had been no burials on this site since 1934 and no layout map was thought to exist. A house adjacent to the property was commonly known to be built on top of several graves! It was clear that the task of moving the cemetery would not be an easy one. Renshaw had an aerial photograph of the cemetery enlarged, and he pored over it, trying to establish a pattern in the raised mounds. [28]

He contacted the young Orthodox priest at the Kenai Parish, and discussed with him the idea of moving the cemetery. The priest concurred that action had to be taken to protect the exposed burial sites and agreed to have the cemetery moved, provided it could be done in a respectful manner. Renshaw contacted his superiors, who balked at the idea of moving a cemetery: they were unwilling to stick their necks out to approve such a renegade undertaking. Undaunted, he contacted the Bureau of Indian Affairs, the highway departments of various states, and other agencies he felt might have encountered the problem of an old cemetery now "in the way." By all the experts, Lavake was advised to leave well enough alone. Cemeteries couldn't be moved, he was told; it simply had not been done before.

Renshaw now faced a situation which required some sort of immediate action on his part. The eroding Russian Orthodox cemetery was threatening to hold up the Urban Renewal bulldozers and his superiors in San Francisco were reluctant to act. The "experts" he had consulted had given him no support so now the decision was up to him. It was a decision that, if handled poorly, could alienate or even enrage an entire community. Lavake decided to go ahead with the move. In his heart he felt that it could be done,

Workers dig up graves in the tide-threatened Russian Orthodox cemetery. A makeshift privacy screen for temporarily storing the remains is seen at right, while the project foreman confers with a representative of the Orthodox church nearby. This photograph was captioned "Ghouls at Work, Urban Renewal Project at Seldovia, 1965" and expressed the feelings of many townspeople about the relocation of the cemetery. Photo courtesy of the Jack and Susan B. English Collection.

and done carefully, with respect for both the dead and their living descendants. He announced to his superiors that the cemetery would be moved. Relieved of the burden of decision and its responsibility, they put up no argument. Meanwhile, Lavake drew up a scope of work and put the job out to bid. From the eight to ten mortuaries who responded, he chose Kodiak Mortuary, and they in turn subcontracted the actual work to Studnick Construction, already onsite.

With time now at a premium, Lavake gathered the necessary permissions for the move and submitted an advertisement to the newspapers. He was required by law to advertise the proposed project so that any who opposed would have the opportunity to make their concerns known. No serious objections were voiced, but the judge gave everyone a turn when, just prior to the day he would issue the court order to proceed, he announced that he was embarking on a ten day vacation!

Despite those delays, the work got underway with painstaking attention. A screen was erected around the excavation site, so as to protect the sensitivities of the public. Each grave was opened and the body was removed and re-coffined before workers proceeded on to the next site. Because some of the burials were very old, the work took on the air of an archaeological dig. Lou Collier remembers the beautiful copper embossed coffins. Lavake recalls the practice of burying people with the tools of their trade. He noted in particular that one of the earlier graves was a female who had been buried with scissors and needles, the objects of her earthly profession. [29]

This dignified air was shattered when local boys vandalized the site one night. For some reason, one of the graves had been left opened and unsecured at the end of a working day. Come nightfall, the young mischief-makers entered the excavation and stole a skull. The mark of their thievery was found the next morning in the shape of a Honda motorcycle key, which they had apparently dropped in their haste to get away. The key was duly delivered to Jack English, who put out the word that he had a certain key. This key, he said, could be exchanged for a certain item (the skull) whose return was very much desired by

The cemetery relocation project continues as the heavy equipment of Urban Renewal changes the Seldovia landscape in the background. This photograph, titled "The Ghouls are still working," is courtesy of the Jack and Susan B. English Collection.

the Urban Renewal project. A place and time for the exchange were given out, and the miscreants' anonymity was assured. It proved an effective method for dealing with the problem, for scarcely a day had passed when the key was gone from its appointed spot and the skull was found in its place. [30]

When the disinterments were deemed complete, the Orthodox bishop from Sitka was summoned. Trenches were dug at the present-day cemetery on Anderson Way, and the deceased were blessed as they were reinterred, safe at rest once again. The town had been terribly uneasy about the whole procedure, but in the final analysis, relocating the graves had in fact pre-empted the natural tidal destruction of the old cemetery.

The snow-covered landscape emphasizes the emptiness of "downtown" Seldovia and its waterfront in the years following Urban Renewal. Photo by U.S. Army Corps of Engineers, Chuck Hendrix Collection, courtesy of Candy Hendrix.

SELDOVIA HISTORIC BUILDING INVENTORY
PARTIAL LIST OF PRE-EARTHQUAKE BUILDINGS STILL STANDING

1) SELDOVIA BIBLE CHAPEL, *Seaward end of town* - This was built in 1944 by Rev. George Tobleman and reputed to have the strongest concrete in town.

2) BUCHMAN HOME, *Seaward end of town* - This residence was built by Paul Petresun for Martha Jensen.

3) OLD CITY CEMETERY, *Seaward end of Main St.* - This cemetery is next to the workshop at author's home. It was an outgrowth of the original Orthodox cemetery and was not moved during Urban Renewal as it was not tidally threatened and was not "in the way" of the dike & fill project on the waterfront.

4) AUTHOR'S HOME, *Seaward end of Main St.* - The log portion was built about 1915 by one of the Balishoff brothers from Kenai. Dovetailed and tapered corners are characteristic of Russian-influenced log building techniques. Recent remodeling has revealed that the rest of the house was built over a two-year period from 1920 to 1921, for and first occupied by Ralph and Juanita Anderson.

5) GRUBER HOME, *Hill above fuel storage tanks* - This was originally the cook shack at the chrome mine on Chrome Bay in Port Chatham. When the mine closed down, the building was hauled to Seldovia on a fish scow and moved into place on the hill above the fuel tanks. The Grubers have added on to the structure.

6) GRUBER/ENGLISH OFFICE, *Below fuel storage tanks* - This was the office of Jack English for many years. During Urban Renewal, it was moved up from the waterfront, out of the way of the demolition crews.

7) WILLARD HOME, *Main St., below Orthodox church* - Built in 1940 to serve as Seldovia's hospital, it had patient wards, staff quarters, and an operating room.

8) WINFREE HOME, *Main St., below Orthodox church* - A 1928 Sears mail order house, it arrived here with the assembly instructions in Danish. However, with the numbers of Scandinavian fishermen living in Seldovia, translation was readily available. It was built for the late Winnie Zawistowski and her first husband.

9) A FISHERMAN'S HOME, *On the old boardwalk* - This was the 1930s home of fisherman Walter "Nig" Lipponcott.

10) LETHIN HOME, *On the old boardwalk* - In the 1930s the original portion of this house belonged to Ed Feldahl, a Scandinavian bachelor and fisherman.

11) JOSEFSON HOME, *Across the slough* - The second oldest house in town, this was built around 1917 and was the home of Emma and Simon Josefson. Traditionally, it was painted robin's egg blue.

12) BURNETT HOME, *Across the slough* - Originally the Hilmer Olsen home, it was built in the early 1930s. Hilmer was a tall Scandinavian who worked on sailing ships for years before settling in Seldovia to trap and fish. Taking advantage of a $30 bounty on coyotes, he is reported to have sat at his kitchen table and shot out the window at them on the beach below. At least two subsequent residents of the Olsen home have reported hearing the ghost of Hilmer rocking in his chair on the top floor.

13) RESSLER HOME, *On the old boardwalk* - This boardwalk home was built atop a fish scow. You can still make out the faint markings on its "bow:" **AYR no.6**. This scow came from the Alaska Year Round Cannery, and was apparently scow number six in their fleet. [This home was torn down during publication of this book.]

14) STANDEFER HOME, *On the old boardwalk* - Scandinavian bachelor fisherman Ed Seaverson built this home sometime prior to 1938 and lived there.

15) SANDLIN HOME, *At the bridge* - In the 1930's the bridge across the slough was a drawbridge type so that fishing boats could pass through. A number of fishermen lived up the slough and tied their boats in front of their homes in the off-season. Mr. Garner was the bridge-tender, and the keeper of the key which activated the drawbridge-works. It is said that after more than one gang of local youngsters cranked the bridge up and then ran off and left it that way, Mr. Garner kept the works locked up and the key under guard at his home. [The unmaintained house was torn down during the publication of this book]

16) ORTHODOX CHURCH, *On the hill above Main St.* - See the chapter "Russian Culture and Influence" for information about this building.

17) BACKER HOME, *On hill above bridge* - This was built in the 1930's for Scandinavian fisherman Jack Wormensen. Jack fished Bristol Bay and Cook Inlet, and crossed the latter in the winter to trap beaver, martin, and other fur-bearers.

18) SUYDAM HOME, *On hill above bridge* - This home was built in the 1930's for marshal Andy Anderson. Andy's wife, Inga, was very short, and hence much in the house was scaled down to accommodate her.

19) NORDENSEN HOME, *Shoreline Dr. vicinity* - This home was built in the 1940's for Nordensen forbearer Grandmother Bessie Lloyd.

As the actual demolition of the boardwalk began, Elsa Pedersen compared Seldovia to a battlefield. "We watched the boardwalk sawed in sections, loaded on trucks and carted away. We saw waterfront buildings demolished, the wreckage burned. We were battered by the clatter of air hammers as dynamite holes were drilled in the cliffs near the waterfront, to blast them away. Cap's Hill in the center of town was broken up and leveled to provide rock fill material for the waterfront road that replaced the boardwalk. The processing plants, the stores, hotel, old schoolhouse and all the old residences in the project area were demolished." [31]

When the last Urban Renewal bulldozer finally left town, Seldovia had a new waterfront, roads to accommodate vehicular traffic, and a modern water and sewer system. Nonetheless, it would be some years before the barren gravel wasteland of the new "downtown" Seldovia would stir again with life.

When one considers aesthetics, Seldovia emerged from Urban Renewal a loser. Gone were the picturesque boardwalk and the quaint and historic clapboard buildings that so charmingly hugged the waterfront and wound themselves about the hilly terrain. Gone was a certain sense of intimacy and a sense of pride in the unique community. Economically, Seldovia lost too, as canneries sold out and left town. Such action cannot be blamed solely on Urban Renewal, however, for the decline in the fish resource was already becoming apparent. It was in terms of the environment that Seldovia "won" from Urban Renewal. No more did raw sewage from homes and businesses outfall onto the beach, waiting to be washed away by the tide. No more did sewage run in open ditches or in pipes into the bay. Urban Renewal brought modern sanitation to the community, and in so doing helped protect the health of Seldovia Bay. With time, what was once a barren gravel wasteland has grown into a picturesque town, with green lawns, flower beds, scores of trees, and a waterfront that is bustling and developing even today.

Since Urban Renewal, Seldovia has turned to logging and tourism, while continuing to support a modest-sized fishing fleet. Cottage industries have largely replaced the big canneries, with many folks consequently being self-employed. Presently, the town is seeing some growth as a retirement and summer community.

Final Thoughts

As Seldovia nears the turn of another century, the daily life of the community is marked by searching and struggle. As neighbors, we struggle to understand one another as we appraise the future from widely divergent points of view. Some lifelong residents' vision of the future is distorted by the veil of the past, while newcomers oftentimes are well-meaning, but have little historical perspective to appropriately guide their opinions on what is best for the community. We struggle to remember that there is value in all opinions. We are not so different from small isolated communities anywhere in our country. In Seldovia, we strive to define the relationship between the ANCSA (Alaska Native Claims Settlement Act)-created native corporation and the municipality. It is an endeavor often fraught with frustration for both sides, as there are few precedents to guide our behavior.

As Seldovians, we struggle to set an economic course for our journey into the future. Reluctantly, we begin to admit that fishing may never again be the prosperous economic base it once was for Seldovia, and we concede that our economic base must expand if we are to survive. Tourism may well be part of our salvation, but development scares us, for it has the power to change the very essence of why we live here. People choose to live in Seldovia because of what isn't here. We have no malls, traffic lights, fast food franchise outlets, rampant crime, nor a host of other unpleasant and impersonal trappings of modern life in the world away from our insular haven. Along with the natural beauty, this simple uncomplicated atmosphere is one of Seldovia's drawing cards for tourism. The cruel paradox of developing a tourism industry is that the very development itself threatens the pure character of the attraction.

The challenges which face us as a community seem never-ending and often insurmountable. Despite this, there is a quiet and lovely continuity of life linking past and future together that, with grace, will prevail. There is still a living link back to Seldovia's earliest times, and a tangible link back to the centuries before we even knew ourselves as "Seldovians." It is this link that may in the end preserve us, for it reminds us that in the long course of human existence on this earth, the problems that seem immediate and overwhelming to us as a community are but a speck in time. We need to hold in our hands the bone and stone artifacts from the daily life of those people who walked our local beaches five hundred years before us. We need to remember that the descendants of Adam Bloch, James Cleghorn, and several other early families still make their homes here and continue to bring forth new generations. Such continuity is indisputable proof that once the very old fabric of Seldovia has wrapped itself around our souls, this is indeed the only place for us to be.

Endnotes

[1] William P.E. Graves, "Horror Strikes on Good Friday," *National Geographic* July 1964: 114.
[2] Graves 114.
[3] Elsa Pedersen, "Kachemak Bay Story," unpub. ts., Pratt Museum, Homer, 125.
[4] Lou Collier, personal interview, 29 Apr. 1994.
[5] Pedersen, "Kachemak Bay" 125.
[6] Pedersen, "Kachemak Bay" 125.
[7] Pedersen, "City Spared Heavy Losses from Quake," *Anchorage Times* 9 Apr. 1964.
[8] Pedersen, "Big Tides Challenge Boardwalk Buildings," *Anchorage Times* 20 Apr. 1964.
[9] Pedersen, "Water Enters Three Seldovia Structures," *Anchorage Times* 18 May 1964.
[10] Pedersen, "Tital Action Takes Out Seldovia Road," *Anchorage Times* 22 Aug. 1964.
[11] Pedersen, "Seldovia Gets Set for Fall Tide Threat," *Anchorage Times* 5 Sept. 1964.
[12] Pedersen, "Seldovia: Old and New," *HEA Ruralite* Nov. 1975: 25.
[13] Lutes and Amundson, *A Feasibility Survey for Urban Renewal*, (Springfield, OR: Lutes and Amundson, May 1964) 11.
[14] Collier.
[15] "Urban Renewal on the Last Frontier," *The Cook Inlet Collection: Two Hundred Years of Selected Alaskan History*, ed. Morgan Sherwood (Anchorage: Alaska Northwest, 1974) 208.
[16] "Urban Renewal" 208.
[17] Pedersen, "Kachemak Bay" 145.
[18] Collier.
[19] Pedersen, "Kachemak Bay" 143.
[20] "Urban Renewal" 211.
[21] Collier.
[22] "Urban Renewal" 210.
[23] Collier.
[24] Pedersen, "Kachemak Bay" 145.
[25] Pedersen, "Kachemak Bay" 146.
[26] Collier.
[27] Collier.
[28] Lavake Renshaw, personal interview, 29 Apr. 1994.
[29] Renshaw.
[30] Renshaw.
[31] Pedersen, "Kachemak Bay" 149.

Old Nicodemus paddles up the Seldovia Slough. Photo courtesy of Mary Glover.

Glossary

Analoi - Term used by the Orthodox priests visiting Seldovia, for "lectern"

Anchor Point -15 miles northwest of Homer on the Kenai Peninsula, named by Captain Cook in 1785; (Orth, p.75)

Archimandrite - Superior of a monastery or convent in the Orthodox Church; (Fedorova, p.282)

Augustine Island - Formed by the Augustine Volcano, it lies 70 miles southwest of Homer in Kamishak Bay; named by Captain Cook in 1778; Russian Captain Teben'kov in 1852 called it Chernobuoroy, from the Russian for "black" and "brown"; (Orth, p.93)

Aurora Lagoon - Lagoon on Kachemak Bay 16 miles northeast of Homer; (Orth, p.95)

Backer's Island - Located southwest of the Seldovia boat harbor; connected by a small isthmus to the mainland; named for former owner Harold Backer

Banya - Term for bath house, sauna or sweat house

Barabara - Derived from a (Kamchatka) Siberian word for a summer hut; "barabara" was used by the Russians to denote Native dwellings; (Fedorova, p.282)

Barabara Point - Located on the south shore of Kachemak Bay about 4 miles northeast of Seldovia; named for the Native dwellings reported there at the turn of the century; (Klein, p.101)

Bear Cove - Near the head of Kachemak Bay, 18 miles northeast of Homer; (Orth, p.112)

Bidarka - [Bidarka, Bydarki]; Eskimo or Aleut kayak, which, depending on size and design, could carry one, two or three people

Bleenee - May refer to "blini"; a crepe dish

Brailer - Bag made of loose fabric or rope woven to form a loose mesh; used together with a crane to lift fish out of the hold of a boat; the bottom of a brailer bag may also be opened by loosening a drawstring

Buhkta - [Bukhta, Zaliv]; Russian word for bay of water

Camel Rock - Located at the northeast entrance to Seldovia Bay, near Linder's Beach (Inside Beach); named because it resembles a camel; (Orth, p.176)

Caribou Hills - Hilly region of the Kenai Peninsula, located about 30 miles northeast of Homer; highest point is about 2800 feet; (Orth, p.186)

Chiton - Edible mollusk enclosed in a shell which is made up of arched, overlapping plates; traditionally a Native food, gathered from the rocks at low tide

Chugach Gulf - From an Eskimo name for Prince William Sound; published in 1826 by Russian Lt. Sarichev; (Orth, p.778)

Chugach Islands - Located at the tip of the Kenai Peninsula, about 23 miles south of Seldovia; a group of islands whose name was derived from an Eskimo word, and was published in 1847 on a Russian chart; (Orth, p.216)

Chugachik Bay - Alternate name for Kachemak Bay; (Orth, p.482)

Chugachik Island - Located near the head of Kachemak Bay about 19 miles northeast of Homer; derived from an Eskimo name and reported by Russian Captain Teben'kov in 1848; (Orth, p.216)

Chugachmiut - Term for Chugach Eskimo

Coal Bay - On the north shore of Port Graham; named in 1786 by Captain Portlock; (Orth, p.226)

Cohen Island - Located on the south shore of Kachemak Bay at the entrance to Eldred Passage; W. H. Dall named the island in 1880 for a trader who was operating in that area; (Orth, p.229)

Cook Inlet - [Cook's Inlet, Cook's River, Kenai Bay, Kenay Bay]; body of water reaching from the Shelikoff Strait north to Anchorage; named for Captain James Cook; (Orth, p.235)

Cottonwood Creek - Stream which flows south and empties into Kachemak Bay about 14 miles northeast of Homer; named by W. H. Dall in 1898; (Orth, p.240)

Creole - Person of Russian and Alaska Native parentage; (Fedorova, p.282)

Dena'ina - [Tanaina, Kenaitsy, Kenaitse, Thnaina, Tinnats-khotana, Tehaninkutchin]; branch of the Athabaskan Indians

Distillate - Liquid fuel consisting of the light ends from the first distilling of crude oil; less refined than gasoline

Devil doll - Small carved doll used by Tanaina shamans for the same purpose as a "devil stick"; (Osgood, p.178-9)

Devil stick - Carved stick of about shoulder height, used by Tanaina shamans "to drive out the evil producers of physical ailments and spells"; (Osgood, p.178-9)

Eldred Passage - Passage between Yukon Island and the mainland; named in 1880 by W. H. Dall; (Orth, p.308)

Elephant Rock - Local name for a rock outcropping on the northwest side of Seldovia Bay, at the entrance to Hoen's Lagoon; at certain tides the rock resembles an elephant with its trunk in the water

English Bay - [Alexandrovsk, Alexandrovsky, Fort Alexander, Nanwalek]; village at the entrance to Port Graham on its south side, also facing Cook Inlet; reported by Lt. Sarichev in 1826 as a Russian post; today the name has been changed to reflect the traditional Native name "Nanwalek"; (Orth, p.315)

Fire Island - Located at the head of Cook Inlet and the entrance to Turnagain Arm; (Orth, p.334)

Fox River - Flows from the Chernof Glacier into the northeast end of Kachemak Bay; probably named in 1894 for an executive of a local mining company; (Orth, p.352)

Gillnet - Method of fishing where the net is more or less a stationary curtain, and migrating salmon swim into it and are caught by the gills

Hesketh Island - Located next to Yukon Island along the south shore of Kachemak Bay; named by W. H. Dall in 1880 for a visiting English yachtsman; (Orth, p.418)

Herring Island(s) - Located at the entrance to Tutka Bay, 8 miles northeast of Seldovia; named in 1880 by W. H. Dall; (Orth, p.418)

Hieromonk - In the Orthodox Church, a monk who is also a priest; (Fedorova, p.282)

Hoen's Lagoon - Located on the west side of Seldovia Bay, behind an isthmus running between Elephant Rock and Point Naskowak

Hope - Gold mining town founded about 1896 and originally called "Hope City; located on the N end of the Kenai Peninsula on the south side of Turnagain Arm; (Orth, p.994)

Housepit - Outline on the ground, often slightly depressed, of a dwelling or barabara; the earth was usually excavated to a depth of several feet before a barabara was built

Hyqua shell - Found along the North Pacific Coast, its slender core was used for beads to decorate Tanaina clothing; the Tanaina traded with the Indians of southeast Alaska for these shell beads; (Osgood, p.51-52)

Icon - [Ikon]; From the Greek word for "picture"; paintings of a religious nature which adorn the interior of a Russian Orthodox Church

Iconostas - [Ikonostas]; Screen made of icons; separates the sanctuary from the body of a Russian Orthodox Church

Jakolof Bay - [Jack's Harbor, Yakoloff Bay]; SE of Kasitsna Bay; named for 19th century resident John Jakolof; (Orth, p.469 and Klein, p.102)

Kachemak Bay - [Chugachik, Chugachnik, Chugachnick, Tchugatchnek, Shugachik, Kachikmat, Kuchekmak]; east-reaching arm of Cook Inlet; (Orth. P.482)

Kamishak Bay - Located on the east shore of the Alaska Peninsula and the west side of Cook Inlet; 88 miles southwest of Homer; Russian name was Kamyshatskaya; (Orth, p.491)

Kamlinka - [Kamleika, Kamleia]; from a (Chukchi) Siberian word, it was used to describe the Natives' waterproof outer garments; typically made of sea mammal intestine; (Fedorova, p.282)

Kaniagmute - Term for a Kodiak Eskimo

Kasitsna Bay - [Kahsitsnah]; Located on the south shore of Kachemak Bay, 6.5 miles northeast of Seldovia; from a Kenai Indian name; published in 1883 by W. H. Dall; (Orth, p.499)

Kulich - Mushroom shaped sweet bread, studded with fruit, frosted and decorated; traditional Russian Orthodox Easter food

Kustatan - Abandoned Tanaina Indian Village on the west side of Cook Inlet, 20 miles northwest of Kenai; (Orth, p.555)

Labret - Native Alaskan lip ornament, made of bone or ivory; prehistoric

Lignite - "Soft brownish-black coal in which the texture of the original wood can still beseen; it is denser and contains more carbon than peat"; (Webster's)

Linder's Beach - [Inside Beach]; located at the north end of Seldovia; named for the late resident James Linder

MacDonald Spit - Mile-long spit on the west side of Kasitsna Bay; named for Captain MacDonald, who homesteaded there; (Orth, p.609)

Midden - Refuse pile (shells, bones, artifacts) left behind from human occupation; can be above or below ground, depending on its age, the soils and climate of the area

Moraine - "Mass of rocks, sand, gravel, etc. carried or eposited by a glacier, either along its side (lateral moraine) or its end (terminal moraine)" (Webster's)

Ostrov - Russian word for "island"; (Fedorova, p.282)

Outside - [Lower 48]; Term used by Alaskans when referring to the rest of the United States

Pacha - Probably refers to "Paska," a sweet Russian Easter bread

Papert - Term for "porch" used by the Orthodox priests visiting Seldovia

Passage Island - Located at the entrance to Port Graham; named in 1786 by Captain Portlock; (Orth, p. 741)

Peugh - Single-tined pitchfork used by commercial fishermen to handle fish; two-tined peughs were sometimes used in the canneries; peughs are no longer in use

Pirok - Russian pie made with fish (salmon) and rice, or meat and rice

Point Bede - Point of land on the southwest coast of the Kenai Peninsula, 13 miles southwest of Seldovia; named by Captain Cook; just a few miles south of what is now called Point Adam; (Orth, p.121)

Point Naskowhak - Located on the west side of the entrance to Seldovia Bay; a Kenai Indian name reported in 1908; (Orth, p.675)

Point Pogibshi - [Dangerous Cape]; located about 6 miles west of Seldovia; from the Russian word for "perilous"; (Orth, p.763)

Port Graham - [Graham's Harbor]; village 7.5 miles southwest of Seldovia; (Orth, p.772)

Portlock - former cannery site on the south coast of the Kenai Peninsula; 16 miles south of Seldovia; est. about 1921; (Orth, p.773)

Powder Island - Island on the E side of Seldovia Bay; formerly known as Nordyke Island.

Potlatch - Traditional native feast held to honor an individual or to celebrate an occasion; accompanied by singing, dancing, and gift-giving; (Osgood, p.149)

Prichetnik - Term used by Russian Orthodox clergy to refer to a local lay church official

Purse seine - Method of fishing in which net is played out from a boat by a skiff; the skiff then maneuvers around a school of fish and back to the boat, forming a purse

Raby Spit - Located on the southwest shore of Seldovia Bay, roughly opposite Powder Island; owned at one time by the late Seldovian Frank Raby

Red Mountain - [Chrome Mountain]; peak about 3500', 10 miles SE of Seldovia; name reported in 1909 by the U.S. Geological Survey; (Orth, p.798)

Scow - Square-ended flat-bottomed boat used for hauling freight or fish; towed by another boat

Shaman - Prior to European contact, the Native shaman was both priest and medicine man; provided a link between the material world and the spirit world; (Osgood, p.177)

Shelikoff Strait - Twenty mile wide passage which runs between the Kodiak archipelago on the east and the Alaska Peninsula on the west; (Orth, p. 864)

Snug Harbor - Located on the west side of Cook Inlet, on the west coast of Chisik Island, which is about 50 miles southwest of Kenai; (Orth, p. 895)

Starring - Russian Orthodox tradition of Christmas caroling; the procession of singers carries a large decorated star, which is spun as they walk and sing

Sunrise - Gold-mining town founded about 1895; located on the north end of the Kenai Peninsula on the south side of Turnagain Arm - about 7 miles from the town of Hope; (Orth, p.930)

Tender - Large boat under contract to a cannery; used for collecting fish from smaller boats and transporting the consolidated catch to shore

Tierce - Barrel capable of holding 42 gallons; (Webster's)

Toyon - [Toen, Toion]; from a (Kamchatka) Siberian word; used to describe the chief of a Native tribe or village; (Fedorova, p. 282)

Turnagain Arm - Stretches from the mouth of the Pacer River to the head of Cook Inlet; (Orth, p.994)

Tustumena Lake - Twenty-four mile long lake about 20 miles southeast of Kenai; (Orth, p.995)

Tutka Bay - Located east of Jakolof Bay; from a Dena'ina name meaning "big enclosure"; (Klein, p.103)

Tyonek - [Taionek]; village about 40 miles southwest of Anchorage on the west side of Cook Inlet; from a Tanaina Indian name meaning "little chief" and an Eskimo name meaning "marsh people"; (Orth, p. 1001)

Ulu - Disc shaped Eskimo knife; held in the palm of the hand and used for cutting, chopping and scraping; a prehistoric ulu was made of stone; a modern ulu has a steel blade

Umiak - Native open-top skin boat, capable of carrying 10 to 12 people; wooden frame with seal skin or walrus skin covering

Wadsworth Creek - Drains into Kachemak Bay just east of Seldovia; named for homesteader Gene "Whitey" Wadsworth

Yukon Island - Located on south shore of Kachemak Bay, about 9 miles northeast of Seldovia; named for the U.S. Coast and Geodetic Survey schooner, *Yukon*, in 1880 by W. H. Dall; (Orth, p. 1068-1069)

Zimov'e - Russian term for a winter camp; (Fedorova, p.282)

Glossary Sources

A History of Kachemak Bay, the Country, the Communities; Janet Klein, Homer Society of Natural History; Homer, Alaska, 1987 References in the glossary appear as "(Klein, p.xxx)".

Dictionary of Alaska Place Names; Donald J. Orth, U.S. Government Printing Office; Washington, D.C., 1967 References in the glossary appear as "(Orth, p.xxx)".

The Ethnography of the Tanaina; Cornelius Osgood, Human Relations Area Files Press (Yale University); New Haven, Connecticut, 1976 References in the glossary appear as "(Osgood, p.xxx)".

The Russian Population in Alaska and California; Svetlana G. Fedorova, translated and edited by Richard A. Pierce and Alton S. Donnelly; Limestone Press, Kingston, Ontario, 1973 References in the glossary appear as "(Fedorova, p.xxx)".

Webster's New World Dictionary of the American Language; 1964 References in the glossary appear as "(Webster's)"

Words that are otherwise defined in the text of the book or are in the realm of "local knowledge" have no source in parentheses. When there is more than one spelling or variation of a word, the variations are shown in brackets.

Index

A

Afognak Island. 127
Akedaknak. 55
Akedaknak/Yukon Island Dena'ina. 56
Alaska Commercial Company . 54 - 55,71,75 - 78,81,99 - 101,110,112,114
Alaska Ecclesiastical Consistory. 74
Alaska Marine Highway. 120
Alaska Seldovia Packers 115
Alaska Western Fox Corp. 103
Aleut. 12,23,54,75,79
Alexandrov, Ivan. 88
Alexandrovsk . . . . 41,44 - 45,52 - 53,74 - 76,78,82,85,90
Anchor Point . . . . 40,43,45,54 - 55,101,110,125,129
Anchorage . . . . 21,115,118 - 120,161,175,181,183,196,200,202,205,208 - 209,220,227
Anderson Dock. . . . . 115 - 118,120,125
Anderson, Alyce. 169
Anderson, Axel 123,137,184,212
Anderson, Carl "Squeaky". 115,142
Anderson, Juanita. . . . . 92 - 93,165,168 - 171,174,184,187,200,207
Anderson, Ralph92 - 93,104,115,117,119,122 - 123,170,181,184,207,212
Anderson, Robert. 212
Anderson, Ted. . . . . . 7,115,119,184 - 185,212
Archimandritov. 121
Archimandritov, Capt. . . . . 46 - 48
Arctic Circle 19
Arctic Small Tool tradition 28
Arndt, Katherine. 52,72
Asplin, Capt. Ben. 119
Athabaskan. 23,53
Atka 45
Aurora Lagoon 28

B

Backer's Island 112,128,220
Bai, Nicholas 78
Balashev, Zachari. 82
Balishoff, Fitka. . . . . 25,58 - 59,65 - 66
Balishoff, Mike. 188
Balishoff, Simeone. 63
Baltazar, George. 182
Balyshev, Elisaveta. 75
Bancroft, H.H. 53
Banks, Della. 39
Barabara Point 26
Baranov, Alexander . . . . 43 - 44
Barnes, R.B. 179
Barren Island. 48,101
Bay of Herring. 46,48
Bayu, Nicholai. 82
Bayu, Pavel. 83
Bayu, Vassili. 85
Beach, Zenas . . . . 158 - 159
Bear Cove. 103
Belkofsky 181
Bell, Frank 204
Belmont, Peter. 137
Beltz, Dr. Melvin. 204,212
Berestov, Theodor 86
Berger, Capt. Heinie . . . . 119 - 120,174
Berglund, Eunice 204
Bergmen, Fred 119
Berlin Museum. 55
Bettman, Sid 181
Bishop Innokentii . . . . 87 - 89,165
Bloch, Adam . . . . . . 57,75 - 76,78,80,86,100 - 101,173 - 174,179 - 180,210 - 211,233
Blodgett, Capt. Perl D. . . . . 110 - 111,114,179
Blodgett, Mimi 179
Blue Fox Cafe 26,107

Bocharov, Capt. Dimitrii 37,40,42
Bogart, Eugene. 174
Borst, Della . . . . 88,165 - 166,168
Bortnovsky, Fr. John . . . . . 75 - 76,78 - 83,85 - 89,173
Bowen, Rofey. 157
Brooks, William 183
Brown, Charlie. 89
Brun, Mervin 192
Burgin, Dr. Isam F. . . . . 103 - 104,107,203
Burgin, George. 212
Burgin, Herchel 212
Burke, Mike 157
Busey, Jim. . . . . 7,93,134,181 - 182,185,191,196,211
Busey, M. Lester. 196
Busey, Mary Louise 196,200,211
Buzard, James O. 177

C

Calhoun, Red. 158
Cap's Hill 233
Captain Sand 55
Caribou Hills 102,217
Carlough, Billy. 109
Chambers, Gilbert M. . 136,148 - 149,181,184
Chatham, Virginia. 205
Chernabura volcano 75
Chignik 174,210
Child, John. 156 - 157
China Poot Bay 178
Chkitukskoe . . . . 52 - 53
Christensen, Annie 169,174
Christian, Joe and Bill 106
Chugach Bay 45
Chugach Eskimo (Chugachmiut) 54
Chugach Islands 102,217
Chugachik 54
Chugachik Bay. 52
Clegg, Asst. U.S. Attorney 177
Cleghorn, Adam 188
Cleghorn, James 103,173,233
Coal Bay 49,174
Coal Harbor. 38
Colberg, Eliza. 120
Colberg, John. 107,109,123
Colberg, Mayjoice 219
Cold Harbor. 174
Cole, Roy 143
Collier, Lou 7,217,224,227,230
Cook Inlet . . 19 - 20,23 - 24,37,40,43 - 44,46 - 49,52,54,57,63 - 64,71,75,102,104,110,115,123 - 125,128,136,143,174,177
Cook Inlet Transportation Co. . 111 - 112,114
Cook, Captain. 37,54
Cooks Inlet Blue and Black Fox Farmers Association 104
Copper River 23,54
Cordova. 107,177,189,218
Corser, Charles 181
Corwin, Lynn. 30
Cottonwood Creek . . . . 20 - 22,24,193
Creole. . . . . 51,53 - 54,72,88
Crow Creek Mining Co. 112

D

Dall, William H. 51,53
Daniels, Viola. 200
Davidson, George 49
De Laguna, Dr. Frederica 7,19 - 23,25 - 28,30 - 31,34,40,54,118 - 119,153,190,192 - 193
De Laguna, Grace 20,22
Demidov, Alexander. . . . . 85 - 86
Dena'ina. . . . . 19,36 - 37,53 - 55,57
Dena'ina. 54

Dennis, H.L. 123
Dillingham. 181
Dimond, Oren . . . . 192 - 193
Dingel'shtet 47
Dixon, Capt. George. . . . . 37 - 40,42 - 43
Doherty, R.G. 179
Douglas, Buckley. 142,195
Dudas, John. 107
Duffy . . . . 180 - 181
Dunning, Lawrence 154,158
Dunning, Lawrence, Jr. 181
Dutch Harbor. 124
Dwyer, Ed. 107
Dwyer, Mrs. 107

E

Earthquake, 1964 12,91
Eklutna. 57
Elizabeth Island 102
Elsos, Agnes 96
Elvsaas, Fred. 7,32,143,206,217
Elvsaas, Gladys. 32
Elxnit, Nick . . . . 56,86,92 - 93,113,115,129,131,135,157 - 158,168,182,188,203,206,212
Emil, John 184
English Bay . . . . 52 - 56,74,101,202,217
English, Jack 7,177,184,206 - 207,224,228,230
English, Susan Bloch . . . . 173 - 175,200
Engstrom, Charlie 123
Entrance Island 107
Eskimo 12,19,22 - 24,26 - 27,34,53 - 56,63 - 64
Estus, W.A. . . . . 138 - 141,187,189
Evans, Mr. 166
Eyak 112

F

Farros, Herbert 88,165
Fedorova, Svetlana. 51
Fields, Capt. Jack . . . . 19 - 21,24,26,175
Filardeau, Joe 102
Filmore, Capt. Albert 180
Fire Island. 112
Fish Creek 9,16
Fisk, Jim . . . . 176 - 177
Fomin, Nicholai 86,88,165
Fort Alexander 55
Fox River 106
Frank Raby Hill 212
Fraser River. 23
Fuller, Elli . . . . 177 - 180
Fur Farmer Magazine 105
Furuhjelm, Enoch Hjalmar 151

G

Garner, Tom. 207
Gherke, Alfred 159
Gilman, Isabelle . . . . 168 - 169
Girdwood 114,174
Glascock, Capt. Charles. 93
Golikov, Capt. Ivan 37,40
Graham's Harbor (Port Graham). 49
Greenland 23
Grewingk Glacier. 37
Grewingk, Dr. Constantin C. A. 37
Groothof, John 115,207
Gulf of Alaska. 19

H

Halibut Bay. 176 - 177
Halibut Cove . . 28,35 - 37,49,90,93,115,122 - 123,176,184,202
Halvorson, Mrs. S. 96
Hansen, Bert 154
Hanson, Olof 138

Happy Valley... 153
Harding Ice Field... 37
Harrington, Red... 155 - 156
Hawes, Robert... 181
Hawkey site... 34,37
Heiner, Clair... 158
Hendrix, Tracy... 218
Henington, Merrill... 209 - 210
Henry China Poot... 179
Herbert, Elizabeth... 105
Herbert, John A... 92,102 - 103,105,112 - 114,128,168,174,179 - 180
Herbert, Mrs. R.J... 107
Herr, Earl... 115,208 - 209
Hesketh Island... 102 - 103,107
Higginson, Ella R... 28
Higman, Dede... 55
Hildreth... 176 - 177
Hill, Jimmy... 66,181,183
Hill, Joe... 94,185,187 - 188,191 - 192,211
Hodel, Joe... 156
Hoen's Lagoon... 25 - 26,201
Hofstead, Thor... 207
Hogansen, Martin... 138
Hogatt, Governor... 169
Homer... 12,16,30 - 31,39,85,101 - 102,113 - 115,120,150 - 151,153,156 - 157,161,174 - 175,200,203 - 205,210 - 211
Homer Spit... 39,49,83,177
Hope... 77,110,114,174,177
Hopkins, Bill... 190
Hoy, Fred... 109
Hulbert, Milo... 96,107,174,181,183,185
Hutchinson and Kohl... 71

I

Iliamna... 54,57,109,115,118,174 - 175
Inglima, Lynny... 218
Inhart, Harry... 104
Inside Beach... 36
Inuit... 52 - 54,57,71 - 72
Iron Creek... 125
Issacson, Matt... 108
Izmailov, Captain... 37,42

J

Jack, Kares... 178
Jackson, Dr. Russell... 205
Jackson, Oly... 205
Jackson, President Andrew... 48 - 49
Jacobsen... 183
Jacobsen, Johan... 54 - 55
Jakolof (Yakolof) Bay... 12,16,27,49,105,149,155 - 157,208,236
Jensen, Ed... 184
Jensen, J.J. "Doc"... 96,203 - 204
Jensen, Martin... 206
Johnson, Capt. Andrew... 180 - 181
Jones, Everd... 212
Jorgensen, Lynn... 143,184
Josefson, Emma... 92
Josefson, Simon... 188
Juneau... 75,152

K

Kachemak... 51
Kachemak Bay... 9,19 - 24,28,30,33,36 - 45,47 - 49,55,58 - 59,63 - 64,74 - 75,84,103 - 104,106 - 107,150,176 - 177,184,205,217,227
Kachemak Tradition... 22,26,28,33 - 34
Kadiak (Kodiak)... 53
Kamenskii, Anatolii... 82
Kamishak Bay... 137
Kanitak, Akaky... 79
Kares, Jack... 177
Karluk... 174
Kasilof... 51,114 - 115,118 - 119,174
Kasitsna Bay... 26,49,127
Katalan's Rock... 210
Katmai volcano... 115
Keller & Fjeldahl... 136

Keller, Archie... 153,158
Kelly, Nick... 153
Kenai... 16,51 - 52,54 - 55,57 - 58,74 - 76,78,81,83,89,114 - 115,118 - 119,128,137,152,174,181,204 - 205,229
Kenai Bay... 37,44,46,51
Kenai Fjords... 39
Kenai Indians... 52
Kenai Peninsula... 19,43,64,154
Kenai Peninsula Borough... 12
Kenaian Temperance Society... 88
Kenaitze... 53 - 54,57
Kendricks, Jack... 203
Kennedy Entrance... 217
King, George... 212
Kirby, Dr... 204
Klein, Janet... 28 - 29,32 - 36
Klondike... 203
Knight, Cathy... 218
Knik... 51,110,112 - 115,169,174
Knik Arm... 111
Knik River... 77
Knyk... 51
Kodiak... 45,75,100 - 101,115,143,174,181,220
Kodiak Eskimo... 54
Kodiak Island... 23,64
Kolomin, Petr... 44
Koniagmiut... 54
Konovalov, Grigorii... 44
Korsnes, Elizabeth... 96
Korsnes, Emma... 96
Koyuktolik Bay... 217
Kroll, Hank, Sr... 192
Kuchekmak... 54
Kukak Bay... 148
Kuppler, G.W... 181
Kustatan... 118,138

L

Lake Clark... 217
Lake Susan... 191,210,212
Latouche... 112
Laurence, Sydney... 179
Lebedev-Lastochkin, Pavel... 44
Leiren, John... 123
Lewis, Harry... 21
Lewis, Joseph S... 176
Libby, McNeil & Libby... 123
Lindemann, Bob and Mary... 30
Linder, Albert... 211
Linder, James... 179
Lindstedt, Carl... 123
Lipke, Adam... 184,193 - 194,208
Lipke, Alice... 94,171,193 - 194,210
Lippincott, Nig... 39,184
Lisiansky... 52
Little Ice Age... 37 - 40
Little Tutka Bay... 129
Lituya Bay... 217
Lloyd, T. W... 26
Lloyd, T.W... 105,185,207
Lone Island... 177
Lookout Point... 36,217
Loussac, Z.J... 202
Lund, Charles... 188

M

MacDonald Spit... 26 - 27,127
MacDonald, Captain... 127
MacKenzie, Margaret... 96
Maitland, Bill... 184
Maitland, Mrs. W.W... 200
Malcolm, H.H... 134,138,148
Malina Bay... 125
Markle, Mr... 181
Mars, Ronnie... 109
Martin River... 106
Martin, Tony... 106,109
Mason, Gene... 140,153
Matanuska... 51
Matt Yuth's Pioneer Blue Fox Ranch... 105

May, Samuel... 179
McCullagh, Mrs. Jean... 200
McCullough, Keith... 103
McIver, Mr... 122
McLane, Stanley... 212
McMeekan, Alice... 96
McMicheal, Amelia... 166,168
McNab, Mr... 122
McPorson, Mr... 85,151
Meares, Capt. John... 37,42
Mercer, Mrs... 180
Mickelsons... 205
Miller, Dick... 208 - 210
Molberg, Mel... 223
Moore, "Buzz"... 158
Moore, Capt. Z.S... 113
Moreira, John M... 177
Morris, R.C... 106,182,196,211
Mother Rick... 65
Moulton, A. C... 180
Mr. Frank... 55
Mrs. Meehan... 27
Mt. Augustine volcano... 75
Mud Bay... 49
Murphy, William... 158 - 159,188
Murray, John... 176 - 177
Myers, Charlie... 135

N

Nakani... 65
Naknek... 181
Nanwalek... 44,52 - 55,74
Nash, Mr... 165,168
Neilsen, Carl... 108
Nelson, Sen. Knute... 168
Newman, Bill... 20
Newman, Ed... 22
Nieuwejaar, Mrs. Erling... 200
Nikita, Hieromonk... 74 - 75
Nikolai... 48
Ninilchik... 49,52,75,110,115,118 - 119,169,211
Ninilchik River... 51
Nome... 80,152,168
Nordyke Island... 185
Nordyke, J.D... 122
Norstad, Axel... 132
Northern Alaska Commercial Company... 77
Northern Alaska Commercial Company... 75,99 - 100
Northwest Steamship Company... 110
Nuka Bay... 101
Nushagak... 173 - 174
Nutbeem, Ted... 123

O

O'Dale, Thomas... 114,174,179
O'Neil (O'Neill), Capt. Fred... 96,125,149,189
Ocean Bay tradition... 28
Ollestad (Olstead), Tollak... 27,103 - 105
Olmsted, H.L... 204
Olson, Grace... 96
Olson, Mrs... 204
Osgood, Dr. Cornelius B... 23,25,57,59,66
Ostrovski... 53
Outside Beach... 28 - 30,57,211,219

P

Pacific Steamship Company... 115
Palmer... 200,208
Palmer, George... 113
Passage Island... 102 - 103
Patton, Casey... 158
Pedersen, Elsa... 7,55,141,205,217 - 218,226 - 227,233
Perault, George... 158 - 159
Perry, Tom... 118
Peterson, Allen... 96,170 - 171,184,193
Peterson, Dan... 132
Peterson, Jettret Stryker... 170 - 172,200
Peterson, Jimmy... 170,212
Peterson, Nels... 158

Peterson, Peggy 170
Petkafsky 174
Petroff, Ivan .... 37,53 - 54,57,72
Pierce, Dr. Richard 40,51
Pilskog, Nellie.................. 170,218
Piper, A.F......................... 108
Place, Dan 185
Point Bede 40
Point Naskowhak................. 8,57,84
Poleske, Lee 152
Polson, Pete 222
Pomery, Harold 224
Port Chatham 45,48,154
Port Dick...................... 109,131
Port Graham 23,38,40,43,49,54 - 56,102,114 - 115,125,138,151,155,159,202,211,217,224,227
Port Wells......................... 217
Porter, Robert...................... 90
Portlock........................ 202,211
Portlock, Capt. Nathaniel..... 37 - 38,40,151
Powder Island............. 135,158,185
Prince William Sound......... 19,21,23,44 - 45,53,55,64,123 - 124,217
Pye Islands 101

Q

Quijance, Kathy..................... 218

R

Raby, Frank 108,123,182
Rapp, F.A. 155
Red Mountain .... 16,154 - 156
Reed, Carrie 54
Reed, Judge J.L. 179
Renshaw, Lavake .... 7,229 - 230
Resurrection Bay 43
Revenue Cutter Service 48
Reynolds, Dr. Larry 205
Ritchie, Judge U.S. 102,181
Riter, Clayton...................... 109
Romanoff, Music 106
Romig, Dr. Joseph 167
Rosenbush, "Rosie".................. 213
Rossiiskoe selenie................... 51
Russian American Company .... 46,51 - 52,54,71,151
Russian Orthodox American Messenger ... 81
Russian Orthodox Church . 17,52,57 - 58,71 - 72,79,84
Ryan, Alec .... 75,81 - 82

S

Sagen, Capt. Lars 154
Saint Nicholas Temperance Society....... 89
Sanak 181
Sanburn, John A. 180
Sand Point 174
Sarakoff, Nick...................... 188
Sarechief.......................... 174
Sarikovicoff, Fr. 182
Schmidt, Mr. .... 75 - 76,173
Schooner Beach ... 55,57,92,113,122,128,220
Scotch Cap 174
Scott, Nell. 200
Seiler, Mike .... 155 - 157
Seldovia Bay.. 16,19,37 - 38,40,44 - 45,47,54 - 56,84,217
Seldovia Native Association .... 12,27 - 28,32
Seldovia River 9,56
Seldovia Salmon Company .... 114 - 115
Seldovia Slough....... 9,26 - 27,39,183,224
Seldovia Village Tribe Museum ...... 26 - 27
Seward ..... 105,109,111 - 113,115,122,152 - 153,165,173,176,179 - 180,189,196,200,220
Seward Commercial Company 110
Seward Weekly Gateway 112
Shadura, Fr. Pavel (Paul) 89
Sharp, Charles H..... 119,149,192 - 193,209
Sheldon, Gary 205

Shelikof Strait 19,148
Shelikov, Capt. Grigorii 37,40,44
Shell, Louis 212
Shil'ts, 2nd Lt. Iakov E............ 44 - 45
Shmaltz, Fr. Gerasim............. 92 - 93
Sholin, Andy.................. 102,104
Shortley, Mrs. M.E. 57,96
Shotter, Mrs. Mable 200
Sidewalk Mink Farm 108
Sitka 75,210,230
Sivertsen, Hans 83,87
Skagway 203
Skilak 23
Smith, Bill 205
Smith, John W. .... 57,80,100 - 101,173
Smith, Mr. 208
Smoky Bay 43
Snug Harbor 101,115,141
Soldotna 205
Soonroodna 55
Sorokovikov, Nikolai 52
South Peninsula Hospital 12
Sparrow, J.J. .... 108 - 109
Spellum, Chris 155
Spradlin, Tim 158
St. Nicholas .... 88 - 89
St. Nicholas Orthodox Church .... 89,91 - 92
Stabenow, Dana 7,218
Standard Oil Company of California ... 115
Sterling Highway 120
Street, Dana 20,22
Stuck, Hudson, Archdeacon 83
Studdart, Bill .... 184 - 185
Studnick, Joe 227
Sunrise 77,110,114,174
Susan B. English School 12
Susitna 57
Susitna (Sushitna) River........ 77,110,112
Susitna Station .... 112 - 113
Svedlund, Mrs. 159
Svedlund, Nels G. .... 158 - 159
Swift, Capt. E.A. .... 111 - 112

T

Tanaina ...... 12,52,54,57 - 59,62 - 64,66,71
Tanaina/Kaniagmiut 72
Tansy, Jack 23,184
Teben'kov, Mikhail D............. 46 - 49
Tehanin-Kutchin .... 52 - 53
Telenok, John 78
Teton Fox Farm 105
Theodosievskoye Brotherhood 82
Thwaites, John 174
Tikhmenev, P.A. 52
Tikhon, Right Reverend 83,92
Tillion, Sen. Clem. 90,224
Tinnats-khotana .... 53 - 54
Tonquin 89
Torgramson, Helen 96
Turnagain Arm .... 109,111 - 112,114
Tustumena 9
Tustumena Glacier.................. 37
Tustumena Lake 23,58
Tutka Bay 23,37,129,158
Tyonek (Taionek) (Tionic) (Tyonic) (Tyonik) .... 51,57,64,110,112 - 114,174

U

U.S. Coast Guard .... 48 - 49
Unalaska 115,181
Unga........................ 89,174,181
University of Alaska Fairbanks 55,75,99
University of Pennsylvania 21
Ursin, Andrew 123
Ursin, Axel 154
Ursin, Dora 86,113
Uyak............................. 174

V

Valdez 112,220
Valentine, Mrs. Mattie .... 179 - 180

Valentine, W.D. .... 177 - 180
Van Fleet, J.R. 155
Van Vranken, Ada................ 167,180
Vickers, C.L. 104
Vinal, W.A. 159,187
Vincent, Mrs. Leon S.............. 200
Volstad, Tim Ray 16

W

Wadsworth, Gene......... 7,39,146,161
Ward, James 114,174
Washington State University 34
Wasilla 200
Waterbury, Russel 188
Webb, Gardo 106
Wells, Frank...................... 109
Western Fur and Trading Company ..... 54 - 56,71,99
Western Union Telegraph Expedition 51
Westward Alaskan 106
White, Capt. Nate................ 49,175
White, Harry 209
Whitehead, Dr. Cary 205
Whittier 217
Whorf, William G..... 114,128,151 - 152,176
Wick, Oscar 119
Wickersham, Judge James 51,177
Wiles, Dr. Gregory .... 37 - 40
Wilkensen, Jack 119
Williamson, F.W. 102
Wilson, Albert. 191,212
Wilson, Dr. 204
Wosnesenski Glacier 38
Wrangell 118

Y

Yakoloff 27
Yale University 25,57
Yaroshevich, Alexander............. 75
Yentna 112
Yentna River 112
Yukon 80,203
Yukon Island 19 - 21,23 - 25,27 - 28,34,49,54 - 55,63,102 - 103,193
Yuth, Matt 188

Z

Zawistowski, Steve .... 7,106,108 - 109,125,193,208,213
Zawistowski, Winnie 108
Zollars, Peter .... 29,32 - 33,35